Arts of Living

Arts of Living

Reinventing the Humanities for the Twenty-first Century

Kurt Spellmeyer

- argues to erase the division bt intellectuals
  & the masses. Don't buy into cultural consciousness,
  theory, etc p(17)
- argues that the humanities are weak bc of their
  profound social isolation (p 17)
- corporatization of the university is good
- a communications hub
- our job is no longer the "safeguarding" of
  the archive (repository of established knowledge
  for cultural normalization). (19)
- The humanities must re-invent themselves (19)
- be service providers in the free market (20)
- connect specialized knowledge w/ the every day
  life world (22)

State University of New York Press

Published by
State University of New York Press, Albany

For information, address State University of New York Press,
90 State Street, Suite 700, Albany, NY 12207

Production by Dana Foote
Marketing by Anne M. Valentine

Library of Congress Cataloging-in-Pulication Data

Spellmeyer, Kurt.
    Arts of living : reinventing the humanities for the twenty-first century / Kurt
Spellmeyer.
        p. cm.
    Includes bibliographical references (p.) and index.
    ISBN 0-7914-5647-1 (alk. paper) — ISBN 0-7914-5648-X (pbk. alk. paper)
        1. Humanities—Study and teaching (Higher)—United States. 2. Humanities—
Philosophy. 3. Learning and scholarship—United States—History. 4. Humanities—
Political aspects—United States. 5. Humanities—United States—History. I. Title:
Reinventing the humanities for the twenty-first century. II. Title.

AZ183.U5 S64 2003
001.3'071'173—dc21   2002036683

10 9 8 7 6 5 4 3 2 1

Contents

ACKNOWLEDGMENTS

This book would not have been written without the help and encouragement extended to me by two people. The first of these is my friend and colleague Richard Miller. Whatever clarity I've managed to give my ideas owes a great deal to the polishing provided by the many hundreds of hours we've spent in conversation. Always generous with his time as well as his ideas, Richard actually read and commented in detail on the entire manuscript in its previous, more sprawling form. Friends like that are truly rare.

The other person who deserves some credit for the virtues of my argument is Barbara Suttman, my wife. Many *thousands* of hours of conversation with her over the twenty-five years of our marriage have constantly reminded me of the huge gap between life as imagined by the university and life as lived by ordinary working people. Precisely because one's partner may have the liberty to communicate insights that one's students might not dare to express, many people besides me are in her debt.

I would also like to thank the National Council of Teachers of English for permission to reprint, in revised form, "Travels to the Heart of the Forest: Dilettantes, Professionals, and Knowledge," which originally appeared in *College English* 56, 7 (November 1994): 788–809, and "After Theory: From Textuality to Attunement with the World," in *College English* 58, 8 (December 1996): 893–913. I would like to thank Brill Academic Publishers, Inc., for permission to reprint "Specialists with Spirit: New Age Religion, English Studies, and the 'Somatic Turn,'" which originally appeared in *Religion and the Arts, 3, 2* (1999): 195–223. Finally, I would like to thank the Hampton Press for permission to reprint "The Arts of Compassion and the Instruments of Oppression: James Agee, Lionel Trilling and the Semiotic Turn," which originally appeared as a chapter in the volume, *The Academy and the Possibility of Belief,* ed. Mary-Louise Buley-Meissner et al. (Cresskill, N.J.: Hampton Press, 2000), 171–95.

PART I

1

Taking the Humanities Out of the Box

The argument of this book is that the humanities must change. It may seem
absolutely unthinkable that our enjoyment of the arts might abruptly die away, or
that we might no longer take an interest in the past or ask ourselves what it means to
be alive, but the unthinkable is now a possibility. Even if the humanities should
somehow survive, we have no reason to assume that they will be best served by our
traditional institutions, in particular the schools and the university. While the humanities as taught and studied today may appear to be perennial and changeless, we
should remind ourselves that in their current form as modern professions they have
existed for less than a hundred years, and precariously at that.[1] Until the turn of the
nineteenth century, the most important branches of the humanities were not English
and history, probably the leading fields now, but rhetoric and classics. Within the
short space of a generation, these two disciplines, seemingly irreplaceable, collapsed.[2] The first vanished altogether until quite recently, after periodic efforts to
revive it; the second has limped on in a greatly diminished state. The same fate could
overtake our leading disciplines now.

That the humanities *are* in crisis everybody understands. In our colleges and
universities, the last thirty years have seen steadily declining enrollments while the
number of majors has doubled, even tripled, in business programs, information
sciences, and other fields.[3] Tenured faculty positions have also disappeared, by some
estimates cut nearly in half, while university budgets have increased more than
eightfold over the same period.[4] But the crisis is not only a matter of numbers.
People working in the humanities, especially professors in the key disciplines of
philosophy, history, and literary studies, have witnessed an alarming erosion of their
influence in a broader sense. Many of these people can remember a time when the
humanities seemed to occupy a central place in the life of their culture as a whole.
Now, the center seems to be monopolized by the frenzied rush for wealth and the
evanescent pleasures offered up by the popular media. While the economic growth
of the last fifty years, unprecedented in American history, has enriched and expanded many social institutions, the humanities go begging.

Instead of addressing these problems, our humanists have divided into warring camps over issues that are largely symbolic—and misconceived. No observer of
contemporary American life can ignore the persistence and bitterness of the "culture
wars." Conservatives like Jacques Barzun, Harold Bloom, and the late Allan Bloom

have all decried what they see as an assault on the stainless monuments of Western thought. At the same time, from the legions of left-leaning academics—the "tenured radicals" of Roger Kimball's polemic—comes a seemingly endless procession of arcane critiques, pompous manifestos, and tendentious revisionary histories.[5] At no prior moment in the last century, not even in the worst years of the Great Depression, has the line dividing American intellectuals appeared more sharply drawn.

The crisis now appears so intractable because both sides insist on misrepresenting the other in crude, moralizing terms, without any serious attempt to explore the social and intellectual history behind our current dilemmas—including the decline of the humanities themselves. And both sides keep looking resolutely backward, conservatives pleading for the same great books, while radicals want the great books as well, though as targets for a harsh "interrogation" rather than as sacred icons. The culture wars notwithstanding, the crisis in the humanities has not been caused by our teaching, or failing to teach, certain books. The humanities are in trouble because they have become increasingly isolated from the life of the larger society. And in fact, throughout the twentieth century, they have chosen isolation again and again, as they continue to do now.

This is not, of course, the story most humanists tell about themselves. Sympathetic observers typically see the crisis in unambiguous terms as an undeserved misfortune. One of these observers, the sociologist Robert Bellah, speaks for many when he attributes the humanities' decline to the decisive triumph of business, "unrestrained laissez-faire capitalism."[6] What this triumph has done, in Bellah's view, is to exclude moral judgment from the conduct of our affairs, not only in the use of new technologies like genetic engineering, but also in our political and cultural lives. Capitalism, according to Bellah, values nothing but self-advancement, and its proponents dismiss as naïve or fraudulent all appeals to disinterested knowledge, long the mainstay of the humanities. In his criticism of the market's crassness, Bellah calls for our return to a more traditional division of intellectual labor, one that will again lift the humanities above other forms of knowledge. Whereas science, technology, and the economic fields offer their best service to society when they restrict themselves to instrumental concerns, Bellah argues that the humanities are uniquely equipped to deal with questions of a higher kind. The sciences and technical fields may tell us how we can concretely achieve our goals, but the humanities alone enable us to decide which goals are truly worth achieving. In the collective body politic, the sciences may be the brains and technology the hands, but the humanities should be the heart and soul.

Ultimately, Bellah offers us an easy choice—between the darkness and the light, between vices and virtues, between our baser instincts and our higher natures. But the matter is not actually so simple. A large body of evidence, too large to dismiss unthinkingly, suggests that the market system has made possible a higher degree of human happiness than ever existed in ages past, when bleak privation and relentless toil made up the human lot. Most people have already forgotten that famine was still an occurrence in some parts of Western Europe well into the nineteenth century.[7] In the United States prior to industrialization, the average male could expect to live to about fifty; today, that figure has increased by almost thirty years, thanks to innovations in public health that almost certainly would not have happened without the much-maligned market. While it is true that economic development does not necessarily bring happiness, numerous surveys indicate that the great majority of Americans find their working lives so rewarding that more than half of them would chose to stay on the job beyond retirement age.[8] Although the shocks of industrial development tore apart our agrarian civilization, reconstructing it in ways often violently opposed by ordinary citizens, this same process also brought new freedoms in its wake. The explosive growth of the middle class and the democratization of schooling and material goods were market-driven developments. And if gender and racial equality should someday become the norm, that achievement will owe as much to the culture of trade, in which every person is a customer regardless of his background or complexion, as it will to the culture of arts and letters.

The market is not all darkness; the humanities are not all sweetness and light. No one can responsibly claim that the modern academic humanities have consistently pursued the common good. Even today, when professors tend to regard themselves as leaders of progressive social change, the army is far better integrated than the faculty of all but a few universities.[9] For much of this century, many academic humanists regarded the spread of access to higher education and the growing cultural power of the middle class with distrust if not outright hostility. Virtually every generation of professors since the end of the nineteenth century has looked back longingly to a time when admissions were more selective, students better prepared, and the study of high culture more richly rewarded than in the fallen latter days. Another way to put it might be to say that every generation of professors has had to educate the children of their social inferiors, and every generation has lamented that development. At the same time, professors have deplored, and often still deplore, the rise of movies, the recording industry, and that Great Satan of the academics—television—although these media have actually occasioned something like a Renaissance, except that no prior civilization in history, not even Europe's Renaissance in the fifteenth and sixteenth centuries, produced art and knowledge of such high quality on such a massive scale. Of course, people have been carefully conditioned never to think along these lines. To equate magazine ads with Renaissance paintings is a kind of sacrilege. To speak in the same breath of Shakespeare and *ER,* or Chopin and David Bowie, is to court derision. Yet the cultural achievements of the twentieth century, no less than the century's achievements in science, are in many ways the most remarkable of all time, as perhaps our children or grandchildren will be ready to acknowledge.

In his defense of the humanities Bellah helps to perpetuate a myth the humanities themselves have created: that the schools and universities are the proper home of our best art and ideas. And at first glance, the myth's truth appears self-evident. After all, whatever most of us know about Mary Cassatt and Pablo Picasso, Virginia Woolf and William Faulkner, Edgar Varèse and John Cage, we learned from college classes and the writings of professors. But the classroom and the textbook have agendas of their own, and in those settings the achievements of a Faulkner or a

Cassatt can appear to belong to places far removed from our own pedestrian lives, when the very opposite is actually the case. William Faulkner had a tenth-grade education, followed later by a year at a state university. He worked as a day laborer, a rural postmaster, a school janitor, and after gaining some recognition, a screenwriter in Hollywood. Until he got to Hollywood, Faulkner probably never made more than $6,000 a year.[10] Next to writing and drinking, his greatest passion was hunting. As Faulkner's finest novels appeared in an astonishing burst of creativity from 1928 to 1936, several distinguished critics of the day, inside the academy as well as outside, wrote about his work dismissively. Somehow Faulkner managed to continue, transforming into fiction of extraordinary depth and beauty the materials provided by life in rural Mississippi, hardly the setting one might expect to produce art of the highest caliber. But where is the proper home of the arts and ideas? Is it Harvard or Yale? Oxford or the Sorbonne? Clearly, creativity and insight can arise anywhere, and so in fact they have. Yet some might say that institutions we have created to safeguard the achievements of Faulkner and others do much to obscure that fact.

The truth is that the modern humanities have largely taken up residence in the university, and there they have remade themselves into specialized professions on the model of physics or medicine. As a consequence, they have a powerful vested interest in persuading us that the arts and ideas come from far away and are created by humans quite unlike ourselves. The arts as scholars often represent them seem remote and difficult, demanding almost superhuman levels of erudition, but such qualities have less to do with the arts themselves than they do with the need to make distinctions between the experts and the amateurs. We might say that the academic humanities use the work of Faulkner, Pollock, and the rest to create a specialized, often rarified knowledge that justifies not only the privileged vantage point of critical judgment, but also tenured positions, research stipends, federal grants, and so on. I believe that most nonspecialists revere a novel like Gabriel García Marquez's *One Hundred Years of Solitude,* or a painting like Georgia O'Keeffe's *Sky Above Clouds IV,* because these works have the power to speak to each of us individually, as if they were actually addressed to us, created for us. Although academic critics in recent years have done much to discredit the idea that works of art possess a universal relevance, we know from our own experience that a novel or a painting, a play or a poem sometimes has the *feel* of universality, the feel, almost, of timelessness. And when a reader shares in this condition, lifted out of real time into Faulkner's Yoknapatawpha County or Marquez's village of Macondo, or into the sky above O'Keeffe's New Mexico, who can be blamed for concluding that this is, after all, the reason that novels and paintings exist?

While Bellah implies that the public has deserted the humanities, we might just as easily argue that the public has been quietly edged out by the "middle men." But the middle men are not always professors. Lovers of classical music may bemoan the catastrophic decline of stations devoted to their tastes, but the nonaficionado who just happens to tune in is bound to be struck by the stilted diction of the program "hosts" and the absurdly grave tone of the proceedings: even funerals might be livelier. Worse yet, innovators are often harshly criticized, as when one well-known Los Angeles station tried to attract a wider and younger audience by interspersing classical music with jazz, world music, and "golden oldies." For some musicians and amateur devotees, the experiment amounted to nothing less than a hideous sacrilege, an attack on the whole tradition.[11] The truth, however, is that Mozart, Beethoven, Verdi, and other well-regarded composers wanted to reach a wide audience and were eager to play "medleys" of their "greatest hits."[12] Of course, the radio has not been the only battleground between the public and the custodians of culture. Faced with drastic cuts in government support but unwilling to go the way of the classical stations, a number of important museums have reached out to new constituencies with shows more welcoming to nonspecialists. Not long ago, the Boston Museum of Fine Arts broke attendance records and nearly doubled museum membership. But almost as soon as the changes had begun, conservatives on the museum's board and among the ranks of its curators clamored for the resignation of the new director, Malcolm Rogers, on the grounds that he was "pandering" to the consumer culture.[13] But here, as in the case of music, the image of the arts as aloof and otherworldly is historically inaccurate. Far from regarding popular attention as vulgar, painters like Monet, Dégas, and Gauguin took great pleasure in a large attendance at their shows and were gratified, as well, by their percentage of admission fees. Much the same held true in the Amsterdam of Rembrandt and also in the Paris of Matisse and Picasso.[14]

As I will argue in Part I, the humanities have fallen from glory because they have chosen to back the wrong side in the great, unresolved struggle of our time: the struggle waged by ordinary citizens to gain control over their own lives. In the first half of the twentieth century that struggle was aimed primarily at formal participation in government—women's suffrage is one good example—and then, in the years after World War II, the struggle expanded to include economic security as well as political rights. But the desire for participation does not stop with the vote and a living wage. If culture is where we live, so to speak, if it gives form to our values and extends them into the future, then the promise of democracy remains unrealized so long as most of us are uninvolved in the making of culture itself.

Our direct involvement in the making of culture—this is what the old humanities have failed to achieve and what the new humanities must undertake if they are to have any future at all. Yet the idea that the making of culture is the sort of thing that *should* engage the ordinary person might strike many critics and scholars as absurd, even dangerous. Surely the most accomplished musicians, not the most eager, should get to play with the city orchestra. Surely there are qualitative differences between a poem like William Butler Yeats's "The Second Coming" and the lyrics on top-forty radio or the verses that self-conscious undergraduates write before they head off to law school. By their very nature, art and democracy are opposites, since anyone can be a citizen and anyone can make a pile of money whereas poets like Yeats come along only once every century or so. To the defenders of this way of thinking, the world of art is necessarily an aristocracy, albeit one of insight, talent, and hard work rather than of birth. And the purpose of scholarship, they tell us, is to protect that aristocracy from the leveling tendencies of the modern world. But are they right? Is it possible instead that our thinking about the arts reflects their origins in an aristocratic outlook we began to abandon politically about two centuries ago but continue to accept unreflectingly in other contexts? People as widely different as the Balinese, the Navajo, and the pre-Meiji Japanese have regarded the making of art not as the purview of a chosen few, but as a normal part of any life well lived.[15] For these people, the hyperspecialization of the humanities in our society might seem as bizarre as appointing one person in every thousand to experience emotions or to see colors on behalf of everyone else. Clearly, no one can feel emotions or see colors on my behalf, and by the same token, the creativity of others cannot substitute for my own creativity.

Of course, culture, politics, and economics all go together. The struggle for control over cultural life remains one part of a larger conflict, so far unresolved. Ordinary citizens have the right to vote, but ordinary citizens cannot command the same attention from our cash-hungry politicians as a Fortune 500 CEO. Although we enjoy a standard of living our grandparents could never have imagined in their most optimistic moments, many people feel perpetually insecure, their livelihoods abjectly dependent on forces beyond anyone's control—or rather, almost anyone's. Far from leveling social distinctions, the twentieth century witnessed the emergence of new hierarchies: political and economic hierarchies, naturally, but also hierarchies of culture. Without sentimentalizing the past, we might say that our forerunners in the late nineteenth century, at least if they were white, lived in two worlds at once, the world of the town and the world of the nation. They knew firsthand the "small world" of families and neighborhoods, of local businesses, arts, and civil society, on a scale sufficiently circumscribed to allow the common person to play some modest but significant role. At the same time, they understood themselves as belonging to a larger entity, the nation, and perhaps because of their security within the smaller world, they could see themselves as players in the larger world as well. But things have changed dramatically. In the last election of the twentieth century, less than half of eligible voters bothered to go to the polls at all; in the last election of the nineteenth century, participation came quite close to 80 percent in the North.[16] The difference reflects the waning of the smaller world, and the removal of significant authority to places distant, unresponsive, and poorly understood. In fact, with the immanent rise of a global civilization, this same process, this distancing of authority, has entered a new and more ambitious phase, one that threatens to do to the nation-state what the nation-state did a century ago to the village, town, or region. While criticisms of global capital have become a stock-in-trade of the humanities, the humanities themselves have knowingly helped to create the paradigms, the "official" attitudes, that have made hierarchy seem essential to the health of the arts and letters.

The new humanities as I envision them in Part II must contribute to the renewal or remaking of our small worlds, the first step in regaining the power to act in the larger world as well. While the humanities in the last fifteen years have seen a clash between conservatives and radicals—the much publicized culture wars—these "wars" might be viewed instead as a minor skirmish between two competing elites, neither with much of a commitment to broad-based, democratic participation in the making of cultural life. Whether disciples of Matthew Arnold and T. S. Eliot, or of Karl Marx and his followers, most academic humanists still presuppose that culture trickles down from the top, or should. Conservatives invoke Tradition with a quavering voice while radicals speak shrilly of combating ruling-class hegemony, but both groups imagine culture as a pyramid, a monolithic system that contains everything and confines everyone, whether or not people consciously acknowledge their containment, and whether or not they collaborate or resist. Needless to say, this image of culture as a pyramid tends to solidify even further the social, economic, and political inequities now in place. It constructs in the realm of ideas an imaginary universe that closely mimics real-world arrangements. But we might think about culture quite differently, in new and potentially more democratic ways.

The first part of this book will retrace the rise of elite professionalism in the humanities. But the second part will explore an alternative to that system, with its representation of culture as a hierarchy or pyramid. Ultimately, I develop a new argument for an idea that originated in the Renaissance, when the old humanities first got their start. In the words of a great philosopher of the time, "The universe is a circle whose center is everywhere and whose circumference is infinite."[17] Or, as I put it in my own words, the heart of the forest always lies wherever we find ourselves. In a genuine democracy, all politics become local politics because the decision making that matters most occurs at the local levels. By the same token, a democratic culture will not teach us to look beyond our actual lives for the solution to our problems: it will remind us instead that solutions of some sort always lie at hand, even when our hands have been tied. Given the degree to which our hands *have* been tied, any discussion of genuine democracy may sound to many ears more fantastic than real, but the loss of faith in our own capacities for action keeps us locked in a vicious circle of dependent thinking that only worsens our real dependency.

The humanities might help us to break out of the circle by reaffirming that the world of immediate human experience is always potentially whole and complete, no matter what our social "betters" happen to claim. Although people living in, say, medieval Europe were far less advanced than we are technologically, we cannot say that our world is necessarily more complete or more alive than theirs. Wholeness, completeness—these are not properties of specific ideas or critical masses of information, but of a certain resonance in our relations to the world. This term "resonance," which I will explore in Part II, comes not from Renaissance philosophy but from Renaissance science, the rediscovery of harmonics. If I hold a tuning fork to the neck of a guitar and then I pluck a string, the fork will begin vibrate on the same wavelength—vibrating, one might almost say, with the same life. Resonance in the world of culture signifies the achievement of harmony—intellectual, emotional, aesthetic, and sensuous—between our small worlds and the larger one. The deeper our experience of resonance, the more encompassing the small world becomes until it seems to connect us with absolutely everything. To expand the small world outward, to make a home of the universe, this should be the function of culture in general, and of the humanities in particular.

I know that some readers will disagree. They will say that experience is unreliable in itself and that none of us can ever be fully human until we have studied Plato's dialogues or Shakespeare's histories. We begin as blank slates on which culture must write, and the better the culture the better the writing. But Plato never read Plato; Shakespeare never read Shakespeare (nor, in fact, had he read Plato). While I hold both figures in something close to religious awe, our conservatives have gone much too far when they insist that Shakespeare "invented" personal identity or that self-knowledge is "impossible" without at least a minimal command of the *Phaedrus*. Clearly, people in places very far from the Globe Theatre have developed complex forms of self-awareness, as the Japanese classic *The Tale of Genji* testifies. And people utterly ignorant of Plato's dialectic have traced consciousness back to its roots in ways that outdistanced even Plato himself, as we learn from Indian philosophy. Certainly culture matters, not least because its transmission gives longevity to our attitudes and activities. Yet to say that culture somehow makes us what we are is to treat it quite mistakenly as a big person, something like a god, with intentions and the power to act. In fact, cultures have no intentions and cultures cannot act. It was surely not an accident that Plato and Shakespeare both lived at times of social crisis when culture itself had to be transformed, and they each did so by working outward from the small worlds they knew best, in Plato's case, Athens, in Shakespeare's, the stage.

Our left-leaning intellectuals also go too far, if not by raising culture to the status of a god than by treating it as something like the devil, always steering us to perdition when we relax and enjoy ourselves. So completely does culture blind and ensnare—the favored term for "culture" now is "ideology"—that even a visit to Disney World becomes a textbook case of mass mind control. The magic castles and the twirling elephant rides may look innocent enough, but as part of the nefarious "cultural text," these "signifiers" secretly inculcate us all with the values of a system built on ruthless exploitation. Yet if culture has this power, hypnotic and seemingly irresistible, how can anybody ever wake up from the ruse, even our academic radicals? The short answer is the correct one in this case: experience itself often discloses what culture has concealed or overlooked. Surely no one who works at Disney World for long hours and low pay, and apparently there are quite a few, needs to "decode" the cultural text in order to know that conditions could improve. Surely no one disturbed by forests razed and wetlands drained, and by miles of traffic moving at a walker's pace in the drenching Florida heat, needs to be lectured on the "social construction" of civilization at the expense of the natural world. Change will come, not when people have learned to distrust the evidence of their daily lives, but when they find the courage and the confidence to see the unimpeachable truth in their own discontents, and also in their own joys.

The proper task of the humanities is to promote this courage and this confidence. I believe that the humanities *will* survive if our schools and universities can offer something that knowledge by itself cannot provide: the experience of freedom, which may be more desperately needed now than any other contribution that humanists can make. But in order to offer real freedom, we need to understand what it concretely entails. In one sense, no society has ever been so free as ours. We can choose our careers. We can live where we want. We can vote, and we can buy more material goods than anyone really needs. We can even change our genders. Yet these freedoms all bring constraint of another kind. The constraints imposed by the modern administered state, a central concern of my chapters 2 through 5, are not the ones that I mean here. I mean rather the constraint imposed on us by culture itself, which is always limited and limiting: if we believe too much in the values of our particular time and place, we become the prisoner of those values. What happens to our robust self-esteem, for example, when we lose our jobs or the good opinion of our colleagues? What becomes of our faith in the American dream when we can no longer do the work we enjoy, when we go broke, or when our youth and intelligence abandon us? No one can live without a culture, certainly, but to live in culture freely is to live beyond it in a certain sense, remaking it as we go along. Instead of accepting what "they say" as truth, we can expand the smaller world, the personal world, beyond the categories made available to us by our language, history, institutions, and normative practices. Only the person who no longer fears the disapproval of others can be truly generous. Only those who no longer have something to gain can help others without falling prey to the self-aggrandizement that makes compassion into a kind of tyranny. To act without concern about self-image, to think without the fear of making mistakes—this is the freedom the humanities might someday offer us.

The reigning philosophy of the humanities today, the much-praised and much-disparaged movement known as poststructuralism, takes us halfway toward the goal of a democratic culture. More keenly than their predecessors generally did, the poststructuralists appreciate culture's limitations, its tendency to become paralyzing, even self-destructive, when inhabited inflexibly. Religious wars, conflicts between rival nation-states, colonialism, racial oppression, discrimination based on sexual preference, and the twentieth-century phenomenon of the gulag—all of these demonstrate quite convincingly the potential of culture to diminish the awareness it supposedly enlarges. Instead of seeing values as universal or foundational, the poststructuralists insist on the importance of acknowledging the varied perspectives and social positions that follow from historical differences. At its most extreme, however, poststructuralism militates against any effort to identify genuine commonalities, which it tends to represent ungenerously as an expression of narrow self-interest masquerading as universal benevolence. For some poststructuralists, there can be no fusion between large and small worlds, only many small worlds clashing with one another. One might reply, as I do in Part II, that the suspicious outlook typical of most poststructuralists undermines their own effort, since their claim to unmask self-interest everywhere must itself be just another mask in the larger charade. But even if the poststructuralists might someday make a better argument for their skepticism than they have so far, their vision of human life could scarcely be bleaker, more repressive, and more alienated, despite their celebrations of playfulness. Some notable poststructuralists have rejected the possibility of genuine equality, of nonviolence, of freedom, of relations unaffected by power; many deny as well that the world in itself, beyond our mediating assumptions, can ever be glimpsed even for a moment; and some insist that it makes no sense to speak of progress, either in the advancement of knowledge or in the arrangements of our practical affairs. Not surprisingly, the thinker most admired by poststructuralists is the nihilist Friedrich Nietzsche, but most poststructuralists are notably less optimistic than the master, who believed that by loosening the grip of culture, humans could live more healthy and happy lives. For many poststructuralists, by contrast, culture's grip can never be loosened. We are, they tell us, trapped in culture, trapped in language and history, so completely that health and happiness are themselves nothing more than socially constructed "representations," never more than the products of a particular time and place. Strangely, Nietzsche *began* his career by rejecting such claims, always popular among antidemocratic German intellectuals.[18] He understood that this position, like the argument that starts with complete distrust, is inherently self-defeating: the claim that everything is representation can be nothing more than another representation, the narrow outlook of a particular time and place.

The humanities cannot offer freedom if they see human life as nothing more than an "effect" of culture, language, or social structures. Some people have tried to extricate themselves from the chic fatalism of the academy by turning to the American pragmatist tradition, with its emphasis on experience and experimentation. The two foremost pragmatist thinkers today, the philosopher Richard Rorty and the literary critic Stanley Fish, have both argued that the poststructuralists fail to push their thinking to its logical culmination. While poststructuralism repudiates the idea of an objective, immutable truth, it still acts as though such a truth exists when it tries to correct our representations on the basis of history.[19] Like Nietzsche, Rorty and Fish have both argued that history is just another story, a story we can tell in many different ways, depending on our assumptions and aspirations. But the two pragmatists have also pointed out that this program for reforming our ideas gives far too much importance to ideas themselves, which are simply the alibis that people invent after they have decided on a course of action. If we want to change society, they argue, then we need to do less tinkering with ideas and more of the hard work of talking with people, building coalitions, changing institutions, and so on. Instead of trying to ground our reforms on some grand historical vision or some quasi-metaphysical critique, we might do better to ask ourselves about the way of life we would prefer right now, a choice that needs no tighter alibi than that we find it worth pursuing.

It seems to me, however, Fish and Rorty's pragmatism offers only a pale and anemic future for the humanities. Basically, their vision of freedom still leaves us more or less disconnected from other people and from the universe. One way to understand the problem is to say that both thinkers have come to pragmatism *through* the poststructuralist movement, and both men are deeply imbued with its "sophisticated" skepticism. In fact, they might be described as skeptics who simply refuse to turn their doubts into a methodology or program, as many poststructuralists do, because poststructuralism has made such a dogmatic and repressive mess of it, especially in its quasi-Marxist incarnations. Although I often agree with them, I intend to draw my inspiration from other strands in the pragmatist legacy. We should not forget that pragmatism has its roots in Emerson's *transcendentalism.* Emerson tended to treat ideas as relative and contingent precisely because he believed that we all have access to a reality above, or perhaps below, ideas, in contrast to his German contemporaries. As he wrote in "The American Scholar," "Man Thinking must not be subdued by his instruments. Books are for the scholar's idle times.

When he can read God directly, the hour is too precious to be wasted in other men's transcripts of their readings."[20] Of course, Emerson's God was not the God of the theologians, but an immanent reality always greater than the conceptions we employ to describe it.[21]

This confidence in a larger wholeness might imbue the humanities with a grandeur and depth—a truly world-embracing resonance—now lacking in the thought of our leading pragmatists, while linking the humanities to traditions that reach beyond the modern West. A familiar image in Chinese culture, roughly comparable in its wide circulation to versions of "the Madonna and Child" in the West, was the "Three Sages," a standard fixture of temples and scholars' studios. Conventionally these paintings showed three men dressed in the distinctive robes of the major Chinese traditions: the Taoist hermit, the Confucian scholar, and the Buddhist monk. The three stand together in a cluster, smiling and staring up at a moon alone in the clear sky. In Buddhist iconography, the moon symbolizes "Buddha nature," the "enlightened Mind." For Taoists, it represents the primordial Great Way, and for Confucianists, *jen,* or humanity.[22] Much like our society today, Tang dynasty China experienced a crisis of multiple and conflicting values, some imported from outside, and some developed internally. The Chinese solution to the problem was not the solution applied by our poststructuralist thinkers—the relentless critique of all values in the name of resistance, transgression, counterhegemony, and revenge. That development would have to await the career of Mao Tse-tung, and when it happened, it left twenty to forty million people dead. But neither did the Chinese adopt the solution proposed by Rorty and Fish, preserving the conventions in an agnostic spirit while living as comfortably as one can. No, the Chinese solution came closer to Emerson's: China's people continued to believe in a "highest truth" beyond contingent expressions, while acknowledging relative truths as well, which were not true in the highest sense, but pragmatically beneficial in particular times and places. While it is certainly the case that this solution did not end all forms of injustices, such as the practice of binding women's feet, the syncretic Chinese outlook might still be said to have produced a more stable and humane society than the West managed to achieve until after World War II, when our colonial domination of the world came to an end.

Whether or not Emerson understood Chinese history well enough to appreciate these parallels, he viewed human culture in much the same spirit, as did his occasional detractor Walt Whitman and also his occasional disciple William James.[23] To appreciate Whitman's celebrations of "the mass man democratic," or James's explorations of a "pluralistic universe," is to revisit an opportunity missed by the humanities on this continent. With its commitment to universal truths, validated by discrediting all alternatives, European philosophy was perfectly contrived to consolidate power in the hands of the very few: one party is always right, the others totally wrong, and the right one should get to call the shots. But pragmatists had a very different goal, convinced as they were that the wisest choices are most likely to emerge from the widest range of possibilities and the broadest participation in the testing of those possibilities in practice. Rather than ask if beliefs are simply right or wrong, Whitman and James each tried in divergent ways to understand the value of differing attitudes in the conduct of everyday life. And rather than divide the world into "masses" and "intellectuals" on the European model—intellectuals, that is, *against* the masses—they tried to be intellectuals of and for the ordinary citizen. With all the discord and dissonance of American life, they could value ordinary lives in this way only by regarding each small world as a facet of the larger one.[24]

Pragmatism's many detractors may not share this faith in the ordinary citizen. In the abstract, they might agree that all people ought to participate as equals in the making of social life. But even those who might assent in the abstract—our leftist intellectuals—tend to regard the average citizen as unprepared to assume full control owing to the persistence of "false consciousness." False consciousness is a term of Marxist provenance that is used to explain why people fail to rise up against oppression in the absence of force. Although slaves in both the ancient and the early modern worlds tried to escape to freedom, industrial workers in the United States have typically refused to overthrow the class of owners who employ them. Since Marxist doctrine holds that every class will automatically pursue its material interests, and since ownership is apparently advantageous to the workers, their failure to rebel must reflect a conceptual confusion—not a conscious confusion but an unconscious one, perpetuated by a duplicitous cultural system. This reasoning leads to the rather un-Marxist conclusion that ordinary citizens, including those who belong to the working class, must first undergo an ideological reformation, a reprogramming, so to speak, before they can act to their own real advantage.

The unmasking of false consciousness has proven enormously fruitful for the humanities in recent years, and humanists have increasingly felt called upon to do the work of "ideology critique." Good intentions notwithstanding, this sense of mission justifies a qualitative distinction between an enlightened minority and a vast, semiconscious majority, largely white, largely middle- or working-class. But even those who belong to oppressed or excluded enclaves within the larger society— women, African Americans, Native Americans, and so on—are viewed by some Marxist scholars as trapped inside false consciousness. Under these conditions the academic intellectual is obliged to play a dual role, laying siege to the dominant culture while assisting in the birth of new and oppositional values. The intellectual must work on behalf of the oppressed, while also exploring the ways in which the dominant culture "represents" or depicts the oppressed within society generally. By deconstructing the representations that the dominant class has created, academic intellectuals will usher in a new society. But I wonder if these intellectuals can actually play such a role, acting as stand-ins for the oppressed. How well, for example, does a white American feminist historian understand the day-to-day realities of a black Caribbean emigrée woman who works as a motel maid in Piscataway, New Jersey? Even if the feminist historian happens to know quite a bit about the lives of such people, no one can speak for the maid as well as the maid can speak for herself. And there is something quite condescending, too, in assuming that the maid's mental condition has prevented her from being heard. It seems far more likely that the maid has not been heard for other reasons, perhaps because of popular indifference but also because our society lacks the appropriate mechanisms. The problem, in other words, is not that the maid has been deceived but that she lacks the power to act in ways that would transform her situation. Many pragmatists would say that people are held down by the absence of real-world alternatives rather than by their conditioning. Academics who act as ambassadors of the oppressed are no substitute for enduring arrangements that might enable the oppressed to explain themselves and pursue their own interests as they wish.

The role of the critical intellectual is problematic for another, even more important reason: critique itself may be just an illusion. After all, when we change our ideas, what have we really changed except for our ideas? Yesterday I may have been an existentialist and tomorrow I may switch my allegiance to the Marxist philosopher Althusser, but what will have really changed if I still get up at six o'clock, arrive at work by nine, put in my eight hours five days a week, and pick up a paycheck twice a month? Even many defenders of the pragmatist legacy fail to understand this crucial objection. The point of thinking is not just to change ideas but to change our actual lives. And in this process of change, ideas may play a minimal role. As Emerson was first to recognize, activity has a wisdom of its own, since activity reveals opportunities impossible to foresee by relying on existing knowledge. This is why when we try to act self-consciously, or with a specific outcome in mind, the result is so often halting and unsuccessful. But when we act in a way that diminishes self-consciousness and the will to control events, our activity takes on an autonomous life and a greater, implicit order can emerge.

Emerson's word for this implicit order was "oversoul," a subject that our latter-day pragmatists have kept carefully offstage as an embarrassment akin to William James's fascination with the occult. "Man," Emerson wrote, "is a stream whose source is hidden. Our being is descending into us from we know not whence."[25] Emerson's discussion of the oversoul remained tentative and imprecise, and today it may appear to resemble the Freudian unconscious, but Emerson would probably object to the view that we can bring the unconscious to consciousness simply by looking inside our minds or remembering details from the past—as would, I suspect, William James. During the last years of his career, after the pioneering work in psychology, James concluded that the unconscious—or, as he called it, the subconscious—is not inside the mind at all, but out there in the world. For James, the subconscious *is* the world, or rather, all aspects of the world that exceed our immediate attention and our cultural conditioning:

> My present field of consciousness is a centre surrounded by a fringe that shades insensibly into a subconscious more. . . . What we conceptually iden-
> tify ourselves with and say we are thinking of all the time is the centre; but our
> *full* self is the whole field, with all those indefinitely radiating subconscious
> possibilities of increase that we can only feel without conceiving, and can
> hardly begin to analyze.[26]

Although self and world seem quite sharply distinct, their distinctness is an "optical" illusion produced by consciousness: there can be no self except as part of this world right here and now. Even memories exist only in the present moment as approximate reconstructions of what happened in the past. From these conclusions it follows that the Freudian practice of analysis, so important to the postmodern academy, cannot achieve what its advocates believe. For one thing, both consciousness and the "unconscious" occupy a perpetually shifting terrain, and what was conscious a moment ago can recede once again into unconsciousness. When we try to bring the subconscious into consciousness, we cannot really go deeper into the mind, since there is nothing to the mind except our awareness of this moment. All we can do is turn our attention to another moment, another disclosure of the world. Introspection, therefore, is a myth. But in this case, what on earth is thinking for? James replies that the purpose of thinking is to deal pragmatically with the next moment. As he puts it, the "concepts we talk with are made for purposes of *practice* and not for purposes of insight."[27]

If James is correct, then the humanities are in trouble. When humanists claim to set aside crude, worldly, practical concerns for the sake of purely "philosophical" inquiry, they actually fall prey to the optical illusion of a pure thinker somehow separate from the world. But this is just what the humanities have done for the last two decades, dominated as most of our disciplines have been by what is called "French theory." The rise of theory is a complex development that I address in Part II, but it might be described unsympathetically as prepackaged analytical systems devised by a handful of European luminaries: Derrida, Foucault, Lacan, Deleuze and Guattari, Habermas, and possibly the latecomer Zizek. I will grant that reflection on our activities is inescapable and necessary, but the term "theory" in the academy today has a more restricted connotation, describing philosophic systems quite divorced from any real-world tasks, except those so grand as to exceed any possibility of realization. And as a pragmatist, I cannot take at face value theory's claim to the status of pure reflection. Like all thinking, it must serve some practical aim—and that aim, or one of its aims at any rate, is to establish as an unquestioned elite the small circle of those who create and use theory.

The exclusionary character of theory, though obvious to nonacademics, is a great, undiscussable secret within the university. While the defenders of theory represent it as "insurgent" and "liberatory," a weapon of the oppressed, it is in fact ideally suited to the life of the hyperspecialist who relies on technical expertise inaccessible to the ordinary citizen. That theory is essentially technical, even mechanical, in character only its defenders will deny. But once a theory has been learned, it lends itself to almost every application with only a few slight adjustments. Michel Foucault can be used, for example, to explain a poet's life and work, or the history of public education, or the caste system of India, or the sexual practices of the British middle class. Because it seems to explain so much so thoroughly, theory can be heady stuff, and perhaps for this reason few of its advocates have come to grips with its tautological character. Whatever its defects, however, theory has admirably served humanists eager to acquire a form of knowledge closely comparable to the knowledge made by the sciences, and in this spirit theory has marketed itself as a science of "signs" and "signifying practices," in other words, of language and culture.

But theory is on the wane, largely because the once exciting research it inspired has progressively taken on the character of an empty ritual, much as communism did in the Soviet Bloc just prior to its collapse. Some disciplines have embraced theory more guardedly than others—philosophy and history in particular—but English departments now find themselves overtaken by profound malaise. The top of the profession has begun to shift toward aesthetics or literary history with fewer Gallic flourishes, while the bottom has turned for comfort to the practice of social critique and the dissemination of "critical consciousness" through the conduit of the classroom. Like theory, the movement gathering around critical consciousness inspires a missionary zeal among its believers, but it also reinstates a familiar division between intellectuals and the masses—that is, those few who have critical consciousness and the many who lack it. Quite apart from the impossibility of defining critical consciousness with precision, or of proving its reality by empirical means, the idea has other limitations as well. Although its defenders often celebrate change, especially change of a revolutionary kind, critique as a practice is quite conservative. Instead of devising real alternatives, a much harder undertaking than critique, the practitioners of critical consciousness have built their careers on scathing treatments of Disney World or *The Simpsons*.

Relevant and trendy as such critiques may seem, they actually reflect the most fundamental problem of the humanities in our time—their profound social isolation. A century ago, for example, works of history enjoyed enormous readerships, sometimes surpassing those of popular novelists. By contrast, most historians today write only for other historians in a language inhospitable to nonspecialists.[28] But this abandonment of the general reader follows from an isolation of another kind. The truth is that people trained in the humanities are often ill prepared to write with any genuine knowledge about science, sexuality, the film industry, urban life, or other pressing current issues. One example is especially telling. Several years ago, a leading journal in a subfield of English known as cultural studies published an article by an eminent scientist who denied that the sciences describe reality.[29] What the sciences describe, the author suggested, is at bottom arbitrary, no less socially and historically constructed than, say, our table manners or sartorial preferences. On these terms, even science cannot operate outside the reach of critique—in other words, outside the reach of English professors. The only problem, it turned out, was that the article, which had gone to press unread by any competent reviewer, was a brilliant parody of cultural studies intended to embarrass the journal and its cutting-edge editorial board. No direct attack, however well-reasoned, could have done half so much to discredit the pretensions of English as the would-be disciplinarian of other disciplines, or the notion that a critic can read whole cultures just as easily as reading a novel or a poem. Sadly, the journal's many supporters have remained undeterred, and the broader implications of the incident remain largely unexplored.

To my knowledge, the other side in this dispute—that is, the scientists—have never argued that their practices are sacrosanct, but they have asked for a degree of informed consideration that current training in an English department, or in most of the humanities disciplines, usually fails to provide. In English, undergraduate education is largely shaped by the imperatives of graduate training, while graduate training is largely shaped by the imperatives of the tenured professor's working life at a major research institution. As individual competitors, professors at these institutions build their reputations by publishing articles and books that other professors read, review, and cite, while departments distinguish themselves in national rankings by attracting eminent faculty and by producing numerous candidates for professorial jobs. The system is completely closed, in other words, and humanists find themselves caught in a bizarre twilight world, knowing too much on the one hand and too little on the other—too much about "cultural diasporas" and "symbolic economies" and too little about the actual lives of international migrants and the real links between the media and the corporate milieu. In a certain sense, humanist inquiry is all dressed up with nowhere to go. Since most of its discourses are quite narrowly addressed to other humanists, and not even to humanists in general but primarily to other specialists, the whole question of pertinence tends to remain unspoken—and unspeakable. To my knowledge, no department of English now measures its success according to its impact on the surrounding community, or by assessing the circulation of its written output in some larger public sphere. The results would be too depressing.

The problem, however, goes beyond inadequate training, deeply rooted as the humanities are in the lofty ideal of "the intellectual," which I regard as a fixture of a heritage now rapidly receding. At the time of Voltaire or Dr. Johnson, perhaps the West's archetypal modern intellectuals, the best that people could hope for was a clubby *republic* of letters—as opposed to a genuine *democracy*—guided by the mere handfuls of men who could then count as educated. But things have changed, and the role of the intellectual, the uniquely educated and cognizant man, is inescapably on the decline, though not for the reasons many people think. The truth is that knowledge of all sorts has become vastly more available than at any other moment in history. More books get printed and more readers read them. Add to this the information that circulates through television, movies, and the Internet, and the growing number of people who contribute to the making of even the most specialized knowledge, and Dr. Johnson's world begins to look like ancient history.

Understandably, this development has caused some trepidation in the traditional humanities fields. One way to explain the rise of theory, for instance, is to see it as our latest bid to recover the authority blown away by the explosion of knowledge in the modern world. The point I'd like to make here, however, is that our nostalgia for the intellectual's leadership role has prevented us from seeing what should be plain—that all this change might be to the good. The problem is that we still think of knowledge in eighteenth-century terms. We still think of it, in other words, as a scarce commodity that must be carefully sifted and weighed before it enters into general circulation. The truth is that the making of knowledge today far outstrips the mechanisms of critical assessment and restraint—not only in sheer volume but in the pace of production. By the time our critics of "popular culture" have completed their harsh assessments of *Titanic* or *Saving Private Ryan,* those films will be old news, and few of our students five years from now will probably have seen them. Even if academic critics were able to speak to and for a society as diverse as ours, they cannot stop the culture machine or slow it down. If anything, criticism has simply become the most discerning type of consumption, a snobbery disguised as principled resistance.

Once we stop conceiving of knowledge as a scarce commodity on the model of ages past, a commodity given value by its scarcity, and we begin to think about it as superabundant, then we can see that no particular knowledge has any value at all. What matters in our society is the ability to produce more knowledge of use to more people, or to circulate existing knowledge in unprecedented ways. Social power comes not from what we know but from what we can do with what we know, from the capacity to act creatively. This is why observers like Robert Bellah are spectacularly off target when they decry the corporatization of the university. In America, corporate money has always paid for higher learning, and if Duke and Stanford aren't good enough examples, then an afternoon's research on the better public universities might clinch the argument. No, the difference is not that universities have suddenly gone corporate, but that they are shifting from being repositories of established knowledge, collected for the purposes of teaching and cultural normalization, to becoming sites of knowledge production and dispersal. What has changed, in other words, is the university's structural relation to society as a whole. At one time, the university imagined itself as a place apart from society. More and more it has come to occupy a central position: once a dusty archive, it has become instead a communications hub. But where does that leave us in the humanities, when the safeguarding of the archive has always been our principal task? While I cannot foresee a prosperous future for all of our current disciplines, I am convinced that the humanities as a whole will have bright prospects if they are prepared to reinvent themselves. But how?

Humanists must learn to think of their fellow citizens as genuine collaborators, not as students to be lectured at, heathens to be converted, or philistines to be shunned. What I mean is not simply that our embrace of criticism has reinforced our claim to a privileged vantage point, but also that we have to stop assuming that others will see our isolation as a reason to respect us. In particular, we need to stop relying on the conception of ourselves as professionals enjoying a monopoly. While it is true that for much of this century professions like medicine had a virtual lock on their clientele, that situation has begun to change. From outside the professions, public resentment has occasioned a significant degree of restiveness; on the inside, the rapid growth of specialized inquiry has inadvertently produced what the sociologist Anthony Giddens calls an "indefinite" pluralism of expertise.[30] A person with cancer can go to an oncologist, a naturopath, or a specialist in Chinese medicine; a person with emotional problems can consult a Freudian psychiatrist, a Jungian psychoanalyst, a clinical psychologist, a neurologist, a priest, a rabbi, or a faith healer. As for the humanities, they have never enjoyed the dominance that once made medicine the envy of the other professions, and in contrast to lawyers as well as physicians, scholars working in philosophy, history, and literary studies have seldom been able to sell services directly to their clients. Those who disagree can put my argument to the test with ads in the Yellow Pages that read "Philosopher for Hire" or "Public Literary Critic." Even with low hourly rates and free consultations, the only calls the freelance humanist is likely to get will be from Oklahoma banks hawking low-interest credit cards. Instead of selling services directly to clients, fields like philosophy and English depend for their survival on the university's bureaucratic structure and prestige, and without these artificial protections, they would largely disappear. Even with them, they may disappear. But at the same time, many universities are overwhelmed by the demand for educated and articulate generalists. At the university where I teach, the English department cannot begin to meet the current demand for people with appropriate preparation in writing for the sciences and the professions. Former teachers in the writing program I direct now work as editors and researchers at salaries comparable to those of eagerly courted new assistant professors. And I suspect there may be a huge untapped market for research and writing services that the university itself might sell.

The humanities must become "service providers" in a free-market climate. I recognize, of course, that in the culture of the humanities, to speak of selling information or skills is almost the same as saying that we should sell our souls, or our children. We might recollect, however, that this circumspection owes much more to Matthew Arnold than it does to Karl Marx. It was Arnold, after all, who first defined the critical intellectual as the person who does no worldly work, and who, by eschewing all practical engagement and know how, can think "above the fray," so to speak.[31] In effect, Arnold establishes a ruinous division of labor. To the sciences, to business, and to government he cedes all worldly action, while securing for the humanities an austerely contemplative role. Men of the world are left to clash on the darkling plain like the ignorant armies in the poem "Dover Beach," while the humanists pass judgment retrospectively from on high. In the early decades of the twentieth century, this division of cultural labor seemed ideal for granting humanities departments a place at the table of leadership, but what do humanists concretely know? And what real-world venues are there for the knowledge that we actually have? Our problem is precisely that the view from above is too blurry and too dark, and that no one below can hear us, or could understand us if they did. We need to step down.

Stepping down, however, may not be so bad. Look at all the work that might get done if we are willing to involve ourselves in an unpretentious way with central problems of our time—globalization, the environmental crisis, the growing split between the haves and have-nots, the erosion of well-defined cultures, the disappearance of the transcendent. The issue here is not simply the old chestnut of relevance—bringing Shakespeare up to date by mixing *Romeo and Juliet* with *Boyz N the Hood.* We need a fundamental change of direction. Painful as it may be to admit it, the present does not wait to be measured by the past; instead, the value of the past—its only value, I would say—is its helpfulness to us right now.

If we can make a real contribution to people's lives today, they may even start to listen to us once again. The reason that political scientists and economists—and some historians as well—turn up as talking heads on the evening news is primarily that their fields have always served as conduits for people who go on to take jobs with the State Department and other branches of government or, just as often, with business; in fact, some of the best scholars in these fields circulate in and of the academy throughout their careers. Although we should continue to build on our past achievements, I suspect that our best future will be found in a different sort of specialization than we have so far cultivated. The specialization of the humanities

Revising the specialization of the humanities

today is disciplinary in nature: that is, historians cover only the subject of history, critics cover only literary texts, art historians cover only art, and the subjects themselves get organized internally in the most predictable ways, by historical periods and geography. But the humanities might trade specialization by discipline for specialization by areas of real-world activity. We might someday see, for example, fields such as "medical humanities," "legal humanities," "economic humanities," "media humanities," each linked to professional or preprofessional programs. People working in these disciplines might be historians, philosophers, and critics all at once. In fact, they would need to combine our traditionally separated disciplines; they would also need to be well versed in medicine or law or economics. Sweeping as such a proposal may sound, we already have many humanists of this kind, although we seldom think of them as humanists. The paleontologist Stephen Jay Gould would belong on the list, as would the physicist Carl Sagan, and the ecologists Rachel Carson and Aldo Leopold. To these names I might add two biologists, Anne and Paul Ehrlich, authors of *The Population Bomb;* a psychiatrist, Robert Coles, who wrote the multivolume *Children of Crisis;* a psychologist, Daniel Goleman, author of *Emotional Intelligence;* the political scientist Benjamin Barber and the management theorist Peter Drucker, whose books are too numerous to be named here. I would also add the names of writers working outside the academy: Bill McKibben, author of *The Death of Nature,* Thomas Moore, who wrote *The Care of the Soul,* and Susan Faludi for her feminist opus *Stiffed: The Betrayal of the American Man.*

To reimagine the humanities along these lines would mean understanding them, not as particular subjects, but as the human dimension of all knowledge. When we begin, for example, to explore the human dimension of medicine, as opposed to more restrictively scientific concerns, we enter into the realm of what I am calling "medical humanities." In that context, we might ask questions about the history of medical practice and institutions; about historical and cross-cultural perceptions of illness, including those represented in literary texts. And we might ask about the experiences of illness and health as people actually live through them. Far from diminishing the humanities, a reform of this kind would open vast new horizons of research to those appropriately trained. At the same time, it would greatly broaden the exposure of ordinary citizens to the legacy of the older humanities as well as to the new scholarship. Where I now teach, the humanities reach in a significant way (that is, in more than two courses on the way to the B.A. or B.S. degree) fewer than 20 percent of undergraduates, and humanities majors account for fewer than 15 percent. At many universities, the figures for majors are even more dismal—sometimes as low as 5 percent. But reforms of the sort I am proposing would bring the humanities to students who now miss or quite intentionally evade them because our disciplines, in their splendid isolation, can often seem irrelevant and needlessly arcane. And if the humanities would benefit, so too would colleges of engineering, schools of medicine, and M.B.A. programs.

As long as we imagine the humanities as branches of a "human science" corresponding to the natural sciences, we overlook what makes the humanities crucially different. We should not dismiss a remark once made by William James, echoing Plato—that all knowledge begins and ends in wonder.[32] For many human-

→ the human dimension of medicine or chemistry

ists today, the experience of wonder is certainly important, but only as a personal consequence of an impersonal enterprise. Yet wonder is never simply a happy accident; it is the motive force behind the making of knowledge itself, and without it, knowledge soon becomes dead and deadening. The distinctive purpose of the humanities is to make wonder possible by insisting, over and over again, on both the openness of our experience and the coherence of the world we encounter through it. The pedant, the dogmatic thinker, is the person who confines himself to knowledge in a fixed and finished form, while carefully averting his eyes from the uncertain, which encircles us everywhere. Only after we have turned from the safety of our systems, paradigms, and formulas, does the process of questioning take on new life, which we may feel to be the life of the world itself. I will grant that the humanities are not the only area of knowledge to inspire and cultivate wonder, but the humanities make wonder possible in ways that may even surpass scientific inquiry, astonishing as science has become. Although science is far more complex an activity than even scholars of science can fully explain, it seems fair to say that it produces its knowledge about the world by stepping away from that world, so to speak, by reducing to small parts the lived world in all its experiential wholeness and immediacy. We might say that the knowledge of science is deep but not broad: even the dizzying heights of cosmology look down on only one narrow prospect, beyond which lies the heterogeneous world we encounter in our everyday lives. Increasingly, what science now addresses lies beyond this world altogether, in the microverse of quantum mechanics and the macroverse of black holes. In my opinion, the breakthroughs of science are the greatest achievements in the twentieth century, but in order for those achievements to acquire human meaning—that is, meaning and "weight" in the realm of values and behavior—the humanities must play a mediating role by "translating" the discoveries of science back into the contexts of ordinary life and language. For this reason, I count much of popular science writing today among the best work getting done in the humanities, and I deeply regret as ignorant, mean, and self-serving much of what passes in the academic humanities for the critique of science.[33] Unfortunately, the current war between the sciences and humanities will end either with the ruin of science, hardly to be expected but still possible, or the complete discrediting of the humanities, which seems more probable all the time. A third alternative is a new partnership between them.

For some time now, the humanities have tried to rival the sciences by imitating their methods, but I believe that this strategy has failed. As I argue in the final chapters of Part II, future education in the humanities needs to include a great deal of actual science, but at the same time, the humanities must rediscover their much-neglected roots in the arts—not in the arts as the subject of either critical study or cultured consumption, but as the actual practice of art making. I believe that the purpose of the humanities is to connect specialized knowledge with the everyday life-world—the world we share as people, not as doctors or physicists or carpenters or sales representatives, and not as women or men or blacks or whites. And if this is true, then the arts have to play an indispensable role, since the arts dramatize the process of fashioning connections among our various perspectives, disciplines, and credos. The arts enact in a highly ritualized way an element of all

the practice of Art making

human culture at its best: the movement out of the self and into the world, and out of the world and back into the self again.

To many people in the humanities, this proposal might actually sound far more radical and threatening than the argument that humanists need to know more science. A great secret of the academic humanities has been their quiet but consistent exclusion of the arts as an activity, as a practice. Most universities keep the less-prestigious performing arts and studio arts at some distance from the more revered and often better paid humanities. Art historians seldom have any contact with professors of sculpture or printmaking, and in English departments, critics and scholars have had a long history of uneasy relations with contemporary novelists and poets. This divorce between the study of art and the making of art is not at all an accident but reflects the way in which the humanities established themselves as distinctive professions. For one thing, the arts bear too close a resemblance to the applied disciplines, which our predecessors brushed aside as déclassé. Since its inception, the modern university has privileged the "cultural" over the "practical," and theoretical knowledge over applied knowledge. While this prejudice has begun to erode, the rise of English, to take just one example, virtually demanded the exclusion or quarantine of "creative writing." Writers had to be put on a pedestal so high that ordinary folk would be induced give up on the thought that they themselves could be writers, or even that they could make sense of the poem or book by themselves. Of course, other, more pedestrian factors played a part as well. Right now, for example, the great majority of our genuinely excellent novelists, and there are quite a few in America today, seldom get taught at universities. And, in fact, if English departments tried to keep up with the pace of artistic production, they would need to double in size or else curtail more than a few courses on historically important writers. The whole system, however, is designed to perpetuate a *manageable* body of canonical work, and one stable enough to ensure the survival of the existing divisions of scholarship in English. No matter how many volumes have been written on similar topics in years past, graduate students who complete dissertations on Shelley have a far better chance of getting a job than those who write on Peter Matthiessen or Jane Smiley. Other disciplines, such as biology, have been forced by the growth of new knowledge to reconstruct themselves almost from scratch, but in English, we may never see any comparable change undertaken voluntarily from within our own departments. English pays a price, however, for this resistance to change. Anyone who bothers to research the titles of recently granted dissertations in the field will probably agree that most of them, with some slight accretions of new scholarship, could have been published half a century ago.

I am not arguing that we should throw out the great books or terminate all historically oriented scholarship, but I believe that the humanities as a whole devote far too many resources to research that has a negligible impact on the real life of our society. If we support disciplines like English because we value the arts, then perhaps we should do more to support the arts directly. When one stops to think about it, novelists might prove to be no less capable than historically trained scholar-critics in the teaching of, say, "The English Novel to 1900." But I would prefer that our doctors, engineers, and web masters had the experience of actually *writing* fiction or *making* linocuts or *taking* photographs, rather than enrolling in an isolated survey course for nonmajors on the grounds that these courses give the student a little culture, or worse, that they are needed in order to rectify the student's political outlook: in my view, nothing could do a greater injustice to the whole tradition of the arts, no matter how well taught such courses might be. At the same time, courses in creative writing or painting or dance might actually stimulate interest in historically oriented study. Indeed, such a result would follow almost inevitably if, as we claim when it suits us, historical scholarship complements and enriches artistic practice.

I recognize, however, that the arts themselves are in trouble, though slightly differently from the humanities. I will certainly not be the first person to observe that art making in America has been captured by an elaborate system that involves elite patrons, exclusionary museums and media outlets, and critical gurus who have, at times, striven mightily to normalize tastes and control the direction of the arts from above. All of these vectors came together most smoothly and effectively with the rise of abstract expressionism, a movement guided by the criticism of theorists like Clement Greenberg. During this period, universities and museums waged a kind of *jihad* on all forms of representational art, which became, absurdly, a straw man standing in for middle-class conformity.[34] Even today, when the arts have grown ungovernably diverse (a triumph for the arts, in my view), many superb artists remain outside the circle of public attention—and financial viability—simply because they fail to do what certain critics sanction. It is my hope, however, that a greatly broadened level of participation might help to save the arts from their sometimes overpossessive guardians.

And perhaps such a change would do something as well to diminish the power of possessiveness in general. Could it be that our infatuation with "theory," no less than our obsession with computers and cars, is an autistic response to a failure of imagination? Perhaps we academics are content to criticize consumer culture ad infinitum precisely because we can imagine no alternatives that have not already turned out badly. And most of the alternatives have turned out very badly indeed. However much humanists may detest the market system, who can forget what preceded its triumph? Facing the "iron cage of modernity," the sociologist Max Weber toyed with a return to charismatic leadership, but Hitler's answer to that call has (I hope) decisively ended a chapter in the history of our illusions.[35] And the same might be said of the great communitarian experiments of our century: Lenin's Soviet Union, Mao's People's Republic, the North Korea of Kim Il Sung, the Kampuchea of Pol Pot. Except for the dream of the market, the benign promise of endless plenty, all our dreams have taken us into dark nights far worse than the fantasies of Bruegel and Bosch. If the triumph of theory signals anything, it signals the exhaustion of alternatives, a failure of the capacity to dream anything truly new.

This is precisely why the otherworldliness of our disciplines now stands us in such poor stead. We look longingly back to Socrates, our first Critic, without acknowledging that he created nothing, accomplished nothing; only at the end of his life did Socrates have a true vision, commanding him to make music. Had Socrates lived and had he learned to embrace the revelations of his dreams, we today might have a very different image of the thinker's task. No matter how much may we dislike it, the world we live in now will remain the way it is, barring a complete ecological collapse, until we can devise something better to replace it. The work of the arts and humanities in our time is to imagine—and create—alternatives that are more satisfying, just, and beautiful.

2

Democracy Sets in the West

From Able Citizens to Ignorant Masses

A way of life ended in America with the close of the 1960s. And like most really lasting changes, this one did not arrive as a cataclysm of the kind that gets boldfaced in the history books—the Fall of Rome, the Norman Conquest, the Industrial Revolution. It came quietly in the guise of confusion and unease. Children denounced their parents, and parents walked out on their children. Harvard professors on television celebrated psychedelic drugs while *Life* magazine ran feature stories on half-naked couples who had gone to live in caves. Blacks in berets were organizing private armies while bombs went off on colleges campuses. No one knew exactly what was happening, and everywhere people tried to make sense of things. One of those people was M. I. Finley, a well-known historian of the ancient world.

In April 1972 at Rutgers University in New Jersey, Finley delivered a series of talks later published, somewhat misleadingly, as *Democracy Ancient and Modern*.[1] I say misleadingly because the talks themselves expressed a sense of crisis that his bland title failed to convey. America was falling apart, Finley implied, because it was no longer a democracy, at least not in any sense that the citizens of ancient Athens would have recognized. Democracy, as Athenians understood it, meant direct, sustained participation—"almost," Finley added, "beyond anything we can imagine":

> It was literally true that at birth every Athenian boy had better than a gambler's chance to be president of the Assembly, a rotating post held for a single day and, as always, filled by the drawing of lots. He might be a market commissioner for a year, a member of the Council for one year or two (though not in succession), a juryman repeatedly, a voting member of the Assembly as frequently as he liked. Behind this direct experience, to which should be added the administration of the hundred-odd parishes or "demes" into which Athens was subdivided, there was also the general familiarity with public affairs that even the apathetic could not escape in such a small, face-to-face society.[2]

Every Athenian boy had a gambler's chance of becoming the equivalent of our President, and every one was guaranteed a seat in "congress" at the time of his coming of age. As radical as Finley's accusation might have seemed, most of his hearers knew from their own experience what he was getting at. Some of them had voted more or less regularly, and some of them, though by no means all, could explain in general terms how bills were drafted, passed, and implemented. But none of them, or almost none of them—and they saw themselves, at least tacitly, as members of the intellectual elite—had ever played any meaningful part in the political life of the nation, the state, the county, or even the towns to which they returned at the end of their working day. Distinguished professors, academic administrators, graduate students—they had no direct control over matters as important as the taxes they paid, the laws they observed, the schools their children attended, the lessons children studied in those schools, or the maintenance of their neighborhoods. Finley was correct then, and perhaps even overly circumspect, when he told his hearers that the power exercised by the least powerful Athenian citizen—unqualified and unmediated power—surpassed their own by many measures.

Government in Athens, Finley explained, was a government *by* the assembled people, who decided on all matters related to law, war and peace, diplomacy, the budget, and public works. From the Assembly no free male over the age of eighteen could be excluded, and everyone had both a vote and the right of *isegoria* or free speech. The bureaucratic administrators of the Athenian state—the holders of city offices and members of the Council of 500—were all selected by lot and served terms of one or two years. Even leading political figures like Pericles owed their power to no civil position, since there was no position for them to hold, but solely to their insight and eloquence as citizens exercising commonly held rights.[3] While Pericles at the height of his influence could generally count on public acceptance of his policies, his proposals "were submitted," Finley notes, "week in and week out . . . and the Assembly always could, and on occasion did, abandon him. . . . The *decision* was theirs, not his or any other leader's."[4]

But, as Finley argues, in America circa 1970 things were different. Many experts on politics believed that no one wanted direct democracy, even if it could be made workable somehow. What popular opinion expected, instead, was effective administration: a government *for* the people but not *by* the people themselves, operating under the guidance of the appropriate specialists. At that particular moment in our history, however, Finley's contrast between the two societies struck a painful chord, especially when the discussion turned to the Athenian invasion of Sicily in 413, which had ended in the army's utter defeat and the loss of 40,000 to 60,000 citizen-soldiers. The war in Sicily, of course, recalled another, still ongoing conflict, and one that looked every bit as ruinous as its classical predecessor—the struggle in Vietnam. Ten years of defeat, deceit, and mismanagement at all levels had made the notion of direct democracy far more appealing to Finley's audience than it might have seemed at the end of World War II, and the differences between Sicily and Vietnam were as painful as the similarities, since the Athenians, at least, had chosen *their* fight, while Americans in their "democracy" found themselves unable to terminate what they never had a voice in undertaking. To many of Finley's listeners, for whom images of body bags were still quite fresh and painful, the modern administered society stood exposed as a colossal failure, and not only with respect to the conduct of war in a small East Asian nation, but also here at home, and at the very moment when its final triumph as the so-called Great Society was supposed to have arrived. Only five years earlier and forty minutes to the north of Rutgers, in Newark and Plainfield, two of the most serious race riots in U.S. history had ravaged once prosperous urban centers, leaving dozens of people dead and hundreds injured. More than a few of Finley's listeners could remember the glow of burning buildings on their television screens, and some of them had abandoned their old neighborhoods for the safety of white suburbs.

The experts had failed, that seemed clear enough, but Finley's audience may not have understood that they were experts, too, and beneficiaries of the same system. Like intellectuals everywhere, they might have preferred to see themselves as heirs to the great Athenian philosophers, critical and independent questioners pursuing truth wherever it may lead. Yet the world they actually inhabited was less like Periclean Athens than its Hellenistic counterpart in the third century B.C.E., under the massive state bureaucracies devised by the successors to the dictatorship of Alexander the Great. Marching south from Macedonia, Alexander's army had conquered the Greek city-states, and from there it had overrun most of the known world—Persia, Egypt, and the Middle East, never stopping until it reached India. The empire built by this violence was not a democracy. In the world of democratic Athens, where even the powerful Alcibiades owned a farm of only seventy acres, politics mattered to everyone—to artists and thinkers as well as more ordinary citizens—because everyone had an immediate stake in the city's political life.[5] But in the centralized and stratified world of Alexander's successors, conquered peoples had no way to make themselves heard except as a rioting mob.[6]

In contrast to the Athens that Finley described, the Mediterranean after Alexander was a society like ours, managed by an elite minority of professionals, as it had to be in states so complex, far-flung, and resentful. And these professionals, like our specialists today, ushered in what some might call a Renaissance, but a Renaissance of a rather curious kind. Professionalism produced the exponential growth of "technical proficiency, the collection and systematization of previous knowledge, and the standardization of products."[7] A geographer correctly calculated the circumference of the earth, and astronomers taught that the sun occupied the center of the solar system. At the same time that scientific learning advanced, innovations of technique and technology—the bill of exchange in banking, the Archimedean screw in hydraulics, the threshing machine in agriculture—transformed Mediterranean economic life. By contrast, Finley's free Athenians were "half educated," as he concedes in response to Thucydides' snide allegations about their ignorance.[8] When they voted to send troops into Sicily, for example, only a handful of citizens could have known much about the location, size, or population of the island. A petty scribe in Alexandria, a major city of the empire, may have known more about many subjects than a renowned lecturer two centuries earlier, yet the Hellenistic cultural renaissance can hardly be described as anything except a period of precipitous social, political, and moral decline.

As an interpreter of his era Finley grasped what many of his contemporaries had not: public apathy about modern politics was a "withdrawal response" to a system of government by specialists.[9] But he did not go on to explore the connection between such a system and the forms of knowledge it promotes. That connection would be made on another occasion by another historian, not a professional scholar like Finley but a self-confessed amateur, the novelist and poet Eduardo Galeano. This is what Galeano had to say about his earliest encounters with their shared branch of learning:

> I was a wretched student of history. History classes were like visits to the waxworks or the Region of the Dead. The past was lifeless, hollow, dumb. They taught us about the past so that we should resign ourselves with drained consciences to the present: not to make history, which was already made, but to accept it. Poor History stopped breathing: betrayed in academic texts, lied about in classrooms, drowned in dates, they had imprisoned her in museums and buried her, with floral wreaths, beneath statuary bronze and monumental marble.[10]

The fate of "poor History" is the fate of a knowledge systematically detached from the issues and urgencies of everyday life, issues like the war in Vietnam. Finley, an unusual specialist in many respects, had carefully crafted *his* remarks for an audience of nonspecialists, but the history embalmed in Galeano's "academic texts" was the creation of professional historians conversing principally with one another, men and women for whom the conversation itself had displaced the world in which such conversations might have obvious meaning and value. While the history they wrote could instruct, it could never move people to action; while they had any number of topics to argue *about,* they no longer seemed to have anything to argue *for.* Alexandrian in outlook rather than Athenian, these historians could trifle endlessly with details and with perspectives on the details; they could spend years debating what various people might know and how they might know it. But in doing so they inadvertently revealed what they most wished to keep hidden away: their profound social isolation. By contrast, the historians of ancient Greece— Xenophon, for example, and Thucydides—were not at all concerned about historical research "for its own sake" or about how we know what we know.[11] As apologists of the old, predemocratic aristocracy, these men understood the connections between knowledge and public life, and both had a stake in telling the story of past events to support their particular social interests. Unlike the latter-day historians who made sure that students like Galeano left the class convinced that history was over, they had purposes rather than perspectives, commitments rather than methodologies; and among their hearers and their readers, surely no one in all of Athens was naïve enough to suppose that the stories these historians told were purely factual or disinterested. History of the sort that Galeano describes, a record of the past with no purpose or point other than to record, was unthinkable for those first historians.

Like people at all times the world over, the Athenians had their experts too.

Plato's Phraedrus was an orator, his Euthyphro a theologian. But the nature of Athenian society gravitated against this tendency, as the historian Jean-Pierre Vernant suggests when he describes their way of life in the centuries before Alexander's dictatorship as fundamentally unhierarchical and egalitarian. "Of course," Vernant writes, "their ideas [about how to live] were bound to change, but so long as the city remained" untroubled by external domination, these "were the ideas of men who saw themselves as autonomous and free within the framework of small independent communities." Just as power in the Athenian city-state belonged to every citizen and was said to have been "placed 'en mesoi'" or "at the center" of the community, so knowledge and culture in general belonged to all. These too were "placed at the center, no longer the privilege of a few families or . . . a class of educated men."[12] But for this very reason—because knowledge and culture belonged to everyone—the Greeks did not share our current sense of ideas as the exclusive property of those who know most or know best. And here Vernant makes a useful comparison—to ancient China rather than to late antiquity in the West. Both Greece and China had, he tells us, mastered the forging of iron at approximately same time, but in China iron smithing remained under government supervision as "an instrument of [state] power," whereas the Greeks saw it as a skill that any person could learn. For the Greeks as for the Chinese at the close of the Bronze Age, no technology brought with it greater dread and greater danger than the forging of iron, but technology, like power, stood *en mesoi*, at the center. Among the Greeks, a blacksmith did his work unremarkably, crafting swords and crafting spoons as an independent artisan in a workshop he often owned.[13]

All of this changed, of course, with the gradual rise of Rome following Alexander's death, and on the final day of Finley's lecture series at Rutgers, when he asked his listeners to consider why intellectual life had declined along with the democratic city-state, he took as one example the surprising atrophy of the Stoic school of philosophers, thinkers we today might compare to the modern world's leftist theorists—radical critics of the status quo. "No authority," Finley observed, had openly threatened the Stoic philosophers in spite of their long reputation for making trouble, and no one had tried to force them to accept "a comfortable accommodation with the rapacious . . . Roman oligarchy."[14] All the same, the Stoics capitulated—without torture, without prison, without the cruelty of exile. That they stopped challenging those in power, Finley suggested, may tell us less about the moral failings of individual Stoic teachers than about the political and social transformation that succeeded in making real freedom look absolutely unattainable. What good did it do for philosophers to ask hard questions when they talked only to one another? And what good did it do to think or debate, when thinking had become an end in itself—had reached, in other words, a dead end. Without a capacity to act upon the world, the students of the great philosophers might just as well have passed their evenings dining out and drinking, or going to the theater, and that in fact was what they did. Public argument had become mere philosophy—just as Plato, a critic of democracy, had devoutly hoped it would—while philosophy in turn became the pastime of bored aristocrats and sentimentalizing antiquarians. The most brilliant minds of the late Alexandrian world, Plotinus and Proclus, wasted their prodigious energies in abstruse speculations while they earned their daily bread relieving wealthy patrons of guilt, anomie, or tedium. If Finley's lectures have anything to say to people now, thirty years after the fact, they call on us to ask ourselves if this is the way many of the best minds of our times earn *their* daily bread. Could it be that knowledge of the kind we most value now—the knowledge of specialists—has failed to make the people of our time either more intelligent or more free, more capable or more confident? Is it possible that our scholars and critics have undermined not only our political ideals but also our own sense of self-worth?

For us now, the best answer to these questions may be found in the sweeping transformation of American life that took place at the turn of the nineteenth century, when the administered society—rule by the best and the brightest—arose from the ruins of an earlier, more democratic culture. As the historian Robert Wiebe maintains in his classic study of this crucial period,

> Small town life was America's norm in the [1870s]. Depending upon the lines of transportation, groups of these towns fell into satellite patterns about a larger center, to which they looked for markets and supplies, credit and news. . . . With farms generally fanning around them, these communities moved by the rhythms of agriculture: the pace of the sun's day, the working and watching of the crop's months. . . . Usually homogeneous, usually Protestant, they enjoyed an inner stability that the coming and going of members seldom shook. Even when new towns were established in fresh farm country, the gathering families brought the same familiar habits and ways so that a continuity was scarcely disturbed.[15]

Wiebe wrote this passage at a distance of several generations from the time he describes, but John Dewey, a young man by the end of the 1880s, could offer a personal testimony to the success of democracy in "small centers," as he put it, "where industry was mainly agricultural and where production was carried on mainly with hand tools." Even if the population was often "mobile and migratory," the "forms of association" themselves proved to be surprisingly "stable."[16]

As Dewey understood, however, and as Wiebe takes care to point out, the small towns of nineteenth-century America were never Utopian communities, harmonious and entirely egalitarian. When we view them from the distance of more than a hundred years—years of unparalleled change—we may be eager to overlook small-scale hierarchies of distinction and wealth less elaborate than ours but also, in certain ways, less open to challenge. Wiebe recounts that some men—merchants, bankers, a handful of prosperous farmers—were addressed by their last names. Others—the craftsmen, the small farmers, the new immigrants—might be called by their first. Yet within these small "island communities," the *relative* equality of face-to-face interactions made it possible for many citizens to perceive the order of their lives as consonant with the order of nature itself, and even as divinely ordained.[17] For most Americans, the town was the world. New York and Philadelphia were themselves little more than large towns by our standards, and in the absence of technologies of mass communication, contacts between the civic "islands" remained hopelessly sporadic, a restriction that worked to disperse and fragment "the power to form opinion and enact . . . policy." For a later, urban generation, "small town America" became synonymous with banality and intolerance—novelist Sinclair Lewis's *Main Street*—but the people of the time saw it differently. Far from perceiving their relative isolation as something to be overcome, Americans in the last third of the nineteenth century often associated their "local autonomy" with democracy itself. Even education underscored this fundamental lesson: at every level from the schoolhouse to the college lecture hall, formal learning inhibited "specialization" and discouraged "the accumulation of knowledge" for its own sake.[18]

Many of our communitarians today—the sociologists Robert Bellah and Amitai Etzioni, for example, —blame the passing of this way of life on the triumph of a new and disruptive "individualism," but Wiebe offers a more complex and, to my mind, more pursuasive explanation.[19] Far from abandoning family, friends, and neighbors, Americans were left to fend for themselves as the center of gravity shifted from the town to the nation-state, from the local market to distant centers of finance, from the country to the city, and from the region to the "cosmopolitan" center. Although people discovered new possibilities once this transformation had over-taken them, many experienced the coming of the new order not as a moment of liberation but as a time of painful crisis. According to Wiebe, "In a manner that eludes precise explanation, countless citizens in towns and cities across the land sensed that something fundamental was happening to their lives, something they had not willed and did not want." Without fully comprehending the forces under-mining their way of life, they fought against "whatever enemies their view of the world allowed them to see." But their world "had already slipped beyond their grasp."[20]

Among the citizens of rural America—roughly 85 percent of all Americans in the 1890s—many associated the coming of modernity with a *loss* of personal autonomy. Even those who held the levers of change, the industrialists and politi-cians, were carried forward by processes they had set in motion but never altogether mastered, so that the period from 1870 to 1900 saw a series of spectacular depres-sions, each collapse producing groping adjustments to the unruly financial system. Anyone familiar with works like Henry George's *Progress and Poverty,* Edward Bellamy's *Looking Backward,* Josiah Strong's *Our Country: Its Possible Future and Its Present Crisis* or Richard T. Ely's *Social Aspects of Christianity*—all influential social criticism in their time—will recognize the popular resistance to moderniza-tion and the popular commitment to the older, agrarian, and largely Protestant order. Yet there could be no going back: whatever new associations people might manage to create, these could no longer have their deepest roots in kinship or a shared sense of place. In some other guise community would have to be invented, but the instability caused by larger social forces made that task into a labor of Sisyphus.

Rather than imagine modernity as a single system, we might remember its early years as a period of conflict among rival successors to the old, agrarian order—

a conflict that continues to this day. The first of the successors were the cultural populists, who tried to create a new and larger democratic community while preserving valued elements of the older local cultures.[21] They saw that people who were geographically dispersed could still be united by comparable experience, values, questions, and aspirations. Prominent in this effort were the "scribbling women" like Louisa May Alcott, Sarah Orne Jewett, Rebecca Harding Davis, and Mary Austin, all writers who achieved a national audience. There were also "regionalists" like Mark Twain, Bret Harte, and Hamlin Garland; African-American writers like Langston Hughes and Zora Neale Hurston; leftist "radicals" like Jack London; and Native Americans like Charles Eastman and Gertrude Bonnin. Although many of the writers engaged in the attempt to reconstruct democracy are now commonly remembered as "regionalists" or "ethnic" writers, these rubrics carry with them the disparaging connotations of provincialism and nostalgia. Instead, we might understand them all as social thinkers who astutely recognized that the best communities draw their strength from differences as well as agreements.

The populists had a rival, however, and one that grew increasingly powerful with the advent of the Progressive movement—the culture of specialization. As the island communities disappeared, ingenious and enterprising minds devised another means of organizing social life, no longer based on consensus from below but instead on administration from above.[22] While the populists used the new mass media of magazines and books to build coalitions by appealing to affinities of experience, the Progressive-era creators of the administered society were busily constructing institutions: government bureaus, professional organizations, educational systems, and of course, corporations, which we might think of as the bureaucratic form of capitalism.[23] And in contrast to the populists, they claimed to draw their authority from their possession of the truth—especially the truth of science—as opposed to popular opinion. From the start, the opponents were unevenly matched. Persuasion demands from the writer skill and time, from the reader sensitivity and openness, while coalitions built over many years sometimes evaporate overnight. Institutions, by contrast, can persist for centuries. Institutions never tire or require sleep; when a human cog wears out, another quickly takes his or her place. Institutions have another advantage as well; the more they proliferate, the more necessary they become.

So much has administration shaped our society that we may find it difficult to imagine what life was like a little more than a century ago, before General Motors, the Federal Reserve, and the American Medical Association. The record of some lives, however, gives us a sense of how it was—the life, for example, of Charles Eastman, a Lakota who had witnessed as a child the "Sioux Uprising" of 1862.[24] In the transition from island communities to their cosmopolitan successors, no one traveled farther or less willingly than the Native Americans, yet in some ways their experience reveals the most about the nature of the change overtaking everyone. The coming of modernity made it possible for Eastman to complete a degree in medicine at Boston University in 1890.[25] Kept out of his profession by the sheer force of prejudice, he eventually earned his living as a popular writer on Indian customs and history. But in moving beyond the boundaries of his ancestral world, Eastman was hardly alone. The same might be said, with slightly different inflections, of African Americans like Charles Chesnutt or W. E. B. Dubois. And yet to suppose simply that these Americans lived *between* worlds is to underestimate the extent to which they tried to create a larger world. By writing in middle-class literary English to white readers, Eastman changed the way those readers understood not only the "Red Man" but also their own society. Describing the events at Wounded Knee massacre, for example, he recalled "the excitement and grief of my Indian companions, nearly every one of whom was crying aloud or singing his death song." Among the bodies Eastman found on the frozen fields was one severely wounded man still living, who begged him to fill his pipe. "When we brought him into the chapel," Eastman wrote, "he was welcomed by his wife and daughters with cries of joy, but he died a day or two later."[26] The newspapers told the story differently, but same social forces that had given the papers their chance to be heard gave Eastman a voice as well.

People like Charles Eastman belonged to the first truly modern generation in America—the first generation to lose a world and then to set out in search of a new one. Eastman's father was a warrior who had spent four years in a military prison and then returned to the Dakota Territory, a newly converted Christian. After building a cabin and learning how to farm, Many Lightnings, or Jacob Eastman, as he called himself by then, sent the boy he now named "Charles" off to school. "You will be taught the language of the white man," he told his son. "The white teacher will first teach you the signs by which you can make out the words in their books. They call them A, B, C, and so forth. Old as I am, I have learned some of them."[27] Believing change to be inevitable, Jacob Eastman wanted his son to have some degree of power over change itself. The white man's "way of knowledge," he was convinced, "is like our old way in hunting. You begin with a mere trail—a footprint." But if "you follow that faithfully, it may lead you to a clearer trail—a track—a road."[28] And once Charles had begun to follow that road, he found himself caught up, like many white Americans, in a process that outstripped all the linguistic and symbolic resources provided by his tradition. While it is possible to see the path that Many Lightnings glimpsed as ultimately leading nowhere, Eastman would not have agreed. The contradictions of modernity forced him to reinvent not only himself but also his own history. He had begun his life in the Wapeton clan, a "Dweller among the Leaves," but in the course of his journey through the modern world Charles Eastman became something else, something that had never existed before. "I am," he writes in the final paragraph of his memoir, "an *Indian;* and while I have learned much from civilization, for which I am grateful, I have never lost my Indian sense of right and justice. I am for development and progress along social and spiritual lines, rather than those of commerce, nationalism, or material efficiency. Nevertheless, so long as I live, I am an *American.*"[29] Eastman ended his life at a boundary that no one before him had crossed—as an Indian and not just a Wapeton, with a kinship to Seminoles and Cherokees his ancestors had never even heard of; a supporter of progress but also a critic of capitalism; a defender of "Sioux" tradition but also a self-professed American.

This was the *promise* of modernity, which Dewey celebrated as the world-transforming "release of human potentialities."[30] But as the power of tradition declined, new obstacles arose. With his medical degree in hand and the highest hopes, Eastman had initially gone back to the reservation, where he married a white woman who spoke fluent Sioux and assisted him in his growing practice. "There was," he remembered, "nothing I called my own save my dogs and horses and medicine bags, yet I was perfectly happy, for I had not only gained the confidence of my people, but that of the white residents, and even the border ranchmen called me in now and then. I answered every call, and have ridden forty or fifty miles in a blizzard."[31] What might have happened if Eastman had remained there we can only speculate, but the Lokota, as wards of the government, were not the masters of themselves, and when Eastman attempted to challenge the dishonest practices of federal agents, he "was promptly charged with 'insubordination.'" The "local authorities," he recalls, "followed the usual tactics, and undertook to force a resignation by making my position at Pine Ridge intolerable." Although Pine Ridge, like all reservations, occupied an ambiguous position between a captive territory and a state populated by full citizens, it might also be seen as one early proving ground for a new and distinctly undemocratic political organization—the bureaucratically administered state. Although the federal agents had never been elected and were accountable only to their own superiors, they exercised on the reservation an authority that no one could successfully resist. Eastman and his wife soon found themselves "hampered" in their work and "harassed by every imaginable annoyance" until, together with their few white sympathizers, they were finally driven off the reservation.[32]

Eastman's struggle with the Office of Indian Affairs was an emblematic moment. In one sense, it was a fight between two professionals and their professions. But if we view the event in the context of Eastman's later life, it places into sharp relief something more than two professions: two very different futures for America, one represented by the freelance writer and activist, the other by the bureaucrat. A century earlier, such a conflict would have been unthinkable. Institutions like the Office of Indian Affairs did not yet exist, and even the professions remained poorly elaborated. Physicians and dentists, often practicing alone without degrees, were hardly distinguished from barbers. Attorneys like Abraham Lincoln learned their law in the courtrooms rather than the lecture halls. And the early forms of the now-ubiquitous research university could be found only in Germany, where wealthy young men like the future historian Henry Adams went abroad to study.

Even then, however, what distinguished the two adversaries—Eastman the university-trained physician and his opposite, the government functionary—from the great mass of other Americans was their possession of a new form of power, knowledge. It was knowledge of a new kind, however, not local and informal but transportable and highly formalized. In the older world of island communities, knowledge had played a different role and had a different character. Describing rural Wisconsin life during the last third of the nineteenth century, the novelist Hamlin Garland recalls that there were "few books in our house":

Aside from the Bible I remember only one other, a thick, black volume filled with gaudy pictures of cherries and plums, and portraits of ideally fat and prosperous sheep, pigs, and cows. It must have been a *Farmer's Annual* or State agricultural report, but it contained in the midst of its dry prose, occasional poems like "I remember, I remember," "The Old Armchair," and other pieces of a domestic and rural nature. I was especially moved by "The Old Armchair," and although some of the words and expressions were beyond my comprehension, I fully understood the defiant tenderness of the lines:

I love it, I love it, and who shall dare
To chide me for loving the old armchair?[33]

Most of Garland's early learning did not come from books at all but from face-to-face interactions, and the knowledge they conveyed was local as opposed to cosmopolitan: more tacit than explicit, more practical than abstract, more fully anchored in a single context than universal. Even the knowledge that came from outside the confines of community—agricultural bulletins and poems like "The Old Armchair"—tended to support the assumptions and practices of everyday life. Far from "pushing the envelope," as we now expect "great" art and letters to do, the poems scattered through the pages of the *Annual* encouraged readers to suspend the critical attitude for the pleasure of identification, the same pleasure that many people still derive from television and the movies. And these pleasures played a crucial role in a world that depended on shared labor, friendliness, and reciprocity. But this primitive economy of local knowledge, highly stable and roughly egalitarian, was destined to be changed, and by forces far removed from Garland's particular island community.[34] With the growth of industry came the railroads and the telegraph lines, and with these came the first mass communications.

When Garland wrote his memoir, *A Son of the Middle Border,* he recalled that during the years of his family's homesteading in Wisconsin's Green Coulee region, there were "piles of newspapers but no bound volumes other than the Bible and certain small Sunday school books." Later, accidentally, he came into the possession of two "miraculous" texts—*Beauty and the Beast* and *Aladdin and his Wonderful Lamp.*[35] After his family had moved to a new homestead in Minnesota, neighbors loaned him several other mass market books, one an "enthralling" adventure entitled *The Female Spy,* the other a tale of the shipwrecked seamen, *Cast Ashore,* although "this volume unfortunately was badly torn and fifty pages were missing."[36] But when Garland started to attend the new public school, his reading became more structured and more clearly an import from somewhere else. From *McGuffey's Eclectic Reader* he "got his introduction" to Shakespeare, the Romantic poets, and the monuments of an emerging American literary tradition: Whittier's "Thanatopsis," Longfellow's "The Village Blacksmith," as well as excerpts from Cooper's *The Deerslayer* and *The Pilot,* although it seemed to Garland that "Professor McGuffey," being "a Southern man, did not value New England writers as highly as [Garland's] grandmother did."[37] While a distinctly national pantheon of authors had yet to be fully consolidated, "local knowledge" was gradually ceasing to count as knowledge at all. Garland recalls, for example, that his family liked to play a trendy new card game entitled "Authors." And to the Garlands, the authors pictured on the cards were "singular, exalted beings found only in the East—in splendid cities. The authors were the first example of what we now call "stars": "men and women living aloof and looking down benignantly on toiling common creatures like us."[38]

In another autobiography of the time, *Earth Horizon,* the novelist Mary Austin remembers the itinerant "professors" who acted as purveyors of the new cosmopolitan knowledge to the towns of rural Midwest:

> [The professor] was still, in [those days], indispensable to a "cultivated" state of mind. . . . Everybody wanted culture in the same way that a few years earlier everybody wanted sewing machines, but culture by this time was something more than it had been a few years earlier, when . . . a school for young ladies in a neighboring town advertised both "solid and ornamental cultures," in the latter classification the making of wax flowers was included. It meant for one thing . . . the studious reading of books. To say that people in Carlinville were, in the late seventies, anxious about the state of their culture, where formerly they had been chiefly concerned about their souls, is to sum up all that had happened to them in the twenty years that succeeded the close of the Civil War.[39]

In a certain sense, the Civil War did not end at Appomatox in 1865 but at Chicago's Columbian Exposition 28 years later, since the growth of an industrial economy went hand in hand with a new cultural and political centralization. If the sewing machine rapidly made its way to midsized towns like Carlinville, Illinois, a mass-market version of "culture" could not be very far behind. As Wiebe has argued, Americans of the day, especially the ones with the greatest social power— politicians, industrialists, the educated elite—associated this transition from community to nation-state with the ideals of social progress and democratization, though in practice its consequences were far less innocent.

With the shift from the local production of culture to its importation from far away came a subtle but long-lasting change in the relations within the island community itself. To be anxious about the state of one's soul was to acknowledge a moral accountability not only to God but to family members, fellow townspeople, friends, and of course, enemies, with whom it was essential to get along somehow. Anxieties about the possession of "culture" imply a very different sense of relations with others—relations that become more and more competitive, hierarchical, and socially isolating. On the one hand, the arrival of a new cosmopolitan knowledge made it possible to look critically at traditions formerly immune to change. Austin, for example, became a feminist by osmosis toward the end of her high school years.[40] But the new economy of knowledge brought, on the other hand, something else, something formerly almost as scarce as the knowledge hawked by the traveling lecturers—and that was ignorance.[41] As Austin understood in retrospect, "The status of being cultivated was something like the traditional preciousness of women: nothing that you could cash in upon, but a shame to you to do without."[42] The cultured person was the one who could recite a verse or two from Longfellow, and without that ability, Austin's fellow men and women—people only a decade earlier as good as anyone else—suddenly found themselves obliged to endure an unfamiliar sense of shame.

A poem like Garland's favorite, "The Old Armchair," did not perform the same social function as a poem by Longfellow. For one thing, Longfellow's work represented a uniquely portable culture, supported by the new public schools and mass-market publications like *McGuffey's Reader*. But the value of Longfellow as *knowledge* in the modern cultural economy derived from his relative transience. Longfellow was "in" but he would soon, predictably, be "out," just as French philosophers like Derrida and Foucault were in a few years ago and are on their way out today. A person might, in fact, come to Longfellow's work so belatedly that an appreciation would make her cultural poverty more obvious. And if the new economy of knowledge created a division between those who had knowledge and those who did not, it brought about another unexpected split that Austin recognized with remarkable clarity:

> Into the widening gap . . . between the generations, our burgeoning system of public education was driving a wedge of books. It drove [them] so fast that by the time [I] was twelve, one book, such as was usually kept in Mother's bureau and given to girls to read when they required it, was not enough to close the gap between young girls and young mothers; tradition was not enough; "Godey's Lady's Book" was too fragile; not even the weekly county paper . . . the "Carlinville Democrat" . . . answered wholly the need of a democratically constituted society for "keeping up."[43]

Carlinville citizens a generation earlier had been inhabitants of a different universe, one in which reading and prayer were practices of self-cultivation that helped to sustain an order perceived as timeless. But for the young men and women of Austin's generation, newer practices brought them into a world where nothing remained the same. And this spirit of change served to devalue local knowledge, not once but again and again. "Keeping up" described a more or less one-way transaction between the Eastern core and the Western periphery, and while the pursuit of culture in Carlinville initially preserved the communal character of the older way of life, the center of gravity had shifted.[44] When the townspeople gathered to discuss literary matters, they did so as the Chautauqua Literary and Scientific Circle, with a reading list developed not in the spirit of public discourse but toward the ends of "adult education."[45] Quietly but also decisively, certain citizens had become "students" while others had somehow garnered for themselves the coveted "teacher" role.

Like many people of her generation, Mary Austin at first felt these events to be enormously liberating. Of her Methodist upbringing, for example, she writes in fairly negative terms. The worst thing about it, she remembers, "was that its stresses were upon what the preacher thought, nor what God thought even" but upon "the judgment of the congregation."[46] With the coming of modernization, however, the power of the congregation loosened rapidly. In spite of prohibitions against the theater, Carlinvillians (as Austin calls them) went to watch traveling performances

of *Uncle Tom's Cabin* and the popular Civil War thriller *The Union Spy.* Eventually
the town would even construct an "Op'ry House" in the shell of an abandoned
church.[47] Yet at the same time as the coming of modernity allowed a certain
spaciousness of experience, it closed off other avenues. Enrolled at the State Normal
School in 1885, Austin suffered some kind of a nervous collapse, ostensibly caused by
overwork. She would later decide, however, that what actually had broken her was
not the strain of learning but the "pedagogical method." "At the normal school," she
wrote, "she was simply redriven over the curricula of public school grades with
immense and boring particularity." History was "reduced to a precise allocation of
names and places, middle initials and unimportant generals," while reading was
"reduced to the rendering of the content of literature in the most explicit rather than
the most expressive verbal terms."[48] On the one hand, modernization had loosened the hold of old assumptions, as honored as they were unexamined; on the
other hand, it replaced the loose, pliant bonds of custom with the iron cage of
regimentation.

In a rather different way, Garland learned the same lesson. As with thousands
of other young Americans of the time, his education had prepared him for a world
that promised far more than it could deliver. After he completed a program of study
at a Wisconsin seminary, Garland went south to the capital, Madison, in search of a
job commensurate with his education. He arrived there, however, only to learn that
"four men and two girls were clamoring for every job. Nobody needed me."[49]
Working several months in the accounting department of a Madison firm, he finally
left to try his luck in the glorious East, but unemployment there was just as high,
and soon he was drifting west again, first to Chicago and then to the Dakota
Territory, where his family had gone to homestead once more. Doing odd jobs until
the winter set in, Garland wrote to town halls in Minnesota and Iowa, and then,
acting on the casual suggestion of a man in Madison, he "tramped" his way back to
Boston hoping to enter college. Disappointed by brief stints at Harvard and Boston
University, which he found pretentious and unfriendly, Garland began to sit in on
the lectures at the Boston Men's Union, nineteenth-century New England's equivalent of a community college. This was the opportunity that changed his life.
Reading voraciously under the direction of his teachers and writing every day, he
managed after only a year to achieve success beyond his own vaulting ambitions,
launching his career as a literary star with essays published in *Harper's Weekly* and
The New American Magazine.[50]

In his migration from obscurity to national prominence, and from the prairie
to the northeast, Garland drifted with the currents of social and economic power.
And the knowledge he acquired along the way was a distinctly cosmopolitan
knowledge—systematic and universalizing. Like millions of working-class Americans, he had been deeply moved by reading Henry George's populist polemic
Progress and Poverty. But the books that Garland valued the most once he had found
his "calling" as a writer were the ones that promised to explain what he called "the
laws which govern literary development"—the laws governing the evolution of
literary forms and subjects. These were books like Chambers's *Encyclopoedia of
English Literature,* Greene's *History of the English People,* and the collected works of

Hippolyte Taine, who developed in his "science" of literature a synthesis of the growing nationalist spirit with the tenets of social Darwinism. "Day after day," Garland recalls, "I bent to this task, pondering all the great Frenchman had to say of *race, environment,* and *momentum.*"[51] Among the most widely influential works of the time, Taine's four-volume *History of English Literature* purported to demonstrate that the culture of every nation expresses a collective personality shaped by the nation's material circumstances. Later, under Taine's influence, Garland had gone on to read the social thinker (and social Darwinist) Herbert Spencer, who became, as Garland said, "my philosopher and master."[52]

For Garland, the power of writers like Chambers, Greene, Taine, and Spencer lay in their appeal to tradition—to a stability and continuity that life in twentieth-century America increasingly lacked. But the "tradition" these three writers traced out in their works was something altogether new, the tradition of the nation and the race. In fact, the new learning they created was exactly the knowledge necessary to demolish local traditions and promote a dehistoricized cosmopolitanism: it was not a knowledge that could be tested against the realities of everyday life, but one that took precedence over the testimony of experience itself. It did not encourage the learner's activity but offered the assurance that "development" was happening according to a colossal master plan. Yet the new knowledge had another function beside the erasing of local memory. By positing the existence of national "personalities," works like Taine's *History* imposed upon their readers obligatory ways of regarding themselves. To be "an Englishman" or "an American" was to be, by the process of evolution, a particular kind of person, with proclivities and capacities transcending all the accidents of individual birth and opportunity.[53]

Garland's early adulthood had been a series of accidents and dead ends, but if his education taught him anything, it taught him that history had a direction. Yet that direction, it turned out later in his career, was not the one he had been told to anticipate. Despite his reputation as a voice of the West, his *A Son of the Middle Border* closes with a growing sense of disappointment about the future, a future he beheld with his own eyes at the Chicago Exposition's "Magic City" where he taken his parents at the end of their lives as exhausted, unsuccessful pioneers:

> Stunned by the majesty of the vision, my mother sat in her chair, visioning it all yet comprehending little of its meaning. Her life had been spent among homely small things, and these gorgeous scenes dazzled her, overwhelmed her, letting [everything] in upon her in one mighty flood. . . . She was old and she was ill, and her brain ached with the weight of its new conceptions. . . . At the end of the third day father said, "Well, I've had enough." He too began to long for the repose of the country.[54]

But it was not exactly the "country" that the Garlands would retire to after one last harvest. Their final homestead turned out to be a modest suburban home in West Salem, Massachusetts, "not beautiful," Hamlin admitted, "but it was sheltered on the south by three enormous maples," and there was space for a garden and a few fruit frees. While Garland's memoir ends on a Thanksgiving evening under a "protecting roof," an optimistic century had come to a close and the result was hardly enlivening. "All about me as I traveled," Garland writes, "I now perceived the mournful side of the American 'enterprise.' Sons were deserting their work-worn fathers, daughters were forgetting their tired mothers. Families were every-where breaking up . . . in [a] restless motion, spreading, swarming, dragging . . . reluctant women and their helpless and wondering children into unfamiliar hard-ships."[55] For many of these Americans, who had begun their lives as townspeople but would end it as an urban proletariat, the city was anything but "magic."

All the suffering, of course, was supposed to pay off. The ideology of progress had taught people like the Garlands to tolerate a degree of misery that no one would have otherwise endured. If technological innovation kept transforming everything, from the rituals of private hygiene to the skyline of the city, the forces of *cultural* change were no less distant and unresponsive.[56] As the sociologist Robert Park observed in 1916, modern life was urban life, and in the city "more than elsewhere human relations are likely to be impersonal and rational," with the face-to-face associations of the town replaced by routines conducted almost exclusively "in terms of [social] interest and in terms of cash"[57]:

> In a great city, where the population is unstable, where parents and children are employed out of the house and often in distant parts of the city, where thousands of people live side by side for years without so much as a bowing acquaintance, these intimate relationships of the primary group are weakened and the moral order which rested upon them is gradually dissolved. . . .
>
> Under the disintegrating influences of city life, most of our traditional institutions, the church, the school, and the family, have been greatly modi-fied. The school, for example, has taken over some of the functions of the family. . . . The church, on the other hand, has lost much of its influence. . . .
>
> It is probably the breaking down of local attachments and the weaken-ing of the restraints and inhibitions of the primary group . . . which are largely responsible for the increase of vice and crime.[58]

As Park had witnessed at first hand during his years as an urban reporter, the life of the rural community had given way to a spirit of "individualism," but unlike many observers now, Park understood that this shift was an unchosen and largely unforeseen result of large-scale economic changes. Strictly speaking, the emergence of the modern "individual" meant a *loss* of personal freedom and self-worth, since the life of the unpropertied wage worker, always only a paycheck ahead of destitu-tion, was precarious in a way that life fifty years before had not been. The "freedom" of the modern urbanite was a *freedom to*—the freedom to work, to sacrifice, to compete, to fit in—but never a *freedom from*. Never a freedom *from* want, *from* anxiety, overt violence, or coercion. And Park understood that this loss of personal autonomy—an autonomy that could be fostered only by the appropriate community structure—had the gravest political ramifications. "Our political system," he wrote, "is founded upon the conviction that people who [make their homes] in the same locality have common interests, and that they can therefore be relied upon to act together for their common welfare." But that "assumption," in the urban setting, was no longer "valid." When millions of Americans lived in hotels or lodging houses, more or less out of their suitcases, "traditional forms of local government [must] fail or break down altogether."[59] The modern city was nothing like the Athenian *polis,* and its inhabitants had ceased to be citizens, because their "primary" institutions—the family, the neighborhood, the relations sustained by friendship and work—had become too drastically attenuated to support any genuine civic culture. Once the imperative to earn a living consumed all available energies, and once every person rose or fell exclusively by his isolated efforts, crisis was the order of the day every day. Modernity brought about what might be called a "total mobilization" of the populace.

While Park explained the nature of modernity as lucidly as any observer of his day, he never thought to call for a restoration of the older, democratic sensibility— the one that Finley would look back upon longingly fifty-six years later. As far as Park was concerned, there could be no going back. Instead, he believed that with the fading of rural traditions, the problems of urban culture called urgently for mechanisms of effective "social control," mechanisms based on "positive law" and informed by expert opinion. "There is," he wrote, "probably no other country in the world in which so many 'reforms' are in progress as at the present time in the United States." And the "reforms thus effected, almost without exception, involve some sort of restriction or governmental control over activities that were formerly 'free' or controlled only by . . . mores and public opinion."[60] Although the tradition of direct democracy—the tradition of the town meeting—"was well suited to the needs of a small community based on primary relations," the city had a distinctive life of its own, whose workings Park saw it as his task to explore. And in the course of his long career he became convinced that the modern city was not an accidental sprawl but a living organism subject to the dynamics of a "human ecology." Park was convinced that the city's life, no less than the life of a natural ecosystem, "involves a kind of metabolism. It is constantly assimilating new individuals, and just as steadily, by death or otherwise, eliminating older ones."[61] Individuals came and went but the system continued because its highest law was the law of competition—and this was nature's law, as well—which protected the whole at the expense of the part, and collective life at the expense of individual lives.

Like Durkheim and, before him, Thomas Hobbes, Park conceived of society as a collective subject, one that "moves" like a person "under the influence of a multitude of impulses and tendencies."[62] But Park was also persuaded that at this moment in the collective subject's natural evolution, the organism had yet to take on its final form. Enormous and complex as the nation-state might be, it still needed a brain, a steering mechanism—what Herbert Spencer called a *sensorium*—and that need would be filled by social scientists such as Park himself, a member of the rising knowledge class. Unlike some other social scientists, a man like E. A. Ross, for example, Park did not envisage speaking directly to the laity. Rather, he claimed for himself a leadership role as a shaper of *policy.* Implicit in his understanding of the social sciences was the belief that the government, guided by the brightest and the best, was obliged to impose on the great mass of uprooted Americans the restraints they no longer had the self-control to impose on themselves. While this arrangement was clearly undemocratic, the conviction that reason, systematicity, and science must replace the "mere" opinion of the citizenry had become so firmly entrenched among the elite that social scientists of Park's generation were obliged to climb aboard or else get left behind. If Park himself had moments of ambivalence, his successors had graver doubts. In their textbook *Urban Sociology,* Nels Anderson and Eduard C. Lindeman, both admirers of Park, could write disparagingly about the "dictatorship of the expert." "Experts and specialists," they argue, "threaten to preempt the seats of power occupied by kings and priests." And yet even while they warn their readers against "the authoritarianism of the professionals," they regard professionalism as the hallmark of "urbanism," inevitable as rain in the spring. Dictators or not, the professions had a right to rule so long as they remained "on the frontier of creative knowledge."[63]

By the 1920s, when Anderson and Lindeman wrote these words, the meaning of the frontier itself had changed. If Americans fifty years before had imagined cultural power as a capacity to take and hold a *place,* the frontier had become a *cultural* boundary separating "creative knowledge" from ignorance. As the cultural populists soon discovered, their small, shared worlds were already on the way to conquest and colonization. What remained, however, was the powerful memory of an alternative. In *Earth Horizon,* Mary Austin recalled a way of life approaching the Jefferson's ideal:

> Of the time and the town of which I write, practically all of its solid citizenry had sprung from the upper bourgeoisie of Northern Europe, or the landless scions of the least privileged aristocracy. They had come primarily from the British Isles, and latterly from Germany, escaping from oppressive militarism and overripe social privilege. With this prospect of reestablishing themselves on the new land, they had driven out the wild tribes, subdued the wilderness, and projected into a servantless society their ideals of culture and social continuity. And except for the . . . faint shadow of social privilege and the saloon, they had achieved world-singular success.[64]

It seems less important that such a world actually existed than that Austin believed it had. Certainly she recognized the failures as well as the success. She remembered, for example, a "pretty young German woman who used to bring her three children to our house until their father recovered from 'one of his spells.'" And she remembered too the "great bloody bruise" upon the woman's face.[65] Still, the "world-singular success" of Carlinville was something she was never to find again anywhere, not in the East and not in her extensive travels through Europe.

The road from Carlinville had carried her very far away indeed. As a girl, Mary had read Ruskin, whose "radical" writings her mother tried to conceal. She had gone on, after her disaster at the normal school, to a small women's college. Married in 1891 to Stafford Wallace Austin, she discovered, as Hamlin had, that the system of education was preparing many thousands of graduates for a world unequipped to provide them with meaningful work. And so like thousands of other men and women of their time, the Austins headed west to California, where they encountered another America. As Austin later wrote, "There were still warm traces at Los Angeles of the old Spanish settlement. . . . One saw Spanish-speaking natives lounging there, and immensely impressive Chinese merchants in silk."[66] While her husband moved unsuccessfully through a series of careers—homesteader, vinyardist, administrator in the district schools—Mary began to write and publish stories about her life out West, and the West became her home. The world that Austin pursued in the course of her career was not the global city of the cosmopolitan intellectual, although she knew that world well, but a place like the town of Carlinville that she had left behind—small in scale and isolated from the larger world, expansive and open inside because it was protected from the outside.

In contrast to a technocratic optimist like Park, Austin somehow sensed that those who entered the clearing opened by modernity would drop endlessly, groundlessly, through an abyss of their own making unless they could restore some enduring sense of relation to other people and to the natural world. Austin's own husband had been such a falling man, perpetually in motion from place to place, job to job, searching restlessly for wealth, recognition, and finally, for something he could never even name, let alone achieve. For a man like Austin's husband, there could be no "world," only a series of disconnected locales; there could be no genuine relations, only a series of arrangements. There could be, in spite of the continuous change, no actual change at all. What could change, under the regime of modernity, was simply the *content* of commodified knowledge, the *objects* of the purchaser's desire; what remained absolutely unchanging was the the sense of displacement from the condition that Austin described as the "true center of her being."[67]

"Man," Austin wanted to believe, was not condemned to fall endlessly through space but might enjoy a "continuing experience of wholeness, a power to expand," again and again, beyond the confines of culture itself.[68] Whether or not we today feel obliged to belittle her "visionary" language, we still have to acknowledge the mood of anomie that Austin's language expresses. *Something* happened to Americans in the period between 1865 and 1920—and not only to Americans but to people around the world. And whatever that something may have been, it produced a mood of worldlessness and groundlessness that came to be the hallmark of modernity and that seems especially anomalous given the potential for emancipation. At the very moment when the triumph of modernity *should have* brought about an unprecedented release of human creativity, millions of readers across the world, from London to Djarkarta to the Cameroon, saw their faded image in T. S. Eliot's "hollow men," men whose voices were "quiet and meaningless/ As wind in dry grass." A spiritual expatriate long before he left this continent for good, Eliot rejected the Progressive legacy of his fellow Americans. "We cannot" live, he argued, "in literature, any more than in the rest of life . . . in a perpetual state of revolution."[69] If Eliot seemed to speak prophetically to so many different readers in so many different locales, this may have been because he felt in an acutely immediate way the oppressive character of change itself, which ceases to be liberating when people can no longer control its direction and pace. But Eliot interpreted the mood of worldlessness as a consequence of "cultural disintegration," the fall of culture from unity into chaos. By turning back to Christian tradition, and by arguing that this tradition must be understood as a legacy free from difference and contradiction, Eliot hoped to restore the sense of groundedness that people like Austin felt themselves to have lost.

No less than Eliot and others, Austin found herself powerfully drawn to traditional societies, not because she considered them to be more coherent, but because they promised her life on a *scale* that made it possible to recover both a sense of genuine community and sense of personal freedom. Her interest had begun as an exercise in a highly visible activism but it rapidly assumed a deeper and more personal form. "At the same time," she wrote, "that my contemporaries were joining labor organizations and aligning themselves with wage-strikes, I took to the defense of Indians because they were the most conspicuously defeated and offended group at hand."[70] And while Austin may have helped them to salvage their past, they gave her a future in return. Among the traditional societies of the American Southwest—societies widely diverse in language and custom living side by side—she found alternatives to modernity so compelling that the day came when she "could no longer call herself a Christian." Through them Austin discovered another way of understanding culture itself:

In the [Navajo] song of Earth Horizon man wanders in search of the Sacred Middle from which all horizons are equidistant, and his soul happily at rest. Once the Middle is attained, all the skeyey rings that encircle earth's six quarters dissolve into the true zone of reality, and his spirit, no longer deflected by the influences of false horizons, swings freely to its proper arc.[71]

What Austin tried to do in her research on Native American societies was to reimagine knowledge and culture in ways that would valorize the local, that would restore a perception of the local as universal *because* of its specificity. Only such a localized horizon, she believed, would enable people like herself—not especially brave, not especially clever—to exceed the reach of institutions that routinely force their "clients" into utter dependency. Throughout the last decades of her life, Austin fought the assimilationist policies of the Office of Indian Affairs, and in New Mexico she helped to revive the native arts of pottery, weaving, and vernacular architecture. When the office accused her of "corrupting" the native peoples by encouraging their resistance to "Americanization," she organized a public outcry loud enough to oust the Commissioner.[72] Unlike Eliot, however, she did not look longingly backward to any prior order for the answers. Instead she looked to the future—or, rather, to many different, local futures. Those futures as she imagined them had at least one essential common element: they would all enable *everyone,* regardless of ability or attainment, to participate in creating the communal life, not only its political and social life but its artistic and religious life as well.

It was this insight more than any other—that culture is not something people "have" but something they must create for themselves—that distinguishes her from many other intellectuals of her time. As she writes in the closing paragraph of *Earth Horizon*—and here the contrast to Eliot looks especially pronounced—"I have seen that the American achievement is made up of two splendors: the splendor of individual relationships of power, the power to make and do rather than merely to possess, and that other splendor of realizing that in the deepest layers of ourselves we are incurably collective. At the core of our Amerindian life we are consummated in the dash and color of collectivity."[73] We encounter the collective, or so Austin believes, within the "deepest layers of ourselves," and we find, by acting in our common world, fulfillment as individuals. To have lost our faith in this consonance between self and world, self and others, was for her the greatest error of modernity, which contrives to impose an order on things that already have an order of their own. The spell of modernity loses its power the moment we are persuaded that the "Sacred Middle" lies wherever we happen to find ourselves. Every place is always the sacred "here"; every time is always the eternal "now."

As things turned out, the spell was not to be broken. Austin's vision of the earth horizon, like her refusal of modernity itself, was possible for her only because she remained outside the institutions that would shape the century to come. Several years after *The Atlantic* had rejected her translations of "Indian poetry" in the mistaken belief that they were spurious, Austin, now vindicated, became the first woman to address the Association for the Advancement of Science. And still later she represented New Mexico at the Seven States Conference organized to debate the proposed construction of Boulder Dam, a project she opposed whole-heartedly. But by 1932, the year that *Earth Horizon* came off the press, the knowledge she had spent her whole lifetime pursuing—a knowledge that arose from her most intimate encounters with other people and with the natural world—no longer really counted as knowledge at all. Within the span of her own lifetime, the word *knowledge* came to exclude virtually everything she had taken to be the hallmark of truth. The age of professionalization had begun.

3

The Great Divide

The Professions Against Civil Society

As the historian Samuel Haber points out, the word *profession* prior to the eighteenth century could describe almost any activity—laying bricks or selling groceries—but by late nineteenth-century America, the difference between a profession and a mere trade meant the difference between power and relative powerlessness.[1] In the preindustrial United States, a person of modest standing could be a preacher and a healer and a small farmer all at once, and his status depended less on his particular tasks than on his place within a system of local alliances and obligations. A century later, however, the person was the job. If professionalism in America began as a relatively democratic phenomenon, allowing the ambitious to rise above the level of their birth, a new hierarchy soon replaced the old one. Physicians finally established themselves as the quintessential professionals, while the generic term "laborer" came to describe those who had failed to gain standing through some form of specialization.[2]

Just as we see in the modern world a widening *cultural* split between knowledge and ignorance, so we see a corresponding *social* divide between an elite class of professionals and the larger mass of ordinary citizens. For much of the nineteenth century, the professions justified their special status by drawing on the older language of a shared community life: in theory, at least, the price for the professions' quasi-aristocratic privilege was their selfless service to the less advantaged, an ideal embodied in the popular image of the gruff, overworked country doctor. But this image of the professional as a public servant was displaced by another during the Progressive Era: the professional as a social leader, operating above the community at large. Education did much to foster such a great divide, with young hopefuls demonstrating their superiority in the competitions and promotions that have become the classroom teacher's routine business. But quite apart from the rituals of schooling, knowledge itself was increasingly shaped by the view from above: instead of addressing fellow citizens for the purposes of persuasion, this new knowledge was addressed to other professionals, who saw themselves as jointly invested with the task of organizing and reforming the masses. In this transformation, medicine and law led the way, followed by a host of new professions like sociology and management, each eager to play an important part in the administration of society.[3]

What first distinguished the new professions from the old was their self-created distance from lay men and women. The success of medicine, for example, had little to do with the quality of its knowledge and much to do with skillful public relations. Dr. Benjamin Rush, a late eighteenth-century teacher at the newly founded medical school of the College of Philadelphia, linked formal instruction in medical practice to an informal training in comportment and sensibility. Future doctors were urged to cultivate a bearing that elicited respect and even awe. "We should," Rush once told his colleagues, "appear to [our patients] as deputies from heaven, commissioned to guard the health and lives of our fellow citizens."⁴ According to Haber, American doctors during the nineteenth century worked diligently to establish "a relation with their patients unlike that between seller and buyer or between politician and voter; rather, they aspired to the traditional relation of protector and dependent," a relation "based upon an intrinsic inequality" that "looked back" to a pre-democratic society of "rank" and "honor."⁵

Medicine now has science firmly on its side, but its emergence as a profession actually precedes its close partnership with the sciences. As Haber observes, the reputation of American medicine in Rush's day made stronger gains than it had seen in several centuries despite its continued loyalty to practices like bleeding and the use of emetics, which killed many thousands of people. If the discredited physiology of humors lingered on in the medical literature until the eighteenth century, when doctors came to regard the body as an "automaton" or self-enclosed mechanical system, this idea gave way in turn to one of several rival successors: to the nineteenth-century innovation of "rational" and experimental therapeutics; or else to neo-Darwinist medicine, which saw contagion as nature's way of eliminating "the low-spirited, the intemperate, and the debilitated."⁶ Well after many scientists had abandoned the miasmic theory of disease, doctors and nurses at Johns Hopkins Hospital still walked their rounds above thick asphalt subfloors designed to protect the wards and hallways from penetration by supposedly deadly "soil gases."⁷

In the race to professional status, other fields may have been more rigorous or more closely allied with "pure" research, but medicine became the most successful at creating an authoritative public persona, the kind that the medical educator William Osler cultivated while making his rounds at the Hopkins hospital. Magisterial in his gray Prince Albert jacket and surrounded by adoring, imitative students, Osler would offer diagnoses liberally mixed with erudite reflections on history, ethics, religion, and culture. His motto was *aequanimitas*—"poise."⁸ By the turn of the century, however, following Osler's heyday at Hopkins, the older image of the doctor as an educated man in the tradition of humane arts and letters was already giving way to another: the physician as a hero of scientific specialization.

As Sir James Paget observed in New York in his opening address to the 1880 International Medical Congress, "As I look around this hall, my admiration is moved not only by the number and total power of the minds which are here, but by their diversity[, for] our calling is preeminent in its range of opportunities for scientific study."⁹ A pioneering researcher who had discovered the cause of trichinosis while he was still a London intern, Paget had become the hero of the younger generation of men who regarded medicine as a true science, and science as inherently specialized. To underscore the need for specialization, he drew an analogy that could hardly have missed its mark with its audience, twenty-one years after the appearance of Darwin's *The Origin of Species*. "Generally," he noted, "those species are the strongest and most abiding that can thrive in the widest range of climate and of food." The "mightiest are those who are strong alike on land and sea; who can explore and colonize, and in every climate can replenish the earth and subdue it."[10] At the task of thriving widely, medicine had already proven brilliantly successful, appropriating breakthroughs made by other disciplines, edging out competing organizations, and establishing an ever-growing range of niches for inquiry and practice.

Still, Paget felt a certain hesitation. While medicine now owed its preeminence to its scrupulous impersonality, it remained for him an avocation or "calling," and he ended his speech by praising its "nobility" rather than its precision. In the final analysis, he insisted, medicine was not about money or power or prestige; it was not even, finally, about knowledge, since knowledge itself kept changing, but about "the nobler ambition of being counted among the learned and the good who strive to make the future better and happier than the past." Paget asked his listeners to regard their work as an expression of solidarity with others and a response to predicaments shared by all humankind: sickness, disability, illness, death. "It is," he said, "surely fair to hold that, as in every search for knowledge we may strengthen our intellectual power, so in every practical employment of it we may, if we will, improve our moral nature; we may obey the whole of Christian love." Yet it was precisely this moral dimension that the new spirit of professionalism, in contrast to the older ethic of the "calling," gravitated against. With the triumph of scientific medicine, what mattered was not the doctor's goodness or kindness or fellow-feeling—his ability as a healer—but a purely instrumental competence.[11]

A comparable change occurred in law. By the end of the nineteenth century, the symbolic distinction between work and profession was matched by a growing distinction between practical know-how and theoretical knowledge. In an after-dinner speech on the teaching of law presented in the 1898 meeting of the American Bar Association, C. C. Langdell, Dane Professor of Law at Harvard, underscored the importance of a final break with the practice-centered system of legal training carried over from Great Britain. While aspiring American attorneys had learned the law as one might learn any other trade, that is, by an on-the-job apprenticeship, Langdell noted that "in all the rest of Christendom law has always been taught and studied in universities.[12] And in universities, he insisted, American legal studies must also make their home, although they would not do so successfully until legal scholars could establish two principles. First, that law is a genuine science, capable of study in a regular and systematic fashion, and second, "that all the available materials of that science are contained in printed books." The law, in other words, had to acquire not only a formal method but a clearly defined subject matter, no less objectively quantifiable than the matter of biology or physics. "Accordingly," Langdell told his colleagues, "the law library has been the object of our greatest and most constant solicitude. . . . We have also constantly inculcated the idea that the library is the proper workshop of professors and students alike; that it is to us all what the laboratories of the university are to the chemists and physicists, the museum of natural history to the zoologists, the botanical garden to the botanists." By underscoring the importance of books and legal libraries, Langdell could distance the law from its embarrassing worldliness, shifting the center of professional gravity not only from practice to theory but also from the courtroom to the university. And for the same reason, he maintained that what qualifies a person "to teach law, is not experience in the work of a lawyer's office, not experience in dealing with men, not experience in the trial or argument of [cases], not experience, in short, in using law, but experience in *learning* law."[13] Removed from the courtroom, to say nothing of the larger contexts of political and social life, law could become a discursive universe unto itself, with its own problems and styles of reasoning, its own questions and disputes.

With the triumph of professionalized medicine and law, other fields of knowledge were obliged to follow their lead, or else risk disappearing altogether. For the humanities, in particular, the transition was fraught with a profound uneasiness. Two years after Paget's address, the renowned philosopher Alexander Bain, in his 1882 rectorial address at Aberdeen University, warned against forgetting the common cultural legacy from which the professions themselves had arisen. "To the Greeks," he told his audience (mistakenly, in fact), "we are indebted for the earliest germ of the university. It was with them chiefly that education took that great leap, the greatest ever made, from the traditional teaching of the home, the shop, the social surroundings, to schoolmaster teaching properly so called."[14] By separating knowledge from everyday customs and values, and by setting the learned apart from ordinary citizens, the Greeks as Bain imagined them had made social and technological progress possible. But there are problems with this argument, apart from its questionable accuracy. On the one hand, Bain insisted that modern society urgently needed the older culture of organic community to counterbalance the fragmentation of both knowledge and society; on the other hand, he saw the Greeks—supposedly the founders of that older culture—as the inventors of specialization itself. For Bain, the way out seemed to lie in a defense of the humanities as a repository of things past, a cultural memory that offered an indispensable sense of proportion. "The mere professional man," he argued, "however prosperous, can not be a power in society, as the 'Arts' graduate may become. . . . His part is to be a follower, and not a leader." "He it is," Bain told his audience, referring to the student of the arts and humanities, who "may stand forth before the world as the model man."[15] Yet Bain could still not say how the humanities should be organized, except as specializations in their own right. While the study of "Spiritual Philosophy" and the "higher literature of the imagination," might impart "the taste of freedom," what place could these have in the new order?

Humanists in America felt much the same ambivalence once the research university began to replace the older and more locally rooted college system. In 1885, sixteen years before his appointment as the president of Columbia, Nicholas Murray Butler observed that the American college had served a unique function precisely because it remained "in close touch with the social life and institutions of the people."[16] Yet even Butler believed the college had outlived its usefulness. "The

American University," he wrote, "may, or rather must, learn the lessons that its German predecessor has to teach"—in particular the lesson of specialization. A neo-Kantian professor of philosophy, Butler was convinced that the German system could not meet the needs of undergraduate education as effectively as the "unsystematic, but remarkably effective" college system, yet he also hoped that the new universities might be able to combine the socializing mission of the colleges with "research of excellence and originality."[17]

Speaking somewhat less optimistically at Vassar College in 1901, Butler expressed new misgivings about the growth of research universities. "A host of knowledges," he said that summer day, "compass about us on every side and bewilder by their variety and interest. We must exclude the many to choose the one. The penalty of choice is deprivation; the price of not choosing is shallowness and incapacity."[18] As Butler could clearly observe, the domain of knowledge that remained at the center of a shared social life was steadily contracting. Butler's response was ambivalent, however, in ways he perhaps overlooked. On the one hand, he argued for the importance of "reflection," by which he meant the ability to step back and consider the direction we have taken. "It is," he wrote, "a frequent charge against us moderns, particularly against Americans, that we are losing the habit of reflection. . . . We are told that this loss is a necessary result of our hurried and busy lives" although "the life which asks no questions of itself, which traces events back to no causes and forward to no purposes . . . is not a human life at all."[19] But at the same time, he wanted to shore up the tradition of belles letters as foundational in a prereflexive way.

Implicit in Butler's argument, and in countless similar arguments for the rest of the twentieth century, was the claim that inquiry in a field like physics is too narrowly focused for reflection on the broader implications of its knowledge or the social consequences of its activities. But such reflection, Butler argued, lay within the purview of humanists, whose concern was not this branch of knowledge or that one, but the way that all the branches fit together. In that case, however—if humanists ought to be generalists—then their field of inquiry should have included a little physics, biology, finance, law, and so on, hardly the stuff of the humanities since the time of Matthew Arnold. Butler took another tack, however: the subject of the future humanities would be literature and the other arts precisely because, as he supposed, the arts reveal universal qualities rather than human differences and particularities. But is science really less "universal" than poetry—less rich and meaningful an expression of human nature? And are the arts any less specialized than the sciences? In effect, Butler wanted to have it both ways, promoting specialization in the humanities as an antidote to specialization in the sciences.

The argument for reflection had another shortcomings as well. People need to reflect on their condition from time to time precisely because contingency is an inescapable feature of human life. We reflect when we have reached an impasse or when the future looks uncertain, and for this reason the process of reflection unfolds without set rules or predictable stages, grounding itself in the urgencies of the moment. No argument, however, could be more at odds than this one with the rage for scientific inquiry that swept across the professions and disciplines. In the study of human affairs, just as in physics or geology, the search for truth became synonymous with the discovery of inalterable laws. The great prophet of the new "scientific" study of human life was the British social theorist Herbert Spencer, whose international appeal grew in direct proportion to the spread of uncertainty and discord along with industrialization.

All this chaos, Spencer argued, was an illusion. During a talk on the subject of "over-activity," given at a lavish New York banquet, Spencer tried to come terms with the unprecedented changes in the modern world. For him, the most extreme examples of these changes were to be found in the United States, which had, he thought, inadvertently produced a hell of brutal competition by encouraging individual happiness at the expense of traditional restraints. "The struggle," he told his audience, "grows more and more strenuous, and there comes an increasing dread of failure—a dread of being 'left'[behind], as the Americans say."[20] For Spencer, the irony of Americans' pursuit of happiness was that it had culminated in their utter enslavement to competition and work, but this irony was not his main concern, although he certainly seemed to relish it. Instead, the crowning insight offered to his wealthy patrons was that nothing could or should be done about it all because competition was in fact nature's law, which society *must* obey no matter what. As he put it, "the life of a society so sways the wills of its members as to turn them to its ends."[21] People, in other words, may prefer to see themselves as the makers of culture, but it is culture that makes them what they are, and nature that makes culture in turn. Perhaps American life would be less brutal someday, but "natural forces" would inevitably decide. When and if change should come, Spencer said, it will come for its own reasons and on its own schedule, in keeping with the tenet of "the survival of the fittest."

For all intents and purposes, Spencer bestowed on society's leaders the scientific equivalent of the divine right of kings: he told them that Nature had chosen them to lead, while the others were destined to be led. At the same time, he dismissed as a sentimental illusion the older social contract to which men like Paget looked back wistfully. The lawyer, the doctor, the economist no longer needed to express solidarity with the aspirations and values of ordinary people. Instead, professionals owed their success to a deliberate repudiation of those values, which were often dismissed as irrational impediments to progress. The authority of the professional now depended on his ability to see objective laws at work beyond or beneath the perceptions of ordinary citizens. In this transformation, however, even Spencer himself was a transitional figure, soon displaced by younger and still more ambitious social scientists. Today, some of us might wish to argue in reply to Spencer that certain people were to blame for the miseries of his era, rather than some deterministic principle of natural selection, but this was not the criticism offered by his successors. For them, the problem with Spencer's argument was that it encouraged too great a passivity on the part of the leaders themselves, especially the intelligentsia. By representing cultural institutions as a product of natural forces before which humankind was helpless, his analysis may have granted to social scientists some degree of foresight, but it left them with no corresponding power. Instead of simply observing nature's work, social scientists of the generation after Spencer proposed to devise technologies of mass manipulation that would allow them to subject their fellow Americans to scientific oversight and planning.

Like Spencer, the pioneering American sociologist E. A. Ross presupposed the reality of inalterable laws governing human interaction, and like Spencer he assumed that accounts of human behavior that began with conscious motives were hopelessly unscientific. As he argued in his pathbreaking study *Social Control,* "It is a common delusion that [social] order is to be explained by the person's inherited equipment for good conduct, rather than by any control that society exercises over him."[22] But Ross also recognized that a social science capable only of announcing the inevitable decrees of nature was no science at all—or, at any rate, not a science that might find its fitting place among the new professions. But the new professionals had other motives as well, aside from their quest for authority. Between 1860 and 1914, the population of New York City grew from 850,000 to 4 million, and of Chicago from 110,000 to 2 million.[23] As the major cities swelled with people, drawn from the American countryside or from villages and towns in Europe, they brought with them folk traditions of personal independence and collective cooperation poorly suited to the authoritarianism of the factory and the ruthlessness of urban life.

In her autobiography *Rebel Girl,* the labor activist Elizabeth Gurley Flynn, whose father had been an impoverished itinerant engineer, remembers moving from rural Concord to the "gray mills in Manchester," which "stretched like prisons along the banks of the Merrimac" and where "fifty percent of the workers were women" earning a dollar for a sixteen-hour day. Child workers ate meals of bread "buttered" with lard, and they went to their stations at the factories thinly clothed against the bitter New England winters. "Once," Flynn recalls, "while we were in school, . . . piercing screams came from the mill across the street. A girl's hair had been caught in an unguarded machine and she was literally scalped."[24] In reaction to such conditions, workers formed huge umbrella organizations like the Knights of Labor and the American Federation of Labor. Acting together with immigrants from Germany, who could draw on the traditions of European socialism, they became an increasingly "dangerous" presence, and during the final decades of the century strikes grew larger, more frequent, and more violent. In 1886, a strike by the Knights of Labor against the Texas and Pacific Railroad closed down the rails from California to St. Louis, and the A.F. of L. strike for an eight-hour workday, which sent forty thousand Chicago workers into the streets, shut down both the rails and the stockyards there.[25]

Such events provided the unstated impetus for the writings of Ross and his contemporaries across the social science disciplines, Progressives who understood their task as the study and resolution of the growing discord. Scrupulously dispassionate, *Social Control* begins, not with events like the Haymarket massacre of strikers in Chicago, but with the abstract "problem of order," and not with little girls tending bobbins fourteen hours a day, but with "men" considered in the aggregate. While Ross conceded that "private property . . . warps society farther and farther from the pristine equality that brings out the best in human nature," he felt obliged as a neutral observer to acknowledge the importance of inequality as "a great transforming force" acting "independently of human will." As he put it, "Equality before the law, political equality, religious equality—-these may delay but they cannot stop the progress of economic differentiation."[26] In contrast to Sir James Paget, who had argued for the sustaining power of Christian love, Ross's research led him to view humankind as fundamentally selfish and violent unless checked by rigid institutions and mores: "Whenever men swarm in new places—Dutch Flat, Kimberley, Siberia, Skagway—the man-to-man struggle stands out naked and clear, and the slow emergence of order out of disorder and violence presents itself as the attainment of a difficult and artificial condition."[27]

Because he regarded social life as necessarily repressive, Ross insisted that it could not be left unmanaged; as a single living organism, society needs the "solid bony framework" of "obedience" even more than the "connective tissue of sympathy." Although some people might still believe in the sovereignty of the "free moral agent," Ross argued that no such person ever existed except on the very borders of civilization or else at times of complete collapse. In reality, society makes its members everything they are through a careful balance of "punishments and rewards," and if force or the threat of force must always remain in play, he also argued that the pressure of the "general will" ordinarily operates to "overpower and regulate" the individual long before violent forms of correction might be needed.[28]

Like many social scientists of the day, Ross claimed to observe rather than prescribe. Specialists in other fields might apply his research to real situations, but his concern lay exclusively with the underlying mechanisms. Far from presuming to judge how much latitude people should be allowed in the conduct of their lives, Ross simply noted in passing that there "are times when society holds the individual as in a vise, and times when he wiggles out almost from underneath the social knee."[29] Yet this stance of studied disinterestedness concealed the real bias of his analysis. By treating a collective abstraction, "society," as though it were an actual person, while reducing actual people to inanimate parts within a larger "living organism," Ross ruled out in advance the possibility that conflict might serve some useful purpose, or that the need for social control imposed from on high might testify to a basic social failure.

In contrast to Spencer's social Darwinism with its laissez faire underpinnings, Ross's thinking lent itself readily to the administration of human subjects, and beyond the university, popular writers like Eugene Wera saw the implications of this approach at once. As Wera reasoned in *Human Engineering,*

> Society is in a continual state of evolution, but its different groups have never progressed equally. Discordance has separated the groups and caused issues to arise which are not clear to us because we interpret them more or less by means of outworn ideas, prepossessions of the past, which confuse our understandings of new principles. Consequently, conflicts between past beliefs and present truths have brought about strained industrial and social situations.[30]

Wera means, but does not say directly, that inequalities of wealth and opportunity have produced class conflict, but he carefully avoids the terminology of the left because he proposes to develop an alternative model of social amelioration, one dedicated to the "scientific treatment" of "human forces" and "the establishment of a new relationship among [the three] competing parties—labor, capital, and society"—a relationship that would serve to "liberate the vital aspirations of a progressive, industrial population."[31] Contrasting his ideal of the scientifically administered society to the plans of radicals in Europe and the USSR, Wera faults their understanding of human nature. What people want, he argues, is not economic equality or control over the means of production, but the sense of self-esteem that comes from performing a socially useful task. Although Wera was prepared to acknowledge the seriousness of worker discontent, he blamed it on a system that had failed to meet the basic need for the approval of others.

While granting that industrialization in its earlier phases had too narrowly served the interests of capitalists, Wera approvingly noted the emergence of a new spirit based upon the "common social interests of employers and employed." And to support this claim, he quoted from recent speech delivered by John D. Rockefeller. "Shall we cling," Rockefeller had asked his audience, "to the conception of industry as an institution primarily of private interest. . . . Or shall we adopt the modern viewpoint and regard industry as being a form of social service?"[32] Rockefeller described himself, in other words, as a public servant. The problem, Wera held, was no longer with capitalism, which had transformed itself in the way that Rockefeller described, but with the workers themselves, who remained more or less unaware of the change. Although labor agitation had formerly served a legitimate purpose, it now injured workers even more than it injured employers by closing off vital possibilities for the pursuit of personal merit.

If Ross's *Social Control* provided the theory, books like Wera's *Human Engineering* put that theory into practice. Like Ross, Wera was convinced that "the social world cannot be built upon the peculiarities of individuals. Indeed, our civilization is based on community of beliefs, ideas, desires, sentiments, and aspirations which bind individuals into collective . . . organizations."[33] But society's "increasing complexity" had made cohesion much harder to achieve than in times past, so hard that it was now essential to "shift social control from the hands of amateurs into those of trained men, in order to realize a systematic integration of the members of society." Toward this end, Wera called for a national organization directed by sociologists, engineers like Wera himself, business leaders, hygienists, economists, ethicists, and city planners. As for the workers, they could be counted on to go along "if employers cooperate in promoting progress in [job] safety, security, health, comfort, justice, and spiritual development."[34] For Wera, the rise of the administered society promised to end the conflicts between workers and management, left and right. As honest brokers with best wishes for all parties concerned, the Progressive Era human engineers would usher in a new social order, not through conflict or government fiat but through the promise of prosperity and "the formation of public opinion." "Persuasion," Ross had written, "is little else than the art of introducing into a man's mind unwelcome ideas so really as not to arouse the will to expel them."[35] Wera too recognized that the smooth operation of the administered society depended on the artful management of public opinion through advertising and the popular media, and through workplace training carefully crafted to form "a correct, collective opinion . . . and a spirit of loyalty."[36]

There was, however, one other important venue Wera left unexplored. In the literature of social control, no other aspect of human engineering could rival the importance given to education, which became at all levels a focus of efforts at "reform." Writing in 1915 as an ally of the nation's teachers, Nicholas Murray Butler had called for a new "science of education" on the model of medical science.[37] Thirteen years later, in *Principles of Educational Sociology,* Walter Robinson Smith, a professor of education at the University of Kansas, joined many others in answering Butler's call, though by that time, sociology, not medicine, had become the model. Like *Social Control,* a work it references occasionally, Smith's *Principles* elaborates a theory of social interaction that buries the reality of riots and strikes beneath the weight of scientific-sounding discourse. "Modern man," Smith blandly notes, "is engulfed in . . . a maelstrom of social forces which complicate his wants, his needs, and his activities."[38] As Smith observed, modern "city life" demands "readjustment in sociability, amusements, and religious, civic, and cultural activities. Tenements and slums [have] multiplied" and "the monotony of narrowly specialized work [has] intensified" while the "massing of the population" destroyed "the familiar restraints on moral conduct."[39] Like Ross, Smith understood that the best solution was an appropriate division of tasks—and levels. As he wrote, "The progress of society from the primitive horde to complex civilization has been brought about by differentiation of social functions and their incorporation into specialized institutions"[40]

In education as in other spheres of modern life, society needed direction, but direction of the proper kind. "In our day," Smith complained, "we find labor unions discussing educational measures . . . manufacturers' associations calling for industrial training . . . propagandists and reformers demanding special instruction to undermine war, the use of intoxicants, narcotics, etc."[41] It seemed obvious to Smith that education could not be abandoned to public debate but had to be reconstructed on a soundly empirical footing. He was particularly critical of reformers who emphasized self-expression under the influence of liberal psychologists. It "remains," he wrote, "for educational psychology to correct this false perspective by a counter-emphasis."[42] Smith regarded the pedagogy of self-expression as especially dangerous because he believed, as Ross did, that humans were by nature almost boundlessly aggressive. "Man," after all, "is a biological organism, and so his fundamental effort is centered in the struggle for existence. . . . Therefore, the first law of societies, as of individuals, is self-preservation."[43] By curbing the excesses of egoism, and by strengthening the student's sense of "community spirit," educators could resolve in the safety of the classroom social tensions that might have otherwise erupted on the street or in the workplace. At the same time, however, Smith wanted to make room for individual achievements of the right kind. As he saw the matter, Progressive education should not produce "dead leveling"—"not equality of possessions, equal rewards for effort, or equal responsibility for service"; instead, education should promote social concord and equality in the opportunity to compete. And once teachers had reined in destructive energies while spurring on competition, they could imbue their average or below-average students with realistic expectations. As for the gifted, they would ripen into the professionals of tomorrow.[44]

While Progressive administrators had vaulting ambitions, the results were arguably rather modest. Between 1900 and 1935, the percentage of students who completed high school increased from 25 percent to only 35 percent. Until the end of World War II, the average American had a ninth grade education, up by just two grades from the turn of the century.[45] But the consequences of Progressive reforms were ambiguous in other ways as well. Progressives would later take credit for changes such as reductions in the work week and the curtailment of child labor, but the evidence strongly suggests that such legislation followed from a partnership between liberal reformers and the workers themselves.[46] In fact, some very prominent Progressives regarded the tribulations of the working class as part of a natural process of winnowing, which they wanted to free up, not arrest. As the historian Donald Pickens observes, "For Americans in a naturalist age," the class-based conflicts of the time appeared to be racial in character and closely comparable to "natural and animal competition."[47] Far from occupying the fringes of reform, a belief in eugenics found broad support among people like David Starr Jordan, the president of Stanford, the ubiquitous E. A. Ross, the feminist Margaret Sanger, the biologist Paul Popenoe, and the naturalist Gifford Pinchot.[48] Even Teddy Roosevelt, the famous antimonopoly "trust buster," was an ardent proponent of eugenics and the superiority of Anglo-Saxons. And what held true for competing races, held true for competing cultures as well. Smith, for instance, compared the "processes of biological selection," which gradually remove "the unfit and improve the human breed," to the "processes of social selection" that gradually eliminate "the unfit traditions, ethical practices, and institutional forms, preserving those best adapted to ensure group survival."[49]

The new professions did not create prejudice, but they gave it a scientific-sounding rationale and turned it into a program of national reform. As the sociologist Nicole Hahn Rafter observes in her anthology of eugenics studies from that time, the burgeoning of eugenics research directly coincides with the rise of the professions themselves, in particular the rise of the "helping professions" such as education, applied psychology, and social work, whose practitioners needed to identify populations that were demonstrably in need of professional help.[50] All too predictably, the preferred subjects for these researchers were the groups least familiar with the mores and rites of middle-class life, and therefore least capable of fighting back, especially rural poor whites. Although marginal economically, the "country folk" of the eugenics studies were, as Rafter notes, economically independent of the growing market society, which explains the researchers' indignation over such activities as berry picking, scavenging, and itinerant farm work. In their determined indifference to the ideology of progress, the "throwbacks" who became the staple of the research—in places like Appalachia, Oklahoma, Ohio, and the Pine Barrens of southern New Jersey—offered Progressives an unparalleled opportunity.

So complete was the triumph of the administered society, a triumph in which fields like sociology played a central role, we may almost forget it did not go unopposed.

Starting at the end of the nineteenth century, there was another option, which we might now describe as the dissident tradition. Although historians have often viewed the dissidents strictly in terms of their resistance to corporate capitalism, many were no less strenuously opposed to the emergent culture of Progressive administration. Strictly speaking, corporations are economic and legal entities, not political or social ones; by contrast, Progressive Era social engineering as well as "radical" dissidence were both cultural and political adaptations to a period of confusion, and they were clearly rivals. If academic Progressives like Ross favored greater centralization and hierarchy, the dissidents hoped to move America in the very opposite direction toward greater equality and broadened participation, much like the cultural populists. Although some of the dissidents saw themselves as socialists, Marxists, or European-style syndicalists, their response on the whole was more complex and less programmatic than observers, then and now, have typically recognized.

Well before there were concrete programs, there was the crisis itself. In *Wobbly,* a memoir of the period, the former labor agitator Ralph Chaplin describes his family's history on the prairie in much the same way as Hamlin Garland did. Chaplin's great-grandfather had fought in the Revolutionary War at Saratoga, and his grandfather fought in the Civil War on the Union side before settling in the open lands of Kansas. After the economic collapse of 1886, Chaplin's father, once a prosperous Cloud County horse breeder, was forced to sell his farm and go to work for the Pullman company. He ended up in Chicago, where he and many others were laid off. "My father," Chaplin remembered, "would get up every morning before sunrise and walk the streets looking for work. Sometimes he would come home grim, hopeful, but empty-handed. Other times he would return after dark, triumphant, having earned enough to buy food for another day."[51]

Another celebrated agitator of the time, Elizabeth Gurley Flynn, recalled moving to New York in 1900 when she was ten, leaving behind "the green hills of New England" for a small windowless flat where on winter days she sat beside her sisters in their kitchen, the one room that her family could afford to heat, trying to complete their lessons by the light of a kerosene lamp.[52] Together with millions of others who made this same migration, Flynn's family found itself in a world where all the old rules had broken down and new ones had to be improvised. She remembered, for example, that railroad workers would steal from their employers, throwing chunks of coal off their trains at night for the poor to pick up the next day. And she recalled, as well, that the wife of the local saloon keeper—always a target of middle-class reformers—made huge pots of free soup and sent bowls to the poorest families in the neighborhood. The poverty of her childhood Flynn compares in her autobiography to a country "so strange and terrible" that "only those who have been there can really speak of it with knowledge."[53]

Anyone who now reviews the surviving writings of prominent dissenters will be struck by how often they relate this same story of loss and displacement. Compare the accounts of Chaplin and Flynn to this record left by another leading agitator of the time, Kate Richards O'Hare:

My earliest memory is of a Kansas ranch, of the wide stretches of prairie, free herds roaming over the hills and coulees; of cowpunchers . . . free and easy of speech and manner, but brave and faithful to their friends . . . of the freedom and security and plenty of a well-to-do rancher's home.

Those were wonderful days and I shall never cease to be thankful that I knew them. Days that laid the foundation of my whole life, gave me health and strength and love of freedom, taught me to depend on myself, to love nature, to honor rugged strength of mind and body and to know no shams in life. . . .

Then comes the memory of a Kansas drought, followed by one of the periodical [economic] panics which sweep over our country. Days and weeks of hazy nightmare when father's face was gray and set, when mother smiled bravely . . . but when we sometimes found tears upon her cheeks if we came upon her unexpectedly. . . . A horrible something that we could not fathom had settled down over our lives, but the day when the realness of it was forced home came all too soon. The stock was sold, the home dismantled and one day father kissed us goodbye and started away to the city to find work. . . . Though I could not comprehend it then the bitterness of it all was seared upon my memory and I never see a strong man vainly seeking and begging for work that my whole soul does not revolt.[54]

The dissident tradition of this period has its roots in the passing of an older way of life often remembered as happier and freer than industrialization could offer. Rather than looking forward to a Marxist utopia, people like O'Hare often viewed their struggle—perhaps with some degree of false nostalgia, but also with some truth—as an attempt to restore what had been taken from them. They understood themselves, not as opponents of distinctly American values, but as the truest defenders of those values. In *Rebel Girl,* Elizabeth Gurley Flynn remembered her grammar school on 138th Street in the South Bronx—P.S. 9—as "a decrepit old building . . . with toilets in the yard." But she also remembered one of her teachers, James A. Hamilton, "who fired me with ambition to be a constitutional lawyer and drilled us so thoroughly in the U.S. Constitution and . . . the Bill of Rights that I have been defending it ever since."[55]

In many ways, the experience of loss and displacement made it possible for the dissidents to reimagine the American life in ways that were more consistent with the nation's founding principles of equality, tolerance, and personal freedom. Drawn out of her isolation by the New York labor movement, the young Elizabeth Flynn soon began to realize that many people—and many different kinds of people—shared the experience she had lived through. At public talks and discussion groups—where texts included Marx, Kroptkin, Jack London, and Edward Bellamy—Flynn met black and Chinese-American activists, and her first boyfriend, the son of a crusading New York City advocate of birth control, took her to meet the notorious Jewish anarchist Emma Goldman. Many of the dissidents were also defenders of women's rights—Kate O'Hare, Crystal Eastman, and Helen Keller—at a time when most of the professions, including journalism, excluded women categorically. Later, as an organizer for the International Workers of the World, Flynn marched with miners in Pittsburgh and Coeur D'Alene, with lumberjacks in Spokane, and with textile workers in Paterson, New Jersey. More was at stake in these activities than the struggle for better wages and shorter hours, although wages and hours were certainly important. Implicit in the culture of dissent was a social vision based on the older ideals of civil society, but now expanded to include people formerly excluded from the life of the small American town. Although the dissenters engaged in struggle, they often perceived it, not primarily as a struggle between classes, but as a struggle to realize an ideal of universal brotherhood. In a talk given in Canton, Ohio, the socialist leader Eugene V. Debs compared the "life of the mind"—the life, we might say now, of professionals—to the life of the "hand," a life dedicated to "service to others":

> [Socialism] has enabled me to hold high communion with you, and made it possible for me to take my place side by side with you in the great struggle for the better day; to multiply myself over and over again . . . to feel life truly worthwhile; to open new avenues of vision; to spread out glorious vistas; to know that I am kin to all . . . to be class-conscious, and to realize that, regardless of nationality, race, creed, color or sex, every man, every woman who toils, who renders useful service, every member of the working class without an exception, is my comrade, my brother and sister—and that to serve them and their cause is the highest duty of my life.
>
> And in their service I can feel myself expand; I can rise to the stature of a man and claim the right to a place on earth.[56]

This is not only the language of Marx, but also the language of Walt Whitman. Although Debs was familiar with Marx's writings, he remained uneasy with the communist ideology, always writing and speaking instead within the context of his local experience. Marx in his later writings seemed to discount the struggle for democratic government, and Marx's concept of the dictatorship of the proletariat was fundamentally at odds with the traditions from which Debs derived his understanding of social justice.[57] When he called for an end to private ownership of the railroads, mines, and mills, he thought of this change as an extension of political democracy to the economic realm.[58] And this was how many others understood him at the time. Debs' lifelong friend Ralph Chaplin placed him in the "tradition of great crusaders and reformers which started with Samuel Adams and Thomas Paine . . . Daniel Shays . . . William Lloyd Garrison, John Brown." Debs, Chaplin maintained, "had more in common with [men] such as these than with the undistinguished Marxist dialecticians with whom he associated—and disagreed."[59]

If we turn to the European sources so popular with academics today— especially Gramsci and the Frankfurt School—it will be difficult to explain much that we encounter in the primary sources of the dissenting culture. We might understand the dissenters, instead, as heirs to the thwarted Populist movement, which had attempted to subordinate economic forces to the will of the people by severing the links between the government and business. The dissenters objected, not exclusively or primarily to capitalism, but to a more general and persistent disempowerment of individuals and communities. As Emma Goldman declared, "The individual is the true reality in life. . . . Civilization has been a continuous struggle of the individual or of groups of individuals against the State and even against 'society.'" Humankind's "greatest battles have been waged against man-made obstacles and artificial handicaps imposed on [it] to paralyze [its] growth and development."[60] In making this declaration, Goldman quite consciously positioned herself against Progressive social theorists like Ross. The "greater the mental charlatan," she wrote, "the more definite his insistence on the wickedness and weaknesses of human nature," and she asked her audience to contemplate "the possibility of an organization without discipline, fear, or punishment."[61] Surveying the governments of her time, she dismissed them all—with a quote from Emerson—as organized "tyranny," and she expressed particular concern about the public schools, which she compared to "barracks" where "the human mind is drilled and manipulated into submission to various social and moral [dogmas]."[62] Ultimately Goldman described herself as a supporter of "that form of trades-unionism which has done away with centralization, bureaucracy, and discipline, and which favors independent and direct action on the part of its members."[63] In a similar spirit, Debs had written, "I confess to a prejudice against officialdom and a dread of bureaucracy. I am a thorough believer in the rank and file, and in *ruling* from the *bottom up.*"[64]

This vision could no more be realized at the time than the Populist ideal that preceded it. For one thing, the dissenting tradition was energetically quashed by a powerful alliance between industry, government, and the new professional-managerial sector. Fifteen days after he delivered his Canton speech, Debs was arrested by officers of the Cleveland Police on treason charges for encouraging resistance to the draft. In April 1919, he went to prison, where he launched his second run for president as Prisoner No. 9653, winning slightly more than 900,000 votes. Chaplin, O'Hare, and Flynn all spent time in jail as well. But the dissenting tradition failed for other, more complex reasons. As Chaplin describes in *Wobbly,* tensions between Marxists and their opponents tore apart the labor movement from within. In spite of early, glowing reports on the success of the communist experiment in Russia, a significant number of people, Chaplin among them, came to conclude that the option favored by Red Left was far from conducive to "rule" as Debs had said, "from the bottom up"—a lesson learned at first hand by Emma Goldman, whose stay in the Soviet Union convinced her that the experiment had gone wildly wrong. If the Soviet Union was able to bend economic forces to its will, it ultimately did so by means of an administrative apparatus even more extensive and inflexible than anything to arise on this continent.[65] One irony of modern history is that although the Soviet Union and the United States were ideological opponents, both developed along parallel lines throughout much of the twentieth century.[66] A man like Ross would have felt quite at home with the Soviet *nomenklatura.* But the ultimate reason for the decline of the dissenting tradition may lie in a failure to compete programmatically with its administrative rival—a failure to develop any viable program other than dissent. It was not simply a practical failure, but an intellectual failure as well. The dissenters did not produce a knowledge of their own, or institutions to disseminate that knowledge.

The rise of the great administrative societies of the twentieth century went hand in hand with a new totalizing knowledge the West had not seen since the Middle Ages. In Progressive Era America, that new knowledge was social Darwinism; in Russia, it sprang from the teachings of Marx. But both societies embraced intellectual systems that explained absolutely everything, from the proper conduct of the economy to the appropriate modes of sexual intercourse. And the ultimate virtue of both systems was that nothing could disprove them in the long run. Against such powerful competitors, the American dissenting culture, with its commitment to equality and participation, was, in the words of John Dewey, "at a distinct disadvantage."[67]

The same year Debs had delivered his Canton speech, Dewey pondered this disadvantage and its causes in an address to the University of California's Philosophical Union. As he observed, those who could reason from first principles or final causes always seemed to be on higher and firmer ground than those compelled to argue in an ad hoc fashion from their immediate experience. But Dewey went on to observe that the desire for a totalizing schema—so often viewed as a sign of rigor or depth—was actually an intellectual symptom of arrested political and social development: an imaginary compensation on the level of ideas for real-world disappointments. Viewed in this light, the whole history of philosophy could be read a chronicle of defeats and the psychological repression of those defeats, since virtually all the great philosophers "have at bottom been committed to [discovering] the principle of a single, final and unalterable authority from which . . . lesser authorities are derived." Greek thought, for example, which began as a liberating challenge to the dead weight of predemocratic Attic tradition, was subverted by the triumph of a disembodied "universal reason" that turned out to be even more oppressive than the old Attic customs. Lacking even this critical impulse, medieval philosophy had exhausted itself in the effort to justify the arbitrary power of the church and the sovereign, while its modern successors, after boldly overthrowing revelation as a source of truth, and divine right as a rationale for political power, recoiled in fear of their own achievement and had desperately set out to restore both the crown and the cross in slightly altered forms.[68]

The one thing that totalizing systems could not incorporate, Dewey insisted, was the acknowledgment of their own limitations, especially their own blindness to the future. If the history of ideas shows anything, it shows that ideas are never universal but inevitably a specific response to specific conditions, giving voice to each thinker's "most passionate desires and hopes, [his] basic beliefs about the sort of life to be lived." For this reason, Dewey argued, no two people can ever really share the same ideas, though they might *use* the same ideas in different ways. The slave Epictetus and the Emperor Aurelius may have both described themselves as Stoics, but they could not have held "just the same philosophy of life." What promoted self-esteem and resistance to oppression in the case of Epictetus instilled a sense of guilt and a commitment to tradition in the Emperor. By the same token, Dewey predicted that when women in America become engaged in the study of philosophy, "we cannot conceive that it will be the same in viewpoint or tenor as that composed from the . . .masculine experience of things."[69] In effect, Dewey tried to offer an alternative to the totalizing logic of the administered society, and he called for a return to philosophy in the "original and etymological sense of the word" as "a form of desire, of effort at action."[70] No less than Debs or Goldman, Dewey rejected "top down" solutions, but he recognized also that real democracy could not be created until the American people understood themselves as inhabitants of a universe that was essentially "incomplete and in the making," without any "fixed order of species, grades, or degrees."[71]

If Dewey criticized philosophy, he also took particular umbrage at social scientists like Ross for regarding it as their "chief problem" to determine how individuals who are "supposedly non-social become socialized" and "how social control becomes effective among individuals who are naturally hostile to it."[72] In Dewey's view, such a pseudoscience does something "even more harmful than the rationalization" of arbitrary authority. "It serves to justify the laziness, the intellectual inertia, of the educational routineer" who would prefer to exempt his own assumptions from critical challenge. Convinced that "individualism" undermines society, the "routineer" not only subordinates himself to a reductive "tradition"—with its canonical texts and its time-honored methods—but he demands that his students do the same for their own good, even when the demand for subordination plainly testifies to the society's continued oppressiveness and the failure of its tradition. The "unsolved problem of democracy," Dewey wrote, "is the construction" of an educational system "which will develop that kind of individuality which is intelligently alive to the common life and sensitively loyal to its common maintenance."[73] But Emma Goldman may have stated the case with greater precision when she wrote, "The problem that confronts us today . . . is how to be one's self and yet in oneness with others, to feel deeply with all human beings and still retain one's own characteristic qualities."[74] What Dewey had yet to recognize, and possibly Goldman as well, was the extent to which the modern regime of the professions served to encourage the habits of the "routineer" while discouraging both a sense of personal worth and also a sense of "the common life." This problem is still our problem today.

The problem is likely to go unresolved until we understand why the professionals won their competition with the cultural populists and with the dissenting tradition. Is the history of the professions just another instance of a *trahison des clercs,* a betrayal of the people by their elite? Or might it be the case that the professions were the most viable arrangement at the time, a first step that could lead—in the future, if not before—to arrangements less exclusionary and hierarchical? On the way to an answer, we might take a second and more careful look at Edward Alsworth Ross, the patriarch of American sociology. Long before he had achieved mythic status—to be precise, at the end of August 1888, after two years of high school teaching in Fort Dodge, Iowa—Ross crossed the Atlantic on a small Dutch liner, the *Edam,* where he lived through his first episode of seasickness. In his autobiography, *Seventy Years of*

It, Ross recalls "the beauty of the steep wooded heights" along the Rhine, "crowned with the ruins of medieval castles." "Is it possible," he asked himself, "that such romance and charm are on the same planet with roaring Chicago?"[75]

Unlike most of the young Americans he would meet abroad, Ross had been born in a sod house on the prairie near Centralia, Kansas, built by his father, a Scots Presbyterian whose family had gone west to dig gold. Sixty-five years later, he still wrote warmly about "oxen yoked to a 'breaking' plow," and he remembered "playing . . . among deer-skin tents with Indian children and dogs."[76] When his parents died—his mother of tuberculosis, and then his father after a long and paralyzing illness—he lived first with his father's sister in Marion, Iowa, and later as a ward of "Squire" Beach in the same town. About the life there, however, Ross remained perpetually divided between nostalgia and regret. On the one hand, he wrote effusively of "a one-room school set down where the native woods gave way to the fields." On the other hand, he felt impoverished by the absence of the enduring "traditions" he would later find in the East and in Germany, and the stereotypical evocations of "golden days" conflict markedly with other passages. "How bare," he writes several pages later,

> those farm years were of cultural opportunity! I attended rural school for only about seventy-five days a year, farm work being too pressing to release me for the summer and fall terms. After I was twelve I got practically nothing out of school, for I was being taken again and again over the same ground. Five times I went through Barnes' *Brief History of the United States,* so that I knew it by heart. Four times I traveled over Ray's *Arithmetic,* Third Part. School libraries were then unknown, so there was nothing to read. There were perhaps six books in the Beach home and after re-reading them for the twentieth time I could draw from them little nourishment for a starving intelligence.[77]

Early in his life, for reasons that his memoir leaves carefully unexplored, Ross developed an overpowering urge to escape—to immerse himself in the cosmopolitan culture that he knew only at second hand—and in 1881, seven years before the trip to Germany, he convinced his legal guardian, a "taciturn" lawyer named Alexander Campbell, to advance him sufficient moneys from his parents' bequest to defray the costs of his enrollment at the public high school in Marion. From there he arrived, the following year, at a newly opened undergraduate institution, Coe College, in nearby Cedar Rapids. At the high school Ross had not known clearly what he was looking for, but at Coe he begin to see the outlines of a larger world with Europe at the center, and it was also the world of professional success. Years later he would still remember with pride his college years: "Competing . . . at Berlin and Johns Hopkins with crack graduates of old and renowned American colleges, never once did I feel myself at a disadvantage."[78] At Coe, and later in Fort Dodge where he was hired to teach by a Presbyterian "college institute," Ross steeped himself in the high culture of Western Europe: De Quincy, Coleridge, Carlyle, Arnold, Goethe, Mommsen, Darwin, Spencer, Turgeniev, Tolstoi, and in German, Kant,

Fichte, Hegel. "Literary German," he recalled, "was becoming child's play for me; I thought nothing of reading three or four German classics a week, besides [subscribing to] a German paper and attending a German Church."[79]

In Berlin, Ross heard the lectures of the historians Zeller and Paulsen; for the first time he read Schopenhauer and Hegel's *Phenomenology of the Spirit.* As he recorded in his diary, "My life nowadays is so beautiful that it seems a dream. . . . I seize eagerly upon everything and work with enthusiasm. I rest myself from philosophy by studying Italian in which I am making astonishing progress. It is my ninth language."[80] From the vantage point of the Botanical gardens, where he would practice his Italian with friends punctually "at one o'clock," Chicago and the prairie must have seemed, as he thought, "another planet." Among the Europeans, Ross became the European of his own imagining, and by doing so he may have hoped to escape the contradiction he had left behind in the United States between individual ascent and communal loyalty.

But Europe had contradictions of its own, about which Ross himself seems less explicitly aware, for there were in fact *two* Europes, one by day and one by night. The one by day was the Europe of Goethe and *wissenschaftliche Objectivität,* the spirit of empirical research. But the other he described in his diary as a place of brutal rituals

> maintained by the student corps in defiance of the vigilance of the police. It is large, unplastered . . . with the painted roof timbers overhead. . . . The first match is in progress when we arrive. At the extremities of the painted rectangle on the floor of the room, about seven feet apart, sit two frightful-looking objects, the duellists. . . . The swords clash in quick hew and parry. Sparks fly, blow rains on blow till the [referees] strike up the weapons. Perhaps one has received a cut and the blood is running down his face. . . . When the duel is over the combatants are unbandaged by their friends and taken to the surgical table where their wounds are dressed. The sewing of the wounds is hard to bear and the boys make very wry faces and even tremble. Meanwhile the swords are filed sharp for the next encounter.

Ross himself looked on the duels with the uncritical passion of a convert. "My blood was fired," he wrote, "and I wish I were a German student that I might feel the wild delight of standing before an opponent and giving and warding off stern blows."[81] In Berlin the students actually received *two* educations—one that spoke passionately for reason, the spirit, and world-historical progress, while the other perpetuated a legacy of "passion," violence, and the struggle for domination. European militarism lived healthily alongside European high culture, though this was not quite the lesson Ross had bargained for.

Yet it might have been the lesson he most needed to learn, for in the high culture of late nineteenth-century Germany he found an intellectual rationale for his repudiation of the "parochial" values of his own midwestern town, since in Europe a similar repudiation of local culture had shaped almost every aspect of intellectual life—the sciences, the arts, *belles lettres.* The society that enshrined airy treatises like

The World as Will and Representation rested on the barely concealed foundations of force and inequality; in the nightly rituals of self-inflicted wounds, Berlin's students learned *their* most important lesson. Bismarck had built the unified Germany of 1871, together with its the system of state education, on the ruins of the democratic revolutions thirty-three years earlier—the same revolutions that had sent many of Ross's German-speaking neighbors in Marion half a world away from the place of their birth. And only a few years before his arrival, Germany had hosted a conference among the great European powers to hammer out the partition of West Africa, where German troops would later engage in their first genocidal campaigns. For a person like Ross, however, the journey to Europe took on the character of a transforming pilgrimage, and when he later enrolled at Johns Hopkins to begin work toward the Ph.D., he was already prepared to assume a special role in his society—the role of the *wissenschaftlich* social manager who saw it as his task to shepherd his pioneer nation along the difficult road to modernization. "After sixteen months," he remembered of the time following his return to the United States, "I came up for my Ph.D. oral examination before a dozen world-famous scholars, only three or four of whom knew me. To prepare myself for the ordeal I knocked off work for a half week, spending my days in the park." Seated at last before the scholars, "I [felt] gay, even saucy."[82] Naturally, he was dazzling.

Ross saw himself as a man for his age, and the trajectory of his career coincides more or less exactly with the rise of the modern academic disciplines and the transplanting of the German-style university to American soil. But if the German institution with its emphasis on pure research was strongly shaped by the crushingly authoritarian climate of Bismarck's Germany—where high culture became a crucial instrument of mass manipulation—the new American university would soon be shaped by different but equally constricting forces, as Ross himself would learn in the most painful way. Recruited as a prodigy by Stanford's president, David Starr Jordan, he arrived in California expecting to play brilliantly the part he had wanted to play since leaving Marion behind. Already an economic sociologist of international visibility, Ross confidently turned his attention to the most pressing public issue of the day, the campaign to return U.S. currency to the gold standard, a change that he feared would enrich the elite while driving the working class deeper into poverty. When his writings and speeches attracted the attention of the Democratic National Committee, and when the *San Francisco Examiner* reproduced a copy of one speech he had delivered before the Committee, Ross became a target of California's celebrated monopolists, close friends of Mrs. Leland Stanford. For more than two years, Ross waged an ongoing battle with his attackers, who used the conservative *Los Angeles Times* to turn public sentiment against him. "Grimly," he writes of that time, "I regarded my scholarly career as . . . at an end and saw myself obliged, in order to support my family, to serve as principal of a high school or become a reader in a publishing house."[83]

In fact, Ross kept his Stanford job—at least until he offended the railroad interests by launching a campaign against Japanese immigration. "I tried," as he puts it in his memoir, "to show that, owing to its high, Malthusian birth-rate, the Orient is the land of 'cheap men,' and that the coolie, although he cannot outdo the

American, can underlive him."[84] Once again his activist scholarship—which coincided with the sentiments of organized labor and the Progressive elements in California politics—set him at odds with the reigning powers, and on this occasion Stanford's president felt compelled to solicit Ross's resignation in the spring of 1900. When Ross refused, he became the focus of a national debate on academic freedom, and he found supporters not only in California but all across the country. Forced to conduct a public inquiry when sentiment turned strongly in Ross's favor, Stanford's board of trustees accused him of sloppy scholarship and unprofessional behavior— using slang in the classroom, for instance, and speaking badly of Leland Stanford— and the board noted that they were, at any rate, under no legal obligation to renew his contract for another year. But a second review committee, made up entirely of eminent American economists who were also "gold standard men," surprised Ross by finding on his behalf, strongly praising the integrity of his work despite their disagreements with his conclusions. His vindication notwithstanding, Ross accepted an appointment at Wisconsin-Madison that he would hold for the rest of his life.

The Stanford case was in fact far more complex than a clash of saints against the empire, pitting capital against the common man and freedom against conspiracy. Although Ross described himself as the defender of workers and farmers against the predations of the "big fellahs," the social theory he developed was profoundly authoritarian. The same man who took heart when the San Francisco papers came to his rescue had written in *Social Control* that "primitive public opinion . . . far from being a wise disciplinarian, meddles when it ought to abstain, and blesses when it ought to curse." While Ross believed that public opinion had a place in political life, he saw it as blind without "the ascendancy of the wise."[85] But who should be regarded as "wise"? The Stanford case was an early round in a more protracted struggle between the forces of "big business"—corporate capital with its middle-class beneficiaries—and an opponent almost equally "big," if somewhat less wealthy, the newly emergent managerial class, the leaders of our own "information society."

It was Ross's bitter fate to be defeated, not by big money but by the profession he had helped to create. As the 1930s came to a close and his best work lay behind him, the academy was losing its patience with activist intellectuals. Increasingly, Ross's social science colleagues saw him as a careless, overreaching generalist—the kind of person who could write glibly about China one year, Mexico the next, and the Philippines after that, always sketching out the big picture at the expense of the crucial details. Ross, they came to think, was not a social scientist after all—not methodical like a scientist, and not sufficiently dispassionate. When he began his career as a sociologist at Stanford, he estimated that there were no more than five professors in the field nationwide, but by the end of the 1930s, sociology belonged to a younger generation with very different values. The rising star of the next generation would not be a brawling activist like Ross, a Midwestern outsider, but the consummate insider Talcott Parsons, who rode out the Great Depression as an assistant professor at Harvard.

Nowhere is the transformation more clearly evinced than in the discourse of sociology itself. For Ross and his contemporaries, the social scientist still spoke as a public figure in a language never far removed, even in *The American Journal of Sociology,* from magazines like *The Atlantic* and *Popular Science Monthly,* where Ross regularly published. Like his contemporaries William James and John Dewey, Ross wanted to reach the largest possible audience, and throughout his autobiography he repeatedly underscores the sheer magnitude of his readership—9,000 for *Foundations of Sociology* on the first printing, 17,300 by 1935 for *Social Control*—and he even pauses in his narrative to calculate the tens of thousands of people he managed to reach through his lectures and public talks.[86]

It was precisely this relationship with the public that Parsons and his generation strongly repudiated. If their prose operates rhetorically to exclude the "lay" readership that Ross was unwilling to neglect, Parsons could do so in part because the discipline had grown from Ross's estimated membership of five to something better than 12,000. Quite apart from the issue of numbers, though, sociology's relation to the public had changed, and for reasons that reflect the influence of events outside the discipline. When Parsons's *The Social System* was published in 1951—the year after Joseph McCarthy's "infiltration speech" to the Senate— professional sociologists no longer saw themselves as positioned to lead a reform of any kind. Increasingly, their work served to justify the existing social relations, as Parsons himself did unapologetically, not simply in the content of their arguments but also in the style. It might even be said that through its language, Parsons's *The Social System* created an entirely new discipline:

> In the first place, by virtue of internalization of the standard, conformity with it tends to be of personal, expressive and/or instrumental significance to ego. In the second place, the structuring of the reactions of alter to ego's actions as sanctions is a function of his conformity with the standard. Therefore conformity as a direct mode of the fulfillment of his own need-dispositions tends to coincide with conformity as a condition of eliciting the favorable and avoiding the unfavorable reactions of others. In so far as, relative to the actions of a plurality of actors, conformity with value-orientation standard meets *both* these criteria, that is from the point of view of any given actor in the system, it is both a mode of the fulfillment of his own need-dispositions and a condition of "optimizing" the reactions of other significant actors.[87]

If Ross wrote *for* the "significant actors" of his day, Parsons wrote *about* them, and he did so in a "metalanguage" that belonged exclusively to sociologists who conceived of themselves as members of the management or "policy" class. Far from working to create a discursive presence, Parsons bent his language—past the breaking point, some might argue—to support the fiction of a perfectly disembodied analysis. By concealing the writer's motives and situation, he speaks in the voice of sociology itself, and by claiming to reveal the essential truth beneath the misconceptions of common sense, he makes sociology invulnerable to the challenge of the reader's own experience, a trait seen in academic writing for most of the twentieth century.

Revealingly, Parsonsian "grand theory" culminated in a preoccupation with refinements to theory itself. As another sociologist, C. Wright Mills, wrote about the generation of Parsons, "The grand theorists . . . are so rigidly confined to such high levels of abstraction that the 'typologies' they make up . . . seem more often an arid game" than an attempt to address "the problems at hand."[88] What Mills saw clearly, and very nearly Mills alone, was the way in which the rhetoric of theory, coupled with the ideology of professionalism, had allowed sociologists to insulate themselves from precisely the crises that they once regarded as their principal business.

"They have," Mills charged of his colleagues, "taken up social research as a career; they have come early to an extreme specialization, and they have acquired an indifference to or a contempt for 'social philosophy'—which means to them 'writing books out of other books' or 'merely' speculating." Once "a young man has spent three or four years at this sort of thing, you cannot really talk to him about the problem of studying modern society. His position and career, his ambition and his very self-esteem, are based in large part upon this one perspective, this one vocabulary, this one set of techniques."[89] As their understanding of social life became increasingly elaborated, their own faith in themselves as active agents diminished. The *more* they could explain the *less* they could act, and in this sense they were, just as Mills alleged, "energetic and ambitious technicians whom a defective educational routine and a corrupting demand" for imitation "have made incapable" despite all their expertise.[90] Perhaps this was the consummate irony of all the modern professions—that their power as institutions came at the price of growing personal powerlessness.

4

The Trouble with English

The Rise of the Professional Humanities and Their Abandonment of Civil Society

If we want to understand the humanities' role in the twentieth century, we need first to understand their uneasy relations to the social sciences, each of them struggling to take root under the shadows of the sciences. Initially, the differences between them were anything but well-defined, and scholars and scientists sometimes published in the same journals. But the comity was not long-lived. At the start of his year and a half abroad, the young E. A. Ross had immersed himself in European philosophy and the *belles lettres* along with his study of economics, but after several months he was unexpectedly overcome by a sense of disorientation and self-doubt. "Soon," he wrote about that time, "I was 'in the depths' and wondered why I shouldn't commit suicide." Like his predecessor the historian Henry Adams, Ross had gone to Europe in search of the certainties missing from the American scene. Once he had dropped into "the depths," however, Ross saw, or thought he saw, an abyss at the core of Europe's intellectual life from which he somehow had to break free. As he recorded in his diary, "My mind still tends strongly toward the practical. The needs of humanity in the present are . . . my [true] concern . . . I shall keep within the sphere of reality."[1] And "reality," he decided during those crucial, bitter weeks, meant the pragmatic pursuit of human happiness through the social sciences. Given Ross's central role in their development, it would hardly be an exaggeration to say that the choices he made more or less decided the course of social inquiry in the United States for almost thirty years, marked as it would be by an avoidance of "philosophic" issues and a commitment to real-world interventions.

Precisely because they were willing to leave behind the heritage of European arts and letters, men like Ross succeeded in making sociology a self-consciously *modern* discipline, scientific rather than "cultural" in the Arnoldian sense, forward-looking rather than tied to the past. As spokesmen for the future, the worldly professions went about their work with sublime indifference to their nostalgic counterparts in the field of English—a point frankly conceded by the scholar M. D. Learned in his 1909 presidential address to the Modern Language Association. The humanities, Learned said, had plainly lost their competition with the "technicals," and the result was a growing cultural crisis:

The demand of the technicals . . . threatens to eliminate all serious study of language, even of English, to make room for the encroaching technical courses. The same spirit in reality prevails in our professional schools [where] the lawyer clamors for more law, the physician for more medicine, while the liberal arts are passed by as unnecessary and—what is to the technical mind far worse—*unprofitable*—all signs not the most promising for a great national culture or for a creative national literature.

It is a vital question for us as teachers of modern languages, whether our national greatness shall go up in airships and build castles in the air to last for a day or record its life in imperishable forms of literature and art and take its part in this struggle between the material and the cultural forces in our intellectual life.[2]

In their misgivings about specialization—the "lawyer's clamoring for more law" and so on—Learned's remarks seem to voice the same nostalgia that Sir James Paget had expressed in *his* speech of 1880, when the old physician looked back to a more intimate age given over to self-sacrifice and charity. The danger of specialization, Paget felt, lay in the forgetfulness of commonalities that transcended differences of schooling or occupation. But this was *not* the argument that Learned made. For him, the greatest danger arising from excessive technical specialization was America's failure to produce the great cultural monuments without which the nation would remain provincial and second-rate no matter how dramatically scientific research might advance. The point, finally, was not to overturn the "technicals," who clearly deserved a future role of some kind, but to pursue a parallel form of excellence, "the higher work of *creation* . . . the building of a national literature."[3] At a time when journalism and popular magazines shaped the sensibilities of most young Americans, and when the works that passed for literature could not compare, in Learned's view, to the run of the Europe's mill, it seemed obvious that the best hope for his country lay with the study of "literary forms" as these had developed in Europe.

By 1910, however, roughly half a century after Thoreau and Emerson, Melville, Whitman, and the early Twain, and two decades following the posthumous appearance of Emily Dickinson's poems, American literature was hardly the wasteland that Learned described. The years between 1899 and 1910 saw the publication of Dreiser's *Sister Carrie*, Kate Chopin's *The Awakening*, Jack London's *The Call of the Wild*, Frank Norris's *The Pit*, Edith Wharton's *The House of Mirth*, and Gertrude Stein's *Three Lives*. Learned spoke highly of Emerson, whom he refers to as "the American Kant," and also of Poe, whose inspiration Learned attributed to E. T. A. Hoffmann. But his argument for the deficiency of the nation's literary life is really about Americans' relative indifference to the great monuments of *European* literature, and so the canon whose works he enumerated at great length began with the *Iliad* and *Odyssey* and concluded with the labyrinth of German aesthetic theory. Whatever Learned might allege, the problem was *not* the waning of public literacy. In fact, Americans of the day enjoyed a rate of literacy that rivaled the Germans', whose achievements had become the envy of the English-speaking world. As one of

Learned's younger contemporaries, Yale's Henry Seidel Canby, observed at that time, "We are the greatest readers among the nations. Everybody in America reads—from the messenger boy to the corporation president. It was never so easy to read as now in America."[4] What bothered men like Learned, however, was the "quality" of this reading. In Canby's words, the "hunger and thirst for the printed page has resulted in a flood of writing that is good, but not too good; clever, but not too clever . . . A year of such indiscriminate perusing, and a man of good natural taste will swallow anything rather than be left without something to read."[5] While Learned predicted a steep decline for America's thin and vulgar civilization, Canby foresaw that ordinary Americans would continue to be avid readers—and the targets of academic scorn. "Not long ago," he wrote, "I saw a college professor drop into a chair at his club, glance over the table of contents of a well-known periodical, and fling it down in disgust. 'I can't read the magazines,' he snorted. 'What's the matter with American literature?'" But as Canby pointed out, the professor, half a century earlier, would have thrown down in the same contempt the latest installment by William Thackeray or Charles Dickens.

"What is it," Canby asked, "that makes us contemptuous when we come to current literature . . . especially to current American literature?" And he offered at least part of the answer when he took issue with James Russell Lowell's dictum that there would never be a good American literature without an American criticism. "If he meant," Canby wrote, "that there must be great critics before there are great writers, the history of many literary periods is against him."[6] While Canby himself believed that the best European writing was better than the best that Americans could offer, he still correctly understood that the contemptuousness of his colleagues had more to do with their own sense of illegitimacy, inside and outside academia, than it did with character of the nation's cultural life. By 1915, as he noted in his collected essays *College Sons and College Fathers,* the teaching of English had become "one of the largest" of all American professions, a close competitor to "advertising, social service, and efficiency-engineering." "Yet already," he went on, "the colleges complain that the popularity of this comparatively recent addition to the curriculum is so great that the harder, colder, more disciplinary subjects are pushed to the wall (and this in practical America!)."[7]

Far more typical than Canby's assessment, however, was the opinion of Learned's successor, Charles Hall Grandgent, whose 1912 presidential address announced the advent of nothing less than a new "Dark Ages." Dark as they were, he told his audience, the old Dark Ages still held to a reverence for learning: Charlemagne in the worst years of medieval "barbarism" had built the famous Palace School where the great Alcuin taught. But in the new Dark Ages, as deplorable in its ignorance as the old one, even this reverence has disappeared, and to make the point concretely Grandgent quoted from the recent conference proceedings of the National Education Association, where high school teachers spoke against an overemphasis on the genteel letters and in favor of a new curriculum designed to meet the needs of everyday life. "Was it thus," Grandgent asked, "in the seventh century?"[8] If American high school students under the new, reformist regime learned some English, some German, a bit of history and elementary algebra, the great

Alcuin had gone through far more demanding curriculum that included grammar, rhetoric, poetry, astronomy, physics, both Testaments, the whole range of science and "general literature." While such a curriculum had made Alcuin nothing less than the wisest of men, it worked its power on the Emperor as well, transforming him from a rude conqueror into a genuine sovereign, one who was "'ever learning, and fond of learning'" and to whom no subject, from architecture to the most abstruse theological discourse, was foreign.

Recent scholarship has called into question much of the portrait Grandgent painted of life in the reign of Charlemagne, who in fact died as unlettered as when he was born.[9] But Grandgent needed to exaggerate the glories of the past in order to show that Americans were deficient in every conceivable way. "Has the world," Grandgent asked his audience, "ever seen a more completely self-satisfied being than an empty-headed American high school pupil? There is," he said,

> a supreme type of self-complacency which is born of sheer ignorance, an ignorance so absolute as to be unaware of the existence of anything to learn. And this self-complacency, I have already said, is not confined to school children: it is shared by old and young. It may be called the dominating spirit of our time. One of its marks is a contempt for thoro [sic] knowledge and a profound distrust of anyone who is really well-informed. An expert opinion on any subject becomes valueless the moment we learn that it emanates from a "college professor."[10]

As Grandgent's audience would have understood quite readily, the opinion of *some* experts might be very well-received, but in matters of culture things stood otherwise. Clearly the most vital centers of American cultural life lay far from the oversight of English professors. "In the field of humor," he complained, "Washington Irving yields to Mutt and Jeff. In religion, we see flourishing sects whose very names seem like a blasphemous caricature." And in the public halls "musicians vie with one another in [the] noisy cacophony" of ragtime and jazz.[11]

In the struggle for greater authority, men like Grandgent represented themselves as Arnoldian defenders of the "best that has been thought and said," and for them "the best" meant the high culture of Europe. Yet the version of Europe that they embraced was in many ways a figment of their own imaginations, excluding as it did the achievements of Europe's finest living writers and artists. "In art," Grandgent said derisively, "the Impressionists have long since been succeeded by the Post-Impressionists, the Futurists, and the Cubists" in an absurd frenzy of innovation.[12] Such innovations flew directly in the face of attempts to sell European culture here at home as older and therefore better, since the Futurists and their rebellious confreres had flaunted—in the very heart of the motherland—the same militant indifference to the past that caused Americans like Grandgent to go red with shame for their ill-tutored countrymen. Europe itself had broken faith with the Europe of yore, and Grandgent was obliged to take sides not simply with the Old World against the New, and not only with the past against the present, but also, finally, against the Enlightenment and everything it represented. The new Dark Age, it turned out, had begun with the French Revolution, which Grandgent saw as the start of a wholesale decline, an "extension and cheapening of education resulting in a vast increase of self-confident ignorance." While Grandgent might admit that the Enlightenment had greatly expanded the sum of human knowledge, the rightful heirs to this knowledge—as he put it, "the large share-holders" in the stock company of Western civilization—were "no longer in control." And for Grandgent, Alcuin notwithstanding, getting back in control was the substantive issue, not sweetness or light or culture or anything else. As he noted with keen regret, "It is scarcely conceivable that democracy should ever relinquish its hold. The civilized world is committed to the principle of majority rule, believing that the supremacy of the many results in the greatest good to the greatest number."[13] If at first the "plebs" had gained some knowledge and refinement through their ascent to political power, the reverse was now true, so that "equalization has come to mean the lowering of the brahmin to the dead level of the intellectual pariah."[14]

The denigration of mass culture allowed scholars of Grandgent's day to wrest literary art from the undergraduate reading societies, a fixture of academic life since Ralph Waldo Emerson's time, and from the even more successful women's clubs operating outside the university.[15] But these founders were less successful in defining what it was about the literary work of art that required such careful handling. For several decades around the turn of the century, instruction in English courses took the form of recitation. Bliss Perry became famous at Harvard for his stirring renditions, and textbooks of the time, such as *The Oral Study of Literature,* made the case for recitation as the most effective way to absorb the taste and wisdom embodied in the great works.[16] In effect, the founders of English had institutionalized the literary connoisseurship of the European aristocracy, as did the related field of art history under the stewardship of founders like Bernard Berenson.[17] A phrase from Shakespeare, an allusion to Dryden, an acquaintance with Cellini or Watteau, these immediately identified a person as a member of the cultured class, whom one detractor at the time, the sociologist Thorstein Veblen, caricatured as a sort of landless gentry.[18]

We might say that the founders of English borrowed the trappings of the older, aristocratic culture in the service of a consummately modern enterprise. But as knowledge became increasingly professionalized, appeals to taste and beauty could hardly justify the expense involved in creating tenured lines for faculty, endowed chairs, and all the other apparatus of a department or discipline. Literary studies had to establish itself as a specialized knowledge with a unique and indispensable social function in the administered society. Scholars like Grandgent responded to these conflicting demands by developing a "scientific" form of historical scholarship modeled on German criticism and philology. In retrospect, the scholarship of this period, with titles like "Spenser's Irish Rivers," and "The Tudor Line in Shakespeare," may seem to exemplify the worst aspects of academic pedantry, but historicism gave English and other humanities both a methodology and a quasi-scientific image. At the same time, it sharpened Grandgent's case against the benighted masses. In a mock dialogue, he made his modernists say, "The past is dead. We will turn our backs upon it, and give ourselves to the living present." "How familiar," Grandgent continued,

> these words have become in the public press and in college papers, and in assemblies of educators! Anything that bears the label of actuality attracts the throng, whether it be on the book-shelf or on the stage, in the public lecture-hall or in the academic class-room . . . "Only the present is real," say the modernists. On the contrary, say I, nothing is more unreal, more elusive, more fictitious. The present is an illusion: it is a perpetually shifting mathematical line dividing the future, of which (humanly speaking) we know nothing, from the past, of which we know much.[19]

The past, of course, is actually no more certain than the present as an object of inquiry, and one might in fact reply to Grandgent that all we ever know about the past is what we reconstruct in our own time. But by representing history as the key to all understanding, Grandgent helped to authenticate a new division of intellectual labor. While the knowledge of the sciences was predictive, extrapolating from the present into the future, the knowledge of the humanities would move with comparable rigor in the opposite direction. Thus the world was divided.

Historicism closely followed science, however, in another and perhaps more important sense. Behind Grandgent's notion of literary history were figures like the French critic Hyppolite Taine, the author of the landmark study, *The History of English Literature,* that so impressed Hamlin Garland. Today we might see Taine's work as one of the more bizarre relics of social Darwinism, but in its time it seemed to achieve a brilliant synthesis of humanistic learning with some of the most important trends in the biology and anthropology. According to Taine, geography and genetic heritage have helped to develop in each race and each nation a distinctive character, starting with a "primitive disposition," an "elementary moral state" that changing conditions have transformed over time.[20] Although this elementary state has its origins in the founding moments of a people, and although it never ceases to undergo transformation, Taine also saw everywhere the signs of an underlying continuity. While geography and history were important, in his view the most decisive of all was race, what we would now call genetics:

> We have here a distinct force—so distinct, that amidst the vast deviations which [the environment and history] produce in him, one can recognize it still; and a race, like the old Aryans, scattered from the Ganges as far as the Hebrides, settled in every clime, and every stage of civilization, transformed by thirty centuries of revolutions, nevertheless manifests in its languages, religions, literatures, philosophies, the community of blood and of intellect which to this day binds its offshoots together. . . . There is nothing astonishing in this extraordinary tenacity . . . of [the primordial marks]. When we meet with them, fifteen, twenty, thirty centuries before our era, in an Aryan, an Egyptian, a Chinese, they represent the work of a great many ages, perhaps of several myriads of centuries.[21]

Taine discerned the traces of his "primordial marks" in all aspects of a culture, but most immediately and revealingly in literary art. Although histories of criticism, for obvious reasons, typically consign Taine to the silence of the footnotes, his influence on the formation of literary scholarship has been significant. Even when critics rejected his pseudo-anthropological method, they accepted his account of literature as the fullest expression of a language, a culture, and a people. While Taine's racial theories are no longer in vogue, many educated readers still believe that literature holds the key to a culture and expresses the best and truest form of a language. A monograph like "Spencer's Irish Rivers" seems trivial until we understand it in the context of Taine's project, where it reveals itself to be a kind of textual archeology, a contribution to what we would now call collective cultural memory.

Precisely because it resonated with the nationalist spirit of the times, Taine's influence, explicit or otherwise, was not limited to scholarship in the field of English. The idea that each society possesses a distinctive sensibility determined by biology, geography, and history is also the guiding assumption behind the historian Frederick Jackson Turner's famous argument that the American consciousness has been shaped most decisively by the experience of the frontier, and that the frontier's closing would transform that consciousness once again. But the reception of these ideas by many historians differed in important ways from their reception among English professors. Although Turner saw culture and nationality in rather reductive ways, his privileging of geography over race gave his work a distinctly egalitarian character.[22] In his narrative, all Americans without exception were the offspring of the frontier, the rough and ready carriers of its liberating values. Even the critics who now assail Turner's thesis tend to share this egalitarian sensibility: rather than denying a decisive influence to the frontier—or the "borderlands," as they now call it—the post-Turnerians simply add that its influence differed among various overlooked groups: women, Hispanics, working-class Americans, and so on. The frontier is still the parent, but now of many different children. We might say, however, that the whole point of English was to work against any such inclusive leveling—a "dead level," as Grandgent described it. In America at the outset of the modern era, the legitimacy of history as a form of expert knowledge depended on its ability to speak, ostensibly, for all Americans, to tell the shared American story. But the legitimacy of English depended on the maintenance of a distinction between the elite and the masses. Perhaps this divergence helps to explain why the discipline of history has a long established tradition of explicitly democratic thinking, whereas such a tradition is conspicuously absent even today from the legacy of English studies, which has been dominated, on the one hand, by the hauteur of cultural conservatives, or on the other hand, by the hauteur of the left, hardly less contemptuous of the ordinary citizen.

While the creation of English as a discipline first required Taine's idea of a distinctive national consciousness, that idea finally stood in the way of the field's full professionalization. In fact, it absolutely had to go. By Taine's account, all Englishmen alike participate in the essence of Englishness. There is always, he thought, "a community of blood and of intellect which . . . binds its offshoots together."[23] But if Taine's claim holds true, then a music hall ditty might matter just as much ethnographically as the "Ode on a Grecian Urn."[24] Absurd as Taine's racialist ideas may seem now, they implicitly underwrote a potential egalitarianism that Taine himself never pursued and that an elitist like Grandgent would never have endorsed. And there were other problems with Taine's thinking, at least from the standpoint of English as a profession. Although he believed in an essential Englishness or Germanness or Frenchness, he never represented these qualities as the product of conscious reform or rigorous self-discipline. The brilliant, superficial sons of Gaul could no more make themselves behave like the stolid, stalwart sons of Albion than the peacock could soar like an osprey. Taine acknowledged as well that the passing of time made a difference in spite of the essential continuities: people living in the modern world could not expect to hold on to the values of the Middle Ages.

It was the potential in Taine's thought for cultural leveling and relativism that eventually produced in English studies a powerful reaction to the historicist approach, a reaction which, perhaps ironically, went by the name of the "new humanism." While people like Grandgent had launched the field of English by imitating the model of the sciences, the new humanists perceived correctly that a scientific outlook could not sustain the *qualitative* distinctions upon which rested the whole tradition of the *belles lettres,* high literary culture. If historical scholarship that Taine inaugurated had its sources in the German Romantics and the research of folklorists like the brothers Grimm, the American new humanists of the twenties looked to the classical Republican tradition—not the faction-torn society of Periclean Athens, but the culture of the Roman aristocracy.

The foremost spokesman for this position was Irving Babbitt, whose influence on the formation of the humanities in America can scarcely be overrated. If Babbitt is so seldom cited these days—if most graduate students confuse him with the Sinclair Lewis character—it is because his ideas have become so much a part of the basic outlook of the academy. Although Babbitt was a professor of French rather than of English, his own field resembled English at the time in its embrace of a German-inspired historicist methodology. What had gotten lost in all this rigor, he insisted, was the humanity at the heart of any living culture. But when Babbitt referred to "humanity," he never meant a universal humanity. In fact, he meant exactly the opposite. On the one hand, Babbitt criticized the historicists as out of touch with times and with a spirit of spontaneity. "We should at least insist," he wrote, "that the college teacher of ancient or modern literature be something more than a mere specialist. To regard a man as qualified for a college position in these subjects simply because he has investigated some minute point of linguistics or literary history—this, to speak plainly, is preposterous."[25] By formalizing literary study and encouraging microscholarship, the historicists had contributed to an increasing rigidification of social life in general. "The risk we run nowadays," Babbitt argued, "is that of having our minds buried beneath a dead-weight of information which we have no inner energy, no power of reflection, to appropriate to our own uses and convert into vital nutriment." By its very nature, the tradition of humane letters put a premium on a balance "between knowledge and reflection," or rather, between knowledge and cultivation.[26]

On the other hand, Babbitt accused the historicists of undermining the basis for indispensable standards. With the rush to imitate the sciences, literary history had displaced the study of literature itself, not just as a subject but as an alternative way of thinking.[27] The historicists had failed to understand that the sciences and humanities had quite different social roles to play: the first to produce new information, the second to provide a framework for putting that information in its socially and morally appropriate place. Babbitt reasoned that when the humanities try to become sciences, they abdicate their responsibility and contribute to a general draft away from all familiar points of moral reference. That such fixed points of reference existed Babbitt was absolutely certain, and he found them in the classics, not only the classics of Greece and Rome, but of India and China as well. The Buddha and Socrates, Epictetus and Confucius—for Babbitt they all taught the same fundamental doctrine, all pointed to the same unchanging human law.

"Man," he wrote, "is a creature who is foredoomed to one-sidedness, yet who becomes humane only in proportion as he triumphs over this fatality of his nature, only as he arrives at that measure which comes from tempering his virtues, each by its opposite. . . . For most practical purposes, the law of measure is the supreme law of life, because it bounds and includes all other laws.[28] As this passages indicates, the source of Babbitt's "law of measure" remains unclear. At times, he seems to indicate that it lies in our genetic inheritance as a species, but to say so would be to concede once again the primacy of science. At other times, he seems to be an idealist in the tradition of Plato, though unwilling to announce outright his faith in transcendentals of some kind. Then again, he could sound like a historicist himself, looking for his certainties in the primordial past rather than in a philosopher's heaven. But whatever its justifications, the value of Babbitt's theory of human nature lay in his turn to high art for moral certainties at a time of cultural crisis. While conceding that philosophers may have the clearest vision of human nature, a vision superior to the critic's, Babbitt still argues that for most people, a sense of measure "will be attained, if at all, by a knowledge of good literature—by a familiarity with that golden chain of masterpieces which links together into a single tradition the more permanent experience of the race."[29] In opposition to the growing liberalization of the undergraduate curriculum, Babbitt insisted that "what is wanted is not a hard and fast hierarchy of studies, but a sense of measure that will save us from the opposite extreme, from the democratic absurdity of asserting that all studies are, and by right should be, free and equal."[30] Literary criticism was not simply a handmaiden to the arts; it was the discipline of all disciplines, and the disciplinarian of society as a whole.

Babbitt's argument with the historicists was not about the value of literature, but about what should be done with it: it was ultimately an argument about how to read. If the historicists transformed the literary text into an artifact for analysis, Babbitt represented it instead as a guide to inner cultivation, not unlike a secular scripture. But Babbitt's leanings, at least in public, were more secular than scriptural. He owed his understanding of self-cultivation primarily to the Stoics, although his enormously wide reading allowed him to draw upon sources from virtually every age and all of the so-called world civilizations. In his view, literature uniquely offers us models of behavior and judgment against which we can measure our own behavior without appeals to religious absolutes. The principal point of reading literature was not pleasure, but self-restraint and self-discipline. Babbitt believed that by rehearsing the thoughts of great minds, we slowly learn to see our small selves in due proportion, but at the same time, we are transformed into better thinkers than we were initially. By imitating great men—by putting their ideas into our heads, so to speak—we become, if not great, then a tiny bit less deficient.

To English as a fledgling profession, no aspect of humanism recommended itself more strongly than its defense of a hierarchy based upon merit, in the best tradition of middle-class competitiveness. For the historicists, the focus of literary study was the race and not the individual. Although Babbitt shares this racialist outlook to some degree, he understands self-cultivation to be an inescapably personal affair.[31] The Greeks and Romans may have been great races, but their excellence arose from the greatness of their leaders, men of exemplary self-discipline. By its very nature, the path they followed could not be followed by everyone:

> The true humanist maintains a just balance between sympathy and selection. We moderns . . . tend to lay an undue stress on the element of sympathy [with our fellow men]. On the other hand, the ancients in general, both Greek and Roman, inclined to sacrifice sympathy to selection [as in] Gellius' protest against confusing *humanitas* with a promiscuous philanthropy. . . . Ancient humanism is as a whole intensely aristocratic in temper; its sympathies run in what would seem to us narrow channels; it is naturally disdainful of the humble and lowly who have not been indoctrinated and disciplined.[32]

As a professing Christian, Babbitt could not entirely countenance Greek and Roman disdain for the uncultivated. But he goes on to argue several paragraphs after this passage that even "God himself is selective ('Many are called, few are chosen')."[33] For Babbitt, the modern principle of "universal brotherhood" is fundamentally mistaken. A society that accepted everything indiscriminately would be no society at all. In every aspect of human life "selection" must operate, and selection itself depends on a hierarchy of values and of the persons who embody them.

From the necessity of moral and intellectual hierarchy, Babbitt infers the necessity of a corresponding social hierarchy. Of course, one might easily reply that in many societies, moral and intellectual hierarchies have gone hand in hand with widespread human misery, and that some quite exacting ethical systems have operated in the service of greater equality. Jews have long affirmed their brotherhood and sisterhood through the observance of common rituals and symbols. In the Islamic world, a rigorous schedule of religious observances has tended to lessen the force of distinctions based on wealth and ancestry, most dramatically during Ramadan and the *hajj* to Mecca. But as an account of the outlook held by the ancient Greek and Roman aristocracies, Babbitt's point is well taken. In the ancient world, the ruling class justified its position on the grounds of its moral superiority, an argument that was by no means original to Aristotle, who espouses it in the *Politics*. Theoretically, slaves and women were inferior to their male masters because they lacked any comparable capacity for self-restraint. Slaves were the strong arms of the ancient world, women the fecund wombs, whereas the masters were society's cool brains.[34]

What Babbitt does so brilliantly is to translate the ancient ideology of self-mastery into the context of American society at the start of the twentieth century. Humanists become, in effect, the new ruling class, not an aristocracy of the blood, but of reason, effort, and sensibility—sensibility in particular. Strictly speaking, the humanities, as Babbitt imagines them, impart wisdom rather than knowledge. Of course, wide reading was required, but the virtue of reading was its power to produce a stable frame of reference, a certain quality of discernment that the great mass of people were bound to lack, given over as they were to riotous change and indiscriminate mingling. Needless to say, Babbitt suppresses the real complexity of classical culture, to which the modern distinctions between "high" and "low" culture do not readily apply. He imagines too that people in the classical world shared a single, unifying outlook, when in fact, classical history presents a spectacle of uninterrupted social conflict. But the appeal to wisdom gave scholarship in the humanities a political and social relevance that historical study could never rival. The critic of literature was nothing less than the exemplary man among men, and as such, he was obliged to lead others in all matters related to the conduct of life. He was the conscience, the soul, of the society.

At the same time that Babbitt raised the humanists above the masses, he raised them above the sciences as well. For the Greeks, working with one's hands was inherently degrading, the activity of slaves and not free men. In Babbitt's account, technology was the successor to the work of the blacksmith and the peasant. Gone from his account was the visionary quality of science, its imagination and intelligence—these belong only to the man of letters, who can withdraw from the crudities of material life. About those critics and poets who called for a marriage of the humanities and science, Babbitt wrote dismissively. What we need, he insisted, is not a marriage but a complete divorce. Implicit in Babbitt's demotion of science was a recoiling from the openness and expansiveness at the heart of the modern adventure. Believing as he did that the acceptance of limitation—of one's natural place in the order of things—held the key to both personal happiness and social harmony, Babbitt saw nothing to be gained from innovation in either science or politics. From his perspective, modernity had to be understood as one colossal error.

For this reason, Babbitt rejected as well the effort to open more widely the doors of higher education. But his rejection was complex, since he understood that the humanist elite could not lead the masses unless the masses had been trained to follow. In Babbitt's writings generally, education became a form of leadership, reinstating distinctions rather than dissolving them. As he argued, "the purpose of college is not to encourage the democratic spirit, but on the contrary to check the drift toward a pure democracy. If our definition of humanism has any value, what is needed is not democracy alone, nor again an unmixed aristocracy, but a blending of the two—an aristocratic and selective democracy."[35] Eighty years later, in *The Closing of the American Mind*, Allan Bloom would offer much same argument, and although Bloom took thinkers like John Dewey to task for the sins of higher education, the truth is that Babbitt's conception of teaching as a covert form of moral and political rule has had a more enduring impact on the humanities than Dewey's thought would ever achieve.[36] Like Bloom, too, Babbitt tended to arouse controversy, especially—and predictably—among the historicists. But much of the fight was pure showmanship. Although the two camps—new humanists and historicists—often behaved as adversaries, staging lofty debates and trading salvos in print, their efforts were in fact complementary and mutually reinforcing, undertaken in pursuit of the same ultimate goal.

That goal, strange as it may sound given Babbitt's classical flourishes, was the appropriation of the arts for administrative ends. By the 1930s, the United States had a well-established culture of the arts, or perhaps I should say that it had many different cultures, as dissimilar as the plein-air painting of California, the Ashcan School in New York, the Arts and Crafts movement, the novels of Jack London and the plays of Eugene O'Neill, and the music of George Gershwin. All occurred without the benefit of the academy, and even the major cultural critics of the time—people like Randolph Bourne on the left and H. L. Mencken on the right—operated outside the university. As academic criticism emerged, its main purpose was to shape artistic practice and popular taste in a new way, not through argument in the public media, but by adjudication from above. Babbitt never dreamed, for example, that he should reach out directly to an audience like Mencken's—direct address to the general public had already begun to grow passé.

What got lost in all of this were the arts themselves—the vibrant culture of the arts outside the academy. But during this same period, the academy was to be the site of a powerful protest to the appropriation of the arts. In an essay delivered at Columbia in 1910, Joel Spingarn, a professor of comparative literature, took aim at both the new humanists and the historicists—at "literary erudition and evolutionary science"—which he accused of sacrificing the arts for other ends:

> Historical criticism takes us away from [the work of art] in a search of the environment, the age, the race, the poetic school of the artist; it tells us to read the history of the French revolution, Godwin's *Political Justice,* the *Prometheus Bound* of Aeschylus and Calderón's *Mágico Prodigioso.* . . . [Humanistic] criticism does not get any closer to the work of art by testing it according to rules and standards; it sends me to the Greek dramatists, to Shakespeare, to Aristotle's *Poetics,* possibly to Darwin's *Origin of Species,* in order that I may see how far Shelley has failed to give dramatic reality to his poem, or has failed to observe the rules of his genre. . . . Aesthetics takes me still farther afield into speculations on art and beauty.[37]

Spingarn did not mean simply that all interpretation is invidious. As he himself went on to acknowledge, *any* commentary whatsoever must stray from the work to some degree, insofar as commentary by its very nature revisits the work from the standpoint of something else. (If only all scholars could be so honest!) But Spingarn recognized also that the existing culture of the arts *already* taught sophisticated forms of interacting with the work, and that people who love and enjoy the arts were already adept, in their own way, as readers. To begin with, ordinary art lovers often approached the arts as a distinctive mode of experience. We now might say, although Spingarn never put it quite this way, that the arts enable us to experience vicariously worlds unlike our familiar worlds. Even in common speech we say that we get lost in a book, or that a painting transports us, or that a piece of music takes us out of ourselves. Everyone who loves the arts has already learned this lesson, the most important one the arts have to teach.

Spingarn was a canny opponent: in reply to Babbitt's new humanists, he pointed to the defects of the classical tradition; and in reply to the historicists, he developed a historical argument. Classical tradition, he argued, had never managed to recognize the arts as anything more than an instrument of the state, a close kin, we might say now, to propaganda. As for the so-called neoclassicists, writers and critics in the eighteenth century who took antiquity as the model, for them the arts were still a means to an end, a handmaiden to philosophy or science. It was only with the Romantics, Spingarn argued, that art acquired the status of a way of knowing in its own right. As the Romantics understood it, this new way of knowing, the artist's way, differs from philosophy and the sciences in its attention to experience at its most particular and individualized. The philosopher inquires and the scientist observes, but the artist *expresses:* the artist adds what the other forms of understanding take away—feeling, memory, sensuous life, combined to make a representation of experiential wholeness. And it was here, in his defense of personal experience, that Spingarn answered Babbitt and his followers most directly, since the arts would be useless as a "guide to life" unless the artist had lived without such guides, if only temporarily, and then passed on the fruits of his experience. The arts begin with personal experience, in all its precariousness, and only later does that experience become a common property of society as a whole.

In his defense of art as an experience, Spingarn did not go quite so far as to jettison criticism altogether. Instead he argued for its reconstruction. The reconstruction that he called for, however, could scarcely be more radical. The "poet's aim," he wrote, "must be judged at the moment of the creative act, that is to say, by the art of the poem itself."[38] But what does Spingarn mean by "the art of the poem"? The list of things he doesn't mean grows longer with every page. "In the first place," he argues, "we have done with all the old Rules," which he dismisses as "a survival of the savage *taboo.*" We have done, as well, with genres. The "separation of the *genres*"—the insistence that "comedy should not be mingled with tragedy, nor epic with lyric"—he derided as another example of classicism's arbitrariness pretending to universality. In fact, Spingarn insisted that any normative account of art is ultimately bound to fail, for "no sooner [is a] law enunciated than it [gets] broken by an artist impatient or ignorant of its restraints, and the critics have been obliged [either] to explain away these violations" or else to invent "new laws."[39] But Spingarn still was not done with being done: gone too was "the theory of style, with metaphor, simile, and all the paraphernalia of Greco-Roman rhetoric" insofar as they treated form as divisible from content and context.[40] Gone was "technique," since each artist must invent a form of expression unique to his own experience. And finally, Spingarn disposed of those staples of historical criticism: "the race, the time, the environment," and the idea of a quasi-natural evolution in art.[41]

After all of that, what remained? A sympathetic reader in our time might be tempted to say that what remained was the record of creative activity embodied in the work. Spingarn wanted us to ask what the writer was trying to accomplish when he wrote this poem or that chapter; he was not asking about literary form or technique or conventions, but about the activity that shapes all of these. Terms like "form," "technique," and "convention" are all attempts to treat as an artifact what is actually a process, and although the critic might reasonably draw on such terms for heuristic reasons, they ultimately falsify the creative or synthetic character of artistic activity. Implicit in this critique of formalism, however, was a more subtle but far-ranging repudiation of critical practice at the time. On the one hand, Spingarn rejected all attempts to judge the artist's activity by standards other than those that the artist has set for himself. But on the other hand, Spingarn recognized that the artist's "standards," so to speak, get defined and redefined in the process of creating, and that so long as the activity continues, the standards themselves will continue to change. In this sense, no work can be said to "fail": implicit in the idea of "failure" there is still a containment, or outright denial, of the radically creative character of art making. Instead of passing judgment on the success or failure of the work, the critic ought to ask what the artist has *discovered*. In a certain sense, this is the only question that can ever be asked of any work of art, and perhaps of any human activity whatsoever.

In contrast to figures like Grandgent and Babbitt, who regarded contemporary developments in the arts with great suspicion, Spingarn was one of the first American academic humanists to ally himself with the forces of democratic change. It might be tempting to call Spingarn a modernist, and to contrast his position with the conservativism of these other critics, but the record is somewhat more complex. I would prefer to think of Spingarn as a democratic theorist of the arts rather than a champion of modernism because modernism often rested quite comfortably with Progressive rule from above or else with a nostalgia for a simpler and more "orderly" time when people knew their "proper" places. While industrial society unleashed powerful forces of change, forces manifest in many different ways, modernism can be explained as an effort to contain those potentially explosive forces beneath a new pyramid of authority. Viewed from this perspective, the administered society might be seen as crowning achievement of the modern age, and critics like Babbitt and Grandgent, though profoundly backward looking, might nevertheless be understood as founders of the modernist humanities.

By contrast, Spingarn proposed a form of criticism that subordinates critical judgment to authorial activity. Although Spingarn's term for this new practice was "creative criticism" it hardly conformed to the conventional ideas about the critic's proper enterprise.[42] Closer equivalents might simply be "explanation," "appreciation," or even "co-creation." "Criticism," as Spingarn defined it, "is essentially an expression of taste, or that faculty of imaginative sympathy by which the reader or spectator is able to relive the vision created by the artist."[43] This is, of course, what every ordinary reader already does. What the critics can add is simply the discursive understanding that arises "when taste is guided by knowledge and rises to the level of thought." In other words, creative criticism *explains* what the writer *shows;* it translates narrative into argument and image into ideas. Whatever else it may do, creative criticism always operates as an unfolding of the author's intentions and achievements. The "greatest need of American criticism," he wrote, "is a deeper sensibility, a more complete submission to the imaginative will of the artist, before attempting to rise above it to the realm of judgment." By "taste," Spingarn did not mean the "good taste" of the connoisseur or collector, or taste in its rationalistic eighteenth-century sense, but that "creative moment of the life of the spirit which the artist and the enjoyer of art share alike."[44]

For many eighteenth-century critics, taste implied something like a *sensus communis,* the judgment of a whole community as expressed by its most learned and receptive representatives. But for Spingarn, taste meant something like "skill at being receptive" or "openmindedness." A person with taste is a person who has learned how to surrender himself readily and easily to the "creative moment of the life of the spirit," a power of identification closely akin to Keats's "negative capability." When this happens, however, the force of social norms—and of conventionality in general—is diminished, if not actually suspended, along with the power of society itself, including the power of professional critics. Perhaps for this reason, Babbitt regarded Spingarn's work as the very archetype of everything destructive in the modern age. It was, Babbitt insisted, "not enough, as Mr. Spingarn would have us believe, that the critic should ask what the creator aimed to do and whether he has fulfilled his aim; he must also ask whether the aim is intrinsically worthwhile."[45] Babbitt warned that when innovation is accepted as the highest standard—as "genius," to use Spingarn's phrase—and when identification with the artist replaces as the judgment of those elevated by long acquaintance with the classics, the result is an overturning of the "two virtues that sum up . . . all civilization, humility, and decorum." Worse yet, Spingarn's expressionism "encourages the two root diseases of human nature, conceit and laziness." Spingarn's "exhortation to . . . let ourselves go amounts in effect to this: follow the line of least resistance."[46] For Babbitt, this was clearly the road to ruin.

But it wasn't. Instead, one might argue that Spingarn's understanding of the arts has triumphed in America's vernacular culture, although Spingarn himself may have done no more than defend and theorize an attitude already commonplace among ordinary citizens. Certainly most people who are not trained by professionals—or trained to be professionals—assume that a painting and a poem exists primarily as special kind of communication, addressed to each of us in our privacy as individuals and inviting our own participation and enjoyment. This is, in fact, the understanding of art that many artists themselves endorse, explicitly or otherwise. But on these terms academic criticism can never claim to be anything more than one person's response in a potentially infinite pluralism of responses, a democracy of responses.

If Spingarn was correct, then the distinctive contribution of the arts is not to provide moral guidelines, nor, necessarily, to "push the envelope" by overturning established habits; rather, the arts offer a unique arena of human freedom, not only freedom of thought and imagination, but also of sensation. While cognoscenti often learn to appreciate art in highly formalized and restricting ways, calculated to legitimize exclusions of various kinds, the work of art is always promiscuous. Strictly speaking, there can be no proper way to view a painting or read a poem: only with the emergence of the administered society does the issue even arise. Instead of telling us how to see or act or think, the arts exist to remind us that our relations to the world are in fact radically underdetermined, and that we are the creatures of what William James referred to as a pluralistic universe. Nowhere else in society is this pluralism so fully allowed free play, but in art something even greater than freedom is at stake—something even deeper than freedom because it is the source of freedom. Whatever else a work of art expresses, it expresses a fundamental trust in those who stand before it. In effect, the work of art dignifies the response of anyone who takes the time to notice it, the learned and the ignorant, the honest and the dishonest, the rich and the poor alike. And this, perhaps, poses the greatest threat to the use of art for the purposes of establishing the humanities as a profession.

Spingarn challenged the modern order—and with it, the rationale for a professional criticism—when he suggested that an unleashing of human powers would enrich, not destroy, society. But he challenged that order in another and perhaps more radical way by dissolving the boundary between art and life. Whatever Babbitt might have thought of a bohemian like Oscar Wilde, he would still have approved of Wilde's notion that life imitates art, or should.[47] But Wilde continued to think of art as something separate from, and higher than, life as conducted from day to day. To see art as experience, however, is to allow that activity of any kind can rise to the level of an art. What lifts it to that level is not the degree of its formalization, or its character as public performance, but the process of discovery that culminates in a heightened sense of contact with the world. On the terms defined by the expressionists, any activity can become an art when we subordinate its instrumental function to this search for a deeper encounter with the world. While some artists achieve a higher level of technical virtuosity than others do, expressionists like Spingarn drive a wedge between technical sophistication and experiential depth: for them, richness of meaning and emotional resonance are not guaranteed by competence or even virtuosity. But if technical sophistication is no guarantee of experiential depth, then how is the critic finally to judge the quality of the work? Ultimately, judgment is an inappropriate response. All the critic has to work with is the artist's statements of intention and the critic's own individual reactions—not much of a foundation for cultural leadership of the kind that Babbitt aspired to, but possibly the point of departure for more generous vision of culture generally.

By privileging experience over technical virtuosity, expressionism transposed onto the sphere of the arts a basic principal of democratic political life. But Springarn stopped short of making this connection explicitly. That task fell to another critic, Van Wyck Brooks. It is clearly no accident that Brooks, like Spingarn, spoke from outside the academy: Spingarn resigned after twelve years at Columbia to enter publishing, Brooks after only two at Stanford, which he left to work in publishing and journalism.[48] Of Brooks, most academic histories of criticism could scarcely be more dismissive, representing him as a youthful radical who emerged from a severe nervous breakdown to become the lyrical apologist for middle-brow tastes—and who suffered the worst of all possible fates from the standpoint of the academy, becoming a literary lion for Book-of-the-Month-Club types.[49] But this assessment of Brooks is far from an impartial one, reflecting as it does a deep distrust of "low brow" and "middle-brow" readers and of their unpoliced involvements with the arts.[50] It reflects, in other words, the specialist's resentment of the self-instructed dilettante.

Academic literary histories typically divide Brooks' career into two parts— the first high-principled and politically engaged, the second characterized by ever-deepening moral compromise—but these accounts overlook both the consistency and the originality of his work. If the early Brooks found Marx appealing, his thinking deviates from orthodox Marxism of the 1910s and 1920s in ways that no scholarship, to my knowledge, has fully considered. Perhaps the most significant document of Brooks' early career was his 1917 essay, "The Critics and Young America," and it is there that he develops an understanding of American history and cultural life that he never abandoned or fundamentally modified. To observers like Grandgent and Babbitt, America was a democracy *in extremis*, throwing off time-honored constraints of reason, taste, and morality. Although Brooks shared their distrust of the marketplace, he saw something quite different in America's life: not self-indulgence but a nearly pathological self-repression, which he traced back to the Puritans. Perhaps influenced by Max Weber, Brooks saw the Puritans as the founders of American society because they were the ones who perfected a thoroughgoing disenchantment of both nature and human activity. For the Puritans as Brooks represents them, the one path to salvation was work, to which all other energies and aspirations had to be sacrificed utterly, as a matter of religious duty. And it was work, and work alone, that secured the believer's membership in the community of the redeemed.[51] Over time, the Puritans' this-worldly philosophy ensured that all of the potential barriers to commercial development and technological innovation fell away: tradition, emotion, even physical needs were brushed aside as fallen and misleading. The result, for Brooks as for Weber, was the modern industrial society.[52]

As intellectual history, Brooks' account may be somewhat fanciful. Certainly much recent scholarship has brightened the dark portrait of the Puritans he painted. In their attitude toward sexuality, for example, the Puritans are now thought to be the liberals of their time.[53] Yet a sympathetic reader might be willing to concede that Brooks's account does some justice to American culture at the turn of the nineteenth century, if not to the realities of America in the 1600s. Certainly no society on earth had seen a comparable transformation in so short a time as America in the last 150 years. In no society had economic forces managed so readily and thoroughly to crush the obstacles in their path. Brooks clearly went too far in his essay when he claimed that "the creative energies of men" had been utterly stifled by this transformation.[54] But later in the same essay he modified his claim by arguing that these energies, though freed up as they had never been before, could express themselves only in the highly constrained and ritualized forum of marketplace competition. The effect was a draining off of the attention that might have been devoted to other concerns, especially the creation of an interior life.

Consequently, Americans were not, as Babbitt had imagined them, barbarians at the gate. They were, in fact, the most cowed and pliable of all possible citizens, a nation of powerless Hamlets:

> The Hamlets of Russian fiction, generally speaking, are social idealists, wrapped up in dreams of agricultural and educational reform; they long to revolutionize their country estates and ameliorate the lot of their peasantry, and they lose their will and their vision because there is no social machinery they can avail themselves of: thrown as they are upon their own unaided resources, their task overwhelms them at the outset with a sense of futility. Turn the tables about and you have the situation of the corresponding class in America. They find the machinery of education and social welfare in a state as highly developed as the life of the spirit is in Russia; it is the spiritual technique that is wanting, a living culture, a complicated scheme of ideal objectives, upheld by society at large, enabling them to submerge their liberties in their loyalties.[55]

Far from having overwhelmed the boundaries imposed by their withered traditions, Americans as Brooks represents them confronted the most powerful institutions in all human history with the fewest intellectual and "spiritual" resources for resistance. If the Russian Hamlets were defeated by the sheer inertia of their underdeveloped societies, their American counterparts were swept helplessly along by ceaseless change on a scale contrived to make even the boldest and strongest feel helpless and inconsequential. And precisely because the forces involved seemed so enormous and so implacable, ideas quickly lost all significance. To be a Marxist or a Jeffersonian democrat, a Populist or a Fabian socialist was simply to strike a public pose that had few real-world consequences. Socialist or not, one awakened at five, got to work by six and toiled till eight in the evening, six days a week, fifty-two weeks a year.

Like Marx, Brooks was concerned with the phenomenon of alienation, but he saw the problem as, if anything, more complex than Marx supposed. It is important to remember that Marx himself regarded capitalism as a liberating force that would destroy the legacy of the feudal past while enabling the conscious self-formation of the working class. But Brooks recognized that in America these two developments had failed to go hand in hand:

> Our [culture] has prepared no pathways for us, our leaders are themselves lost. We are like explorers who, in the morning of their lives, have deserted the hearthstone of the human tradition and have set out for a distant treasure that has turned to dust in their hands; but having on their way neglected to mark their track they no longer know in which direction their home lies, nor how to reach it, and so they wander in the wilderness, consumed with a double consciousness of waste and impotence.[56]

In our time, following W. E. B. Dubois, the term "double consciousness" has come to signify the special self-awareness of people who have had to see themselves through the eyes of their oppressors but who retain an alternative self-image. Brooks described another double consciousness, however, one in which a dissatisfaction with the status quo led to an intensified sense of personal disorientation and worthlessness. The slave at least understood his condition as injustice, and this recognition made possible the formation of an interior life, as many slave narratives attest. But modernity in America fostered a psychic life in which the sources of identity lay always outside the self, in the arena of public striving. Instead of producing a contempt for society's norms, the experience of powerlessness intensified a desire for recognition and approval—for wealth, for fame, for rank, for academic degrees and other honors.

Americans became real to themselves by winning the approbation of powerful authorities and large masses—the more powerful or vast, the greater the reality achieved. Nowhere did Brooks see this dynamic at work so fully as in the literary life of his society. Typically, the arts of the day were equated with a soothing realm of wish fulfillment. In the words of the novelist William Gillett, cited by Brooks in his essay, "modern life is full of problems, complex and difficult, and the man who concentrates his mind on his problems all day doesn't want to concentrate it on tediously obscure poetry all night." But even when art strove to rise above the level of entertainment, its makers were deeply hungry for the approval of those whose opinion mattered most in everyday affairs. "The result," Brooks wrote, "can be seen in such novels" as William Dean Howells' *A Modern Instance,* where "the tragedy is not viewed from the angle of an experience that is wider and deeper" than the conventional thinking, "but from the angle of Ben Hallek, the epitome of Boston's best public opinion. Boston passes judgment, and Mr. Howells concurs."[57] To put the problem in Freudian terms, although Brooks himself did not do so, the life of the American was all superego and no id: all public striving and no interiority. Americans, one might say, lived outside of themselves, in the eyes of others, and the worst fate for an American was to live and die unknown.

As for ideas and philosophic systems, which might in other circumstances provide some shelter from the glare of public visibility, these were put on and taken off like so many articles of clothing. "How natural," Brooks wrote, "that the greatest, the most 'difficult' European writers should have had, as Carlyle and Browning and Meredith had, their first vogue in America! How natural that we should have flocked about Ibsen, patronizing Nietzsche, found something entertaining in every kind of revolutionist, and welcomed the strangest philosophies."[58] In a world completely dominated by the logic of the marketplace, ideas mattered only as "cultural capital" or "symbolic commodities." Among Europeans, ideas were often programs for practical action, for a reconstruction of social life, if necessary, from the ground up. But in America, even the most radical ideas could be swiftly domesticated in order to reinforce existing divisions and proprieties. By valuing Nietzsche over Emerson, or Browning over Longfellow, a person gained in stature rather than placing his reputation at risk. To read daring authors was to seem daring, or "counterhegemonic" as we now say. But no one expected the Nietzschean to leave his wife, quit his tenured job, and go to live alone at Sils-Maria—only a madman would do that.

For Brooks, the fundamental problem was a dissociation of ideas from both social action and personal experience. And he concluded that the place to start was with the recovery of personal experience, since social action in and of itself would not break the spell of the Puritan superego—would not free Americans from their psychic dependency on purely public forms of identity. Brooks argued for the intensification of self-consciousness through an ethic of self-expression, which he found increasingly evident in the dissident subculture of his times. "Undoubtedly," he insisted, "the gospel of self-expression, makeshift as it is, has revealed a promise in America that we have always taken for granted but hardly reckoned with. Isolated, secretive, bottled up as we have been in the past, how could we ever have guessed what aims and hopes we have in common." While Brooks acknowledged that this new "gospel of self-expression" had produced a vast flood of undisciplined emotionalism, and "if it [was] often lazy and willful, if its smoke [was] only at intervals illuminated by flame—well, was it not so with the Oblimovs of Russia?"[59] In essence, Brooks argues that Americans could not develop an interior life unless that life was freed from the continuous public scrutiny and censure that had played so prominent a role in American cultural history, not only through the medium of the marketplace but also through the church, the family, and certainly the school. If anything, the market had triumphed so swiftly and completely because the obstacles had been cleared long before by these other institutions, which also viewed the individual as nothing more than a object of collective manipulation. Perhaps the greatest irony of America's "democratic" spirit of inclusiveness is, as Brooks recognized, its unwillingness to allow for the "antisocial" or "isolating" impulses that might ultimately make possible a deeper, richer psychological and cultural life.

Brooks's career began with this analysis, and much of his subsequent work was not, as some historians of English have supposed, an attempt to abandon this original formulation, but instead an effort to define the appropriate role for the "man of letters." Initially, Brooks followed the lead of figures like Herbert Croly and Randolph Bourne in his conception of the intellectual as an oppositional voice pitched against the drone of hypnotized masses. But I would like to conjecture that as Brooks' career developed, this role began to seem less and less appropriate given his own reading of American cultural history. By playing the role of public superego, the supposed radical critic remained well within the bounds of conventional "Puritan" culture. In a certain sense, the radical critic might be said to play the same role as Jonathan Edwards on the pulpit, leading the congregation through a process of self-searching, disclosure, repentance and restoration to the body of the church. If, as Brooks understood, criticism in America had simply secularized this process, then the man of letters had to play a rather different role, a role that had much in common with Spingarn's idea of creative criticism, although Brooks himself never cites Spingarn in his early essay.

In his later career, however, Brooks tried to put into practice an ethic of interpretation that privileged creative activity over ethical, aesthetic, or political correctness—arguably a version of the "creative criticism" called for earlier by

Spingarn. Although his critics accused him of whitewashing American history, it might be fairer to say that he wanted to tell the story of his society in a way that would emphasize its achievements rather than its failures, and its awareness rather than its blindness. Anyone who reads his later work in a spirit of generosity will probably appreciate its innovative qualities. Rather than pass moral judgments, as he did in his earlier writing, Brooks attempted to develop accounts of social and cultural life that explain why certain works rose to prominence at certain times. Writers as divergent as John Dos Passos, Mary Austin, and Henry Miller won his respect.[60] The spirit of these accounts was historical and sociological rather than critical in the literary tradition; in fact, many people felt that Brooks had ceased to qualify as a critic at all. Certainly he had given up on the critical pretense of Olympian impartiality. Long before it became fashionable to do so, some of Brooks's later writings foregrounded his own presence in the text, an approach that his detractors associated with the middle-brow genre of journalism. But perhaps the feature of his later work that has most troubled academic critics is the absence of what we now call "close reading," interpretation that is minutely keyed to individual passages and sentences in an author's work.[61] Instead, Brooks invented a genre of his own, perhaps one more appropriate to a general audience, which combined aspects of biography, cultural history, and personal memoir. Only with the coming of postmodernism would scholars in the humanities undertake comparable experiments.

For all of these reasons, it was not Brooks who finally determined the shape of academic criticism in America, a shape it retains more or less to this day. In fact, it was not a critic at all, or at least not a critic primarily, and not a university professor, but the man whom many people regard as the greatest English-language poet of the twentieth century, T. S. Eliot. Even more improbably, he accomplished this feat in an article of barely seven pages and fewer than 4000 words. The article, "Tradition and the Individual Talent," has probably been read by every graduate student in English since the early 1950s, and every generation of critics following that time has drawn on its central tenets, consciously or unconsciously. Not simply the founding document of professional literary studies in America, it was also one of the two or three most powerful and persuasive statements of the high modernist outlook. One might argue that the essay itself would never have exerted so great and lasting an influence had its author not played, before and after, so central a role in the world of high culture. But the essay in its own right effected a truly brilliant synthesis, combining in a highly original way elements of both the historicist and the humanist positions. The essay had another virtue as well. That so distinguished a poet should defend criticism as an elite activity, and on terms so ideally suited to criticism as a profession, appeared to obviate once and for all Spingarn's charge that the academic critics had turned their backs on the creative culture of the arts. Here was an artist— and one of the best—clamoring for more criticism.

We cannot fully understand the success of Eliot's essay until we recognize that many advocates of modernism saw their movement as the founding of a new high culture in reaction to what one modernist philosopher, José Ortega y Gasset, referred to as the revolt of the masses.[62] Although other self-professed modernists may not have shared this view, Eliot spoke powerfully for those who resented what Babbitt had earlier decried as "leveling." Eliot's motive in writing "Tradition and the Individual Talent" was not primarily to legitimize academic professionalism, although it certainly had this effect, but to provide a philosophical justification for qualitative distinctions between elite and mass culture, and for a deeply conservative account of cultural leadership. Of course, elitism can be justified by appeal to radical values as well: in the discourses of the Communist Left and of proto-Fascists like the Italian Futurists, intellectual elites are often represented as the champions of change, struggling heroically against the hidebound and blinkered populace. But it was Eliot's stress upon the conservation and continuity of culture that made his argument especially appealing to academic critics, whose situation and training best suited them for a custodial role, and not for the role of innovator or vanguard. Fundamentally, Eliot's manifesto justified in the field of culture the same top-down administrative structure that had expanded into every other area of American life. Although Eliot could not have foreseen the massive consolidation of authority that took place over the next fifty years, he helped to lay the groundwork for it.

But Eliot's essay recommended itself for another reason. It provided the rationale for a distinctly nationalistic or chauvinist model of culture, as opposed to one more universalist, internationalist, or anthropological in its premises. In many ways, his language hearkened directly back to Taine. As Eliot argued, "The poet must be very conscious of the main current" of his culture:

> He must be aware that the mind of Europe—the mind of his own country—a mind which he learns in time to be much more important than his own private mind—is a mind which changes, and that this change is a development which abandons nothing en route, which does not superannuate either Shakespeare, or Homer, or the rock drawing of the Magdalenian draftsmen.[63]

Tradition, as Eliot uses the word, first gained currency in the nineteenth century as a way of generalizing about the actual behavior of real-life people. In this context, "tradition" operates as useful shorthand—akin to what Max Weber called an "ideal type"—designating a more messy, varied, and complex reality. In this sense, the word describes probabilities of behavior: given past evidence, we might expect *most* people in a certain place at a certain time to do a certain thing. But Eliot stands this relationship on its head by treating culture as the cause of human actions, while these actions are treated as predetermined effects. To a greater degree than even in Taine's writing, culture for Eliot became the real actor in human history, whereas humans were reduced to the mere products of culture, almost the instruments of culture, although some instruments, as he imagined them, express their culture—their *tradition*—more fully than others do.

Instruments may seem too strong and polemical a word, but is it? Throughout a long career Eliot made no secret of his belief that ordinary people are deficient. He referred derisively, for example, to "the confused cries of the newspaper critics and the susurrus of popular repetition that follows."[64] Eliot might have said that all human beings without exception are the products of their national traditions, whether they as individuals happen to be inferior or superior. But inferior people listen poorly, so to speak, to the voice of their culture: though they are inescapably instruments, they are careless and untuned instruments, the kind who may not even know what *susurrus* means. (I must confess that I did not until I looked it up.) While such people embody and express their tradition unreflectingly, others bring it as completely as possible into conscious awareness, and by this effort they become fully realized:

> Tradition . . . involves a perception, not only of the pastness of the past, but of its presence; the historical sense compels a man to write not merely with his own generation in his bones, but with a feeling that the whole of literature of Europe from Homer[,] and within it the whole of the literature of his own country has a simultaneous existence and composes a simultaneous order. This historical sense, which is a sense of the timeless as well as of the temporal[,] and of the timeless and of the temporal together, is what makes a writer traditional.[65]

Some people have read Eliot as a traditionalist in the ordinary sense, one who wants to protect long-established cultural forms from the ravages of time, but this is a goal that Eliot explicitly rejects. "We have seen," he writes, "many such simple currents soon lost in the sand."[66] The kind of traditionalism that Eliot endorses places past and present into a conscious dialogue, so that one enlivens and informs the other. When past and present come together in this dialogue, the temporal can be experienced as timeless, as part of an eternal continuity. By contrast, ordinary people live exclusively in the present, and their perceptions are impoverished by fleetingness and triviality.

Eliot is clearly a masterful writer of prose as well as of poetry, and his language is so seductive here that one can easily overlook what is most problematic about his argument. Is it really possible, for example, that a person can know "his own generation" with anything like inclusiveness and precision—can know, that is, the values and attitudes of, say, thirty million people who all happen to be born at roughly the same time in roughly the same country? Is it really possible for one to have "a feeling for the whole of the literature of Europe," starting with Homer, and what does it really mean to "have a feeling"? How much knowledge of history is adequate, and how much is too little, if we want to achieve a sense of the timelessness hidden in history? The argument invites other objections as well. For example, even people acquainted with very little history can feel deeply connected to their traditions, whereas people in quite traditional societies may have no conscious awareness of "tradition" at all.

Still, Eliot has a point: when we view present events as a part of a historical continuum, they can seem less fleeting and inconsequential, and also much less frightening. Death too seems less final, somehow. But for the profession of English, and for other humanities disciplines, the enormous appeal of Eliot's argument owed much to the distinction it made between elites and the masses, and between historical insight, which Eliot represents in quasi-religious language, and the blind "presentism," so to speak, of the person on the street. Eliot's essay does not simply establish a hierarchy; it defends that hierarchy in a time-honored way, associating differing positions on a scale of social power with differing degrees of interior illumination. In the West, the linkage of authority to one's inner state reaches back at least to the Greeks, who justified on psychological grounds the superiority of their archons or aristocrats, fitting masters of women and slaves because they had first become the masters of themselves. But the most notorious example of this linkage is the Indian caste system. Of course, the excellence of the Brahmin was imagined as a hereditary trait, whereas the membership in Eliot's aristocracy is open to anyone willing to engage in the appropriate ascetic discipline, making it, in a certain perverse sense, a democratic aristocracy of the sort that Babbitt called for. But the logic of inner worthiness was essentially the same, rewarding the master with preeminence on the basis of his "self-sacrifice."

In the case of the Greeks, the master sacrificed himself to Reason; in Eliot's essay, the artist or the critic sacrifices himself to Tradition. "No poet," Eliot writes, "no artist of any art, has his complete meaning alone. His significance, his appreciation is the appreciation of his relation to the dead poets and artists. You cannot value him alone; you must set him, for contrast and comparison, among the dead." But a reckoning with the dead is not simply a heuristic device employed for "contrast and comparison." The dead—or rather the monuments of culture they erected— constitute "an ideal order among themselves, which is modified by the introduction of the new (the really new) work of art among them."[67] But how does one create such a work, a work that counts as "really new"? Not simply by mastering, say, the craft of poetry, or even by studying the great works of the past, though the poet must thoroughly know all of those works. The literary artist writes great works only by the means of a particular discipline:

> What is to be insisted upon is that the poet must develop or procure the consciousness of the past and that he should continue to develop this consciousness throughout his career.
>
> What happens is a continual surrender of himself as he is at the moment to something which is more valuable. The progress of an artist is a continual self-sacrifice, a continual extinction of personality.[68]

Of course, many artists—many great artists—have described their creative activity in quite different terms. If we look, for example, at English-language poets who have written on their art—Sir Philip Sydney, Wordsworth, Coleridge, Shelley, Frost, Stevens, Snyder, Ginsberg, and Rich—it may seem that tradition as Eliot understands it plays a far smaller role, if it plays a role at all. And at any rate, how can the critic really tell from the poem the extent of the poet's communion with the past? Is explicit reference to the past an adequate sign of communion? In fact, no one, however discerning, can reliably detect from the reading of a poem the inner condition of its author. A poet writing on loneliness may be surrounded by family and friends; and a poet who manages to "lose himself in tradition" may be quite selfish and self-absorbed, and not at all successful in the extinction of personality.

While Eliot appears to describe poetry in general, and while he later went on to apply his standards to English-language poetry of many different historical periods, he actually described poetry as he wanted it to be rather than as it has actually been. Eliot tried valiantly to persuade both critics and poets of his day that all other standards for judging literature are ahistorical and unartistic. He took aim, for example, at Irving Babbitt when he derided "any semi-ethical criterion of 'sublimity,'" and he rejected Spingarn's position when he writes that the poet has, "not a personality . . . but a particular medium" to "express."[69] More was at stake in these remarks, however, than the judgment of poetry: the real issue for Eliot was nothing less than the fate of the West. Eliot wanted innovation, but only innovation that could not threaten his "ideal order," his beloved "tradition," by which he actually meant the values of people most like himself. Perhaps on some level Eliot understood that this "tradition" was in fact his own invention, but what he wanted, finally, was to guarantee that only the most cautious and cultivated people would have a hand in the making of the dominant culture. Whatever fears he may have harbored about the future of poetry, Eliot feared most that the "hollow men"—the ignorant, inferior people—were going to take over, and that the result would be sheer anarchy. Somehow, society had to put on the brakes, and to the brakes he invented he gave the name "tradition."

The emphasis on tradition explains why criticism played so prominent a role throughout the discussion. As a matter of fact, Eliot's essay was not primarily addressed to poets at all, but to critics, whom he enlisted in a general scrutiny of culture. "Every nation, every race," he declared in the essay's second paragraph, "has not only its own creative, but its own critical turn of mind."[70] No wonder the essay spoke so powerfully to the academic humanities! Not only did the essay raise the critic up to equality with the artist, but it also heralded the critic as the master of a much larger domain than the arts alone. By arguing that the monuments of high art always constitute the most complete expression of any culture as a whole—a claim to be echoed many times since then—Eliot hands over to humanities departments the keys to the entire edifice. No less than scansion or narrative structures, politics and the economy fell within the critic's rightful purview. And while art making and criticism remained distinct activities, the critic's authority derived from the same regimen as the authority of the poet's—the "continuous extinction of personality."

Eliot would later abandon much in this line of thinking. Increasingly, he came to believe that the salvation of Western civilization lay in submission of a rather different kind, no longer to the secular tradition of the arts but to the sacred revelations of the Christian faith.[71] But for many scholars in the humanities, Eliot evoked in a single sweeping vision the best future they could imagine, one almost perfectly adapted to the tasks most readily undertaken from within the university. One particular virtue of this vision, quite apart from the authority conferred upon the critic, was its emphasis on the past at the expense of the present. The explosion of art in the twentieth century—the incredible proliferation of schools and styles along with the sheer number of writers, painters, dramatists, and so on—strongly gravitated against the consolidation of culture at the top. But Eliot offered a principled rationale for ignoring the vast preponderance of artists and their works. Instead of trying to do justice to the ongoing development of the arts, as Brooks did in some of his later work, scholars could devote whole lifetimes to commentaries on the familiar classics—the "canon." In this way, the needs of professional scholarship might be persuasively represented as a lofty commitment to the highest standards.

Almost as quickly as Eliot gained ascendancy in English, his ideas migrated into other disciplines. The modernist art historian Clement Greenberg began his career as a follower of Eliot, until Eliot's anti-Semitism drove him into the arms of Kant.[72] It was, perhaps, Greenberg's struggle to get out from under Eliot's historicism that explains the strongly cognitive and psychological orientation of much high modernist scholarship in art history, as witnessed by Gombrich and Arnheim. But Eliot's influence may also have made its way, if less directly, into philosophy. Just as Eliot tended to emphasize the conventional and historical character of literature, so the philosopher J. L. Austin tended to treat language in much the same way. Our "common stock of words," Austin wrote,

> embodies all the distinctions men have found worth drawing, and the connexions they have found worth making, in the lifetimes of many generations: these surely are likely to be more numerous, more sound, since they have stood up to the long test of the survival of the fittest, and more subtle, at least in all ordinary and reasonably practical matters, than any that you or I are likely to think up in our chairs of an afternoon.[73]

Whether Austin knew Eliot's essay, or whether these ideas were just in the air, the relations between words and people here closely follows relations of another kind— between individual citizens and the institutions that precede, control, and at last outlive them. Austin's point is not so much that the past must remain unchanged, but that the process of change should be turned over only to the very few. It was the modern way.

5

The Poverty of Progress

James Agee, Lionel Trilling, and the Alienation of Knowledge

"Education" as it stands is tied in with every bondage I can conceive of, and is the chief cause of these bondages, including acceptance and respect, which are the worst bondages of all. "Education," if it is anything short of crime, is a recognition of these bondages . . . and a deadly enemy of all of them.

—James Agee, *Let Us Now Praise Famous Men*

The astonishing observations above tell us something, of course, about the outlook of the person who offered them, James Agee, a journalist widely admired in the decades after World War II. But they also tell us something about a change in social life occasioned by the flowering of the Progressive vision. In politics, that flowering assumed the form of the modern liberal state, a government administered by un-elected specialists, while in culture it produced high modernism, less highly for-malized in its arrangements but no less subject to rule by expertise. One result of these developments, the result Agee found most troubling, was a related change in education, a change that devalued learning for the sake of schooling. Real learning, Agee felt, had become virtually impossible inside the vast, cumbersome machinery of the schools. By the tens of millions, students memorized facts and mastered skills, but these facts and skills actually contributed to a growing sense of "bondage" and disconnection from the world. Agee saw this disconnection outside the schools as well: in their secret hearts, he thought, all Americans felt it, a feeling they could put aside temporarily but could never altogether lay to rest. Today we might see Agee as one of the administered society's most original critics, though not by virtue of his insights into policy or grand structure, about which he probably knew no more than any other journalist. But Agee saw, or thought he saw, into the soul of modernity: the psychic life it had produced on an unprecedented scale. At the same time, he tried to look beyond its founding fictions—the search for progress as an escape from basic human limitations, and the worship of material abundance at the expense of more enduring kinds of happiness.

In the sweltering months of July and August 1936, two journalists on the payroll of *Fortune* magazine—one a respected writer born in Tennessee and the other a Chicago-raised photographer of modest but growing reputation—arrived in central Alabama to do a story on the Cotton Belt's nine million tenant farmers. The photographer, Walker Evans, made a darkroom in his Birmingham hotel, but the writer, James Agee, took up residence on the scene, living alongside a tenant family, renamed "the Gudgers" in the book he later wrote.[1] That Evans and Agee should have gone to backwoods Alabama—hardly the kind of place where "news" gets made—hints at how deeply unsettled American life had become, so unsettled that *Fortune* was lurching visibly to the left with stories on restive, overworked laborers, on abuses of the prairie soil that brought the Dust Bowl in their wake, and on the all-American childhoods of FDR's socialist deputies. At no other moment in its history did *Fortune* send a message so mixed, with photos of seamstresses bent over their machines, while advertisements on the opposing page showed slimmer, younger women lounging at the beach or reclining on the shoulders of handsome men in fast new cars. No one could tell, just then, which way of life the future would bring—more of the Satanic mills or the bright, open road to incalculable wealth.

Despite the atmosphere of uncertainty, the editors commissioned Evans and Agee to turn out a story that must have seemed already as good as written. That story was the familiar one about progress and poverty: without good food, without new clothes, without a decent place to live or a proper education, life would be brutish, nasty, and short. Whatever the differences might have been between the people who hated Roosevelt and the ones who were prepared to redistribute the nation's wealth, they were united on the value of progress and the sordidness of any world without it. To tell this distinctly American story for the millionth time was the task of the two journalists, yet it was ultimately one they never got to complete, not for *Fortune* at any rate. Back in New York with sheaves of notes and rolls of gelatin silver negatives, they discovered that Ralph Ingersoll, their supportive editor, had fallen from the good graces of the magazine's Republican owner, Henry Booth Luce. Depression or not, Luce resolved that *Fortune* would celebrate the romance of big capital, and so its pages did forever afterward in the bright, upbeat spirit that has since become that publication's hallmark. But even if their story had somehow survived the purge, Agee and Evans were poorly disposed to recount it in the standard fashion: if they were not Republicans by anybody's definition, neither were they New Deal Democrats, and the final product of their months among the "cotton tenants"—the book *Let Us Now Praise Famous Men*—might be read as an attempt to show that these supposed antagonists, the defenders of big money and the saviors of the little guy, were really the most intimate of co-conspirators.

Exploiters and improvers were allied, Agee believed, in a basic disrespect for the tenant farmers and their way of life; for what we, in our more anthropologically minded time, might refer to as their "cultural" legacy. Despite the enormous odds against it, Agee—a country boy uneasily civilized by private schools—quickly learned to admire that legacy. No one, I think, has described lives like theirs with greater honesty and feeling than this sometime poet. Coming from Harvard, and from the small but enchanted circle of New York intellectuals, he should have found in subjects so profoundly disadvantaged a vindication of everything he possessed: education, taste, relative wealth, and the mobility of the modern urban professional. But Agee actually saw himself as more impoverished than his subjects, a person who had paid an unfair price in self-denial for every one of his "advantages."

The irony of Agee's life lay in this painful contradiction: each advance in his own education and career had been accompanied by a growing panic at his state of worldlessness—his sense of belonging to no one and to nothing. An alcoholic at twenty-eight, Agee had already begun to suspect that the problems of America went deeper than the financial pages could explain and would not be repaired with a rise of the median annual income or a Bolshevik revolution.[2] In some way that it took years for him to clarify, the sharecroppers embodied everything he feared about himself, the self he had learned at school to keep concealed. What he wanted to rediscover a thousand miles south of his adopted metropolis was precisely what he wanted to rediscover in his own past: some trace of a basic dignity that everyone had overlooked. And he pursued this dignity to the point of nervous exhaustion, convinced that if he could unveil it in the cotton farmers, men and women who were all but universally despised, then others might acknowledge it in him.

As a journalist, Agee was supposed to craft the conventional documentary. His subjects—men and women living abjectly on the land—had become quite familiar to most middle-class readers through the Progressive narratives of rural depravity that were a staple of popular and scholarly publications for almost twenty years. Even by the late 1930s, many readers might still have associated people like "the Gudgers" with the slogans of eugenicists and social engineers, although everyone in those Depression years had learned to look with greater "toleration" on the urban jobless and the honest agrarian poor. The staff at *Fortune* may not have wanted cold statistics, but they expected their men in the field to furnish as dispassionately as they could an image of lives emptied out in a cycle of endless work, and robbed of meaning by a lack of contact with the higher things: good books, elevated company, the fine arts, and great ideas—the amenities that money alone could buy. As the readers of *Fortune* knew, it was culture that made people everything they were; it was education, knowledge, manners, poise.

If Agee did not see matters quite that way, he certainly understood what the toil of the farmers had cost them, growing other people's crops on other people's land only to remain perpetually in debt. And he found their predicament, like so many other things, "awful" beyond his capacity to describe:

> On the day you are married, at about sixteen if you are a girl, at about twenty if you are a man, a key is turned, with a sound not easily audible, and you are locked between the stale earth and the sky; the key turns in the lock behind you, and your full life's work begins, and there is nothing conceivable for which it can afford to stop short of your death, which is a long way off. It is perhaps at its best during the first two years or so, when you are young and

perhaps are still enjoying one another or have not yet lost all hope, and when there are not yet so many children as to weigh on you. It is perhaps at its worst during the next ten to twelve years, when there are more and more children, but none of them old enough, yet, to be much help.[3]

What the tenant farmers felt most immediately, as Agee describes them anyway, was not a loss of nobility or an absence of refinement, but their own, very tangible powerlessness. For them, living was the experience of an unalterable fate, a cycle of perpetual debt.[4] Yet Agee saw something else besides their oppression. The same labors that made a prison of their hours and days seemed to him nothing less than a "dance"—"slow, gradual, grand, tremendously and quietly weighted":

> Annie Mae at twenty-seven, in her angular sweeping, every motion a wonder to watch; George in his Sunday clothes with his short cuffs . . . Mrs. Ricketts, in that time of morning when from the corn she reels into the green roaring glooms of her home, falls into a chair with gaspings which are almost groaning sobs . . . Miss-Molly, chopping wood as if in each blow of the axe she captured in focus the vengeance of all time.[5]

In this brief passage Agee showed his readers two very different kinds of work: one instrumental, work done *to* the world; the other connective, work done *with* it. The first was the work of people who were forced to fight, quite literally, for their survival, who labored for others until their bodies gave out and who would have at the end nothing to show for their efforts. In this work, they treated the world as an instrument, just as they themselves remained the instruments of others. But Agee showed his readers a second kind of work, for which the English language has no fully appropriate word: the work of connecting with the world, breathing into the routine of planting corn or chopping wood the animating force of emotions and desires, whether noble or crude, beatifically calm or suffused with "the vengeance of all time." With our penchant for objectivity, we might discount as insignificant or unreal the inner life of the tenant farmers, but it was Agee's intention to teach us otherwise. He wanted his readers to see with him the work of perception that lifted people beyond themselves into an existence indestructibly alive.

And for Agee, the discovery of this other, connective work—by means of which the self and the world draw together—reassured him that the doors of his own perception were not yet closed, when he had every reason to suppose they had been shut and locked. His "education" had taught him, after all, to believe that the hunger for connection with the world—for a sense of presence, of participation— was a hunger for something that would never be found. Agee knew his Freud and his Marx; he knew the modern (and now, postmodern) tenet that "reality will always be unknowable," as Freud once declared, and that we are condemned, at best, to an endless tinkering with the symbols and structures handed down to us.[6] But once Agee had arrived in the Cotton Belt, where his formal education ceased to apply and a new process of learning began, he could no more take his cue from this "Modern Library Giant"—as he called Freud, referring derisively to a popular edition of his works—than he could from the style sheet at *Fortune*.[7] But Freud was not the only Giant Agee refused to worship. The second of the epigraphs that opens his book, just after a passage from *King Lear*, is Marx and Engle's famous call to arms from the *Communist Manifesto*, "Workers of the world, unite and fight. You have nothing to lose but your chains, and a world to win." To these lines Evans and Agee appended a caveat: "These words are quoted here to mislead those who will be misled by them. They mean, not what the reader may care to think they mean, but what they say" and "it may be well to make the explicit statement that neither these words nor their authors are the property of any political party, faith, or faction." The world to be won was not the Marxist utopia, which might still be a thousand years in coming, and not the Christian heaven either, but a dimension of experience in this life accessible to every person everywhere, without the cost of confession or conversion.

If nothing in Agee's education had prepared him for the tenant farmers, nothing in the culture of modern America had taught him to value this dimension of everyday life for its own sake, without reference to anything higher or better. To Americans of his time, few experiences could have made less sense than to lie down willingly, as Agee did, in the moist, chill Alabama night on a bed of unwashed sheets, which he remembered as "coarse and almost slimily or stickily soft":

> The pillow was hard, thin, and noisy, and smelled as of acid and new blood; the pillowcase seemed to crawl at my cheek. . . . There was an odor something like that of old moist stacks of newspaper. I tried to imagine intercourse in this bed; I managed to imagine it fairly well. [And then] I began to feel a sharp little piercings and crawlings all along the surface of my body. . . . I struck a match and a half dozen [bedbugs] broke along my pillow: I caught two, killed them, and smelled their queer rankness. They were full of my blood.[8]

Unable to sleep, Agee got up, lit the lamp and searched his body for fleas and lice; checked the bed, where the bugs were waiting, and finally admitted to himself that he would never "beat them."[9] Walking out of the room to the porch, he unintentionally woke the dog, and then, urinating into the dust beside the house, he listened to the sound of a river roaring somewhere in the dark. After watching the stars and "nodding at whatever [he] saw," Agee returned to his bed and put on both his long coat and his trousers, the cuffs tucked into his socks as protection against the bugs. "It did not work well," he recalled, and he spent the duration of the early summer night scratching and shifting his posture, covering, uncovering, tucking, and untucking. Yet at that worst possible moment, he unexpectedly felt himself overwhelmed by a sense of presence exceeding all his frustrations and expectations. "I don't exactly know," he wrote, "why anyone should be 'happy' under these circumstances, but there's no use laboring the point: I was: outside the vermin, my senses were taking in nothing but a night-deep, unmeditatable consciousness of a world which was newly touched and beautiful to me."[10]

Precisely because every person is endowed with this capacity for connecting with the world just behind or beyond our representations of it—what Agee called the "actual" world—the narrative in *Let Us Now Praise Famous Men* does not begin with a "before" and "after" framing some transformative epiphany when the scales fell from the author's eyes. To be educated one must first be ignorant, and it is the existence of something called "ignorance" that Agee wanted most of all to deny. At the start of his account, neither he nor his subjects are living in ignorance, and the conditions for the exercise of their connective power lie around them everywhere. As he wrote,

> In any house, standing in any one room of it . . . it is possible, by sufficient quiet and passive concentration, to realize all of [it] . . . and to realize this not merely with the counting mind, nor with the imagination of the eye, which is no realization at all, but with the whole of the body and being, and in translations of the senses so that in part at least they become extrahuman, become a part of the nature and being of these rooms.[11]

In reply to the apostles of progress, who were prepared to believe that the cotton tenant farmers had descended to the level of savages, Agee told his readers that the real savagery was "culture" itself, once it had become fixed and sacrosanct in the forms of Science and Art. But deliverance from savagery, as he discovered there in central Alabama, started when his own education no longer told him what counted as real and he was forced to live from the "whole of the body"—a life that began with the failure of knowledge, the failure of the codes and symbol systems at his disposal. This contradiction—between things as they unfold from moment to moment and things as they are "supposed" to be—made it possible for him unlock the prison house of language, convention, and history, if only momentarily. And in this process of unlearning, he experienced a "translation of the senses"—their cleansing and renewal through contact with a world too concrete and complex, too open in the absence of any systematic coherence, for even the most fluent language to express. The greatest lesson of Agee's pilgrimage to Alabama was this: that the absence of control and certainty made him feel more alive, when all his years of schooling had taught him exactly the opposite. As for the schooling, it had taught him only "acceptance and respect," which he now saw as "bondages." With the translation of his senses, which Agee tries to commemorate on every page of *Let Us Now Praise Famous Men,* the "big ideas" that have preoccupied entire generations are unveiled to us as the momentary images—the play of shadows on the wall—that everyone knows they are, and that everyone has been schooled to treat reverentially as more solid and real than experience itself.

So well had Agee's readers learned this reverence for big ideas that almost no one of his generation understood what he wanted to say, and his book, when it came out, sold less than a thousand copies.[12] But the coup de grâce was delivered post-humously, twelve years after Agee's death, in an appreciation of his "great" book by the self-proclaimed liberal critic Lionel Trilling, a man committed to preserving the best that has been thought and said for those who could not think or speak half so well. Agee, Trilling wrote, was an unreformed romantic, idealizing people more deserving of our pity, or perhaps a stern reproof, than of starry-eyed admiration—

people, in other words, who needed badly to be lifted up by the mechanisms of liberal meliorism.[13] No one, to my mind, has more cruelly betrayed Agee's intentions than this ostensibly sympathetic critic, but Agee himself would probably have found the betrayal unsurprising, given his distrust of the culture-mongering that became Trilling's stock-in-trade.[14]

Never for a moment did Agee suppose his subjects to be "innocent," as Trilling alleged, not even when he wrote this of one black couple: "The least I could have done was to throw myself flat on my face and embrace and kiss their feet."[15] Agee was far too thoroughly educated to see his subjects as good or beautiful in some vague, hopeful, starry-eyed way. What he revered in them, however, was their unconditional "actuality," their sheer presence in the world, beyond praise or blame, approval or loathing. And his awareness of this sheer presence he found no less resonant, complete, and inspiriting than the creations of the "great artists" that Trilling idolized—Beethoven, Cézanne, Kafka, Blake, Céline. Agee saw the creations of these artists, all the symphonies and poems, paintings and novels, as the products of this same experience of connection, forgotten by the priests of the cult of "Art," who were more concerned with erecting icons of authority and permanence than with understanding how it could be that such "great" works had come to exist at all. "Official acceptance," Agee wrote, "is the one unmistakable . . . sign of fatal misunderstanding, and is the kiss of Judas."[16] But if Agee saw the worship of Art in this way, as a kiss of betrayal, he did so because its cult operated with breathtaking efficiency to conceal those acts of everyday attention that are no less complex and momentous than Blake's *Songs of Innocence and Experience* or Cézanne's *The Bathers*. Had he lived to reply to Trilling's critique, Agee might have said that it was in fact men like Trilling who were guilty of idealizing "mere" human beings. When Trilling charged, in effect, that Agee overlooked the tangible failings of his rural subjects, Agee might have responded that the lovers of Art had always willfully magnified the differences among people while failing to perceive, with the appropriate awe, the marvelous, perpetual renewal of life through those moments of surprise, loss, and connection that happen every day.[17]

But Trilling, I believe, was compelled to misread Agee's work as he did because it laid the ax so unsparingly to the whole edifice of modernism, with its faith in the cultural leadership of the many by the few: perhaps in Agee's unhappy Ivy League persona Trilling saw an image of himself, but an image naked where Trilling wanted to be clothed, and small where Trilling wanted to loom large. I do not mean simply that Trilling also felt himself to be a person on the "outside," the Central-European Jewish immigrants determined to make it in the ultra-Anglo-Saxon milieu of English departments at midcentury; I mean, instead, that Trilling continued throughout his career to imagine education, and the discourse of educated people, as distinct from his own experience. To live by experience, in his view, was to be subjective in an irresponsible way—to be partial, provincial, close-minded, as unrepentant as a Shylock.[18] The best hope for a world of tolerance, of fairness and generosity, was the cosmopolitan faith in a cultural tradition that transcended local knowledge and regional loyalties, to say nothing of emotions and the body's appetites. The pursuit of truth as Trilling understood it required that all people surrender equally whatever belonged to them alone; like a great nineteenth-century novelist or man of science, or a great critic like Matthew Arnold, the cosmopolitan of Trilling's liberal imagination always tried to begin with those assumptions and beliefs that everyone could accept unreservedly, and from that basis, Trilling felt, larger commonalities might be pursued.

With the advent of postmodernism, Trilling's liberal confidence in a universal tradition has begun to wear thin, while Agee's world-embracing skepticism may seem less cynical than powerfully humane. Yet that was not how matters looked at the time. Only a dozen years after Agee's stay in Alabama, it was his skeptical way of thinking that seemed ready to disappear. With the Depression over and World War II at an end, Trilling could announce in 1949 something like the end of history. "In the United States today," he wrote, "liberalism is not only the dominant but even the sole intellectual tradition."[19] Yet Trilling recognized a danger ahead, arising from contradictions at the heart of the liberal regime. On the one hand, liberalism encouraged a unique respect for freedom and difference—for "contingency and possibility, and [for] those exceptions to the rule which may be the beginning of the end of the rule."[20] But on the other hand, he noted that the preservation of liberal culture required an everexpanding "organization" of experts and administrators to plan, survey, educate, enforce, and punish. While these two different aspects of liberal culture looked dangerously incompatible, Trilling regarded it as the critic's task to maintain an equilibrium between the need for fixity and the desire for change, between the value of diversity and the imperative of order.

If Agee seemed deeply pessimistic, Trilling seemed hopeful, even smug. But Trilling was also afraid, and in a way that Agee was not. For his part, Trilling saw the great novels of the previous century as the finest expression of liberal culture's universalizing impulse, the one place where crucial questions about "manners"— about classes, culture, and social life—could be freely entertained and decisively adjudicated on everyone's behalf. Trilling argued that in acknowledging the novel's special role "we can understand the pride of profession that moved D. H. Lawrence to [proclaim], 'Being a novelist, I consider myself superior to the saint, the scientist, the philosopher and the poet. The novel is the one bright book of life.'"[21] It went without saying that Lawrence's "pride of profession" somehow carried over from novelists to the critics and scholars of novels. But Trilling on many occasions also remarked that the novel and its solutions looked increasingly irrelevant to an American scene growing more fractious and decentered every day.[22] The novelist might speak for everyone, but who, finally, would be listening?

Brilliantly successful in so many ways, the modern administered society still contained within itself a fundamental contradiction: the migration of power to the upper reaches of society had created an empty space on the ground level that even postwar prosperity could not altogether fill. Most Americans experienced this empty space less as a crisis of meaning than as a vague sense of paralysis or dissatisfaction. Liberalism, we might say in the language of political theory, slowly erodes the sources of own legitimacy—in particular those sources that sustain motivation, except, of course, for money. But Agee was not a political scientist and he tended to describe the problem in different terms. The crisis Agee faced in writing his book, though he never quite explained it as I have here, was the crisis of no longer knowing how to make sense of things when his education had succeeded too well and he awoke one day to find that the world had disappeared—as a *world,* coherent and welcoming. The question that the Gudgers ask themselves in the book, and that Agee repeated as a kind of choral refrain, is "How did we get caught? How was it we were caught?"[23] In asking this question at various moments in their lives, the tenant farmers expressed an unambiguous frustration at their poverty and power-lessness, conditions that modernization had set out to eliminate. But the irony of the question, at least as I am reading Agee here, lay in his awareness that he was caught more completely than they were, since he had learned from his own unhappiness that the achievement of "freedom," wealth, and sophistication did not bring an end to *his* poverty, which was a poverty of spirit.

Agee knew, of course, the talismanic significance that education held for the tenant farmers, who worked slavishly under the large landholders because the system of cotton tenantry had in fact replaced the last generation of slaves. But unlike slaves, the mostly white tenants—who were free men and women legally—viewed their situation as somehow their own mistake, the result of a failing or a weakness on their part. Without access to information about the real causes of their predicament, information never taught in school at any rate, they were obliged to begin every day of their lives as Annie Mae Gudger did, filled with "utter tiredness . . . since she [had been] a young girl."[24] For her, living in a decade when few working-class Americans had even started high school, the idea of a classroom, of books and lessons, held the promise of escape into a life so different from her own that she could hardly imagine what it might be like. In a certain sense, education might have kept that promise, as Alabama's large landowners had foreseen in 1894, when they overturned the law banning child labor and enforcing attendance in the schools. If the Depression later made the public schools a showcase for Progressive reform—though not the schools in Alabama—Agee feared that the change would only reinforce the great divides separating rich from poor and white from black.[25]

Back in New York to complete his manuscript, he remembered Annie Mae's daughter, Maggie Louise Gudger, as a girl "fond of school, especially of geography and arithmetic." She wanted, he recalled in his book, "to become a teacher, and quite possibly," he predicted, "she will."[26] But her brother, Junior Gudger, whom we would now identify as learning disabled, was still struggling to read and write after three years in the first grade, and Agee doubted that most of the local teachers had the training to provide the specialized help he needed. There were other "difficult" cases as well. A neighbor's child, Margaret Ricketts, "quit school when she was in the fifth grade because her eyes hurt her so badly every time she studied books," while her sister, Paralee, who could read with ease, also quit shortly after because Margaret's absence made her lonely. And why not quit, when the children of the Ricketts family were looked upon as problems by authorities at the school. "Their attendance record," Agee wrote, was "extremely bad; their conduct . . . not at all good; they [were] always fighting and sassing back"—but not simply because their parents were so poor and they lived so far from school. They were, Agee recalls, "much too innocent to understand the profits of docility"—"sensitive, open, trusting, easily hurt, and amazed by meanness and cruelty."[27]

To say, as some Marxist historians do, that the purpose of education is to impart a false consciousness, painting over the grossest exploitation to conceal the mechanisms of "hegemony," is to oversimplify the complex, conflicted motives of everyone involved in Agee's narrative. The stories the children read and the subjects they studied in their textbooks did not evoke a mystifying falsehood but overwhelmed them with details that erased the world and sapped their power to respond creatively. They read poems by Vachel Lindsay and Robert Louis Stevenson, and sanitized versions of Joel Chandler Harris's fables—"Brother Rabbit's Cool Air Swing."[28] They studied Nature and they studied Science. With the help of a mathematics textbook that went on for 500 pages and weighed more than 18 pounds, they learned to solve problems involving various proportions of mixed nuts, which they had never eaten. But the text that Agee turned to as the most eloquent example of modern education in the liberal state came from their reader in geography:

1. *The Great Ball on Which We Live.*
    The world is our home. It is also the home of many, many other children, some of whom live in far-away lands. They are our world brothers and sisters. . . .

2. *Food, Shelter, and Clothing.*
    What must any part of the world have in order to be a good home for man? What does every person need in order to live in comfort? Let us imagine that we are far out in the fields. The air is bitter cold and the wind is blowing. Snow is falling, and by and by it will turn to rain. We are almost naked. . . . Suddenly the Queen of the Fairies floats down and offers us three wishes.
    What shall we choose?
    "I shall wish for food, because I am hungry," says Peter.
    "I shall choose clothes to keep out the cold," says John.
    "And I shall ask for a house to shelter me from the wind, the snow, and the rain," says little Nell with a shiver.[29]

Is this, however, really what the children would ask? Do food and clothing and shelter really make a world, together with the expertise to provide these items, or is it not the case that our equating of such items with the world—and the world with a "great ball," the cartographer's ultimate abstraction—is the worst poverty of all? If Agee's observations tell us anything, they tell us that he looked with the keenest attentiveness on the deprivations of his subjects, noting, for example, how difficult it was for the tenants to buy the few books their children owned. But he wanted his readers to understand that a disaster more fundamental than material deprivation had already overtaken everyone, not simply the tenants, and not simply the teachers of their children, but also his fellow Americans in the prosperous

Northeast. "It is," Agee wrote, "as harmful to the 'winners' (the well to do, or healthful, or extraverted) as to the losers."[30]

The disaster was this: as the price of their ascent, the privileged and the dispossessed alike had lost the capacity to break through the wall of culture into the openness at the heart of things. As Agee had realized in his time spent with the tenant farmers, this openness lay around him everywhere and could be glimpsed "suddenly . . . by any one of any number of *unpredictable* chances: the fracture of sunlight on the facade and traffic of a street; the sleaving up of chimneysmoke; the rich lifting of the voice of a train along the darkness."[31] What offended Agee most about America's "democratic" education was its concealment of this openness from the poor, who could escape their situation only if they had trust enough in life to try something else, embracing an unknown future with no more than empty hands and the clothing on their backs. But the point of public schooling as he witnessed it was to crush this basic trust beneath an enormous weight of information, closing the future down one detail at a time.

In the refrain "How did we get caught?" Agee posed a question that addressed his readers far more urgently than it did the subjects of his report. How, he asked, has it happened that people like ourselves—educated, leisured people who should by rights be profoundly happy—live as unhappily as the Gudgers, in spite of all our comfort; why do we, who have had the benefit of every opportunity, feel as unfree as those who have no opportunities at all? And Agee's answer takes him back to education in the broadest sense: while the schools incrementally sever our connections to the world, the media instruct us throughout our lives to search for compensations rather than to make the effort to recover what we have lost.

Fortune too was a kind of classroom, after all, and the most basic lesson taught there in the Depression years was the existence of two worlds, each carefully juxtaposed page after page: on the one side, subscribers could read stories of drying croplands or the backbreaking harvest of the cotton; on the other, the glorious advertisements. What the ads evoked for the journal's readers was less a place they actually knew than some better place—a utopia of capitalism—designed by its creators to stimulate the reader's fear of the world pictured on the other side of the page, where disappointment and privation were the order of the day. Of course, the ads might be selling nothing more exotic or ethereal than Buick sedans, but the cars were just the vehicle for the expression of something else: an entire world without Agee's "actual"; a world of empty "signifiers" swept along in an endless, playful circulation. For tough-minded manufacturers and nervous market analysts, the ads operated as a soothing counterworld, where everything that could be imagined was evoked exactly as if it were real. The ads promised an experience of presence—an encounter with the "whole of consciousness," as Agee had put it—but they told their readers to pursue that goal by refusing the immediate, the world here and now.[32] Tacitly but firmly, the words and images made the case that fulfillment always lies *out there,* in that other, better world of pure representation, where a silent Buick races down a dustless road. But Agee warned that from such dreams we will unpleasantly awaken. To believe the ad and to buy the car—or the cigarettes or the scotch—is to court the most acute disappointment; to find oneself in a condition even worse than when one started, because then, at least, one had hope. Desired but never possessed, the product must remain an unattainable idea.[33]

Agee discovered in Alabama that the recovery of connectedness begins with a refusal of this allure; as he kept telling his readers throughout his book, an awareness of bare presence can be achieved only by the means of a discipline as discouraged by the schools as it is by the media—a ceaseless effort to turn awareness to the here and now. Viewed in this way, he told his readers, the unexceptional prospect of "a street in sunlight," passed over perhaps a hundred times before, "can roar in the heart of itself . . . [as] no symphony can."[34] But here Agee's powerful language may fail to express what understatement could disclose more credibly, given the cynical temper of our times. Some years before Agee's death, an Austrian philosopher of a very different temperament, Ludwig Wittgenstein, would observe in a similar spirit, "If anyone should think he has solved the problem of life and feel[s] like telling himself that everything is quite easy now, he can see that he is wrong just by recalling that there was a time when this 'solution' had not yet been discovered; but it must have been possible to live *then* too . . . and even at that time people must have known how to live and think."[35] This, it seems to me, comes closest to what Agee meant: there has always been something right here, right now that thinking and acting could never improve upon, something that is the *ground* of thinking and acting. Prior to the advertiser's world-denying image, prior to the expert's instrumental expertise, there has always been another and more basic-form of being in the world, one premised on the notion that "the place I really have to get to is," as Wittgenstein insisted, "a place I must already be at [right] now."[36]

The problem went beyond *Fortune* and its advertising, which could be dismissed as fairly trivial, reaching right to the foundations of modern intellectual life, to the ways of knowing and forms of truth that people held in highest esteem. Agee believed that any better future would require a different kind of understanding than the knowledge produced by the scientist who "dissects" or by the artist who "digests." Both the artist and the scientist in modernity actively cultivate alienation by suppressing the actual for the sake of the ideal. In his attention to the moment Agee thought he had discovered an alternative, an understanding that emerges when the boundary between self and world has temporarily dissolved. Rather than imposing his will upon the world, an undertaking bound to end in disappointment anyway, Agee wanted to transform himself through the attempt to see and hear, to taste and touch, without the violence of utopianism. "In a novel," Agee wrote, "a house or a person has his meaning, his existence, entirely through the writer. Here [in actuality] a house or a person has only the most limited of his meaning through me: his true meaning is much huger." The difference between fiction and the world lies in the real presence of George Gudger, who exists, "in actual being, as you do and as I do, and as no character of the imagination can possibly exist."[37] It is this recognition of "actual being" surrounding us everywhere, always *more* than words and *more* than ideas, that canonical art and big science conceal, and the price we have paid for the one-sided triumph is an enormous augmentation of the power to dream and the power to act without any clear sense of who we are or where we should go.

Other people of the time shared Agee's sense of dissatisfaction. During roughly the same period, the Marxist Frankfurt School in Germany had developed comparable ideas about the need "to suspend or destroy imagination," as Agee had written, in order to awaken from the dreams of modernity. There were important differences, however. Perhaps because the Frankfort theorists lived and worked almost exclusively within the ranks of other German intellectuals, they tended to privilege what they did best—criticism and critique—as opposed to face-to-face engagement with people like the Gudgers. As Agee came to think in the writing of his book, to interrogate ideas in an analytic spirit is not finally to escape from worldlessness but to simply become more conscious of that condition. The rejection of modern culture had to be followed by a different kind of activity, one more creative and world embracing. The point of listening, say, to a piece of music is not to deconstruct its constituent parts—to hold oneself at the distance; the point, Agee insisted, is to get "inside the music" so completely that you are "not only inside it, you are it."[38] Heard in this way, the music becomes a question, like *Let Us Now Praise Famous Men* itself, a question addressed to the reader, though not in the sense of something that has to be solved and put away, but as something that demands to be *lived through*. Every musician and every dilettante lives through music in this way. It is only the scholar, the professional critic, who prevents himself from listening.

Trilling was wrong about Agee: he was by no means a romantic. What Agee wanted to explore was not a world without culture, a primitive, Edenic condition, but a different and less helplessly prostrate relation to the products of human ingenuity. He asked how human beings, who depend on culture inescapably, might go about creating such marvelous things as poems, novels, symphonies, paintings, electric generators, and cities without allowing their creations to become burdensome and paralyzing. If he rejected the path of detachment and critique, he also rejected the modernist fascination with form as a substitute for personal connection. At a time when "form" had become the operative term in architecture as well as literary criticism, city planning as well as aesthetic theory, Agee saw formalism as deeply conservative, an attempt to reduce the present to a repetition of the past. This attempt, he believed, could no more do justice to an ever-changing reality than to the human longing for freedom. Only by acknowledging real contingency—by allowing the moment to reveal an intrinsic order of its own—could people use culture without being used by culture in turn. Formalism was not the cure but the illness, and its champions had raised their neurosis to the level of a methodology.

Agee believed that we can live in a condition of "not knowing." The unknown, the unsaid, and the unthought—these seem meaningless to the modern mentality, but Agee wrote in praise of "bareness" and "space" precisely because they seemed to hold "such greatness" that he could not "even try" to explain their fundamental character.[39] In the process of completing *Let Us Now Praise Famous Men,* Agee came to understand that the greatest eloquence, and also the greatest sensitivity, could never be achieved by filling all the spaces up with words, forms, and ideas, but by leaving a "bareness" for the others who would come later. And is it not this bareness, he asked us, that gives value to the things that people treasure most? People and events, poems and plays, stone walls and friendships, forests and journeys—whatever remains most durably in the fabric of memory and feeling— all seem to exceed or exhaust our powers of interpretation: something more can always be learned, can always be said. Finally, they exist and we exist with them. For Agee, this was salvation.

There can be, I believe, no way of life more deeply antithetical to Agee's reverence for sheer presence than our current social order, which derives its nearly irresistible power from its world-evading character. Modernity promises connection but produces the very opposite, and this situation may explain why Trilling felt himself called upon to charge Agee with "a failure of moral realism." Like Freud, whom Trilling praised as the greatest thinker of the twentieth century, Trilling considered *some* refusal of connection to be the essential underpinning of culture in both senses of the word, as Arnold meant it and as anthropologists do. And this conviction makes Trilling, rather than a romantic like Agee, our great ancestor in the humanities, even at a time when liberalism has become the target of every professor's critique.

Trilling was convinced that we *must not* get the sort of "wholeness" Agee wants; what the continuity of liberal culture instead demands is a willingness to accept the next best thing, and that next best thing is the vicarious experience of wholeness through art. The arts, and culture generally, must create desires that life itself cannot possibly satisfy, but which spur us on, all the same, to an ethical obligation that stands as a modern, secular substitute for God's covenant with his people: a law to be pursued but never finally, bodily lived through. For Trilling, however, even the idea of a covenant must be reduced to the status of a metaphor. The purpose of art is not to restore what Wordsworth—one of Trilling's inspirations—described as the "visionary gleam," but to demonstrate again and again that this gleam has "fled," and to teach us the wisdom of resignation to our inescapable abandonment. It is this conviction at the heart of Trilling's liberalism that allows him to maintain with serene confidence that the real subject of Wordsworth's "Ode on Intimations of Immortality" is not immortality after all, but the value of literature as a path to maturity in a disenchanted world.[40]

Trilling's Wordsworth is not the poet of nature, with or without the capital *N*, but of reality, which means something quite different from Agee's intimations of sheer presence. To clarify the character of this reality, Trilling draws on *Civilization and Its Discontents,* where Freud describes the inevitable waning of the child's "oceanic" sensibility, the false and immature impression of "limitless extension and oneness with the universe."[41] Despite his powerful nostalgia for an oceanic oneness, Trilling's Wordsworth recognized that "we fulfill ourselves by choosing what is painful, difficult, and necessary, and we develop by moving toward death."[42] Although Wordsworth may begin his famous poem by affirming that the "child is father to the man," he knows that if there is one thing a person can never be again without looking like a fool, it is a child; and Trilling goes on to insist, by the same reasoning, that for all its reliance on a "theistical metaphor, the Ode is largely naturalistic in its intention"—largely committed to the inevitability of human homelessness.[43]

Quite apart from what Wordsworth intended, Trilling's version of the Immortality Ode teaches us the same lesson conveyed by the advertisements in *Fortune* magazine: in the absence of a world, we have consoling images of one. If Trilling differs at all from the casual reader of *Fortune,* he differs in his belief that satisfaction ultimately lies not in breaking through the artifices of cultures but in wanting the things it is responsible to want—not communion but a toaster. And then, when disappointment follows as it must, maturity comes from recognizing disappointment as our human lot. Yet this is the lesson that Agee thought of as his deepest injury, and that Wittgenstein rejected when he wrote that philosophic problems could be resolved only by transforming the way of life from which they arose. Like Agee, Wittgenstein knew that the pleasures of art could never substitute for this essential transformation, but even Wittgenstein seemed not to understand how a way of life might be renewed once it has fallen into disrepair.[44] The path back to coherence, Agee believed, lay ready at hand in the careful observation of experience itself, and he believed that this insight might give birth to a new way of life, a new society. For him, the point of culture should not be to manage neurosis, as Trilling held, but to cure it, not to balance contradictions but to dissolve them.

As a teacher of English at a university, I seldom read Trilling today without regretting the subtle persistence of his legacy, not only in higher education but in our society as a whole, which endlessly reinstates, in a hundred different venues and a hundred different ways, the logic of worldlessness and homelessness. And I am increasingly persuaded that those of us who have followed the avant-garde of the postmodern humanities in taking the so-called semiotic turn—its turn away from experience to the somber pleasures of "textuality"—may have unknowingly revealed ourselves to be Lionel Trilling's most obedient disciples, more obedient than any of his contemporaries. There were certainly alternatives at the time, however, and in unexpected places. Here, for example, are the words of one critic of Trilling's generation who refused to believe that poetry could offer only an image of unattainable freedom and happiness:

> By making forms [the poet] understands the world, grasps the world, imposes himself upon the world. But the "made thing" that the poet produces represents a different kind of form from all the others we know. . . . The form of a [poetic] work represents, not only a manipulation of the world, but an adventure in selfhood. It embodies the experience of a self vis-a-vis the world. . . . The self has been maimed in our society because . . . we [are losing] contact with the world's body, los[ing] any holistic sense of our relation to the world. . . .So in D. H. Lawrence's poem "Cry of the Masses":
> > Give us back, Oh give us back
> > Our bodies before we die.[45]

The writer of these sentences was Robert Penn Warren, a fellow traveler among the New Critics, reviled by most academics today, and he read them aloud to a Harvard audience almost twenty years ago, at the beginning of the end of high modernism. To me, someone convinced that the disappearance of the world is the symptom of a social pathology, the most striking quality about Warren's talk is its consonance with Agee's work of forty years earlier. Of course, Warren invested poetry with an importance that Agee would give it only ambivalently—Warren even goes so far, quoting Harry Levin, as to call poetry the "richest and most sensitive of human institutions."[46] Agee, I think, would disagree, as he would with the New Critical faith in the power of form. Worse yet, Warren celebrates a relation to the world—imposing, assertive, possessive—that Agee found repellant. But Warren demonstrates, all the same, an understanding of the modern situation nowhere evident in Trilling's work.

"The self," Warren writes, "has been maimed" by its disconnection from the "world's body."[47] Like Agee, Warren recognized that the world's body, in its resistance to our projections, schemes, and demands, holds the key to the freeing of our own bodies—and that a medium like poetry, apprehended as *experience* rather than as a system of signs or symbols, can provoke in the reader "a massive reenactment, both muscular and nervous" of "the rhythms of the universe."[48] However mistaken he may have been to claim that poetry is the most fully human of human activities, Warren's ideal poet does what Agee tells us that everyone should do, using words, symbols, and ideas to move beyond words, symbols, and ideas. Professional critics may teach otherwise, but poems are never "about" poetry: they are about the arbitrary limits of ourselves and the possibility of surpassing those limits. The same might be said about philosophy or history or the fine arts.

And what holds true for Warren's ideal poet holds true for his ideal readers of poems. To read a poem, on his account, is to overcome the perception of the poem as a *poem* or of a word as a *word*. The act of reading should culminate experientially in a disappearance of the text into the world from which it came, and also a momentary disappearance of the reader into that same source—what Warren called an "adventure in selfhood." But this is seldom the way we speak about poems now, with the rise of semiotics and its poststructuralist successors, for reasons that the passage below makes clear:

> [One] insidious legacy of the New Criticism is the widespread and unquestioning acceptance of the notion that the critic's job is to interpret literary works. . . . In this critical climate it is therefore important, if only as a means of loosening the grip which interpretation has on critical consciousness, to take up a tendentious position and to maintain that, while the experience of literature may be an experience of interpreting works, in fact the interpretation of individual works is only tangentially related to the understanding of literature.

Here in the academy today, there can be no more talk about such things as the "world's body." What this second critic, Jonathan Culler, wants instead of experience "both nervous and muscular" is a distanced, objective, highly professionalized study of the signifying systems that produce individual literary works in a rigidly deterministic fashion.[49] "At its most basic," Culler writes, "the lesson of contemporary European criticism is this: the New Criticism's dream of [an] encounter between innocent reader and autonomous text is a bizarre fiction. To read is always to read in relation to other texts, in relation to the codes that . . . make up a culture."[50] While literature can, and probably must, be experienced through acts of interpretation, the proper object of professional study as Culler sees it is not meaning or "felt life" but the signs and codes that predetermine the nature of meaning and feeling— the systems and structures of signification that make reading possible.

Culler seems to build his edifice on the most solid of foundations, but by his own reasoning there can be no objectivity of the kind he claims: no such thing as an encounter between an innocent theorist and an autonomous textual system. Like the interpreters he disparages, Culler too offers an interpretation, and only one of many: unavoidably the network he describes is a conjecture, an inference of his own fashioning. The question, then, is not whether Culler has found the truth—the ground floor of all reference—but why he would want to claim a privileged status for his preferred interpretation, and why he excludes so assiduously the meanings ordinary readers might assign. Why, in fact, is he averse to meaning altogether? Agee would have known the answer.

A century from now, historians may ask themselves what disasters must have happened in the brief period that begins with Trilling's declaration of liberalism's ascendancy, circa 1950, and that concludes with hyperspecialization—the turn to signs and systems undertaken by critics like Culler. Whatever answer they might provide, it will be clear that people living and working during those years were forced to address a major collapse of confidence in some of their society's most fundamental institutions. Although the rise of academic theory has many causes, it coincides with a widespread erosion of faith in the administered society, a crisis that began with the conflict in Vietnam and that has steadily deepened since then. But our turn to "the text" has not taken us anywhere except back to the dilemmas and disappointments of Agee's day. When Culler shifted from the isolated literary work to the "text" of culture, he assumed that this larger text could be known with a precision and completeness never hoped for by the New Critics. But the history of literary criticism since the rise of the structuralist enterprise has been a history of growing disagreement and disarray, not of greater concord on the question of method. As each new mode of reading supplants the next—structuralism supplanted by Foucaldian archaeology, archaeology by deconstruction, deconstruction by poststructuralist Marxism—it becomes more and more obvious that there will never be a science of meaning or ideology, since the "cultural text," no less than any poem, is subject to an infinite number of inescapably circular readings, each beginning with some root metaphor (words are signs, words are weapons, words are tools, words are displacements, words are money) and each amenable to extension outward from an individual poem or novel to explicate all notable forms of representation. It is possible to conclude from this trajectory that we are learning more and more about "textuality." But it is also possible to say that the quick succession of critical trends exposes a continuing failure to decide what poems or novels or plays are really *for* in the absence of a living world.

Our great mistake, Agee might say, was to imagine that the codes and signifying systems, conventions or laws of structural transformation might give us a
permanence lacking in our contingent, unpredictable everyday lives. He was convinced, in fact, that only an embracing of contingency might save us from our own
worst impulses by overturning the terrible certainties that make one particular chair
just a chair, one particular tree just a tree, one particular person just a tenant farmer.
Agee knew that all the things humans do in their everyday lives—preparing food or
performing open heart surgery, writing novels or repaving roads—might be understood as acts, as arts, of compassion when they make possible an encounter, first with
a world beyond the self, and then with the world *as self*. But Agee also recognized
that the products of those same arts, if they are treated as permanent, obligatory
systems, might be fashioned into instruments of our own self-oppression.

Nowhere did Agee see this transmutation more openly displayed—this negative alchemy by which the gold of human life is turned to lead—than in education.
From the Cotton Belt to Harvard, the pedagogy was exactly the same: *take the most
splendid examples of humankind's encounters with world, which are always achieved in
the uncertainties of a moment that will never return, and reduce them to an abstract
formula that can be repeated ad infinitum.* By this venerable means one can, of course,
produce many millions of young men and women with all kinds of advanced
degrees, but at the same time society pays a certain price, since the construction of
such knowledge creates a growing sense of unreality. And the haunting intimation
that the real has dropped from sight keeps driving us back, in the most vicious of all
vicious circles—since it consumes the best minds generation after generation—to
the search for an even better method. On the one hand, institutionalization demands
that the production of knowledge be made routine, but on the other, as Agee
warned, learning of the kind that restores our sense of connection to the world is the
mortal enemy of routine.

To read Agee now is to understand how completely our nation has chosen
schooling over learning, and how far we have to go if we hope to transform the
instruments of alienation into something else. In the university today, the university
of theory and "the text," people like Agee have no voice at all. As for Agee himself, he
remained throughout the brief span of his alcoholic life a gentle, gregarious revolutionary condemned to a solitude he found unbearable. Perhaps the crowning injury
of his life, which occurred in the hours leading up to his last, fatal heart attack, was a
televised debate with an academic historian, Alan Nevins of Columbia, who berated
him in front of a national audience for the liberties he had taken in a television play
about the life of young Abraham Lincoln. The professor savaged Agee for assuming,
groundlessly, that Lincoln had engaged in a torrid affair with a woman who, in fact,
was nothing more than a friend. Witnesses recalled that Agee, visibly sick and tired,
had looked as though he were about to cry.[51] Some may find it ironic that an
academic historian only a few years ago would make virtually the same argument
that Agee made, going on to win praise from his colleagues. Of course, Agee's
reconstruction was methodologically flawed.[52] Praised and then largely forgotten, he
has become the unfortunate subject of psychologizing biographers.

Those of us who regret that this humble messenger arrived at so inauspicious a moment should remember the trust he never ceased to demonstrate in the face of his despair about modernity: a trust in himself and in others, as beings capable of living fully in the world—but also a trust in the world as a home, as a body, complete beyond our power to diminish it. Only a decade before *Let Us Now Praise Famous Men* went to press, another professor, not of history this time but of English, had complained about the detestable recalcitrance of that world. "Life," Joseph Wood Krutch had written in exasperation, always "baffles and seems almost to mock. It refuses long to remain consistently one thing or another and it seldom puts us in one mood without violating it soon after," reducing everything to the "hideous confusion" of nature.[53] Krutch thought that art was often better than life because art could be more orderly, but Agee tells us that "confusion" is our saving grace, and he warns that order has become our labyrinth. Beyond the labyrinth, in the place where our knowledge and our mastery fail, the world has been waiting for us. It is still waiting.

Part II

6

The Wages of Theory

Isolation and Knowledge in the Humanities

When conservatives like Allan Bloom and Roger Kimball try to make sense of the humanities' decline, they blame the 1960s, which they see as a time of unbridled self-indulgence that overturned all standards of good judgment and good taste.[1] In their nostalgia Bloom and Kramer seem to forget that the administered society, the edifice on which the modernist program reposed, was not a foreordained outcome of our social evolution but a fragile compromise between working Americans and their wealthy counterparts after a protracted era of violence. It was also quite short-lived.

Even before modernism's crowning moment, the election of John Kennedy, the edifice showed signs of strain. Returning black GIs did not share equally in the post–World War II affluence and they often found it difficult to reconcile America's rhetoric of freedom overseas with the denial of genuine freedom at home. While young white Americans enjoyed a much higher level of wealth and opportunity than young blacks, they too felt a sense of disappointment, a factor often overlooked in accounts of the time. One way to understand the discontent of people like the Beats and later the hippies is to place it in the context of mass education and its consequences. The passing of the GI Bill made higher education a reality for many millions of Americans who would otherwise have never attended college, and the children of these GIs went to college in even larger numbers. Yet mass education did not produce any significant change in the political life of Americans, and although the middle class expanded during these years, upward mobility did not always bring the imagined satisfactions. People who might have worked in factories a generation earlier wound up moving paper in cubicles, and not necessarily for more money than their blue-collar counterparts. Books with titles like *The Organization Man* and *The Man in the Gray Flannel Suit* reflect a vague sense of powerlessness in the midst of prosperity.[2] And even that prosperity was imperiled. From the late 1960s on, the actual earning power of the American dollar began to erode, so that women were slowly but steadily pushed out of the house in order maintain an acceptable standard of living for their families.[3] In a manner typical of the period, the experience of powerlessness was misinterpreted as a cultural development rather than a political or economic matter. The problem, as critics of the time tended to see it, was the banality of the nine-to-five job and the stifling pressures of conformity. This emphasis on culture reached a reductio ad absurdum in the mid-1970s with Herbert Marcuse's *Eros and Civilization,* the bible of the Sexual Revolution, which proposed to overthrow capitalism by setting free the libidinous impulses of the masses.[4]

Nevertheless, for just a moment Kennedy's Camelot promised to bestow on the humanities the glory they had always coveted. Kennedy himself toyed with the role of a man of letters and had even written two bestselling histories, *Why England Slept* and *Profiles in Courage,* while Jackie made a reputation for herself as a gracious patron of the fine arts. The liberal historian James Schlesinger Jr. was a visible presence in the President's brain trust along with other academics like the economists John Kenneth Galbraith and Walt Whitman Rostow, in addition to the former Harvard dean McGeorge Bundy. The poet Robert Frost read "The Gift Outright" at Kennedy's inauguration, and Frost became an unofficial spokesman for the administration, even talking politics with Khrushchev during a visit to the Soviet Union.[5] The choice of Frost was not primarily a matter of the President's personal tastes, which leaned in the direction of Frank Sinatra. Arguably, no other writer of the time was more widely identified with American values and American culture, rough hewn, deeply rooted, and rock-ribbed, a scion of Old New England (although Frost was born in San Francisco). Suddenly culture had become a national asset like bauxite or oil. As Kennedy once told a *New York Times* reporter, "I think it tremendously important that we regard music not just as part of our arsenal in the Cold War, but as an integral part of free society."[6] This was the logic, two years later, behind the founding of the National Council on the Arts and the National Endowment for the Humanities. And these were the years that also witnessed a dramatic increase in the number of undergraduate and graduate humanities students, and in the number of jobs for humanities professors. As the Cold War guardians of national culture, and indeed of the culture of the whole free world, professors often felt themselves to have a clear mandate. In English departments, for example, academics of the day had every reason to believe that they were shaping the literary tastes of the entire country: they even began to speak about their "canon" of great works in much the same way as theologians speak about the Church Fathers.

Because of the university's relative isolation, crisis came to it more slowly than to the outside world. Almost alone among literary critics of his day, Robert Penn Warren tried to address the "race problem," but for the most part, the fragmentation of the larger society did not make itself felt in English until long after the march on Birmingham.[7] Only in the 1980s were there significant calls for an enlargement of the canon to accommodate those figures omitted from the earlier, modernist visions of American high culture—American Indians, African-Americans, Asian-Americans, women, working-class intellectuals, and so on. The popular media, by contrast, especially magazines and movies, responded in a much more timely way. James Baldwin's brilliant and smoldering essays appeared in publications like *The New Yorker.* Michael Harrington's *The Other America,* on the problem of chronic poverty, caught the President's attention, and in 1963, a runner-up for an Academy Award (losing out to the epic of empire *Lawrence of Arabia*) was *To Kill a Mockingbird,* which dealt with racial prejudice in a small southern town.[8]

Why change came so late to the university had to do with its most basic structures. Undergraduates concerned about the problems of the time and eager to address them in the context of humanistic inquiry had to undergo a long apprentice-ship, beginning with five to ten years of graduate study culminating in the Ph.D. If a student had started graduate school in 1964, the dissertation might have been completed around 1970. In the normal course of a young professor's life during that period, two or three articles would have followed over the next five or six years with their heavy teaching obligations. Exemplary junior faculty might have seen their first book in print about 1975 or so, but the first book was almost always a version of the dissertation, and dissertations tend to reflect the outlook of their faculty directors as much as the outlook of their authors. Only later, with tenure and the security it brings, could the young professor start a second book more directly involved with problems of urgent concern almost two decades earlier. But other factors inhibited change as well. Young scholars engaged with, say, the later novels of Thomas Hardy, or relations between Native Americans and European settlers, would have written their early articles in response to scholarly debates that might be ten or twenty years old by the time those articles appeared in print—debates that may have started in the Eisenhower years. And of course, there is always resistance to new ideas. Eminent scholars whose sense of literary tradition or historical significance had been shaped in the late fifties or early sixties might be expected to resist ways of thinking that diminished the importance of their own life's work. A historian devoted to diplomatic history—the history of great leaders, treaties and battles, councils and summits—might with some reason feel threatened by scholarship tightly focused on the everyday lives of ordinary people in the conviction that great men are not truly representative of the life of their times. By the same token, the scholar who rose to fame by arguing that Herman Melville was the greatest prophet of democracy can hardly be expected to welcome a reassessment that makes Melville an apologist for conquest, slavery, and other misadventures. No one will be surprised to learn that people in different eras might think differently about the same events or the same authors, but the structure of the university tends to preserve the perspectives of one era beyond its natural life. At the same time, the structure of the academy exacer-bates tensions by giving the greatest measure of power to those already relatively powerful. The scholar who rises up through the ranks typically sits on the editorial boards of important journals and helps to determine what opinions ever see the light of day. These determinations decide in turn who among the younger scholars will survive the quest for tenure by getting their ideas into into print. Structurally, few other institutions are as unreceptive to change.

Had the university been different, the fall of Camelot might have brought about fundamental change. What would have happened, for example, if we orga-nized the humanities not by disciplines and historical periods but by areas of pressing concern? In the Kennedy years, those areas would have included the struggle for Civil Rights, the conflict with the Soviet Union and the threat of nuclear war, the persistence of poverty, and American involvement in Southeast Asia. It might also have included cultural developments that crossed traditional boundaries, linking literature to the visual arts and to music. In our time, the areas of pressing concern would certainly be different, but by making these the focus of humanistic education, we might offer far better service to civic life in a democracy.

This is not what happened when Camelot fell. Although Kennedy was shot in 1963, the world he helped to create survived him for several years. Camelot truly came to an end in 1968, the year of Tet offensive in Vietnam, an engagement that left 500 U.S. soldiers dead and more than ten times that number of North Vietnamese troops. When Tet was over, hundreds of thousands of noncombattants had lost their homes, or their lives. A month afterward, in the hamlet of My Lai, American soldiers murdered 200 civilians after inflicting on at least some of them a series of sadistic beatings and rapes.[9] Back at home, Benjamin Spock, the nation's pediatrician, and William Sloane Coffin, Yale's thoughtful and respected chaplain, were indicted in Boston for conspiracy to incite resistance to the draft. In April 1968, Martin Luther King led a civil rights march in Memphis that turned into a violent confrontation between whites and blacks.[10] Only a few weeks later, King himself was shot on the balcony of his motel. Riots erupted in Baltimore; Boston; Chicago; Detroit; Kansas City; Newark, N.J.; and Washington, D.C. Students at Columbia occupied campus buildings. About a month after that, the former U.S. Attorney General Robert Kennedy was also assassinated. But the violence of that year reached beyond the United States. Students and workers clashed violently with authorities in France, nearly toppling the government, and there were serious clashes in Italy and Mexico as well. On the other side of the Iron Curtain, 1968 was the year of the Prague Spring, when President Dubcek declared Czechoslovakia's independence, followed by the Soviet invasion. Half a world away, China's ruinous Cultural Revolution moved into full swing.

These events were so important that it may come as a surprise to learn that they are linked in the minds of many academic humanists to a milestone of a very different kind: the publication a year before the global shocks of a book entitled *De la grammatologie,* by a then-obscure French philosopher Jacques Derrida.[11] In that book, the author challenged the idea that perception can ever occur without the mediation of language, or as he put it, of "writing." Although animals, which lack language, sometimes appear to perceive the world much as we do, Derrida refused to consider writing on these terms, as a product of biology, brain function, evolution, or social history. Instead, he began with the assumption that language is the starting point of everything else—science, history, common sense, and even the new field grammatology itself. All these fields, he wrote, exist only in and through writing, and to imagine the human world before or without writing was in his view sheer nonsense. There is, he declared boldly, nothing outside the text.

The world was on fire; in the meantime, theory had descended on in the humanities.

The hardest questions can look like the simplest ones. For example, what was "theory"? In its heyday—the decade after 1968—"theory" could mean almost anything, from Gilles Deleuze and Félix Guattari's "nomadic science" to Jürgen Habermas's seemingly endless defense of "communicative rationality."[12] No matter what the word might have meant, however, scholars somehow sensed theory's importance, and they knew, if they knew absolutely nothing else, that theory had to do with "the text." Now, more than thirty years afterward, people somehow sense that theory's time has run out, yet "theory" today is anything but dead. When the feminist Judith Butler sets out in *Gender Trouble* to rethink sexual identity, she calls on Derrida. When the critic Homi Bhabha, in *Redrawing the Boundaries,* starts to map the new terrain of the postcolonial world, he goes back to Roland Barthes and Mikhail Bakhtin.[13] Luminaries like Butler and Bhabha tend to see themselves as renewing theory or else adding something to it, but the truth may be far more complicated—and also far more troubling. The humanities today may be *trapped* in theory because academics refuse to give up on the authority it once seemed to offer them.

I can still remember my own first encounter with theory, which occurred at a moment of great urgency in my life as well as in my profession. As theory itself has taught its devotees, such small moments, multiplied many times, are what we mean by "history." My first encounter with theory happened on a bleak January afternoon at a downtown Princeton bookstore where I went following the conclusion of a uniquely unpleasant event. That event was the most recent meeting of New Jersey's Basic Skills Advisory Council, which our governor had charged with assessing the public schools, and on which I held a seat as the director of the state's largest college-level writing program. Fourteen years and many millions of dollars into a campaign of twelfth-grade exit testing, the council had assembled the data to "prove" that thousands of graduates from the poorest urban neighborhoods—in Camden, Newark, and Jersey City—were functionally "illiterate." But the data themselves were *all* we had; none of us knew why the scores were so low, and no one could explain with much clarity—although we were supposedly the best in our fields—how we should respond.

Our silence left me demoralized. As the snow piled up against the windows of the store, I found myself increasingly disturbed to think that we had measured the decline of "literacy" without ever knowing what the word really meant. Even more disturbing was the Council's public confirmation, carried everywhere by the local media, of deeply entrenched beliefs about New Jersey's "skills deficient" citizens—largely black or Hispanic, and almost always working class. After a decade in remedial teaching, I knew just how deep these beliefs could go, so deep that they shaped not only the policies of the state but also much of the standard scholarship. One authority whom I had been made to read when I was in graduate school spoke for many members of the profession when he argued that the children of the "culturally deprived . . . do not just think at an immature level: many of them . . . do not think at all."[14] And they could not think, this distinguished educator went on to allege, partly because of their genetic heritage, which he cited in a footnote on black migration out of the postslavery South, and partly because their language lacked "the formal properties necessary for the organization of thought."[15] A decade later, on that January afternoon, absolutely nothing had changed; from our data we expected to learn more or less what the distinguished educator had learned from his, and the solution he had proposed was our state's approach as well: to begin instruction at a cultural zero point, proceeding as if these "children" had, in his words, "no language of their own."[16]

Like most of the Council's monthly meetings, the one in January dragged on so long that none of us felt much relief when it wound down, and I spent what was left of the afternoon browsing numbly through the kind of "difficult" books I would otherwise have looked past. Somewhere in the store a string quartet was playing crisply on a laser disk, and it struck me as I stood listening that even if I traveled to the ends of the earth—to the Outback or Ulan Bator—I could not possibly be more distant than I was just then from the people we referred to as "skills deficient." Camden and Jersey City were a million miles away, but the book I bought that afternoon, with the enigmatic title *Truth and Method,* helped me understand what reading was and why no two human beings could *ever* read the same passage in quite the same way. And on another afternoon three months afterward, as I slogged through the book's last hundred pages or so, I realized that the author, Hans-Georg Gadamer—a protégé of Heidegger, not an instructor of "basic skills"—had given me the intellectual means to change nearly everything about what I did and who I was.

For the first time in my professional life, I found it possible to see the "skills deficient" differently, not as isolated individuals who had missed the chance for cognitive development, but as members of communities *strong* enough to survive despite enormous outside pressure. Although Gadamer himself would almost certainly demur, given his commitment to an elitist view of culture, his work still helped me to recognize that people everywhere were historical beings no more capable of falling outside language and tradition than they were capable of falling outside time. Whether writing or thinking, speaking or acting, people are "always already" inside a linguistic world, and so thoroughly inside that we might say, as Gadamer did, not that we speak a language but that we ourselves are spoken.[17] Where the educator I once read in graduate school had diagnosed a fundamental poverty, Gadamer's "hermeneutics" had revealed a rich plenitude; when the educator called for a program of "no-nonsense" academic discipline, Gadamer invoked the vastly more humane ideal of learning as a journey and a conversation, an endless "fusion" of life-world "horizons."[18] Looking out from the horizon Gadamer opened for *me,* I recognized more clearly than I ever had before that teaching any subject was a violent, useless act unless all the parties involved could find the means to enlarge their particular lived worlds—worlds that were full and real in different ways but *equally* full and real. As Gadamer wrote in a passage that I am sure I will never forget, we always end our journeys of the word and the mind by "returning home."[19]

Theory's detractors sometimes allege that it changes nothing, but theory in my life has had far-reaching consequences. I acted on the insights theory offered me, and my actions touched the lives of many thousands of high school graduates whose experience at the university might have been far more damaging than it turned out to be. For an entire generation in English departments, I believe, the encounter with theory followed a course like the one I have just retraced, an odyssey from silence, boredom, and paralysis to a sense of purpose and "empowerment," as we used to say.

Yet it seems increasingly obvious now that something has gone terribly wrong with theory.

When the German sociologist Max Horkheimer used the word *theory* in the 1930s, he had in mind a pragmatic, hard-nosed skepticism directed against institutions like the university itself, with their tendency to perpetuate inequality through supposedly objective and high-minded practices.[20] But theory in the decades after 1968 rapidly became the central pillar of a staid orthodoxy: no one in the humanities could speak and be heard without resorting to theory. When the critic Robert Scholes observed in 1985—and quite approvingly—that teachers should "read theory to 'keep up,' " he reminded us, without meaning to, of just how far theory had traveled since Horkheimer's time, when "keeping up" was a suspect idea.[21] Derrida may have started his career laying claim to the "margins" of "the text"— where alternative perspectives could survive—but by the late 1980s, the margins had become prime real estate in English and related fields. Overnight everyone claimed to be writing *en marge,* from the margins. Instead of qualifying our statements, we were taught to put them, as Derrida did, *sous rature,* under erasure, half-retracting whatever we had just maintained; instead of saying that a fictional character's behavior looked ambiguous, we learned to say that she "is placed under the sign of ambiguity." Much of the appeal implicit in such jargon had to do with its ability to make the old and stale seem shockingly new. Fresh life could be breathed into *Paradise Lost* by showing that it implicitly anticipates Karl Marx on class struggle, while papers on Shakespeare reveled in epistemological puns: "Coming Apart at the Seems: Hamlet in Search of le Signifié." But theory had other virtues. As the tool of a self-styled critical avant-garde, it landed Yale deconstructionists in *Time* magazine, while the founders of cultural studies—second-generation theory mavens—made fashion statements for the curious New York press in their silk Armani jackets, sleeves rolled up in the style of *Miami Vice,* a much-discussed postmodern cops-and-robbers TV show. Trivial as these events might seem, they tell us something essential about theory and the movements that have followed it. For the first time since the quiz-show days of Charles van Doren, scholars who might have started their careers with books on Donne's debt to Plotinus or Trollope's comedy of manners saw the chance for something like celebrity by deconstructing the "signifying practices" of Rousseau or Bugs Bunny, or by "unpacking" the lyrics of 2 Live Crew.

Yet there has been, I think, more to theory's success than the lure of celebrity can explain—and this "more" has to do with the character of theory as a resource for preserving the humanities' prestige. Like every other form of knowledge in our age of expertise, theory gets produced by specialists. But theory differs from an article in *Harper's* or a report on the *CBS Evening News,* whose writers are no less specialized than academics are, because theory is uniquely the discourse of privileged *and* declining institutions, whose concerns have grown so distant from everyday life that a sense of crisis overtakes the specialists themselves. To justify the privileged status of their work, these specialists must show that their thinking is somehow *superior* to common sense—more inclusive, more penetrating, more rigorous. Even theorists themselves come close to granting this point when they drag out the oft-repeated maxim that critique is a response to crisis; what they fail to add is that the crisis lies within the humanities themselves. But theory is, I would say, an autistic response. It wins the battle for prestige by losing the war for public relevance. Does anyone seriously believe, for instance, that most undergraduates will ever read another word of theory once they start their working lives, selling insurance and composing public relations brochures? The sciences, by contrast, have pursued the lower road—pragmatic, prosaic, and worldly—without any corresponding risk to their high status; for the better part of a century, popular writers on science have brilliantly managed to bridge the gap that divides abstruse research from wide public understanding.

Within the academic humanities, theory and its successors have taken shape in the space opened up by the conflict between our hunger for prestige and our loneliness in an age of mass communications; yet the purpose of theory as we have often practiced it under a variety of names is not to make intellectual life more open and democratic by enlarging the circle of participants, but to invest our disciplines with an aura of unassailable majesty. Theory makes a *weapon* of our marginality by reversing the relations of power between us and a public inclined to dismiss our achievements and concerns out of hand. And while every work of theory turns the tables on its readers, repaying curiosity with a slap in the face, one work that points to this quality with particular (and unintended) candor is Gayatri Spivak's infamous essay on "The Breast Giver," a short story by the Bengali writer Mahasweta Devi. Before looking closely at Spivak's essay, though, I should explain that the story can be read straightforwardly as an account of a woman's unhappy life when the death of her husband forces her to sell her services as a wet-nurse. As Spivak herself concedes in a brief aside, Devi meant the woman to personify the troubled nation-state of India, from whom all its "children" take, giving nothing in return.[22] But Spivak reads the story quite differently:

> Thought as *jouissance,* is not orgasmic pleasure genitally defined, but the excess of being that escapes the circle of the reproduction of the subject. It is the mark of the Other in the subject. Now psychoanalysis can only ever conceive of thought as possible through those mechanics of signification where the phallus comes to *mean* the Law by positing castration as punishment as such. Although the point is made repeatedly by Lacan that we are not speaking of the actual male member but of the phallus of the signifier, it is still obviously a gendered position. . . . Thus, to call Mahasweta's preoccupation in ["The Breast Giver"] with *jouissance* in the general sense "writing like a man" [as Lacanians might] is to reduce a complex position to the trivializing simplicity of a hegemonic gendering.
>
> In ["The Breast Giver," the protagonist's body], rather than her fetished deliberative consciousness (self or subjectivity), is the place of knowledge, rather than the instrument of knowing.[23]

To a reader unfamiliar with the conventions of high theory and its offspring, cultural studies, Spivak's interpretation is bound to seem like a parody of academic criticism at its worst. Readers have to make more than a modest reach, after all, if they want to trace out the connections between Devi's simple allegory and the grand themes that matter most to Spivak herself—"writing," psychoanalysis, ideological reification, and the highly disincarnate form of ecstacy that French critics, sad to say, call *jouissance*. But theory's advocates would probably reply that Spivak's tendentiousness is just what we need. Like every text that tells us more than we already know, she confounds our familiar points of view, and by doing so forces us to see not only the story but also ourselves in an unexpected light.

Such, at least, has been the prevailing party line, but how true is it, actually? New ways of reading stories can be wonderful, yet over and above its novelty, Spivak's text subjects its readers to a violence that practitioners of theory and its more recent avatars take great pains to deny. Reading Spivak *hurts*—hurts beginners, anyway—precisely because her prose demands that we relinquish a large measure of our agency, our sense of control over ourselves, our circumstances, and the ideas we encounter. But the reader's loss of agency does not follow simply from the convolutions of her prose. That loss of agency results, instead, from the double bind in which Spivak's rhetoric locks every reader generous enough to give her work a hearing. On the one hand, her explicit argument promises something like a mass emancipation from traditions that have failed to make a place for people like Mahasweta's protagonist, the much-invoked global "subaltern." But Spivak's rhetoric, on the other hand, compels its readers to abandon Mahasweta's words in order to wander through the labyrinthine speculations of theory's founding giants: Foucault, Derrida, Volosinov, and Lacan. And the result is not emancipation but a forced admission on the reader's part that even when these eminent intellects make very little sense indeed, they still somehow think more usefully than the ordinary person ever could. If there are any subalterns to be found in Spivak's study, one of them is surely the reader, insofar as Spivak's practice of theory does to that reader what educators do to the people they have stigmatized as "remedial," the sort of people I have spent much of my life teaching. By refashioning the character of "literacy" itself, the practitioners of theory have learned to transform whole shoals of articulate Ph.D.s into stammering "illiterates." But Spivak is no less diminished than we are, to the degree that she feels compelled to write about a simple parable of Indian political life in a language that makes India unspeakable. And, in fact, Spivak's largely Western audience comes away from her tour de force knowing something more about the Paris scene but absolutely nothing new about the people who live their lives in the villages and cities of West Bengal.

What disappears from Spivak's text is not just the reader's world, but also any sense of the world that produced Mahasweta's own narrative. And this violent act, which destroys and co-opts at the same time, is the quintessential gesture of both theory and remediation. In each case, as well, the motive is the same—the maintenance of a boundary between the experts and amateurs, "ignorance" and "knowledge," mystification and enlightenment. Constrained as she is by the language of theory, Spivak has chosen to be heard at a certain cost to others—by speaking the argot of hyperspecialists and by laying claim to an insight that transcends the experience of absolutely everyone except a few cognoscenti like the ones she dutifully cites. While attempting to make room for the excluded and disempowered, the theorist continues to occupy a privileged place indistinguishable from the scientist's role as uniquely objective observer, or from the philosopher's pretensions to pure reason. The theorist still plays at being Socrates, with the reader standing dumbly in as Glaucon, while the truth itself remains always somewhere else, far removed from the reader's here and now. If this displacement of the here and now is theory's greatest strength, it is also theory's greatest danger. Looking up from the campus at Santa Cruz or down from the august brownstones on Columbia's Morningside Heights, can we ever know how things appear to those standing somewhere else? But the problem is more serious than our failure to see the lay citizen's point of view. Over the last fifteen years or so, theory's universalizing ambitions have given us the spectacle of upper-middle-class white North Americans using French philosophers (most of them males) to make sense of narratives by and about "Third World women." We can be sure, as well—and this strikes me as even more depressing—that at this very moment, college teachers from Cairo to Kuala Lumpur are busily stuffing their syllabi with readings that their counterparts in Paris would sniff at sourly as old news. Far from breaking with the legacy of colonization, this arrangement has simply reinstated it with a vengeance, so that the grandchildren of the Asian and African subjects who began their schoolday paying homage to "our forefathers the Gauls" now bone up on Derrida or Foucault. And the lesson we need to draw from this disastrous turn of events is that knowledge as we produce it in the university—even when it takes the form of critiques of global inequality and oppression—helps to perpetuate a truly global system of intellectual dependency.

We will never understand how theory has gone wrong until we view its rise against the backdrop of the changes I describe in part I, changes brought about by the passage from the relative coherence of nineteenth-century communities to the fragmentation of "postmodernity." Partly because of this social history, those of us now working in universities respond to fragmentation much as our predecessors did half a century ago: we still want to take charge; we still want to "make a difference." We want to fight the noble fight of "organic intellectuals," deeply rooted in the local scene just as Antonio Gramsci, the Marxist hero of many academics today, was deeply rooted in prewar Turin. Yet when we speak *ex cathedra* to our fellow citizens, we speak as their social betters, not as their friends; and as powerful authorities, not as fellow sufferers. At the university where I work, the average full professor's salary is $65,000 higher than the state's average family income.[24] At places like Stanford or Harvard or Yale, the disparity is even greater. The world within which we operate today is much less like the one evoked by the Brazilian educator of the favelas, Paulo Freire (another favorite of many academics), than it is like the one described by Gary Marx in an essay on his life as an academic sociologist:

> In 1970, there could not have been many sociologists just three years beyond the Ph.D. who were as professionally satisfied and optimistic as I was. . . . Immigrants, gold miners, and aspiring actors might head west, but as an ambitious academic born on a farm in central California, I had headed east to where I thought the real action was—Cambridge, Massachusetts.

I had a job at Harvard with a higher salary and a longer contract (negotiated under threat of deserting to another Ivy League school) than the other assistant professors in the Department of Social Relations. I taught only one course and had a mammoth corner office, where I was protected from intruders by my own secretary in an outer office.

My book *Protest and Prejudice* had sold fifteen thousand copies and had been translated into Japanese. Various chapters had been reprinted in more than twenty books.[25]

Even when we want to play an "oppositional" role, our disciplines continue to operate within a system carefully designed to preserve what the sociologist Pierre Bourdieu calls "distinction," our symbolic distance from the people below us on the ladder of opportunity and cultural capital.[26] But this distance becomes glaringly obvious, as it does in Marx's narrative, only at the points of greatest tension between what we want to think about ourselves and what we actually do. Although Marx wrote a dissertation on political insurgency, he completed his research with the aid of highly competitive fellowships; although he sided with landless peasants, he cut a sharp deal with Harvard; although he argued for cooperation and equality, he beat out his colleagues in the fight for a big office. I cannot help but think of another Marx, shut out of the academy, hounded across the English channel and living in London as his children died from illnesses that he lacked the money to treat. But to dismiss *Gary* Marx's behavior as hypocrisy is to miss the essential point. Sociologists can write the most scathing critiques, or they can take on the more conventional role of Parsonian apologists for the status quo, but in either case they often leave unchallenged—and unchanged—the basic relations of productive life, including the production of knowledge itself.

As the historian Samuel Haber observes, the modern professions in America grew up along with the industrial economy as a reaction to the social leveling that followed the decline of the old elites.[27] For a brief period at the end of the nineteenth century, one kind of labor had begun to look very much like every other kind, but in response to this leveling, doctors and lawyers, engineers and college teachers drew on the older ideology of "station" to create another hierarchy: doctors no longer "did work," they had a "profession." Yet the price that doctors paid for their privilege— ostensibly, if not always in fact—was a life of unstinting service to the very people they perceived as their social inferiors. Things are no longer so simple, though, if they ever were. While Haber identifies the *origins* of the professions, his findings do not help us understand how the professions operate today, when their power no longer relies, as it once did, on the persistence of organic communities and the social contract they once preserved. Gary Marx, after all, sounds less like a country doctor than a famous film director or a legal top gun. Students and colleagues may have learned important things from his work, but no one benefited from that work quite as tangibly as Marx himself, and we need to consider why.

One account of the professions today would place them, over their protests perhaps, in the context of the "information society," where they represent a segment of the larger class of "knowledge workers." As another sociologist, Bernice Martin, has observed, this new class "stands structurally between the owners of capital and the proletariat," above whom the new class has raised itself, not by means of its knowledge only but also by its expertise: its capacity, that is, to generate novel *kinds* of knowledge, virtually nonstop. Within premodern societies, the learned man was typically the master of information valued for its immunity to change; one had to know Plato, Aristotle, Greek and Roman grammar and rhetoric. Today, however, the value of knowledge rapidly decays once the luster of its novelty has dimmed. For this reason, the power of the knowledge class lies in the production of *estrangement* or existential emptiness rather than in the preservation of stability—in the "ability to assemble a bricolage of . . . symbols into customized packages that are in some sense [perpetually] unique."[28] Advertising operates along quite similar lines, so that Ralph Lauren never simply sells a line of towels but manufactures an entire artificial world combining shirts and towels, ties and drapes, to evoke nineteenth-century Nantucket or Sante Fe in the spring. And this new economy of bricolage may account, as well, for the dizzying succession of movements and schools, positions and counterpositions on parade at places like the annual conference of the Modern Language Association, where theory and its successors have long enjoyed preeminence. While we may someday discover that Ralph Lauren's publicists secretly get their ideas from Umberto Eco or Jacques Derrida, it seems more likely that the tidal wave of change has overtaken *us* in the humanities rather than the other way around. We have had to change our knowledge in order to "keep up." The truth be told, we could not have continued to rely *credibly* on knowledge of the older, pretheoretical sort—premised as it was upon the maintenance of tradition when "knowledge" everywhere else has come to mean the opposite: the new and transformative. Right now, apart from the students sitting in some English class, fewer than a hundred Americans are reading *Paradise Lost* or Daniel Dennett's latest book on consciousness; at the same time, 30 million people are probably using the Internet. Seventy million may be watching TV. Theory has been our answer to this predicament. What we have tried to gain, however, is not the open assent of a mass audience but the means of controlling popular culture from on high and from behind the scenes. Theory promised to deliver into our hands the hidden mechanisms that drive the mental life of the whole society.

    This attitude toward "the masses"—an attitide of contempt coupled with the aspiration to unilateral control—is altogether typical of the knowledge class as Bernice Martin has described it, but nowhere does the family resemblance become more evident than in our conflicted attitude toward teaching. For our predecesors at the close of the nineteenth century, the idea of a conflict between scholarship and teaching would have seemed almost unthinkable, precisely because they saw themselves as preservers of a culture they *shared* with the young men under their tutelage. By imbuing undergraduates with the sensibility of the Anglo-Saxon elite, our predecessors reinforced the boundary between the ruling class, sequestered on the campus green or else on their estates, and the swelling ranks of the great unwashed, more or less silently debarred. Today, we draw the boundary at a different place, but we still draw a boundary. We do so partly because the great unwashed have come inside the university itself—literally millions and millions of them—and partly because we ourselves no longer serve the same "custodial" function that our predecessors did. Consequently, we no longer set out to make all our students into younger versions of ourselves; rather, we create within the university the distinction that most matters in the world at large—between the knowledge experts and the laity.

Charles Sykes's notorious exposé *Profscam* is clearly wrong and unfair about many things, but he points to trends that simply make no sense unless the university has indeed given up on its earlier goal of passing on common values. These trends include the swelling ranks of "world class" faculty who seldom set foot in a lecture hall, and the burgeoning of quasi-independent research institutes throughout decades of rising tuitions and declining teacher-student ratios. Sykes notes that in 1986, fewer than two-thirds of the faculty at the University of Wisconsin did any teaching at all, while at the same time, the shortage of seats in required classes meant that the average student had to spend more than five years en route to a bachelor's degree. Irving Shain, the former chancellor at Wisconsin, told Sykes a story that might apply, with a few variations, to almost any field today. "In the beginning," Shain recalled, "every biology student got to disembowel a frog of his own." But "because of insufficient funds, the university had to cut back to one frog per class." Now they have "a movie of someone dissecting a frog and they show it over and over."[29] Compelling as this story seems—to me, anyway—I still think that we would be mistaken to accept Sykes's view that changes of this kind are primarily caused by the egoism of professors and the shortsightedness of deans. Rather, the decline of teaching points to the exclusionary character of the disciplines, whose power derives from their control of a specialized field and the things that define it, among them tenured positions, editorial boards, endowed chairs, and a body of primary material widely recognized as their property.

In an influential essay on the state of criticism, one preeminent literary theorist, Jonathan Culler, openly expresses about teaching what many people think but hesitate to say. While observing that fellow theorists like Stanley Fish and Robert Scholes have given their work a "pedagogical and democratic inflection," Culler represents their forays into pedagogy as distinctly "double-edged":

> For the most part, [the] appeal to teaching is a conservative, even reactionary gesture: the suggestion that thinking and writing about literature ought to be controlled by the possibilities of classroom presentation is usually an attempt to dismiss new lines of investigation or abstruse critical writing without confronting them directly. . . . Few would seriously suggest that physicists or historians should restrict their work to what can be communicated to 19-year-olds.[30]

Whatever one might think of Culler's priorities, he spells out with great precision the value system that obtains in the humanities today, if not at every college and public university, then certainly in the preeminent schools that send quantities of newly minted Ph.D.s across the continent. And yet, to argue against theory for the sake of teaching is still to misjudge the professional terrain, just as Marshall Gregory does when he writes, in the *ADE Bulletin,* about the mismatch between his training and his day-to-day professional life:

> As a student deeply immersed in nineteenth-century British studies and literary criticism, I certainly expected at the end of my doctoral labors to be effortlessly translated, like Enoch, into a higher kind of academic heaven-haven, levitated up and out of my library carrel at Chicago . . . and gently lowered into another library carrel at good old Research U, presumably in a beautiful city with a good symphony and affordable housing.

Gregory goes on to say that none of his professors at Chicago "ever suggested to me the reality that I would find in [an actual] classroom, much less helped me to prepare for it."[31] But Gregory fails to appreciate that the system is working *properly* when it generates this contradiction, just as the system works properly when students leave English 101 and never write again, or when they finish college without having learned where Paraguay is, or when they wake up on the morning of their graduation wondering what in the world they can do with a degree in history, besides, that is, managing a Wendy's and wishing they were back in their medieval seminar. While it is certainly true that our current system of "public" education furnishes the professions with a venue for the recruitment and training of new members, the primary purpose of a course like "The Baroque" or "Introduction to Epistemology" is not to disseminate expert knowledge but to ensure lay support for further specialized inquiry. The point is not to produce three or four hundred additional colleagues every semester—an economic disaster for any profession—but to persuade another generation of nonspecialists that the subject properly belongs to someone else.

Yet the worst casualties of this division of cultural labor may not be the students but those of us who teach them, to the degree that our lives as professionals have been shaped as decisively by our isolation as by our structural privilege. If my own experience is typical, the first lesson we have learned on the path to the Ph.D. is the obligation to play a role cut off from the worlds outside the university, since we share these mundane worlds with nonspecialists, while our knowledge is supposed to reinstate the crucial distinction between unreflecting experience and the quasi-transcendental insight that flows from detached and disciplined reflection. So completely have we come to presuppose that understanding and estrangement go hand-in-hand that even a person like the critic Edward Said, though a tireless upbraider of professional isolation, still celebrates the intellectual's state of "homelessness" as a mark of ethical superiority.[32] It seems to me, however, that academics cannot afford to take for granted their ethical advantage.

At a moment in our history when many observers have commented on the accelerating breakdown of communities and the spreading mood of cynicism, we need to ask if learning as we now imagine it helps to strengthen our students' sense of agency and self-worth while replenishing the fragile sources of compassion and mutual aid. Or have our preoccupations actually served to discredit local ways of life on behalf of the new and steeply hierarchical knowledge society? Positioned at the

threshold between the specialists and the laity, teachers of undergraduate humanities might begin to explore these questions by openly acknowledging the divided
character of their own situation. Nothing could be less helpful, in my view, than to
embrace once again an image of academic intellectuals as representatives of "Culture" on the one hand or "the People" on the other. Instead, we need to understand
that the triumph and persistence of theory, like the call to "revive" books in an age of
television, is symptomatic of a widening gap between the concerns of elites who
produce what counts as humanistic knowledge—the Marxist Fredric Jameson and
the conservative Gertrude Himmelfarb *both* belong to this new elite—and the needs
of those to whom this knowledge gets parceled out. Precisely because I believe, as
John Dewey did, that a knowledge made for others is no knowledge at all, I want
my students to use the work of specialists to complicate their own self-understanding, but I also want those students to preserve an attitude of profound skepticism toward the authorities whose job it is, no matter what the ideology of the day
might be, to turn out properly tractable subjects.[33]

Of course, humans do not live by skepticism alone. The case can be made that
the most important social changes of our time are not taking place inside the
academy, but in the private lives of women and men who have begun to explore new
and uncoercive forms of interaction—as couples, families, support groups, "salons,"
and congregations—and in our courses we too might explore interactions of this
same uncoercive kind. That these experiments are still largely confined to the
private sphere only shows how far the so-called public sphere—the classroom
perhaps most glaringly of all—has to go before it might be regarded as "democratic"
in any credible sense. And yet the openness that people have begun to pursue in their
private lives they increasingly expect in the public sphere as well.[34] The enormous
popularity of Bernie Siegel, a physician who supports patients in their desire for
more active control over their own medical treatment, testifies to a significant
change in popular attitudes toward the system of professions.[35] Since medicine has
set the pace throughout the past century for all the other kinds of expertise, we may
have some small reason to be hopeful. But whether academic intellectuals, who have
historically marched in the rear guard, will support a more equitable distribution of
cultural power remains an open question. Labor reform, women's suffrage, and the
civil rights movement—achievements the academy would like to take the credit
for—each took root far from the campus and long before academics snatched them
up as badges of honor. Yet in deciding where to place our loyalties, professors should
remember that they have choices other than the two most obvious ones: continuing
the legacy of theory or else turning in their resignations. If they want to start playing
a different role, then perhaps they need to make a different kind of knowledge.

What this different kind of knowledge might concretely look like is the
subject of the next chapters, but my own profession's history may provide some
preliminary clues. English in the bad old days was elitist without apology, but its
faculty developed a culture of teaching designed to instill a *felt* sense of being at
home in the world, a sense quite unlike the nervous style of our own times, with its
penchant for abstraction, self-doubt, and critique. No matter how much smarter our
work appears when we set it beside the amateurish scholarship of an earlier day, our

knowledge is no more egalitarian—and in fact, it may prove much less amenable than theirs to any future culture of democracy. For all its truly vicious blindnesses, and I scarcely wish to downplay them here, the sensibility of our predecessors had its foundation in their class's claim to agency or freedom as a natural right, a claim I regard as spurious not because such freedom is illusory but because those men retained it for themselves alone. What would happen, however, if we now set out to revive the "aristocratic" sense of the world as home while repudiating its exclusiveness? Wouldn't such an undertaking need to start where theirs did long ago: that is, with an attention to emotional, sensuous life, because our thinking and our acting have their origins in this crucial source? Or, to put my question just a little differently, at a time when knowledge rather than force of arms has become *the* instrument of domination, won't a democratic counterknowledge need to take root deep beneath the barren surface of "the text"?

About ten years ago, a friend of mine, a physicist and astronomer, had flown from New Jersey to Flagstaff for the most important moment in his professional life. Many times at the start of his career he had applied for a week on a telescope in the hills, and then, once a panel had accepted his request, he patiently waited almost two more years before his special moment arrived. By then, of course, other things had a happened to him: marriage and a child, and the slow and painful struggle for publication. Now the decision on his tenure was coming up. He was buying a house and he worried about that; he had done some good research, but he had doubts about his future. Still, the moment, *his* moment, was about to occur, and when it did, everything would take place as he had planned. To his amazement, though, absolutely nothing did. The weather turned bad; he waited. It got worse, and he waited, and he kept waiting until his five days were gone.

Along with his clothing and some technical notes, my friend took several novels and a book of poems—to read, he supposed, while the data came pouring in. But now that there would be no data at all, he leafed through the anthology and tried to find a passage that could put his mind to rest. The tension throbbed like a thousand volts through his chest and arms, but he found one poem that switched the current off. And the two lines of the poem that brought him the deepest calm were the ones he remembers even now. They were lines almost every English major knows, about "the still point of the turning world . . . The inner freedom from the practical desire."[36] It was a poem about the tyranny of time, read by a man whose time was literally running out.

It goes without saying, however, that the way my friend spoke about T. S. Eliot's poem was not the way most critics handle poetry today. The salient features of a poem, they might insist, have no more to do with the reader's world—with his perennial fears and his immediate desires—than they do with the poet's own intentions. Those of us in English might say instead that what matters most is a poem's place within a *system* of conventions and codes—the same system within which we ourselves think our thoughts and look out at the world. The poem is a text and the world is a text, and even you and I are ensembles of texts, each of which keeps getting refigured in an endless circulation of signs and tropes. Granted, one reader might bring to the poem certain memories and feelings quite unlike another reader's; still, the theorist's appropriate concerns cannot lie with the particulars of an individual response but with the discursive constraints that define how everyone will respond more or less.

Yet something gets lost when we travel with these critics, something essential to much more than poetry. As a person who has never cared for Eliot, I have probably read *Four Quartets* fifteen times without finding solace in his rather bloodless evocation of the still point in a turning world. Other readers, I know, feel quite differently, among them my friend the physicist. But this distinction is precisely the one that gets lost in the flattening of our world into a text—the distinction between my friend's experience of the poem and my lack of any such experience. What gets lost in the semiotic universe is the crucial distinction between "codes" or "signs," which simply "signify," and the living words that foster a "felt" resonance between ourselves and the world.

The poem, we might say, "spoke" to my friend: for him, it had a certain resonance. But what does it mean for words to resonate? One reason why no answer lies ready at hand may be that our thinking about words has grown mechanistic and impersonal on the model of a science, as though people can never think reliably except at an enormous distance from their sensations and emotions. I find it more than slightly ironic, though, that with all our attention to structures and codes, conventions and tropes, the *real* sciences keep telling us simple things we seem unwilling to hear. Many paleoarchaeologists now believe that language did not arrive on the scene at a single juncture in our prehistory, but gradually developed, as all forms of human culture have, through endless interactions with our habitat, renewed and refined over thousands of years. Yet the prehistory of humankind is something more than the idyllic narrative of our gradual "adaptation." Language and culture begin, we are now told, with a *shift* of habitat—out of the trees and down onto the plains—a shift so drastic that it forced a fundamental change in almost everything we did: how we stood, how we moved, how we slept, even how we dreamed, perhaps.[37] Our language and our culture start, in other words, as responses to human *suffering*. And although they enable us to transform the world—through the use of tools, for example—they primarily enable us to transform ourselves.

But even to say this is still to remain under the spell of semiotic idealism, because many of the changes that language brings about occur on a level the "linguistic turn" cannot even start to address. So long as our language remains routine—*only* an array of "codes" and "signs"—its essential character is concealed from us, but when words begin to resonate, we undergo a bodily and emotional transformation. To be insulted, to be caught in an error or in a lie, to hear unexpectedly that a loved one has died, is to *feel* intensely even before we are able to *understand* exactly what has happened. Your face flushes, your eyes water, your heartbeat picks up, the muscles in your stomach clench and unclench. We have all been carefully trained to dismiss these reactions as incidental to the dynamics of "textuality," but signification cannot occur without an experiential anchoring, since we know and remember only what has changed our lived relations to the world.

Such change can assume a negative form, as in the heightened sense of pain produced by the experience of challenge or frustration. Or, as in the case of my friend, change can produce that attunement with the world—that sense of connection—to which we give the name of pleasure.[38]

The roots of language lie in suffering, as I said, but the roots of the self lie in attunement and release. Our conviction that the self is enduring and real—is more than an ensemble of random events—depends on our ability to move past suffering, not once but again and again. It can scarcely be an accident, I think, that psychotics are often the childhood victims of a violence that fragments the self so completely there will never be a lasting synthesis. Nor is it merely coincidence that people who endure prolonged physical pain are often at a loss to describe their personal history, not because they have repressed it but because meaning follows from our felt connections with things—connections that intense pain erodes and erases. Several years before his suicide, the novelist Primo Levi recalled that the occupants of the concentration camp where he was imprisoned were exposed to such relentless pain that escape and resistance had become unthinkable: the world itself had vanished from their horizon of consciousness.[39] It is only through our journeys out of suffering into pleasure that each us can become a self. And it is only through these journeys toward coherence in ourselves that we can move beyond the self, as when a baby finds its parents' presence "transferred" to a blanket or a favorite toy.[40] Repeated many hundreds, many thousands, of times, the transition from the parent to the blanket, and then from the blanket to the home and neighborhood, weaves together unconnected places and events into a coherent "life-world," a place where memory, resonance, meaning, and ultimately love become ever-present possibilities.[41]

If the body, and not language, is the source of the self and the doorway into the living world, it is also the ground of all conviviality. With a spinal tumor blocking more and more of the signals sent from his arms and legs to his brain, the anthropologist Robert Murphy described his loss of motor functions as a "deepening silence." "As my body closes in upon me," he wrote, "so also does the world. . . . To fall quietly and slowly into total paralysis is much like either returning to the womb or slowly dying. . . . This growing stillness of the body invades one's apprehension of the world . . . and I must continually fight the tendency for this growing passivity to overcome my thoughts." But "there is," Murphy adds, "a perverse freedom" in "such a deep quietude."[42] Regrettably, this freedom is the only one that we in the "radical" academy now seem to recognize. But are we really so radical? Our desire to live amid "free-floating signifiers" has a history that predates Derrida and Lacan. Plato inaugurates philosophy in the West by denouncing the senses as inimical to knowledge, which he equates with an abstract order that dissolves the knower's individual identity. But the era of theory ushers in a different and postmodern form of otherworldly knowledge, one that offers us a multitude of "subject positions" while persistently subverting their embodiment. We have many, many different *roles* but increasingly, no *selves* because the formation of a self requires that our actions help to sustain a continuity between the present and past, feeling and thought.

There may be, however, a continuity of a still deeper and broader kind, overlooked when we start with the assumption that the text gives shape decisively to all of our interactions with the world. What are we to make, for instance, of music? We could always speak of it as another language, but the language of music clearly works in ways quite different from the languages we speak and read. While fair-minded people can be counted on to admit that musicians express *something* when they play, what in fact gets expressed is processed by many different portions of our brains and not primarily by those that process language. In response to music, patterns of brain activity are not only the same across cultures but even across species. Recent studies point to striking similarities between the brain responses of humans and whales, especially activity in the limbic system, the most "primitive" area of the brain. Perhaps the "primitive" source of our responses explains why music influences how we think, feel, and see, as well as how we hear. Given the appropriate accompaniment, a banal scene in a movie can brim with pathos; moments potentially tragic can strike a listener as absurd. We might speculate that music has this effect because it structures feeling more deeply than words: we might even speak of music as the language of feeling.[43]

And then, too, we have painting and sculpture. In the creative process of many visual artists, the language of words typically plays a peripheral role, when it plays any role at all, and many artists describe their process of creation as a matter of suspending the desire to explain. Although academic critics have convinced us that the work of art conveys a verbal meaning or commentary, the truth is that the painting or sculpture always *says* just what it *is*. This is why, of course, artists often leave their works untitled, and why Picasso, among countless others, could insist that "people who try to explain pictures," as he put it, "are barking up the wrong tree."[44] If the visual arts speak to us in some sense, they do so in the language of color and shape, texture and rhythm. But my use of the word *language* here is metaphoric. Needless to say, the word *red* can never be red, unless we actually print it in red ink; the word *rough* can never be rough, or *dark* truly dark.

What holds true for these arts holds true for science as well, unlikely as that may seem. While no one would dispute that scientists rely on the written word, the practice of science places language and the senses into conflict with each another, in order to revise the image of "reality" that language holds in place. If the inquiries that scientists undertake really were linguistically determined through and through, then experiments would be superfluous, just as medieval philosophers supposed. Instead, the research done by scientists has expanded and reshaped language itself, often in quite radical and unforeseeable ways, as words like *quark* and concepts like *chaos* demonstrate. This revision of language by experiment has even reached the point that some fields now arrive at conclusions that strain against the limits of expressibility: physics tells us, for example, that the universe is finite but unbounded, that certain objects have mass but no weight, and that single, moving particles can travel in more than one direction at a time. While those of us in English might shore up our self-esteem by replying that the basis of the sciences—mathematics—qualifies as a language too, it comes closer to a language of images than of words, a language of pure forms and relationships.

The language of the text is just one part of a more complex expressive universe sustained by all our senses and by our various forms of intelligence—

emotional, aesthetic, spatial, linguistic, and so on. And the place where they converge phenomenologically is the body, which we should not make the mistake of reducing to the corporeal body alone—the hands I see in front of me, the skin I feel, and so on—since the body extends well beyond the skin into the sensible world. And at its center, the body is unperceivable, always deeper than the conscious awareness that the body itself orchestrates. We might, in turn, understand both science and the arts as traditions of "orchestration," each with its respective limits but each drawn by the promise of connection with things. Our words come alive—become embodied—when they help us to realize this promise; when they help in their way to harmonize our many different forms of contact with the world. But so long as we disparage any of these forms of contact, or insist on the subordination of one form to another, we forestall the convergence that gives language and culture their living force. I scarcely need to add that the privileging of particular forms of contact corresponds to the privileging of particular people over others, as the metaphor of the "body politic" implies. To be raised above others in this way is not without its costs. Inequality produces isolation, for example. If the rise of theory is a symptom of the humanities' isolation from the larger society, it also reflects the disciplines' isolation from one another, intellectually as well as institutionally. While a reuniting of the *faculties* in both senses of that word may not produce utopia exactly, we can be sure that just as the reign of the text has had far-reaching consequences, so too would a greater continuity.

Continuity, of course, is troublesome; continuity makes people far less tractable than they might otherwise be, and so it seems imperative that we ask ourselves if the humanities have a vested interest in the current, disconnected status quo. Whether the venue is an essay by Judith Butler or an advertisement for Guess jeans, isn't the logic unnervingly similar? Each encounter with the text underscores the reader's lack, the learner's insufficiency—his mistaken belief in personal agency, her failure to be thin and tall enough. And this failure, this lack, initiates an ordeal of involuntary change that never leads us back to a still point in the turning world, but only, once again, to a sense of insufficiency. As the philosopher Susan Bordo maintains, social power in our time often operates by colonizing the self, first evacuating and then reconstructing it, as we see in mass pathologies like anorexia nervosa.[45] The eighteen-year old girl who learns from the ad that she looks somehow wrong can stick a finger down her throat five times a day. But a similar dynamic may be at work when a frightened student or a younger colleague feels compelled to talk the current theory talk. In both cases, the novice learns to accept a condition like the one that Murphy describes, in which the world sustained by experience withdraws. Night might be day; right be left, with everything displaced and put *sous rature,* under erasure, à la Derrida. Under these conditions, however, texts no longer speak to us. Instead, they insist that we permit ourselves to "be spoken"—as Gadamer once claimed approvingly and as I once believed. They actually demand that we *remake ourselves* in conformity with the project of the theorist. And our reward for submitting to this painful regimen is seldom the renewal of connections to actual others, the people we happen to know in daily life. Don't we learn, instead, to serve an anonymous "they"?: for the graduate student, something called "the profession";

for the anorexic girl, an admirer in whose radiant gaze she will be real at last. When a baby turns to the blanket as a surrogate for a parent's arms, the transitional object works because the blanket provides a *genuine* satisfaction—a continuity in the baby's felt life. But in the culture of postmodernity, the objects of desire almost never culminate in a concrete satisfaction for *us;* instead, they feed a thoroughly commodified social self whose needs become more pressing than the needs of our own bodies, as every person knows who works twelve-hour days for the sake of rewards as intangible as "reputation" and "career."

But think, if you will give yourself the freedom to, about the different kinds of pleasure that people get from their most mundane involvements with the world— watching leaves shake in the hot summer wind, listening to the sound of rain, tracing the smooth, wet curve of a child's spine with the palm of a soapy hand. And think, if you can stand it, about all the essays written ten or fifteen years ago that began by "deconstructing the subject," or that called themselves "archaeologies"; or all the dissections of "cinematic gaze" that open with a summary of the "mirror stage." The authors of these works are not simply sycophants or opportunists. To write in this way is to *become* Derrida, to *become* a second Foucault or a little Lacan. In the same way, Madonna's fans dress like Madonna, walk and talk like her, and read books about her life.

I see it as crucial to recognize, though, that these practices of impersonation are not new to the academy. Well before the present postmodern interlude, scholars made their reputations, as many still do now, by writing themselves into the lives of their great man. The Beckett specialist somehow became his incarnation; the Stevens scholar learned to speak in Stevens' voice. The time has come to acknowledge that academic literacy, at least as we have constructed it so far, is deeply involved with the same culture of disembodiment that makes possible Elvis look-alikes and the stalking of the stars by their admirers, who cannot break free from obsession except by murdering their idealized alter egos. While we might prefer to dismiss as naïve all the people who watch movies like *Terminator 2,* we in the academy unknowingly share their fundamental orientation. No one goes to the theaters for emotional catharsis, as Aristotle thought the Athenians did, and no one could be more absurdly deceived than we are when we interpret the bad android's metamorphoses as signifying the protean character of late capitalism. The cultural force of film derives, instead, from the chance that it offers the viewer to become someone else—to leave behind everyday existence for an imaginary realm, and this is exactly what we do when we read poems as texts and not as speech addressed to us, commentaries on the conditions of our actual affairs.

Textuality is one way to know the world, but language does not become a text until we contemplate it from the standpoint of alienation. Language becomes text, I am trying to suggest, only after it has failed to correspond to the character of our lived worlds and then, instead of making changes in our actual lives, we autistically suppress the world itself. But when our words do their proper work by making the world more fully present to us, they disappear below the surface of consciousness, and their disappearance indicates that we have moved beyond our isolation. In an essay on the Western Apaches' sense of place, Keith Basso remembers learning from one old man that their landscape is everywhere made meaningful to them by a fabric of ancient narratives. "All these places have stories," the old man told him; and the stories, Basso learned, hold the Apaches' universe together, so tightly together that word and place can no longer be distinguished.[46] For the Apaches, stories bring about a fusion of horizons far more radical than the one that Gadamer describes, linking culture to nature and perception to shareable myths and histories.

But what future might such stories have in our society, where our Great Mystery is not the earth and its perennial rhythms but the frenzy of exchange? People who find themselves at home in the world are typically poor consumers, and the academy needs to sell *ideas* just as Detroit sells cars and Fifth Avenue sells clothes. Deferral and displacement, *différance* and the endless play of signs—this is not how things really are but how things seem in a society where domination takes the form of control over access to the world itself. It should come as no surprise that the postmodern condition resembles nothing so much as Robert Murphy's mental state in the last months of his life. "Given the magnitude of this assault on the self, it is," he wrote, "understandable that [a] major component of the subjective life of the handicapped is anger."[47] And if anger is, as some might say, the prevailing mood within the academy, it is also the ruling passion of our society as a whole (with the possible exception of greed). To pursue attunement, to renew emotional coherences, is not simply to challenge the existing order, but to help fashion an alternative.

For all the radical academy's celebrations of resistance and revolt, no alternative is more revolutionary than our resistance to disembodiment and the pursuit of wholeness in our immediate experience. But how might such a wholeness lie within our reach, when theory and critique have unmistakably become the preeminent forms of knowledge in our time, as highly valued by Peter Drucker, the Wall Street savant, as they are by neo-Marxists like Etienne Balibar?[48] If theory and critique free us from nothing finally, and even contribute to a routinizing of expression unparalleled in our history, then perhaps the way out lies in a domain that the linguistic turn has caused us to overlook: I mean the domain of the arts, understood not as the cunning lies told by oppressors, nor as the property of specialists whose goal is technical virtuosity, but as traditions of attunement with the world, available to everyone everywhere though nowadays diligently suppressed.

"Art" as I want to define it here is what the political scientist James Scott calls a "weapon of the weak."[49] Far from enticing us to overlook contradiction, practices that rise to the level of an art respond to cognitive dissonance by taking us beyond ourselves and back into the world. Initially, this movement can feel like a loss, as when a writer seems to drop the thread of her argument or when a painter's subject, so long looked upon, suddenly becomes unseeable. What disappears, however, is not the world, but the constructions—the established ways of seeing—that prevent us from embracing it, as it is right now. This is why, perhaps, great artists have so often claimed to break free from conventions of every kind. "No theories! Only works," Cézanne wrote in his dairy. "Theories corrupt" the "shimmering chaos" that "we are."[50] And this is why, perhaps, art as an activity has been so thoroughly suppressed—*especially* in academic postmodernity—because it unfolds in an open space that no one can own or close down.

Regrettably, that open space is not the one in which professors tend to do their work. Anyone can see this when he contemplates the testing empire of the Educational Testing Service (ETS) and the new alliances of schools and industry, as can anyone who thinks about the sophisticated inertia of our professions and the spread of electronic media that encourage mass passivity. Anyone can see, in other words, that our society is unprepared to value Cézanne's shimmering chaos over the steady light of instrumental certainty. But whether we like reading by that dull gray light or not, there is a violence at the heart of our society, where the powerlessness of the many sustains the power of the few. And in the absence of any real alternatives, this violence will continue to overturn every kind of knowledge that we manage to devise, Platonic truth as well as deconstructive play. What our society needs most urgently is not another theoretical "advance"—toward some new critical gimmick called "grammatography," let's say, or "psycho-dialectical" materialism—but a better understanding of the practices through which everyone might enter the open space where Cézanne felt himself at home. Yet, in order to discover and protect such practices, the humanities will need to undergo a change more profound than many people might like. Cézanne's art was alive because he placed it at the center of a still larger art of living, and we can neither rediscover nor sustain what he achieved unless we become students of *experience*. When I say "students of experience" I do not mean armchair readers of the "social text," but scholar/teachers committed to discovering how people actually *feel*. Asking this, we can begin to imagine what a culture might look like when it no longer serves the purpose of domination. Far from bringing the humanities to a dismal close, the search for practices of human freedom might give us the future we have never had, a future outside the university.

7

World without End

Criticism or Creation in the Humanities?

When people outside the university think of the humanities, they still commonly imagine them as a creative enterprise. They remember "great artists" like Leonardo, Shakespeare, and Beethoven as visionaries who enlarged the range of human experience. More and more, however, people working in the humanities see their own tradition in a somewhat different light, not as essentially creative but as critical. Eighty years ago, when professors, sometimes even in the sciences, might be novelists and poets on the side, it was still possible to conceive of scholarship as an *interpretive* act: like the artist or the poet, the scholar was obliged to assemble or combine things in original ways. But now, the paradigm of knowledge as interpretive, which had its sources in the culture of the fine arts, has given way to the quasi-scientific paradigm of knowledge as criticism. If, as I maintain in the previous chapter, we have become the prisoners of theory, then we have also become prisoners of a critical role that is as sterile as it is spellbinding. The way out of our confusion, I'm convinced, begins with a something like a counterspell, a disenchantment of the practice of critique itself. Far from offering a cure to our infirmities, critique is actually the illness.

Just now I described the current humanities as quasi-scientific because they have set out to discover laws of meaning comparable to the laws of physics or chemistry. For many academics, "criticism" properly describes the rigorous study of the codes, signs, and signifying systems that they regard as the atoms or molecules of cultural life. While it is true that some critics working in this tradition have challenged the objectivity of science itself by "unmasking" its allegiance to particular values and traditions, we might understand this practice of unmasking as an effort to beat the sciences at their own game. After all, when a critic of science finds a masculine bias in articles describing the "penetration" of a "passive" egg by a "mobile" sperm, the critic's discovery lays claim—at least tacitly—to the same status held by the argument that water is really H_2O.[1] Both of these arguments, the one for H_2O and the one for a male bias in research on reproduction, offer accounts that the reader is supposed to understand as more rigorous if not also more real than the thinking of the average person: ostensibly, the sexist bias is *really* there.

The rigorous character of criticism in our time has freed it from the charge that the whole enterprise is little more than opinion, egoism, or propaganda passed off as genuine knowledge. In the humanities' long rivalry with the sciences, they appear to have gained a second wind, almost a second life. Yet criticism differs from the sciences in at least two crucial and quite damaging respects. First, by its very nature, criticism is reactive, having to content itself with evaluation after the fact, while ceding to others the fashioning of fresh ideas and the building of new institutions. Second, criticism remains firmly tied to a much older view of "contemplation" as distinct from, and superior to, real-world activity.[2] We might say that criticism is like a science that leaves experiments to others, turning its vast erudition and energy to a skeptical reading of the lab reports.

Perhaps the most telling example of this reactive and world-evading tendency is the case of deconstruction. Thirty years after Derrida's work first made its appearance in the English-speaking world—and with a little help from Woody Allen—people who have never heard of "grammatology" now speak about "deconstructing" whatever or whomever they happen not to like. Of course, Derrida took pains to distinguish de-*construction* from merely *destructive* criticism.[3] As he describes it, deconstruction presupposes that in every conflict, the two sides or "binaries" actually create and sustain one another. There are, in short, no "clean hands," no positions finally detachable from counterpositions. The point, then, is not to avoid "error" but to see both members of the binary from some alternative perspective. Instead of destroying a belief, the deconstructionist *transvalues* it by giving that belief a new place in a network of relations and meanings, often with an eye to past inequality and injustice. But as Derrida's own voluminous output demonstrates, the real-world consequences of deconstruction are rather hard to pin down. When the deconstructing ends, what exactly has gotten done? By destabilizing long-established binaries, the deconstructionist might be "creative" in a certain restricted sense—he or she might add something new, that is, to the range of available alternatives—but Derrida's signature gambit in reply to my admittedly unfriendly question would be to deconstruct my basic contrast between "the critical" and "the creative." He might point out that in order to argue for a more "creative" enterprise, I already need to launch a critique of my own, a critique, at least, of him.

As always with Derrida, his thrust would be impossible to parry: no matter what position one argues for, it can always be shown to depend on—and to be contaminated by—the position one wishes to argue against. The "natural" can be shown to be an inescapably human value; "nonviolence" must exclude violence violently. But by proceeding in this fashion, by deconstructing my key terms, what would Derrida have concretely accomplished? Quite possibly, the answer is nothing at all, if accomplishing something means transforming the character of actual life. (I can already foresee a deconstruction of this last phrase, "actual life.") It seems to me that Derrida tries to solve problems that are institutional, cultural, economic, or psychological by means of purely semantic innovations. Even the most brilliant deconstructions of the "black"/"white" racial opposition, for example, have left virtually unchanged the social *fact* that many blacks and whites in America still see themselves as blacks and whites and still constitute "two nations" economically and culturally, just as the sociologist Andrew Hacker has contended.[4] Ultimately, deconstruction may change nothing other than words—and not even words in common parlance outside the graduate seminar room.

Nevertheless, in an institution like the university, which rewards the rapid production of books, articles, and talks, the longstanding appeal of deconstruction should be obvious: semantic changes, after all, are the easiest ones to mass-produce within the Ph.D. machine. But deconstructive criticism has had at least two powerful rivals in our time, although they each lead us down the same cul-de-sac. The first of these is the German Marxist tradition of "critical theory," which seeks to lay bare the subtle workings of capitalist ideology. In what might be the single most powerful statement of this entire tradition, *Negative Dialectics,* Theodor Adorno raises the practice of critique to genuinely metaphysical heights.[5] Arguing that every affirmative claim without exception is complicit in an encompassing structure of inequality and deceit, Adorno insists that nothing short of a relentless debunking of all so-called truths will usher in the Marxist millennium. At the same time, we must quash our vestigial longings for "affirmative culture"—by which Adorno means commitments of some more worldly kind. Unlike many deconstructionists, critical theorists still believe in an ultimate, knowable reality, although they hold that the nature of this reality will become clear to us only at the end of a long historical struggle. Until the culmination of that struggle, we must continue working to expose the gaps between our gratifying images of the status quo and the grinding inequities they conceal.

The other great rival to deconstruction is the tradition launched by Michel Foucault, who began his career as a voice in the antipsychiatry movement of the 1960s. Following his early research on the social history of "madness," Foucault turned to the study of other institutions organized (or so he thought) in ways comparable to the mental hospital, especially the prison. What Foucault claims to discover in all of these institutions is a common strategy for covert domination: while appealing to reason and the general welfare, elites in the modern world have surreptitiously managed to achieve a near-total control over the populace. Although Foucault in his later work becomes more hopeful about the possibilities for resistance to these controlling elites, he continues to promote anarchistic resistance and subversion as the ethical positions most appropriate to the intellectual's vocation, although Foucault would never have defended himself on ethical grounds, since he famously refused to commit to any quasi-universal principles or programmatic political objectives.[6]

In the humanities for the last two decades or so, Derrida, Adorno, and Foucault have ascended to the heights formerly reserved for the great philosophical system builders like Rousseau, Locke, Kant, and Hegel. And as thinkers—original and prolific—they are certainly without peer in the last half of the twentieth century. Yet despite the brilliance of their work, they might still be profoundly mistaken about the value of the adversarial role each of them has largely chosen to play, a choice which makes it hard to see how their ideas might eventually contribute to some enduring social enterprise. A Foucauldian university? A government on the principles of negative dialectics? A deconstructive ethics? Though Derrida keeps trying to develop one, a truly deconstructive ethics would still need at least one transcendental term—one thing beyond critique—if only "deconstruction" itself.[7] Even for those of us who want our flights of speculation cut free from the nagging pressure of reality, the otherworldiness of our major intellectual traditions today might well give us pause. I want to argue in the following chapter that the humanities' embrace of criticism and critique is another consequence of the bureaucratization of culture—in fact, the single most destructive consequence. Not only has the triumph of critique diminished the humanities by misrepresenting a universal capacity, the capacity to understand the world, as the purview of a tiny intelligentsia, but it reinforces the corrosive cynicism that now threatens to overtake our society— and a whole planet that increasingly follows our lead. What we might call the democratization of the humanities, their transformation into arts of living accessible to everyone, will not begin until we have freed ourselves from the illusion that criticism and critique are necessarily the best paths to the changes we wish to see.

I fully recognize how shocking, irresponsible, and even absurd this last statement must sound to many people now working in the humanities. They will respond that criticism alone has power to shatter the stultifying uniformity of "hegemonic" ways of thinking—capitalism, racism, classism, sexism, and so on. They will argue that because of their efforts, the university has become a more open, tolerant, and varied place than it was thirty years ago. But isn't it possible, instead, that the university's receptiveness to multiple cultures, values, and identities owes primarily to developments that our academic critics have done little or nothing to help along—in particular, the unparalleled growth in college admissions, which has opened our universities not only to Americans of every kind but also to college-age people across the globe. There are those who believe, however, that even if criticism did not *create* our current diversity, the predicament of multiple cultures now makes criticism indispensable. We still need it to keep things open to new perspectives, they say. But this is not the role that our academic critics have played. In reality, the triumph of criticism has created a tensely constricted atmosphere in which everyone feels vaguely accountable to the figures who call themselves "critics." And who can fail to notice that in our time, academic criticism has tried to extend its grasp far beyond poetry and novels into medicine, law, anthropology, popular culture, the hard sciences, and so on. Far from decentering authority, as it pretends, criticism looks distinctly imperialistic in its stultifying consensus and its aggressive seizure of new territory.

We should bear in mind, however, that the triumph of criticism and critique is not limited to the academic humanities, expressing as it does a more widespread confusion. Not only the humanities but virtually all the arts now valorize critique as their principal task. At least in part, this conception of the arts as fundamentally critical reflects their new and quite recent role as "professions" with distinctive forms of specialist knowledge—knowledge distanced from, and implicitly better than, the common sense on which ordinary people rely. If the various branches of the fine arts have had anything in common with one another for the last hundred years, it is their determined withdrawal from the rhythms and the values of everyday life. In the nineteenth century, a composer like Giuseppe Verdi could still take pleasure and pride in his popularity among Venetian gondoliers, who reportedly sang his librettos as they pushed their boats through the canals, but today, Top-Forty radio has become anathema to most "serious composers." In the same spirit, many contemporary writers and visual artists regard themselves as adversaries of a debasing "mass culture," which they tend to see as debasing precisely because of its popularity. We should recognize, however, that this withdrawal from the everyday world can go hand-in-hand with an aestheticizing of the mundane, an attitude not so different from the appropriation of African artifacts as examples of "l'art sauvage." While James Joyce, perhaps the novelist held in highest esteem by most English professors, devotes the whole of his masterpiece *Ulysses* to a day in the life of a small-stakes Dublin P.R. man, Joyce himself never wrote a book that a real-world person like Leopold Bloom might actually read. At the same time that *Ulysses* glorifies the ordinary, Joyce has taken extraordinary pains to keep it at an ironic and "artified" distance. It is not my purpose to speak ill of Joyce. I believe that he meant to write nothing less than a new *Divine Comedy,* a work that would reveal a hidden coherence beneath the apparent fragmentation of modernity. While admitting that modernity *looks* fragmented, Joyce points in *Ulysses* to a continuity of narrative form and symbolic image reaching back to the time of Homer. But the coherence that Joyce shows us remains hidden from everyone in the story he tells. Bloom, Stephen Dedalus, Molly, and all the rest live within an eternally recurring order of which they themselves remain wholly unaware, and in this regard, *Ulysses* expresses, perhaps despite its author's intentions, the typical modernist condescension toward the "lay" social actor.

We might speculate that the notorious difficulty of Joyce's masterpiece has something to do with the growing isolation of artists in general. Aesthetic or intellectual difficulty, in other words, is often an index of *social* distance, much as contempt typically arises from the fear of rejection. But the critical character of the humanities today may reflect a still more fundamental aspect of the modern world. It's worth remembering that even Joyce could not quite believe in the Homeric substructure of *Ulysses:* ever the ironist, he leaves us wondering if all the learned references are only a joke. And it is this inability, or unwillingness, to affirm anything unequivocally that prevented *Ulysses* from playing in its time the part the *Divine Comedy* played in Dante's. We might say that Dante imagined an order— with saints on high, no less—that he deeply wished to be true but recognized as nothing more than an expression of hope. But "hope" is too strong a word to describe Joyce's tongue-in-cheek references to Greek mythology: if anything, they heighten the reader's impression that modern life is absolutely absurd.

The significance of this disparity between Joyce and Dante can scarcely be overestimated. Until quite recently, as everyone knows, the West's major institutions still played a conserving role, engaging in a cautious dialogue with the forces of change. An institution like the university, for example, which stood firmly at the center of aristocratic culture, understood its task as the preservation of a "heritage," of "civilized" values, in the face of potentially reckless innovation—an arrangement that the educator and critic Matthew Arnold could still heartily endorse toward the close of the nineteenth century. In contrast to the Oxford don, however, the artist and the philosopher truly lived and worked on the margin, and in this way, as Nietzsche saw, such outsiders helped to "inoculate" society against potentially fatal disruptions.[8] One might argue that Dante played exactly this role—forcing people to ponder the contradiction between the way they actually lived and the tenets of the faith they supposedly revered. But what if Dante had described his Paradise as a late medieval version of Coney Island, with his angels dressed like 1930s Bowery bums? What if he had followed Beatrice from Purgatory while facetiously suggesting in a aside that she was, after all, something of a pious fool? Wouldn't a vision of this kind have functioned like a slow-acting poison instead of a vaccine?

In our time, the balance of cultural power between creation and criticism has shifted, with consequences no one can foresee. What does it mean, for example, that the writer of the following words has probably been read by practically every English major in America since the 1940s?: "Our nada who art in nada, nada be thy name, thy kingdom nada, thy will be nada in nada as it is in nada."[9] These words come from Ernest Hemingway's classic short story "A Clean, Well-Lighted Place," about the personal and social aftermaths of World War I. Official culture, we might say, now speaks in the voice of radical skepticism, while affirmative voices find the centers of authority less and less congenial. Even when Hemingway's words were first published in the 1920s, he had already made his way to the center of literary authority. It may true that Joyce, Hemingway's contemporary, had once lived in relative poverty while teaching for the Berlitz School in Trieste, but people in the know still understood that Joyce and a few others like Hemingway were indeed forging the "uncreated conscience of [their] race."[10] The conscience they were forging, however, was profoundly destabilizing. Even apologists for modernism have been prepared to admit—and to celebrate—this point: as Irving Howe once declared, modernity differs from earlier periods precisely because it repudiates the very notion of an official style or a normative order.[11]

This stance of repudiation is not simply a matter of literary style. Who can fail to notice the absence of a genuine conservative sensibility anywhere in the contemporary West? In the United States, for example, the so-called conservatives are at least as committed to a program of radical social transformation as their liberal counterparts. It was not the conservative philosopher Edmund Burke who inspired Newt Gingrich and the "Republican revolution" of 1996, but the right-wing futurist Alvin Toffler. To say simply, as some left-leaning critics have, that both the Democrats and the Republicans serve the interests of the marketplace is still to miss the essential point: even the radical left must appeal to an ideal that Paulo Freire, a Marxist educator, has described as "revolutionary futurity."[12] As Freire explains in his usual turgid prose, the "liberation" of "consciousness" enables people

> to apprehend [their] situation as an historical reality susceptible of transformation. Resignation gives way to the drive for transformation and inquiry, over which men feel themselves to be in control. If men, as historical beings necessarily engaged with other men in a movement of inquiry, did not control that movement, it would be (and is) a violation of men's humanity. . . . This movement of inquiry must be directed toward humanization—man's histor-

ical vocation. The pursuit of full humanity, however, cannot be carried out in isolation or individualism, but only in fellowship and solidarity.[13]

The truth is that the capitalists Freire inveighs against are no less committed to "transformation" than he is, though they value fellowship and solidarity somewhat less. If anything, capitalist societies have proven *more* receptive to "problemposing," as Freire calls innovative thinking, than their socialist counterparts. And like Freire, defenders of the "free-market system" are deeply committed to the idea that humankind has a "historical vocation," a destiny that requires a continuous labor of reform, undertaken by the whole population. These ideas are so widely shared in the modern world that it may seem odd to remember that people in ages past would never have grasped the idea of "humanization," the idea that people are not yet fully people, or that life is not yet fully life.[14] Although the classical societies of the Mediterranean and the Far East developed elaborate practices of self-cultivation, they perceived their efforts not as a way of becoming human, but as an expression of a human nature they already possessed—*dunamis* for the Greeks, *tao* for the Chinese, *dharma* for the societies of India. Traditional societies like these look back to a "Golden Age," as Plato did in his myth of Atlantis; and so, in a rather different way, did the medieval Christian, for whom the central event of his history, the death and Resurrection of Jesus, already lay in the past. For these people, the fulfillment of human life came from conformity to some ostensibly agreed upon "pattern of culture," in the anthropologist Ruth Benedict's famous phrase.

Of course, no sensibility could share less common ground than this one, not only with modernity in general but also with the humanities in our time. Surely no generation of humanists has placed greater faith than ours in the power of negativity, resistance, and subversion. Yet it seems to me that we might think more carefully than we have about the sources and the consequences of this faith. Clearly, the old world passed away for good reason, with its iron-clad customs and invidious taboos, and the death of that world has promised new freedom to nearly everyone— to exploited working people, to the hundreds of millions of the colonized, and to innumerable women trapped in lives of mute servitude. But has a true rebirth followed the passing of the old order—a renewal of vision and the power to act? Or has the rise of critical culture had the very opposite effect, widening the circle of despair and immobility? If, as I believe, the answer is "no" to the first question and "yes" to the second, then our critics have outlived their usefulness. Unthinkable as it might seem right now, the time has come for us to promote a different sort of activity, one much closer to the arts than to the critical "interrogation" of "texts." Here I want to press the case that criticism itself is not a neutral tool or a portable strategy, amenable to everyone everywhere, but an activity that belongs to an unhappy historical moment, and to a form of institutional power that has proven both destructive and profoundly inegalitarian. But I also want to argue that the humanities' own roots in the arts—which is first and foremost a legacy of making and doing—offer us the chance to assist in the birth of a genuinely new way of life. As I hope to show, the choice before us now is basically an ethical one, between the prestige of our academic professions, which we have tended to imagine as an aristocracy of the mind, and the welfare of our whole society. I believe that the society that values the participation of the many above the "excellence" of the few might discover once again the crucial freedom—the freedom, one might say, to make reality itself—that the reign of criticism has withheld from almost everyone.

So completely do we in the humanities now buy into the idealized image of "the critic" that even with our penchant for interminable self-reflection, we still tend to take that image at face value—so completely at face value that almost no one can say with much precision what criticism is, and is not. One influential American critic, Frank Lentriccia, has defined it as "the production of knowledge to the ends of power and, maybe, social change."[15] This is vague, to say the least, but among criticism's leading figures, the term has never ceased to transform itself from one sort of thing into another. Quoting Derrida in her famous introduction to *Of Grammatology,* Gayatri Spivak describes it as a way of "reading that *produces* rather than *protects*"—that dismantles "the metaphysical and rhetorical structures which are at work in [the text], not in order to reject or discard them, but to reinscribe them in another way."[16] A second deconstructionist, Paul de Man, had a slightly different take. For him, a "critical act of interpretation" is one that allows us to see "how . . . language always reproduces [a] negative movement" toward a confrontation with the "nothingness of human matters."[17] For the Marxist critic Fredric Jameson, criticism is the insurgent political act of connecting the particulars of language and culture with their determining but often unconscious sources in material life.[18] In a similar spirit, the disciples of Foucault understand criticism as the uncovering of what he calls a "positive unconscious of knowledge"—an uncovering, that is, of the struggles for institutional power that have shaped "discursive" knowledge.[19]

It seems obvious that for each of these critics, the word *criticism* means something quite unlike what the other critics mean, and from this I conclude that there is no inherently critical practice or state of consciousness. If we want to explain how so many different people can all travel under the same name, then we need to think less as philosophers and more as historians. Like the idea of "the artist," "the scientist," or "the businessman," the idea of "the critic" has a specific lineage, and one might credibly say that this lineage, in the English-speaking world at any rate, begins with Matthew Arnold's founding essay, "The Function of Criticism at the Present Time."

That Arnold has fallen from favor everyone in the academy knows. The same argument that for so long buoyed up his reputation now sinks him to the very bottom—the argument for "disinterestedness," for the "free play of the mind":

> It is because criticism has so little kept in the pure intellectual sphere, has so little detached itself from practice, has been so directly polemical and controversial, that it has so ill accomplished, in this country, its best spiritual work; which is to keep man from a self-satisfaction which is retarding and vulgarising, to lead him towards perfection, by making his mind dwell upon what is excellent in itself, and the absolute beauty and fitness of things.[20]

Any number of latter-day critics have heaped whole mountains of contempt on Arnold's effort, so frankly expressed in this passage, to avoid entanglement in affairs of a transient and partisan nature. Like the narrator in his famous poem "Dover Beach," the Arnoldian critic stands on the cliffs, somberly turned to the "darkling" plain "where ignorant armies clash by night." For critics now, however, Arnoldian repose looks more like a retreat. Today's critics *want* to leave the cliff and clash on the plain; they value controversy and polemic as instruments of freedom. Put simply, they see Arnold's brief for "disinterestedness" as an elitist attempt to denigrate liberating social ferment as morally disreputable and intellectually bankrupt. And because poor Arnold as a thinker often falls so far below his own standard of excellence—because his arguments often seem so thin and his evidence so flimsy— he has offered any number of our critics an irresistibly lumbering target.

But these scornful critics are his heirs, all the same, and the parts of his argument they want to leave in ruins are largely the extraneous parts. Ultimately, the agenda behind "The Function of Criticism" is not to justify the free play of the mind: free play is simply an alibi for something else—and that something else is the vocation of the critic as a social leader, indeed, as moral guide to the whole of British society from the Prime Minister on down. Without actually pointing fingers, Arnold makes it quite plain that *everyone* except the critic is more or less a Philistine, and that Philistines cannot be trusted to rule, not even to rule themselves. While it is true that Philistines have been successful—all those scientists, newspapermen, states- men, and lawyers, caught up in the hurley burley—they are still unfit, Arnold tells us, *precisely because of their success,* which he associates with a corrupting self- satisfaction. Clearly, Arnold walks a rhetorical tightrope in making this potentially explosive case: by praising the accomplishments of his readers, on the one hand, he tries to forestall their resentment at being criticized; on the other hand, he needs to convince them that they cannot—must not—trust their own hearts and minds.

But Arnold's argument is precarious in another and still more important regard. Why is it, after all, that in talking about the limitations of his age, Arnold makes *so much* of its successes, when he might instead have gestured to all the *failures* of Victorian society? It seems to me that pointing merely to these failures would not work for the purposes of his argument because *anyone* could recognize them easily. In order to justify the special authority of the critic, Arnold has to show that critics see something ordinary people cannot see. And that "something," as he defines it, is intangible: what the critic possesses is not knowledge per se but a critical sensibility, a disposition available only after special training. As he takes care to underscore several times, the critic's sensibility has nothing to do with competence in "the political, social, [or] humanitarian" spheres.[21] Instead, the critic speaks from a condition that those of us in English would now describe with such buzzwords as *marginality, otherness, border-crossing, alterity,* and so on, surprising as that may sound. In a later work, *Culture and Anarchy,* Arnold makes a case for the value of the crtic's task to society as a whole. Yet this value, however public and practical, still derives from the same "outsiderness" he attaches to the critic in "The Function of Criticism."[22] In a sense that Arnold never permits us to forget, the great achive- ments of art and letters stand above or beyond ordinary affairs: they serve as a transcendent pattern for society, not its mirror image. Otherwise they would not qualify as guides to "perfection."

As I have said, Arnold offers an easy target to those who have grown impatient, not only with life on the cliffs, but also with literature itself, and who now lay claim to "culture" in the broadest sense as their legitimate domain. Yet Arnold's detractors often seem to want it both ways: on the one hand, they still believe that the critic brings something to the discussion that the lawyer, the doctor, or the politician is simply unable to bring. But at the same time, these detractors reject Arnold's brief for "disinterestedness." If disinterestedness does not exist, however, then it's hard to imagine what the critic can offer that any other person cannot. One can denigrate the knowledge of the lawyer or the doctor or the diplomat as merely "instrumentalist" or practical; it's much harder to imagine what we in the humanities have to say about racism and the law, or about globalization, or about the future of the nation-state, without a great deal of "instrumental" knowledge. We might answer that the critic is different because the critic is a kind of perpetual amateur—a proposition I endorse—but in that case, we have no need for a *profession* of criticism, since professions are by nature the domain of specialists. Arnold, of course, faced much the same objection, but in response he could fall back on the value of the great works. If those works are not really "great," however, if they are—as our critics now tend to claim—nothing more than partial and polemical images of the usual human blindness, then once again, the critics find themselves without a rationale.

In spite of current anthologies like Hazard Adams's *Critical Theory Since Plato,* professional criticism is a distinctly modern enterprise, and although Arnold clearly was no Hegel, he played a crucial role in placing the critic on an equal footing with the other leaders of the administered society—the scientist, the historian, the philosopher, and so on. Like Emile Durkheim, his counterpart in sociology a generation later, Arnold created his field and then secured the first academic appointment in it. But if Arnold invented criticism for the modern English-speaking world, he also shaped the activity itself in a decisive way, fusing under one rubric two quite different practices—that is, the practice of literary study and the practice of social analysis. In other places, such as Germany and France, the role of the social critic developed along other lines. It's worth remembering, for example, that few of the Continental thinkers most influential in poststructuralist English departments— Derrida and Foucault, Deleuze and Guattari, Althusser, Gramsci, and Bourdieu, Adorno and Habermas—had a background in literary studies.

In part, Arnold's yoking of social critique with literary criticism reflected the special place of literature in the vernacular culture of his society, a culture shaped by earlier critics like Addison and Steele, Hazlett, Coleridge, and Lamb, but in part it also reflected the relative absence of specialized inquiry in Britain, as compared to Germany and France. That Charles Darwin, perhaps the most influential British thinker of the nineteenth century, should make his livelihood from gentleman farming, or that he should publish his magnum opus with an eye toward securing a large middle-class readership, speaks volumes about the unique place of the British man of letters. When Hegel wrote, by contrast, he wrote for a minuscule elite— and he had to, or else he would have ended up in a Prussian jail. But even given

Britain's large lay readership, Arnold was no Darwin, either, and his argument received only a tenuous assent, when it received assent at all. For Thomas Henry Huxley, the scrappy champion of science who debated Arnold, the claim that knowledge of the *belles lettres* entitled one to the status of a secular sage seemed ridiculous on the face of it. And Huxley was not alone, as we can see from the reviews of *Culture and Anarchy* in its time.[23]

Not only have we today inherited the ambiguous role that Arnold created, but we have also inherited his tenuous defense of the critic's authority. And with the rise of academic criticism in America, the claim becomes more, not less, precarious. In an age dominated by the sciences, an argument for the *sensibility* of the critic is unlikely to carry much weight, even when we give that sensibility new-sounding names such as "critical consciousness" or "oppositionality"—terms that define, after all, not a method but an attitude, and one not far removed from Arnold's "sweetness and light." Although many people look back to Lionel Trilling's career as the high-water mark of English studies, he was dogged by the same credibility gap that Arnold tried to overcome. Toward the end of his career, Trilling became less and less certain about the relevance of his own writings in a society increasingly defined by its mass culture. Mistakenly, he predicted the death of literature, when in fact literature was alive and well. If anything was in trouble, it was the image of the literary critic as a universal authority.[24]

The other option for the humanities, the one that Trilling found unattractive, was defined somewhat earlier by John Crowe Ransom in his 1937 essay "Criticism, Inc."[25] There Ransom makes an explicit case for specialization on the pattern of psychology or sociology. What makes criticism possible, in Ransom's view, is the distinctness of its object, the literary work, and the rigor of its method, which should become "more scientific, or precise and systematic."[26] In effect, his essay urges readers to accept the disappearance of the universal critic writing directly to a general readership. At about the same time, other disciplines begin to take a similar turn. In sociology, the ultraspecialist Talcott Parsons broke with prior generations—Lester Ward and E. A. Ross, for example—who wrote what we would now describe as "activist interventions" in the public sphere. About ten years later, the generation of Margaret Mead—whose *Coming of Age in Samoa* rose to the status of a national best-seller—stepped aside to make room for the structural-functionalists in anthropology. Comparable changes occur in history and philosophy as well. But the situation of English was distinctive in one crucial regard. Most people knew little about the Samoans and they regarded sociological studies of mass psychology with a distant curiosity at best. But literature, at least in the mundane sense that includes such things as detective novels and children's books, already lay very much within the possession of ordinary citizens. People rely on doctors to prescribe mysterious medicines, and they still need brokers to help them buy stocks, but no one outside a university really needs a literary critic to explain *Sons and Lovers* or "Mending Walls" or *A Streetcar Named Desire*. And consequently, the more a discipline like English labored to become a science of scansion, narratology, or semiotics, the weaker its connections to the lay culture of literature.

One way to understand the history of academic English—and much the same

might been said of the other humanities disciplines—is to see it in a continuous
vacillation between its two irreconcilable impulses. The closer English draws to the
lay experience of reading, which is resolutely unmethodical, the less it resembles the
sciences; the more it resembles a science, the less justified it seems in claiming a
connection with literature itself, as we see every time the Modern Language Association gets pilloried in the media for conference presentations like Nancy Miller's
infamous paper "Freud's Micturating Penis." Even Northrop Frye, arguably the
greatest academic critic of the twentieth century, failed to overcome this contradiction when he developed a methodology based on the idea of *cultural* evolution.[27]
According to Frye, primitive myths evolved into the Bible, which evolved into
modern literature, which has evolved, yet again, into criticism. What troubles Frye's
attempt at a Darwinian schema, of course, is the persistence of all these forms
together, instead of a clear-cut, evolutionary succession. When Frye confronts modern popular culture—the music of Paul Anka, in one instance—he gives way to
terrified derision, as though the order of nature itself had been reversed.[28] Having
argued for the steady growth and increasing sophistication of humankind's imaginary life, which he equates with a steady growth of freedom and moral responsibility,
Frye is forced by rock and roll to conclude absurdly that human beings also have an
"evil imagination" that mimics and subverts the "good" one—something like the
nineteenth-century popular idea of *de*volution.

　　Much the same problem might be said to confront Fredric Jameson, perhaps
Frye's most brilliant successor on this continent. Like Frye, Jameson wants to see in
literary history an evolutionary schema at work, though he defines evolution in
terms borrowed from Marx rather than from Darwin—in terms, that is, of class
struggle and the march toward a communist utopia. But such a claim seems on the
face of it even more tendentious than Frye's. Can we really say all literary works are
"about" class struggle in some way? The easy way out would have been for Jameson
to answer, "No," and to argue as many Marxists before him did, that literature is
often a frivolous bourgeois enterprise, an evasion of the violence at the heart of the
capitalist system. Instead, Jameson assumes a much more difficult stance: while it
may true that literature *tries* to evade the tensions at the heart of the world it
describes, these tensions leak through—and precisely when the writer seems most
assured that everything has gotten wrapped up neatly. As everyone in English
departments knows, Jameson is the critic of the "political unconscious," the term he
invented to describe this subtle leakage of reality into the consoling fictions of the
middle class.

　　Like Frye, Jameson is a critic of lapidary ingenuity, but as in Frye's case,
ingenuity alone cannot overcome the problems created by Arnold's legacy. For one
thing, Jameson's argument *is* tendentious. If we want to find evidence of class
struggle, we are almost sure to find it when we dig deeply enough, but what if we
reject the proposition that class struggle holds the key to history? What are we to
make of the fact, as well, that no one prior to Jameson himself understood literature
as he does? If no prior reader noticed the "leakages" he describes, then can we say
that these leakages really existed? Jameson might reply that the leakages happen
unconsciously, but how we can be sure that they are not simply artifacts of his own

wishful thinking? There remains a still more basic problem with Jameson's work, however: his "political unconscious" is political in name only. Actually, no one can derive a concrete politics—a concrete plan for real-world activity—from Jameson's writings. Despite his commitment to Marx, Jameson's attempt to practice exegesis as a political act flies in the face of Marx's own claim that philosophy is impotent precisely because it only interprets the world instead of transforming it.

Given the tiny readership of literary criticism, and also of most of the works that criticism addresses, a program of the kind that Jameson has undertaken is truly an impotent gesture. But the practices of a few academic litterateurs, while insignificant in and of themselves, may bear witness to outlooks and assumptions that reach far beyond the graduate seminar into society as a whole. Ever since Arnold's day, the humanities have claimed to provide space for reflection while the world at large rushes headlong into folly after folly. But we should not accept this story at face value. Perhaps critique and criticism were already thriving—in forms we so far have overlooked—long before they became preoccupations of our radical antiquarians.

"Our nada who art in nada, nada be thy nada." These words express more than the mood of the years following World War I; they express the spirit of modernity in general. One might even say that the "Great War" and all our subsequent wars were not accidents or interruptions on the journey to utopia but the most complete and dramatic expressions of the modern spirit, which creates the future by actively destroying the present and the past. Of course, apologists for modernity have worked hard to downplay the perpetual destruction, but destruction is an essential part of our society's quest for "progress." A world always building and growing is also, it seems, a world always in ruins, including the ruins of all former values and loyalties, as Hemingway perceived. But something else, something new, has happened since Hemingway's time: we now take the ruins with us wherever we go. When progress-minded Westerners travel abroad, they see pretty much what they want to see, but the bad news keeps mounting up from places like Pakistan. Recent events have brought Pakistan to public attention, but most Americans still know very little about the region in which they abruptly find themselves engaged. Nor do most Americans understand the causes of the instability that has overtaken not only Central Asia but much of the so-called developing world. In a controversial book published five years ago, the journalist Robert Kaplan warned that Central Asia would soon become a region we could no longer avoid precisely because our influence there had preceded our active involvement. As Kaplan pointed out, the investor who arrived in Karachi these days would find more and more computers, fax machines, and Fotomats, and more and more chic restaurants. But at the time Kaplan was writing, three-quarters of the city's garbage lay rotting on the street while the basic systems for delivering water and power were breaking down with increasing frequency. Despite the frenzied pace of investment, unemployment in Pakistan hovered somewhere between twenty-five and fifty percent, and one million of Karachi's nine million residents lived in shantytowns. Within two generations, Pakistan has been transformed from a village society in which crimes like murder, robbery, and drug addiction were statistically insignificant to an urban dystopia increasingly defined by the global phenomenon known as "gangsterism."[29] And gangsterism we might understand as an attempt to reconstruct something like the older, premodern social loyalties, but under extremely unstable, competitive, and dangerous conditions. Of course, a person need not travel to Pakistan to see gang-sterism in full flower: we have it right here. One might even say that we invented it.

Bad news arrives from other places as well—from southern Mexico, for example, and from Brazil, Peru, the Philippines, much of Africa, and the Russian Republic—though most of it, for us in the humanities, sounds like old news. Having read the writings of François Lyotard, the preeminent theorist of "postmod-ernity," we already know that the "postmodern condition" will soon be a global one, and that the world's only hope lies in the practice, *our* practice, of criticism and critique.[30] But is that practice actually our best hope today? Or could it be that criticism has helped to *make* the wreckage we find in Pakistan and in other places around the world? Could it be that Western critical intellectuals now play much the same role as the Western investor in Karachi, and that far from resisting the forces of decline, we are quite actively complicit with them?

At least one observer of the "global society" offers some suggestive insights. A former UN development officer and now a professor at the University of Lisle, Serge Latouche, speaks about "the Westernization of the world," by which he means not simply the West's economic domination but also its peculiar cultural hegemony— "peculiar" because it largely sustains itself through the negation of established values. Anyone who bothers to look at the world financial situation today can see that "development" has actually impoverished numerous Third World societies; in fact, until the recent G-8 debt amnesty, levels of indebtedness among the Least Developed Countries (LDCs) rose progressively since the 1980s, as have, in most places, levels of unemployment or underemployment.[31] It's worth noting also that the number of people in "extreme poverty" today exceeds the entire world's population only a century ago.[32] In addition, It is easy to show that societies often join the world economy by first destroying their own locally based economies, and that this change often accompanies a decline in the general health and well-being among the bottom half or so of the populace. But these facts are all fairly well known. Latouche's unique contribution is to note that the economic aspects of development must be accom-panied by a distinctive social regime as well, a regime that actively promotes "deculturation," the distmantling of long-established arrangements in the name of reason, truth, and the social betterment. And to underscore the point, Latouche quotes, not an opponent of development, but a prominent French defender of the process, Raymond Barre:

> Economic development of an underdeveloped people by themselves is not compatible with the maintenance of their traditional customs and mores. A break with the latter is a prerequisite to economic progress. What is needed is a revolution in the totality of social, cultural, and religious institutions and habits, and thus in their psychological attitude, their philosophy and way of

life. What is, therefore, required amounts in reality to social disorganization. Unhappiness and discontentment in the sense of wanting more than is obtainable at any moment is to be generated. The suffering and dislocation that may be caused in the process may be objectionable, but it appears to be the price that has to be paid for economic development.[33]

Left-leaning observers might like to think that the "total revolution" Barre celebrates must assume a right-leaning or pro-market character, but in order to see that this is not so, one has only to consider how closely Barre's language follows Freire's in the passage that I quoted earlier, and how often socialist revolutions have taken "deculturation" to radical extremes, especially in China and Cambodia.

But even in less extreme instances, as for example India, we can readily see the emergence of what the physicist and ecological activist Vandana Shiva calls "monocultures of the mind." And as her extensive evidence suggests, these monocultures become dominant through a practice of critique not unlike those familiar to "postmodern" academics:

> Over and above rendering local knowledge invisible by declaring it nonexistent or illegitimate, the dominant system also makes alternatives disappear by erasing and destroying the reality which they attempt to represent. The fragmented linearity of the dominant knowledge disrupts the integrations between systems. . . . Dominant knowledge . . . destroys the very *conditions* for alternatives to exist, very much like the introduction of monocultures destroying the very conditions for diverse species to exist.[34]

As Shiva points out, most "local knowledge" systems are often incapable of meeting Western standards of rationality because they are so deeply embedded in complex but local relations. Western knowledge, in contrast to many forms of local knowledge, is eminently transportable, high theory in the humanities being one good example; "big science" in the West another. And the transportability of Western knowledge is not at all incidental, since it makes possible ways of thinking and acting appropriate to both monoculture and international circulation. People who depend on the forest for staples of their diet are not thought to have either an agriculture or an economy, or for that matter, any knowledge worth preserving. And the erasure of their local knowledges goes hand in hand with the dismantling of their material way of life.

Latouche suggests, and I agree, that from the failures of development we learn much more about ourselves and our society than we do about other peoples and cultures. In particular, we see up close, and without apologetic blurring of hard edges, the process undergone by the West several centuries earlier. As another French observer of development suggests, deculturation should not be perceived as a peripheral consequence of modernity; rather, it is the process that lies at modernity's core. This second observer is the sociologist Alain Touraine, who represents development as a process even more violent than Barre's favored term, "deculturation," can express. For Touraine, the operative term is "revolution":

[Modernity's] belief in [all-embracing] development, [its] Enlightenment philosophy, which dominated the principal centres of industrial development in
Great Britain and then in the United States . . . produced a model of social
and political action which can best be defined as revolutionary. At the beginning of the seventeenth century, Descartes sought to construct rational
thought from the standpoint of a *tabula rasa,* freed from all received ideas and
customary habits of thought. More than two centuries later, the song which
would become the most universal symbol of the workers' revolutionary movement, *The Internationale,* proclaims, ["of the past, let us make a *tabula rasa.*"]
The absolute opposition between reason and tradition, between science and
religion, entails [a still more basic opposition] between the future and the past,
and it founds the general call to destroy the past which would later be found
in [the economist Joseph] Schumpeter's definition of capitalism as creative
destruction.[35]

Touraine argues that it was the West's misfortune to conceive of reason, not as the
product of one particular historical tradition, but instead as the negation of all
traditions across the board. For Descartes and those he inspired, reason, in order to
be reason at all, had to do more than simply offer a pragmatic correction of past
beliefs: these men insisted that reason return them to an absolute foundation, which
they identified with the complete undoing of all "merely" contingent arrangements.
Conceived of as a perpetual return to the *tabula rasa,* critical reason could be nothing
less than revolutionary—as opposed, that is, to producing incremental change in a
pragmatic spirit of compromise. And as Touraine insists, "revolution does not come
from kicking down the door; it destroys the very building which is seen as an
obstruction on a road which leads somewhere else."[36]

Incisive as I find Touraine's analysis, it overlooks one important feature of
modernity identified by the British sociologist John Tomlinson. Although many
observers have understood the Westernizing of the world as a substitution of *cultural* imperialism for its older, *political* counterpart, most people outside of Europe
and the United States have not experienced the West in the oppressive way Touraine's account might suggest. As Tomlinson points out, the Westernization of the
world has gone so far so fast precisely because those we dominate brace themselves
for an assault that never comes—the imposition of an *alternative* culture, thick,
heavy, and inescapable. What occurs instead at first feels like a liberation, a loosening of rules and boundaries, when it gets noticed at all.[37] People in thrall to arbitrary
customs are almost sure to welcome the opportunity to choose some more preferable
arrangement, and so they should. But what happens to those same people when
change is no longer linked to *choice?* What happens when change overtakes us
whether we like it or not, in ways we can neither foresee nor control? In that case,
change plays much the same role as immobilizing custom once did: we must
struggle for sheer survival in a world we never made.

People outside the university might think of criticism as the anodyne task of
people who read novels, poems, and plays for a living, but Latouche, Touraine, and
Tomlinson help us recognize that the practices of our critics are simply one minor

variation on a much more encompassing theme. In our world, criticism is largely the prerogative of the administrative class; it is also the means, in one form or another, by which the members of that class maintain their position of advantage. Consider the case of the humanities themselves. In theory, the emergence of culture professionals—modern art historians and historians, philosophers and literary critics, educators, social workers, and therapists—should have produced a nearly absolute uniformity of value and taste, and to a certain degree it did. By the end of the 1930s, we see the consolidation of a national pantheon of "great writers" and "great artists"—the so-called "canon." In effect, the cultural leadership set about to redistribute downward the entire intellectual heritage of the Western world. But what would have happened if they had succeeded? If they had, the culture leaders would have undermined their own authority, since the persistence of that authority required their fellow citizens to remain culturally "poor." Supposing that the day arrived when most Americans had actually read Plato, Shakespeare, and Emerson, and supposing they had all completed something like Art History 101 and "The Development of Europe"—what would be left for the cultural leaders to do? As I have argued, the solution lay in redefining the consumption of culture in ways that would place it once again beyond the grasp of ordinary people. And criticism was the means by which this came about. Everyone might look at a painting, but not everyone could really "see" it; everyone might be able to read a novel, but genuine understanding was a difficult task that required oceanic erudition and a special sensibility informed by semiotics, phenomenology, dialectical materialism, and so on.

In the larger sense, however, as a wide-ranging social practice, criticism has another, far more important application—the perpetuation of the consumer culture. In any manufacturing society, people must keep buying goods and services or the economy will collapse. And in a credit economy like the one that has emerged since the 1960s, an economy in which personal borrowing has fueled unprecedented economic growth, people must keep borrowing as well. Needless to say, they have done so with a vengeance. As statistics consistently indicate, all but the top fifth of Americans live on the razor's edge of ruin, with earnings barely able to keep pace with rising debt.[38] Precarious as the system has become, it will work smoothly so long as the wheel of consumption keeps turning, but there is always the danger that people will begin to long for liberation *from* the market, especially amid a surfeit of goods bordering on sheer absurdity. One way to prevent these defections has been technological innovation, but even the new marvels of technology cannot stimulate demand by themselves. While mainstream economists tend to see new technologies as responses to genuine needs, other observers of the market have long pointed out that needs must be created where there were none before, and the principle means of doing so is through advertising. But even these observers have often overlooked the fundamentally critical character of the entire system. The stimulation of the market through the stimulation of desire must begin by deconstructing the present and the past, which are always represented as inferior to some future situation. Every advertisement, we might say, is a critique, a deconstruction, of the reader's immediate world, which it displaces from an imaginary center to an imaginary margin.

Although we in English think of ourselves as "oppositional," critical movements like deconstruction have actually arisen from the larger social milieu created by advertising and from the de(con)structive tendencies of modernity in general. While we might like to imagine mainstream American society as strongly committed to "foundations" of one kind or another, poststructuralism turns out to be nothing more than a bookish version of the reality that ordinary people had come to accept long before Derrida. It seems clear, after all, that academic critique today is a "disembedding" mechanism; that is, social or cultural criticism works by isolating some aspect of its subject, disembedding it from its ordinary setting, and then placing it in another context where it abruptly looks untenable, even absurd.[39] One might say that deconstruction "takes the words right out of your mouth." But this is also exactly what advertising does, though deconstructionists do it to language and not, in the manner of advertisers, to entire ways of life. Like deconstruction, advertising *also* makes our familiar worlds look shabby and odd. And like the writings of our deconstructionists, commercials create on a small scale a crisis of meaning or reference in which old contexts for judgment become abruptly uncertain. Strange as it may sound to say so, both advertising and deconstructive criticism are examples of what I want to call "the social production of emptiness," the radical disembodiment of everyday life.[40]

Criticism turns the wheel of consumption: what holds true for suburbanites remodeling their kitchens holds true also for the radical academy. And what holds true for suburbia, increasingly, holds true for the farthest ends of the earth. In our time, criticism's revolutionaries have appropriated a new role for themselves: as the arbiters of truth, they no long preside over the nation-state alone, as did thinkers from Voltaire to Sartre, and from Kant to Heidegger. Instead they increasingly see themselves as speaking for the world as whole. If reason as Descartes imagined it had to be all-destroying, it also had to become all-inclusive eventually. In this sense, globalization is not simply an economic phenomenon, any more than imperialism was. We might think of the emerging global society as fullest possible realization of the ideology of the *tabula rasa*. Within the academy today, the ideal of the critical intellectual as a "cosmopolitan" ally to the downtrodden everywhere may enjoy such wide appeal because it so easily glosses over the starkly unequal relations of power, both here at home and abroad. As I argued in the previous chapter, academic intellectuals in the United States represent one segment of the information society's new elite. But the emergence of the American "knowledge class" is simply part of a larger, global transformation. In the near future, the knowledge class will have gone international, much like the religious intelligentsia of the later Middle Ages, who all had the same basic schooling whether they happened to come from Tuscany or Frisia or Yorkshire. Today, they all speak English rather than Latin, and in this process, which is already quite far advanced, American universities, together with a few European ones, have come to play a central role in the actual education of the global elite, but also in the production and dissemination of specialized knowledges through scholarly journals, research institutes, and the control of key presses at Oxford and Harvard, Berkeley, Chicago, Duke, and Yale. Of course, not all universities are created equal in the race for global domination. Recent evidence suggests, for example, that top American high school graduates a generation ago were much more willing than they are now to attend local public universities.[41] What we are seeing is the rise of a two- or three-tier university system in which the most prestigious schools produce the leadership segment of the global knowledge class, while other schools are turning out the technicians, local functionaries, mediators, and small, independent entrepreneurs. And where in this hierarchy will we find the leading critics? At the top, of course.

If modernity has been our destination, then critique—the deconstruction of our everyday arrangements—was the vehicle that carried us there. And now, with the throttle wide open, we can stop this perpetual destruction of beliefs, this endless return to the *tabula rasa,* only at an enormous cost, since critique has actually become the source of our society's power and wealth. Think what would happen to the economy, for instance, if clothing manufacturers stopped inventing new styles, or if cars were designed to last fifty years, or if people found a way to content themselves with the number of possessions their grandparents owned. Our entire civilization would collapse. By means of advertising and technological obsolence, the social production of emptiness has become inescapable, while the future once imagined by the prophets of the industrial revolution— a world of abundance and equality, in which only our machines will do any work—seems more remote than ever.

By embracing critique so unthinkingly, academic humanists have largely overlooked what is most distinctive about their own place and time—its extraordinary instability. Good descendants of the Enlightenment, these humanists have understood the pursuit of a better world as a heroic struggle against deeply held values and long-lasting social arrangements. This is why the Marxist revolutionary Antonio Gramsci pays so much attention to the traditional or "fossilized" culture of the "man-in-the-mass": even in the factory towns of Italy, tradition remained a formidable part of Italian life, obdurate and immobilizing. For Gramsci, the task of the intellectual was to loosen the iron grip of tradition and to make possible a reimagining of social arrangements.[42] Unfortunately, back here in the United States, intellectuals who admire Gramsci and other heroes of the left tend to see things from the same perspective. In their writings, these leftist intellectuals often treat the lay citizen as a version of the man-in-the mass, deeply in thrall to tradition with a capital *T.* Consequently, they see their task as twofold: first, to shatter the structure of reified consciousness, and then to work toward something better through the process that Adorno calls a "negative dialectic," which will enable us to walk backward into an earthly paradise, like Walter Benjamin's Marxist Angel of History.[43] Even in our aesthetic theory we tend to draw on this same perspective. We like to think of artists and their academic explicators as participants in an ongoing avant-garde, while we imagine ordinary citizens as continuously scandalized by counterhegemonic innovation.

But when we look at American history and at social life today, this paradigm seems stunningly inappropriate. Hasn't the very idea of an avant-garde lost its credibility, and not because our fellow citizens are terrified by innovation, but because change of virtually every kind—social and economic, technological and cultural—has far outstripped anything imagined by barrier-breaking artists and revolutionary thinkers of the twentieth century?[44] Does anyone seriously suppose that a cutting edge performance artist can do something more shocking than we see in Quentin Tarentino's popular movies, or in the real-life story of Jeffrey Dahmer, short of actually killing herself and then getting revived in front of her audience? But even that gambit would probably leave most spectators yawning. And who can forget that the productions of the avant-garde are themselves speculation commodities within a highly evolved market system, and that these productions are not at all likely to bring the system to its knees?

What holds true for the arts holds true as well for our profession's practice of critique: events outdo us at our own game. The cultural disruption caused by the Yale deconstructionists seems in retrospect pretty tame when we consider that if the information superhighway really gets off the ground, it may not only diminish forever the status of the canon of Great Books we have so earnestly debated, but it will produce an enormous generational split between those who grew up on the net and those who did not. But the Internet is simply one of countless innovations that make Foucaldians look like fuddy-duddies. Think about genetic engineering and its likely consequences, or about the global demographic explosion just now overtaking us. Think also about places like Pakistan, which may be dissolving into an ungovernable mass of warring localities, all locked together in a conflict over diminishing resources. To bring to places like these the gospel of critique is less like pouring oil on the waters than it is like pouring gasoline on a house afire.

Outside the university, I suspect, nobody really needs to hear about the instability of meaning, that staple of poststructuralist self-promotion. The *tabula rasa* has too thoroughly done its cultural work. It's important to recognize, however, that academic intellectuals enjoy a unique degree of stability. In the absence of arrangements such as tenure and the lingering prestige attached to membership in the professoriate, most people today have far fewer resources than academics do for dealing with the frenzied proliferation of values and identities. We should never forget that the university is one of the most powerful and protected institutions in our society. And despite recent declines in public funding, universities have expanded enormously over the last twenty years, absorbing many of the social and cultural functions previously discharged by other, independent institutions or simply by individuals working on their own. Precisely because the university has become so powerful, those of us living inside it can contemplate groundlessness and marginality with a voyeur's sense of excitement. But for many of our fellow citizens, marginality is social death and groundlessness starkly paralyzing.

One key indicator—mental health—is especially suggestive. Statistics indicate that the rate of depression in the United States has risen steadily since World War II. More striking still is the global spread of this disorder.[45] According to Arthur Kleinman and Alex Cohen, schizophrenia is on the rise throughout the developing world, and they predicted in 1997 that by the year 2000, this disorder would afflict 24.4 million people, a 45 percent increase over the number afflicted in 1985. Mainland China, the "reforming" market society that Western business looks to hopefully, has a suicide rate twice the rate here in the United States. In fact, 40 percent of all the world's suicides now occur in prosperous China.[46] As Kleinman and Cohen observe, "the very economic and industrial development that has bene-fited some has also engendered massive social changes. Rapid urbanization, chaotic modernization, and economic restructuring have left many developing countries reeling."[47]

But here in the United States all three of these forces—urbanization, modern-ization, and economic insecurity—have been in play for more than a hundred years; at the same time, the institutions that once compensated for the disruption of social life, institutions like the family, the neighborhood, the church or synagogue, and yes, certain federal programs, are more or less on the ropes. What's the result? Few people in the academy may have taken note of Elizabeth Wurtzel's Generation-X best-seller *Prozac Nation: Young and Depressed in America,* but the book strikes me as culturally important because to be young in the United States has come increasing to mean being depressed as well.[48] Academics of my generation, who entered college in the middle of the 1970s, may find it difficult to understand the pervasiveness of radical anomie, which Wurtzel began to experience during her first years in high school. It would be easy to dismiss her narrative as self-pitying teenage angst, the kind of despair that young people cultivate in order to shield themselves from the pressures of socialization. It might help to know, however, that Wurtzel never manages altogether to outgrow these sentiments. Something that should have happened—the forging of some sense of connection to things—failed to happen, and she descended deeper and deeper into terrifying bouts of manic depression. But whether or not Wurtzel is self-indulgent and self-promoting, whether or not she could have gotten a grip on her emotions, her narrative speaks powerfully about a condition that is as statistically significant as it is officially ignored.

One lesson that we might learn from *Prozac Nation* is the redundancy of promoting "critical consciousness" in the humanities. If anything distinguishes Wurtzel's depressive episodes from her saner moments, it is the onset of an acute self-consciousness combined with a pitiless critical intelligence. Instead of reaching for yet another smart critique in response, we would do well to recognize that our various critical traditions already presuppose a *positive* commitment to some project or agenda, and beyond that, a powerful sense of connection to other people and to the world. Precisely because we find the idea of critical consciousness so compelling, we should ask how we formed our own prior commitments. Knowing that an unrestrained market economy can encourage alienation and selfishness does not automatically make one a better citizen—one might just as easily wind up as another Ivan Boesky. To be a better citizen, one probably needs to possess a certain modicum of optimism about the future, a certain confidence in ordinary people, and a basic trust in the ultimate goodness of life itself, a trust that clearly borders on the sheerest naïveté. But I'm certain that critical consciousness did not produce this outlook in anyone who maintains it. And I'm increasingly persuaded that when we pin all our hopes on the power of critique, we simply worsen the present climate of anomie and cynicism. We have forgotten that commitment and solidarity are not givens but formidable historical achievements that people must recreate again and again. Yet such acts of recreation seem to me more difficult to undertake today than they might have been a century ago, under materially harsher conditions. Postmodern society, after all, strongly privileges playfulness over commitment, rhetoric over belief, surface over depth, text over experience, public opinion over private conscience, and professional alliances over civil solidarity. While scholars working in the humanities like to see themselves as agents of change, they have failed to recognize that change itself has become an instrument, a weapon, of the powerful.

For many people—the literary scholars and culture critics alike—the way out has been Gerald Graff's famous dictum, "Teach the conflicts," by which he means the conflicts that preoccupy academic professionals.[49] It seems to me, however, that Graff's advice does not acknowledge as openly as we should the limitations of the humanities themselves, at least in their current form. In effect, Graff's dictum sanctions as important and edifying absolutely anything professors choose to do so long as it involves multiple positions of some sort. I applaud the attempt to get beyond the crude indoctrination that masquerades as "emancipatory politics," but Graff's advice still presumes a qualitative distinction between experts and lay citizens that I simply cannot accept. Is anyone really *unfamiliar* with conflicting viewpoints, and does anybody need special training in how to think them through? In other words, do English professors—or for that matter, historians or philosophers—uniquely possess a certain intellectual skill that ordinary people lack, an attribute called "critical consciousness"? I'm convinced that the answer is no. Wouldn't chemists and merchant sailors and city councilmen also say that they sort through conflicting claims? Nor can "critical thinking" be a particular *kind* of thinking; couldn't we explain it quite easily, instead, as rather ordinary intelligence applied to rather commonplace contradictions? And precisely because contradictions will never cease to arise until culture and nature are at last reconciled (in other words, never), no one needs to *teach* criticism and no one needs to *learn* it. All we have to do is look carefully at the problems that confront us every day.

As I see it, there are at least four problems—really four crises—that our society cannot afford to ignore at the beginning of the twenty-first century: (1) the incipient population explosion, which may have consequences even more drastic than those produced by World War II; (2) the emergence of a global society, with all the cultural and economic disruption it entails; (3) the widening gap between rich and poor everywhere on this earth; and (4) the disappearance of nature—the disappearance of any world outside the sphere of human making and doing. I'm sure that other "crises" might be added to the list, but I regard these as the most important ones because they have enormous consequences at all levels, from the conduct of the nation-state to the raising of children. Events like the terrorist attacks of recent years might be seen as causally related to several of the crises at once. For almost everyone, I think, the importance of these developments is self-evident, just as the importance of the Industrial Revolution was clear to almost everyone at the time. But like the Industrial Revolution, the crises on my list are in some ways unprecedented, so much so that they threaten to overwhelm the conceptual resources at our disposal. Not simply economic in character, nor cultural nor political, they may force the humanities to pursue again what they once aspired to: a more encompassing vision, a sense of the whole and not of parts in their isolation. I recognize, of course, how hard it might seem initially to address questions of this multifaceted kind from within, say, an English department, where we have for so long isolated literature from real-world concerns. If the New Critics made the world behind the work disappear into the bloodless abstraction of "form," we nowadays reduce both world and work to the spectral schemata of "the text" or the rote paradigms of "theory." But perhaps the time has come to reconnect literary works to the problems they were written to address. When one stops to think about it, there is something quite ridiculous about teaching Wordsworth's *Prelude* or Carlyle's *Sartor Resartus* or D. H. Lawrence's *The Rainbow* as either monuments of stylistic virtuosity or else as blind productions of vast, impersonal forces, when these documents surely stand among the most instructive examples that we have of creative responsiveness to the crises of times past— and among the best materials we might draw on in responding to our current predicaments.

For those of us in English, however, teaching this way means teaching fewer literary works each term, and teaching more of other genres in dialogue with them—history, sociology, anthropology, and even the sciences. That this approach has never been our standard practice before should not put us off. Doesn't a person really need to know a little about Irish history in order to understand Yeats, or something about the Harlem Renaissance in order to appreciate the achievement of Langston Hughes? And then there are connections with our own time. Who can read Joseph Conrad today without thinking of the global economy; who can close the covers on *The Prelude* now without asking why our interactions with the natural world have turned out so very badly two centuries later?

But what about the poem or the novel in and of itself: the arts on their own terms? Many people think of the arts and humanities, after all, as a soothing time-out from the troubles of daily life, an island of tranquil permanence in a storm-tossed sea of change. Yet the truth is that a literary work has no meaning "in and of itself." If the history of English studies shows nothing else, it shows that the most accomplished readers can disagree about almost every implication of the text at hand—a point underscored not only by the chaos of theory in our time but also by the chaos of the scholarship that preceded theory. What a poem or novel *says* is unambiguous, unless the typesetter makes an error. But what a poem or novel *means* depends on the uses we wish to make of it. We can use it for entertainment or moral edification or aesthetic enjoyment or political intrigue or historical understanding or simply to kill time. When we look for a single determinate meaning— when we look to the work in and of itself— we have made a category mistake: art, we might say, is better understood as a verb rather than a noun, as a behavior or activity rather than an object. Instead of asking *what* art is, we should ask, as Nelson Goodman tells us, *when* it is.[50] And the answer is that art becomes "art" when it allows for a transformation of conventional ways of thinking by suggesting a greater degree of meaningfulness than everyday life has taught us to expect. By reading Wordsworth along with modern environmentalists, for example, we can deepen and broaden our understanding of human interactions with the natural world. We are not, of course, obligated to read Wordsworth in this way, but that's exactly why we stand to benefit.

It is the fundamental openness of the arts that releases thought into a realm of speculation or play where new horizons can present themselves—a realm not opened up to the same degree by readings in sociology or demography.

We should, in other words, put aside aspirations like the one that has driven us in English to pursue some ultimate science of reading, a project better left to genuine scientists, or else to pure metaphysics. I want to ask a question different from the one we have asked before, not "How *must* we read?" but "When we read in certain ways, what are the likely consequences?" In other words, I vote for a *pragmatics* of reading, and I believe that a strong pragmatic argument can be made—in our distinctly paralyzed and disembodied time—for ways of reading that restore a sense of connection to things, and with it, a greater confidence in our ability to act. Connection, of course, is never unambiguous, but that's all to the good as far as I'm concerned: I want my students to find connections for themselves between the writer's work and the crises of the day, and between the writer's time and their own. And once students find these connections, they will have carried out the most essential work of the arts, whether or not their activities qualify as "literary."

Truth be told, the literary arts are alive and well, but not where those of us in English typically look for them. While poetry and poets flourish, and while novels, good novels, get turned out by the wagonload, the most important thinking of our time is done in nonfiction prose—the essay—much of it the kind of journalism that we in English never teach. But we should. At least since the time of Lionel Trilling, English professors have tended to see the novel as the forum in which great issues of the whole society get worked out. For roughly the space of a century, from the time of Sir Walter Scott to the time of Charles Dickens, the novel may indeed have played such a role, but by the last third of the nineteenth century, works of deliberative prose, large and small, had already begun to enjoy preeminence. Surely the most important works of any kind to emerge from the nineteenth century, that is, the most influential works, were Charles Darwin's *The Origin of Species* and Marx and Engel's *Communist Manifesto*. Works of nearly equal importance in our own century would range from Rachel Carson's *Silent Spring* to Friedrich Hayek's *The Road to Serfdom*. But in trying to compose a list for our century, the problem is not that important works are so few but that deliberative prose has triumphed so completely that we may not know where to start or where to end. The deliberative essay is *the* genre of our time: we might call it the language of those who live among the ruins and now speak about how best to rebuild.

I am really asking for a new humanities. It's well worth remembering, however, that much of the infrastructure needed for such a change already lies waiting for us. At almost every college and university, there are general humanities courses and there are writing courses as well. And it is these, by virtue of their peripheral place, that may offer the best future for the humanities as a whole because it's here that we can "teach the crises" with the freest hand. Take what I am calling the disappearance of nature—the coming environmental crisis that is the subject of several research writing courses at my institution. Right now, to consider one especially important example of this phenomenon, China is constructing the world's largest dam, the Three Gorges project, which will displace tens of millions of people, at a minimum, while flooding some of the world's greatest architectural monuments and wiping out a number of unique species, among them a rare fresh-water dolphin. Absurdly, the government agency responsible for building the dam has had a disastrous record of collapses and of high-fatality floods, a record so bad that even the World Bank—famous for its massive botches—has declined to participate. At the same time, the Chinese scientists who studied the likely consequences of the dam and had the courage to publish the results found themselves summarily jailed.[51] They wound up in jail because the success of the dam has become a litmus test for the Party, which oversaw the manufacture of millions of inefficient, ozone-destroying refrigerators that cannot even operate some of the time because of chronic power outages. And if the Party fails to meet pent-up expectations for a better life, expectations it worked hard to create, the response could make Tienanmen look like a rather tame affair. In setting out to understand an event like this, we and our students might learn something about Chinese history and politics, about Chinese art, philosophy, and literature, about the ecology of China, and about the origins of ecology in general. We might explore the relations between culture and economics, and ecology and politics. If we want to play the part of experts, of course, we are bound to be disappointed, but my point is that expertise often finds itself at odds with a more encompassing perspective. Knowing more never hurts, but knowing more than someone else about some arcane detail does not necessarily furnish a more coherent view of things, especially of things to come. The professional's escape into microscholarship may shield research from untrained or uncongenial eyes, but a problem remains that no amount of prior knowledge and no refinement of method can solve: we can never predict infallibly how the future will turn out. The Three Gorges Project might prove to be the greatest ecological disaster in world history, or else it may end China's practice of burning millions of tons of sulphurous coal each year.

I can already hear the objections—that English is not political science or engineering. Those who are uneasy with my argument will be eager to point out that the attempt to expand the scope of our concerns has already cost English much of its once adequate reputation. Given the well-known tendency of cultural studies to cross disciplines in a shallow, conceited, and ill-informed way, these colleagues will insist on a return to "what we do best," the teaching of poetry, drama, and novels "in and of themselves." But it seems to me that this appeal to specialization (yet again!) betrays the best that the arts and humanities have to offer—in particular, their refusal of specialization, their insistence on a "fractious holism."[52] Although teaching the crises would entail for most of us a serious program of retooling, I'm more than confident we can do it; we have done it where I teach, and credibly enough to win respect from specialists in other fields. If we want to steer a careful course around the shipwreck that is cultural studies, we might start by refusing to assume that our study of Clifford Geertz or Hayden White somehow makes the knowledge produced by other disciplines superfluous. If we can give up on the illusion that everything is "text," then we might find ourselves prepared psychologically to admit that reading Donna Haraway is *not* the same as understanding primatology, and that Deleuze and Guattari know little—actually, nothing, despite their pretensions—about contemporary physics or math.[53]

To teach a crisis like the death of nature, however, we also need to think about knowledge itself in a different way. I submit that the Three Gorges project is a *kind* of problem different from the "death of the author" or the "undecidability" of textual meaning, topics of concern to our theorists. Debates over subjects like the death of the author need to be seen in the context of the avant-garde tradition. That tradition, as I have suggested, encourages us to associate freedom, or the power to act, with the destruction of constraints. When we talk about gender, for example, we take on faith that the undoing of the male/female binary will be intrinsically liberating, and in a certain sense it is. It allows a "woman" to enter a "man's" profession, for example; it allows a "man" to enjoy a "woman's" pleasure. But this pursuit of the *tabula rasa* is a strategy best adopted by people who already know what they want or who have, at least, some sense of what they need to do. Feminism, we should remember, didn't lead contemporary women into the workplace—it followed them there. Like every ideology, it arrived on the scene after the material fact.

The same might be said of critical movements like deconstruction, which gave critics an impressive rationale to express the commitment they already held. But I would like to suggest that the *tabula rasa* does us little good when we don't know where we're headed or what we ought to do. It's difficult to see, for example, how the practice of ideology critique or deconstruction would help us *at first* to make sense of the Three Gorges project. What we need is not a way of destabilizing a solidified position, a way of folding the "margins" back into the center: that approach only works retrospectively but never as events actually open up in front of us. What we need is a means of surveying the whole while placing ourselves somewhere within it—a way of working from a multiplicity of perspectives toward coherence and then to commitment. I don't mean to suggest that we need to reach consensus about whether the dam should get built or not. But even in order to disagree, we already need to see the project within the context of some coherent world. Yet it is in the very nature of postmodernity to evacuate our sense of worldliness, leaving us with an ensemble of unrelated items floating in thin air. And because academic intellectuals are the principal heirs to the *tabula rasa,* we tend to prefer a worldless state rather than to bring things together again. But if we wish to play a more constructive and useful role than we are accustomed to playing, then we need to find some alternative to the paradigm of "creative destruction." With apologies to Nelson Goodman for the second time, we might speak of this new paradigm as "worldmaking"—fashioning the fragments around us into worlds coherent, livable, and emotionally resonant.

The problem at the end of the twentieth century was not that we were squirming helplessly under the dead weight of tradition, but that we had lost the capacity to imagine ourselves as genuine actors in as genuine world. If it makes sense anymore to talk about a *Zeitgeist,* a spirit of the times, ours is marked by a profound cynicism—a point that endless amounts of research have confirmed. Worse yet, virtually all of our most powerful institutions count on the persistence of that cynicism. It's well-known, for example, that the purpose of negative campaigning is not to draw in new supporters but to dishearten and paralyze all but the true believers. The federal government's bureaucracy, which moneyed interests now control almost entirely, also counts on the apathy of the citizens whom it manipulates. But the marketplace itself thrives on cynicism: shopping is what we wind up doing when we have no better options, when the possibility of any other relation to the world has become so remote that buying a new shirt or a pair of socks feels somehow like contact.

I am trying to suggest that we will not have done enough if we simply follow the program I've sketched out so far, the program of teaching the crises. We still need understand how hard it has become to maintain the sense of a world that we require in order to form a commitment or reach a conclusion. Yet it is just this problem that much of current practice in the humanities blithely overlooks. On the one hand, our poststructuralists never tire of insisting on the impossibility of knowing anything for sure; on the other hand, the academic disciplines have routinized thought and expression to a degree probably unequaled since the Middle Ages. While differences of outlook must be respected, and while all knowledge will prove fallible sooner or later, uncertainty should be the means to an end and not an end in itself. How many times, after all, has each of us has lived through the experience of encountering a new problem, feeling overwhelmed, and then, when clarity seemed unattainable, suddenly discerning in the tangle of details the outline of some informing order? Whatever we may claim, our great secret as writers and thinkers is actually our trust in the *coherence* of this world. True, our distrust never leaves us completely—mine never has, at any rate. But the life of questioning has taught us, all the same, that the moment of understanding, of coherence, *always* arrives.

And this small fact, so easily overlooked, carries with it enormous implications, since the ideology of criticism has presupposed an adversarial relation to world, which must be put on the rack, so to speak, until it grudgingly divulges its secrets. At the heart of criticism, we might speculate, is the fear that the world has betrayed us and will never stop betraying us unless we make the most heroic efforts. In this light, we might approach criticism and critique as symbolic acts designed to assuage our sense of helplessness, not by holding at bay the forces of change but by bending those forces to our will. Yet our gambit has had some unwelcome effects. Far from freeing us of our adversarial role, this attempt to beat the world at its own destructive game only intensifies our sense of separation and distrust.

And consequently, we have failed to look closely enough at the phenomenon of change itself. It may be true, as Marx and Engels once wrote, that "all that is solid" now "melts into air," but the world, as a living whole, never stops returning *as a living whole,* even while the parts keep changing.[54] Of course, we *love* those "parts"—those particular people, places, and events that rest so heavily or happily in our memories. And yet no matter what we do, they will pass away. The most enduring works of art, philosophy, statecraft, and science cannot prevent the things we love from vanishing, and even those "enduring" works will disappear. If this earth lasts long enough, even Shakespeare will be forgotten. What we have failed to notice, though, not simply in the humanities but throughout the whole culture of modernity, is the world's luminous persistence in the face of all this destruction. This marvelous world, which time keeps destroying from one moment to the next, never ceases to come back in its wholeness even when we ourselves will have ceased to come back. And this persistence of the whole, in spite of endless change, is the distinctive concern of the humanities. To think the whole—this is our most important job.

In fact, we have no choice, since understanding itself is first and foremost a creative activity rather than a critical one. By this I mean that the act of understanding always begins with a unique kind of courage—the courage of naïveté—to which the culture of criticism is allergic. The person who tries to understand, really understand, must believe, sometimes against all odds, that events *are* understandable, that things fit together somehow, and that human beings have the capacity to discover more or less how they fit, even when we know on some level that reality is always greater than our ability to represent it—and this too is a lesson of the arts. But now the critic rushes to remind us that every artist will be shown sooner or later to have overlooked or denied something crucial. And in this sense, the artist is indeed always wrong and guilty when dragged before the bar of criticism. But the willingness to create despite the certainty of failure, and to do so even from the depths of moral error, is precisely the artist's distinctive contribution. For this reason, what matters most about writing, painting, or performing is not the technical virtuosity of the product—and certainly not its fidelity to somebody's politics— but the ennobling, constructive quality of the practice itself. And if this is true, then the *real* product is not the poem or the painting, but the generous, grateful relation to the world that art making dramatizes and renews.

Our profession has devoted so much of itself to criticism and critique that we know almost nothing yet about art as a way of being that allows our participation in the world's own creativity. Nor are we prepared to acknowledge the universality of this experience. Is it really so absurd to suggest that humans carve sculptures or compose music or write histories or pose philosophic questions in much the same way as birds sing or spiders weave webs? Perhaps all humans have a basic need for the sense of connectedness that the arts and humanities provide. And perhaps, by encouraging the arts in the broadest possible way—as creative activities and not just as objects of study— the humanities may become "agents of social change" in a sense more profound than that stock phrase now generally suggests. As Ellen Dissanayake has observed, the "satisfaction of the human need for being bouleversé"—for being carried beyond the confines of the self through practices like art making—"seems to be provided for in most societies and can be traced, in theory at least, back to very early times." Dissanayake warns us, as well, that where repressed or denied, this desire "is likely to take . . . socially destructive forms," as it has in our time, I would argue, to an unparalleled degree.[55] The need for connection will not be denied, and if the humanities can't provide it, then some other institution will. And to dismiss as "essentialism" the very idea of a "basic human need" is to overlook some cross-cultural similarities that are simply too close to overlook.

An English romantic might have written the words that follow, but their author was in fact a Ching dynasty artist remembered in Chinese tradition as an "expressionist." "The ancients," he wrote, "were able to express through brush and ink the forms of hills and streams [because] . . . they had gone through awakening and growth and life, recorded in the work they left behind, and had thus incorporated into themselves the substance of the hills and streams."[56] In our moment of self-styled postmodernity, Shih T'ao's claim is bound to strike many critics as suspect, absurd, even silly in the same way that much of Wordsworth or Alan Ginsberg or Gary Snyder might strike them as well. Yet it seems to me that our perennial cynicism has nothing to do with truth; it reflects instead the fairly obvious constraints imposed on us by our institutional history. We have always known on some level that criticism by its very nature requires us to withdraw from the experience that artists work through, but we have often mistakenly believed that our austerities would culminate in an understanding superior to the artist's own self-understanding. And when poets and painters try to explain what they do, their sometimes inarticulate accounts appear to confirm our prejudice. But their discourse is inarticulate only on the terms defined by criticism itself. We have yet to learn—and even to hear—their other, unfamiliar language, but we will never hear it unless we are prepared to stop thinking like critics and to begin thinking like Shih T'ao, with his "hills and streams." Unless we are prepared, in other words, to value participation and empathy over mastery and detachment.

8

Specialists *with* Spirit

The Humanities—Outside the University

Where the fulfillment of [one's work] cannot directly be related to the highest spiritual and cultural values . . . the individual generally abandons the attempt to justify it at all. . . . About those living in the final stages of this process, it might truly be said that they are "Specialists without spirit, sensualists without heart."
—Max Weber, *The Protestant Ethic and the Spirit of Capitalism*

The modern world is a disenchanted world, and modern knowledge is a disenchanted knowledge. For a long time now, those who claim this modern knowledge as their property—Western intellectuals and their non-Western imitators—have found it all but impossible to believe in any significant correspondence between the inner life of human beings and the realities of the universe itself. Human beings may value compassion, understanding, and creativity, but critical reason values none of these. And the result has been profoundly corrosive. What becomes of the Sistine Chapel or *War and Peace,* after all, when we remind ourselves that the God of Michelangelo and Tolstoy is only a myth, if not an outright fraud? What happens to our families when we describe them as an "economic unit," or, even worse, as prison-houses of male dominance and sexual repression? What happens to love, to beauty, to freedom, to human dignity? Strange as it may sound to say so, perhaps the last great attempt by intellectuals to resist the disenchanted modern way of thinking was the Marxist experiment, which undertook a synthesis of scientific materialism and quasi-Christian eschatology. Marx proclaimed that evolution was not blind and heartless, as so many thought, but was leading humankind irresistibly to a heaven on earth. Given the alternatives, no wonder his gospel found so many adherents.

Not everyone, however, could share Marx's optimism. There was, for instance, Matthew Arnold. Superficially a conventional Victorian and a defender of human values against the ravages of science, Arnold was nevertheless a man who had looked deeply into the abyss. The idea of truth that he developed, especially in *Culture and Anarchy,* breaks radically with premodern traditions while maintaining

a traditionalist veneer.¹ Arnold never ceased to reference scripture and to range
learnedly through the classics, but at the same time, he represented culture as a
contingent human artifact, invented and sustained without guarantees. Along with
Darwin and Thomas Henry Huxley—two men with whom he is seldom paired—
he was one of the first thinkers in the English-speaking world to perceive that
history was open-ended, and that things could go irreparably wrong for the whole
human race. When Arnold turns to the past—"the best" that has been "known and
thought in the world"—he does so in the shadow of Darwin: the past was not a
revelation of timeless truth but a "fossilized" record of human success amid a much
more extensive geology of violence and ruin. Arnold became a defender of tradition
precisely because he recognized the real dangers posed by change. Although critics
have often belittled him as naïve and banal, he actually enshrines in the humanities a
ruthlessly critical outlook: as the guardians of "the best," humanists must expose and
reject everything not "the best," a principle that means, in practice, that cultural
innovations are always deficient until proven otherwise. This is, of course, the logic
behind the so-called canon in English—with membership limited only to the greatest and most enduring writers—but it has also helped to shape the outlook of the
humanities as a whole. In Arnold's work, the critic operates like evolution itself,
winnowing out everything deficient and insubstantial. And the result that Arnold
promises is "sweetness and light," by which he means the most humane and enabling forms of culture. But this is a strange formulation. From skepticism comes
conviction; from distance comes warmth; from rejection, solidarity; from conflict,
gentle kindness. Arnold wants to believe, and wants us to believe, that the evolution
of ideas, if handled properly, will lead, if not exactly to a paradise on earth, then at
least to a somewhat better world than blind exuberance could create.

The term "disenchantment" is not Arnold's, however. That term was brought
into circulation by another great apostle of skepticism writing fifty years later, the
German social theorist Max Weber.² Like Arnold, Weber adopted studied dispas-
sion as a methodological principle, but he recognized some of the dangers overlooked by his British predecessor. For one thing, Arnold seemed convinced that a
critical spirit could preserve the crucial balance between reason and feeling, the
"Hellenic" and the "Hebraic."³ But Weber saw that the critical outlook had driven a
wedge between mind and heart. In contrast to Arnold, he understood modern
rationality to be primarily repressive and manipulative in spirit, aimed at "control of
the terrestrial world." And Weber argued as well that the skeptical mind-set had its
origin in quite specific social structures—hierarchical and bureaucratically administered. "Rationality" was actually the way of thinking most amenable to the administrator who saw others as his instruments and who justified his control by appeal to
abstract principles of fairness and efficiency rather than to personal loyalty. Under
these conditions, an emotional life of any kind was available only to underlings, who
had neither power nor knowledge. By contrast, the bureaucrat could appeal to
reason alone and consequently find his actions drained of all existential meaning:
ultimately and inescapably, to be a specialist was to act "without spirit." But in
Weber's disenchanted world, the administered underlings were scarcely better off.
While emotion still had a place in their lives, the experience of powerlessness

ensured that it would assume a pathological form as an "increased tendency toward flight into the irrationalities of apolitical emotionalism." At times, Weber appeared to long for a repudiation of the administered society and a return to charismatic leadership based on "the personalistic orientation of individual heros."[4] At other moments, and in his actual civic life, he seemed to have favored a liberal, parliamentary democracy that would make administrative institutions more transparent, responsive, and accountable.

While we today in the humanities may still believe in Arnold's version of the humanist's task, the truth may lie closer to Weber's view than many of us care to admit. Whatever their differences, moreover, both thinkers force us to choose between quite similar extremes: elitist culture or utter anarchy, the dangers of charismatic leadership or the "iron cage" of a bloodless human calculus. In disparate ways, both authors—the literary critic and the sociologist—justify the social and cultural isolation of intellectuals as an absolutely crucial antidote to the unbridled self-deception of the masses. For both figures, truth lay along a razor's edge, which the intellectual could walk safely only by the most scrupulous practice of self-questioning, self-criticism, and self-denial. But Weber was ambivalent in ways that Arnold was not. Though Weber walked the razor's edge as skillfully as anyone ever has, he also perceived quite clearly that the balancing act was bound to fail sooner or later. The intellectual could not really lead a society from which he was himself so completely estranged, nor could he even address it.[5] Ultimately, the knowledge he created would have value only for people like him, and in fact, this was to become the fate of academic sociology, arguably the discipline that has undergone the sharpest decline over the last thirty years. While some sociologists have tried to break free from this isolation—Robert Bellah, for example, and Anthony Giddens—the field by and large has not followed their lead precisely because the whole tradition of academic inquiry has shifted its focus in the opposite direction, away from civic life and toward the model of top-down administration.

Culture or anarchy, soulless specialization or the Nazi trials at Nuremberg—these are not the only options. When Arnold was old and Weber was young, a middle-aged American, William James, saw another possibility. One way to understand what James set out to do is to place it in the context of Emerson's attempt to develop a philosophy consistent with the lived experience of democracy, of personal freedom and civil equality. As Emerson correctly recognized, much of European philosophy had laid the groundwork for totalitarian governments by assuming that incompatible beliefs could not be equally true, and that the ability to distinguish true from false was a rare and difficult achievement. Emerson had challenged the totalitarian tradition by standing German idealism on its head: if the Germans believed that all of history's differences and disagreements would culminate in the realization of a single, universal Truth, Emerson argued that the ultimate reality expressed itself *through* difference, not in spite of it. For Emerson, the world of human disagreements was not the reeking muck out of which the lotus of transcendent clarity arose; instead, this world was the flower. In self-reliance and self-expression, the transcendent achieved its fulfillment in ways that were bound to differ from one person to the next.

By the time of William James, however, the absolutist spirit of traditional philosophy was not the only, or even the principal, challenge to the practice of freedom. The new challenge came from another quarter—the rapidly ascendant sciences with their belief in a single empirical reality.[6] We might say that in his development of the new field of psychology as well as in his philosophical writings, James transformed empirical science just as Emerson had transformed idealist philosophy, placing its language and concepts in the service of democracy. James insisted that ideas had to be understood empirically as "tools" designed to foster motives and inspire actions. Just as certain procedures in science—say, exposure to ultraviolet light—might be expected to have very different effects on living tissue than on inorganic substances, so certain beliefs might in one context inspire courage and self-sacrifice while in another they might foster selfishness and world evasion. It seemed clear to James that concepts and words are never the same as things: the French "un arbre" is not a more apt description of a tree than the English term "a tree." But the same holds true for culture as a whole. Is it better, in some absolute sense, to sleep on a mat on the floor, as many Asians used to, or to sleep on a bed? James would say that we need to understand the different ways of sleeping as different adaptations to different material conditions, while assessing the relative merits of each in terms of their experiential effects—the promotion of physical health, psychological well-being, and so on. What James attempted, in effect, was a materialism of ideas.

Fittingly enough, when James argued for a "pluralistic universe" he offered an empiricist rationale:

> No one of us ought to issue vetoes to the other, nor should we bandy words of abuse. We ought, on the contrary, delicately and profoundly to respect one another's mental freedom; then only shall we bring about the intellectual republic; then only shall we have that spirit of inner tolerance without which our outer tolerance is soulless, and which is empiricism's glory; then only shall we live and let live, in speculative as in practical things.[7]

James recognized that an "intellectual republic"—a democracy of intellectual life—required the willingness to allow all perspectives to have a "vote," so to speak, and not to be ruled out as illegitimate in advance of the process of trial and error that changes minds and creates new areas of agreement in the absence of force. Moreover, he believed that the broadest possible range of outlooks was the most conducive to the flexibility and adaptability in cultural life as a whole. By contrast, James saw the skepticism of conventional philosophy as maladaptive, leading to the rejection of potentially good ideas before they had the chance to prove their usefulness. In keeping with his understanding of cultural innovation as a natural, continuous process, rather than an exceptional event, he argued that the best response to a diversity of ideas was syncretic and creative, not critical.

James wrote at a time when the university was still very much an open-ended enterprise. In a single career, he had studied medicine as well as philosophy, and had taught in several fields at Harvard. And while actively engaged in these areas of knowledge, he helped to develop the new discipline of psychology, in which his two-volume study was for decades a central text. That such polymaths appear less frequently nowadays has something to do with James's extraordinary gifts, but the structure of the disciplines themselves also works against such eclectic inquiry. Perhaps "eclectic" is not the best word, however; James himself might have preferred "holistic," since he believed that "the sentiment of rationality" was closely allied with a holistic impulse.[8] As he reasoned, "The facts of the world in their sensible diversity are always before us, but our theoretic need is that they should be conceived in a way that reduces their manifoldness to simplicity."[9] And the achievement of this simplicity was accompanied by a particular mood or state "in which we might say with Walt Whitman, if we cared to say anything about ourselves at such times, 'I am sufficient as I am.' This feeling of the sufficiency of the present moment, of its absoluteness" James saw as the core of rationality.[10] If "rationality" to Weber meant the fragmentation of the world into mutually exclusive compartments, for James it meant the very opposite—wholeness. Both Weber and James were wide-ranging intellectuals, but they worked toward radically different ends. Weber's research, though ambitiously interdisciplinary, presupposed that holism of the kind to which James aspired was no longer possible. By contrast, James could still imagine himself as a person among people, and he felt comfortable writing to large general readerships about the limitations of Hegel, the physiological sources of mental illness, the political consequences of the Spanish-American War, and the history of religion. Of course, religion was a topic crucial to Weber's thought as well, but if Weber saw religion as finished, an empty shell, James considered it to be the living heart of a living culture—not religion as doctrine or institution but as the mode of experience most directly concerned with the pursuit of wholeness. The believer, as James put it, hopes to find that his personal life "is coterminous and continuous with a *more* of the same quality, which is operative in the universe."[11]

In a certain sense, both figures have turned out to be prophetic. Weber foresaw not the reality of our entire culture but the reality of intellectuals working within the massive bureaucracies that we think of today, mistakenly, as places open to the "free play of the mind"—colleges and universities, disciplines and departments. James's work has also proven prophetic, although it predicted intellectual life *outside* the university. America today actually has two quite separate traditions of humanistic thinking, one academic and elitist and the other public and democratic. The first of these is represented perhaps most visibly by "theory"; the second by a robust and complex discourse often disparaged with the term "New Age." Viewed from Weber's disenchanted world, this new knowledge is bound to appear un-methodical, unscholarly, uncritical, undertheorized, overdetermined, and utterly interpellated (as our Marxist critics like to say) by capitalism, patriarchy, and a host of other ideological bugbears. Or it may simply look stupid. But to a degree that its learned critics fail to recognize, the New Age may be James's legitimate heir and the best humanistic thinking that our time has managed to produce—that is, if we judge it pragmatically and not by some absolute criterion.

From the standpoint of the academy, the discourse of the New Age, our "other humanities," is bound to seem profoundly troubling. For one thing, its leading figures are enormously popular, at least in comparison to ours; for another thing, they are closely identified with religion, and this is probably a graver sin than popularity. For many intellectuals today, outside the academy as well as inside, religious values of even the vaguest sort are *always* construed as fundamentalist: in the words of Katha Pollitt, "a farrago of authoritarian nonsense and . . . the eternal enemy of human happiness and freedom."[12] But when we permit ourselves to think along these lines, we ignore the highest aspirations of many millions of our fellow citizens, and we lose the chance to see at work "the genius of democracy," as Walt Whitman once put it—the creativity of ordinary citizens and not of specialists and hierarchs.

What are we to make, for example, of the Promise Keepers, the Christian men's movement whose ecumenical rallies routinely drew twenty times the attendance of the national conference of English professors? Or of N. Scott Peck's *The Road Less Traveled,* on the best-seller list for more than 500 weeks? Or of the impressive sales figures for Thomas Moore, a former Catholic monk; Betty Eadie, a Christian visionary; and Deepak Chopra, an M.D. and television celebrity who combines standard Western medicine with ayurvedic practice? Whether we take our cue from William Kilpatrick on the right or from Mark Edmundson on the left, it would be easy to denigrate these developments as symptoms of a spreading irrationality, a rebirth of "Gothic" fatalism in an age of mass culture.[13] Even the small handful of observers who have managed to look sympathetically on the growing presence of New Age "religion" find themselves at a loss to explain what they observe: is it just another well-hyped trend or an indication of some genuine cultural change?[14]

For the people committed to this change, however, there is much less ambiguity. One bestselling writer on women's spirituality—Marianne Williamson—describes it as a revolution. "A mass movement is afoot in the world today," she writes, "spiritual in nature and radical in its implications":[15]

> Most people feel it, some deride it, many embrace it and no one can stop it. . . . We are turning away from a purely worldly orientation. We seek an ancient God and a modern God. We feel a current of change, a cosmic electricity running through our veins. However disparate our personalities and interests, we all agree on one very important point: Mankind has come to a major crossroads. . . . From channeled entities claiming to hail from the Pleiades to fundamentalist Christians, from the prophecies of Nostradamus to visions of the Virgin Mary . . . come predictions of global shift, perhaps cataclysm, in the years ahead.[16]

To my ear, this passage echoes Engels and Marx, but the revolution that Williamson foresees is aimed at modernity as a whole—Max Weber's "iron cage"—and not just at our economic order. For readers inside the university, her call to arms may sound absurdly grand, and also absurdly indiscriminate, bringing together in a single movement people no one might foresee sitting comfortably on the same side—Zen Buddhists and spirit channelers, devotees of the Blessed Virgin as well as charismatic Christians, Hindus, and Jews, like Williamson herself. The academic term for all of this might be "mystification," but in view of Williamson's enormous readership, such a dismissal seems like mystification on *our* part, although we have, perhaps, good reason for averting our eyes. The resurgence of religion now underway poses a challenge to our authority that seems unparalleled historically. When Jerry Falwell's Liberty University or Pat Robertson's *700 Club* takes on "secular humanism," they still engage with us on the intellectual ground that we ourselves have defined— pitting, for example, "creation science" against its Darwinian predecessor, or promoting certain triumphalist versions of Western history over those now favored by academic historians. I believe that the challenge we now face, however, is quite unlike the ones offered by these familiar, and eminently orthodox, opponents: a challenge posed not simply by a knowledge that rivals ours—the Bible versus Freud or the power of positive thinking counterposed to Marxist dialectics—but a different *way of knowing.*

I found myself face to face with this different way on a recent trip to one famous New Age sacred site—the *Santuario* in Chimayo, New Mexico. Although its reputation as a "power place" ought to have prepared me, I was surprised by the long line of worshipers shuffling in and out of the church's huge wooden doors. People lit candles and said prayers, and there were so many candles the day I went that the main room smelled hot and sweet with paraffin. The church had some kind of altar—I can't quite remember it now—but no one seemed to pay it much attention. What they had come for, the real *Santuario,* waited in a small room to the left, mostly unadorned, with a hard dirt floor. At the center of room was a hole in the ground into which the pilgrims reached to touch soil alive with a mysterious curative power. Most of them bent down and barely touched the hole's rim; a few took away some grains of earth. Respectfully, I turned around and walked slowly out, but once I had passed through the great doors again, I found myself standing under cool cottonwoods, unexpectedly entranced by the chatter of birds, who had been drawn, I guessed then, by the small rushing stream, now partly covered with a concrete walk.

For me, the striking thing about the crowd at the shrine was not its size— much smaller than the average line at a multiplex cinema. What impressed me the most was the diversity of the worshipers. Some of the pilgrims were Hispanic and some, in a state with the second lowest average income nationally, must have belonged to the working poor. But many of the visitors were very clearly middle class, and many were the kind of "Anglos"—trendy, clean, and tasteful—one might find on the streets of Santa Fe. It seemed that all kinds of people came to worship there, but what exactly were they worshiping? No one who saw the figurines clustered on the altar, or the ornaments on the walls of the nave, could have ignored the earthy, earnestly Catholic quality of the place. But where were the priests? Could it be possible, I asked myself then, that people now journey to the shrine because religion has survived only as nostalgia, only as the *idea* of religion? Or is it rather that religion occupies a new place in our lives at the start of the twenty-first century?

Perhaps the best way to map the terrain of religion in popular culture might be to start with the places where academics schooled in Weber's "rational" tradition enjoy something like a common ground with the people we are trying to understand. And one area of striking commonality, improbable as it may appear at first, is *The New York Times* best-seller *Care of the Soul,* by Thomas Moore, a psychoanalyst and cultural critic. As Moore's title openly acknowledges, he stands in the debt of Michel Foucault's *The Care of the Self.* In addition to drawing on Foucault from time to time, Moore makes use of a wide range of figures from the university canon—Plato, Sophocles, Ovid, Augustine, Pico and Ficino, Goethe, Novalis, Keats, and even Oscar Wilde. Moore knows Latin and some Greek, and like a critic or a theorist in the humanities today, he sees his task as teaching people how to read the world—to provide them, as he says, with a "hermeneutics of experience" in the service of a *technē tou biou,* a "craft of life," another idea taken from Foucault.[17]

Moore sounds distinctly Foucauldian too when he suggests that our commitment to rationalism has itself become irrational, producing new forms of regimentation in the name of progress and the general welfare. Like Foucault, Moore wants to promote alternative knowledges that will better serve the people now excluded from our society's games of power. While his purpose is not to abolish specialization, we can understand his work as an effort to recast social life in ways conducive to a greater degree of public participation. And like Foucault, as well, he understands that the emergence of these "alternative knowledges" begins not with critique, as many intellectuals now presuppose, but with the search for new ways of life. Foucault's emphasis later in his career on the importance of a *technē tou biou,* the artful shaping of everyday experience, might at first glance seem to signal a turn away from his earlier concern with relations of power; and, by extension, Moore's use of Foucault terminology might seem to confirm the charge, made by some of Foucault's critics, that he had given himself over just before his death to the charms of the "California lifestyle."[18] But Foucault in his late work attends so scrupulously to "the care of self" precisely because he understands, in a spirit very close to William James's, that knowledge is finally just an alibi that enables us to live as we want, or we need. Moore might never put it quite so bluntly, yet the question that he poses is the same one James posed: not "What is truth?" but instead "How should we live?"[19]

These concerns and commitments identify Moore as "one of us" in quite important ways, but the differences are as instructive, I think, as the numerous similarities. While noting his debt to Foucault early on, Moore takes care to underscore a crucial distinction as well, because Moore is decidedly not a poststructuralist like Foucault:

> The word *self* implies an ego project. Soul is nothing like ego. Even the Jungian idea of Self, carefully defined as a blend of conscious understanding and unconscious influences, is still very personal and too human in contrast to the soul. Soul is the font of who we are, and yet it is far beyond our capacity to devise or control.[20]

For Foucault, of course, the soul is not the "font of who we are"; it is the voice of society inside our heads, as he makes plain in *Discipline and Punish*. But Moore employs the term "soul" in a different way, to define those particular sources of the self—if I can take a term from the philosopher Charles Taylor—that are strong enough or deep enough to help us resist the assault of a corrupting socialization. And unlike Foucault, Moore suggests that there is not a single "order of discourse," within which we are condemned to hang like spiders in the webs of our own spinning. For Moore, instead, there are *two* distinctive orders and these two orders are at war—the first created in opposition to the nature of things for the purpose of domination, the second fashioned through a dialogue with the world in the pursuit of cooperation and happiness. While Foucault advocates the production of count-erknowledges that mimic and undo authority, Moore argues for what he calls "care," which is not just another knowledge, even a subversive one. As Moore understands it, the term "care" describes a condition or outlook that becomes possible when we voluntarily forsake the will to power, because the source of genuine care—genuine connection to the world—does not lie in what we con-sciously want, but in a collective unconscious, which speaks for and from the body through the interior language of myth.[21]

The interior language of myth. How long has it been since the academic humanities could find this idea believable?—so long, I suspect, that we may fail to recognize its primary inspiration, Carl Jung. Like Freud, who survives among us primarily in the work of Jacques Lacan, Jung understood the "inner life" as a distinctly *mythic* realm, midway between consciousness and the unconscious, and between the subjective and the communal. As Moore says, "Myth reaches beyond the personal to express an imagery reflective of archetype[s] that shape every human life."[22] But Jung departs from Freud, and even more from Lacan, in his account of myth as a *somatic* memory of humankind's interactions with the natural world. And here, in this turn to the body, Moore has a second precursor, Norman O. Brown, who observes in a passage that Moore quotes several times, "What is always speak-ing silently . . . is the body. . . . The true meanings of words are bodily meanings, carnal knowledge; and the bodily meanings are unspoken meanings."[23] The care of the soul begins, in other words, with the sacralization of everyday life at its most immediate and sensuous—and in this search for transcendence by means of the mundane we can hear one additional voice, Paul Tillich's, a third major influence on Moore and, more diffusely, on the New Age in general.[24]

While it is true that Moore holds Foucault in high regard, his *real* loyalties lie with Jung, Brown, and Tillich, whose temporal distance from us is as important as their distance from us in outlook. One way to understand the movement that Moore represents is to see it as a resurgence of a sensibility defeated first in the churches by the religious right, and later, in the academy, by the advent of French theory and the waning of "myth criticism," which survives outside our institution in the enor-mously popular output of the late Joseph Campbell, a favorite target of poststruc-turalist critique. But even those new-religion practitioners unfamiliar with Jung or Brown—Pentecostal or charismatic Christians, for example, who are not to be confused with fundamentalists—share a commitment to experience as potentially redemptive. If we asked them to justify rituals like taking up serpents and the laying on of hands, the Pentecostals would emphatically accept the judgment of one New Age writer, Sam Keen, that "Mainstream religion in America" has become a distinctly "out-of-body" affair.[25]

Even more than the emphasis on the "everyday sacred," this attention to the body—this "somatic turn," if I can draw on as Douglas Robinson's term—has engendered an unprecedented change.[26] If there is any concern that nearly all the new-religion writers share, it is the search for "technologies" of the body that produce a heightened sense of connection to other people, the world, and in some cases, God. Moore describes that search using Foucauldian terms while adding some important reservations, but to people like Deepak Chopra and Jon Kabat-Zinn, Foucault would seem too much an idealist for his thinking about the body to play a role in their work. While both Chopra and Kabat-Zinn have been trained in traditional Western health professions—Chopra as an endocrinologist, Kabat-Zinn as a psychologist—their use of non-Western traditions permits them to understand the body in ways that remain all but impossible in the academy, dominated as our discourses are by language-centered paradigms. But Chopra understands the body as capable of "talking back" to language, and he regards illness as a consequence of our refusal to listen to these wordless communications.[27] Precisely because the ayurvedic tradition of India sees illness as a product of the discrepancy between culture and nature, it continually seeks to refashion the first in accordance with the second. A poststructuralist might counter, quite predictably, that ayurvedic medicine is itself culturally determined through and through—and quite different in its particulars from, say, the nature-centered therapies devised by the ancient Taoists of China. But the *popular* response to such obvious discrepancies obeys a different logic, one that is syncretic and pragmatic rather than analytic and deconstructive. James would approve. Far from concluding that the body is cultural "all the way down," to paraphrase the anthropologist Clifford Geertz, many Americans respond to the diversity of healing traditions by concluding that every tradition makes some degree of pragmatic sense, and that the differences testify to the *limitations* of culture and the *primacy* of nature. It is this syncretic pragmatism that allows Chopra to blend insights from Indian tradition with those from China, Islam, and the Christian West.

To see the body in this peculiar fashion—as the source of a truth that discursive intellect can never do more than approximate—is to turn one's back on much of Europe's dominant idealist tradition. Although exceptions certainly come to mind—such as the medieval Christian mystics and the eighteenth-century Hasidim—the founders of Western thought from Plato on have typically described the task of culture as the suppression, discipline, or transcendence of the body. But the changing perception of the body today also breaks with our more recent history, in that people writing for mass readerships appear to have lost their confidence in "textuality," the belief that the act of reading, in and of itself, can transform our lived relations to the world. While this belief in reading as an inner discipline is at least as old as Augustine, who virtually *invented* it for the West, it has persisted, in various secular forms, despite the Enlightenment's turn to "objectivity" and the modernist-progressivist assault on private life.[28] However radical some poststructuralists may sound when celebrating the absence of foundations or the inexhaustibility of subject positions, they typically remain committed to a Freudian variant of this ancient textualist paradigm: yes, the body *is* animated by biological "drives," but language and culture—in other words, "the text"—give order to the chaos of the body itself. We should never forget that Freud attributed neurosis to our *misreadings* of events, or that the corrective he devised was a text-centered practice, "the talking cure," by means of which internalized contradictions could be reinterpreted and consequently "resolved." But the talking cure, with its emphasis on the retelling one's story in a more truthful way, no longer makes sense if one has ceased to think of language or culture as the key to one's experience, its maker, its master, and its judge.

Perhaps the best example of this departure from textuality is the therapeutic method developed by Jon Kabat-Zinn, a Buddhist lay practitioner. In contrast to the Freudian legacy, Kabat-Zinn's approach does not aim at reinterpreting the past by uncovering repressed contradictions, but instead undertakes to undo and reconstruct habitual patterns of behavior in the present, from one moment to the next. If the past belongs to psychoanalysis, so to speak, then the present moment falls to the discipline that Buddhists like Kabat-Zinn refer to as the cultivation of "mindfulness" (*vipassana*).[29] To some degree, this departure from traditional Freudian analysis reflects the nature of Kabat-Zinn's specific clientele, who are usually people racked by physical pain rather than by problems "in the head." But Kabat-Zinn's approach to therapy would appear to presuppose that even the problems in our heads have their sources in our bodily dispositions.

The practice of traditional psychotherapy requires that both analyst and patient learn to treat experience as text, as a narrative pregnant with hidden meaning like the stories told to Oedipus as he tries to lift the mysterious curse on Thebes. But for Kabat-Zinn, therapy involves setting aside the narrative impulse and becoming increasingly attentive to the comportment of the body in its everyday activities. By watching the breath, by noting the mental and physical impressions that arise with each moment, one learns how to *regulate* attention—and how to develop styles of worldly comportment that escape the stranglehold of pain and the fear of pain. In *samadhi,* a state of wordless and impersonal concentration, pain recedes into the background, like a voice once shrill and deafening but now reduced to a quiet murmur. At the same time, people in *samadhi* no longer see the events unfolding around them as moments in a linear progression that may bring more pain or else the promise of some absolute cessation. Rather, each moment is simply "now," within a cycle of endlessly returning nows. The point is not to escape time nor to follow it backward like Ariadne's thread; instead, one strives to maintain the rhythm of *samadhi* itself, returning over and over to the now.[30]

It seems to me that this reorientation, a shift away from words and signs to sensation in the present, may represent the great divide between the postmodern era and its possible New Age successor. But so completely has textualism dominated our thinking in the academy that we have forgotten, if we ever knew, that "reading" the world as if it were a text is only one of many available ways to make sense of experience. And far from constituting a transcultural universal, the mode of worldly comportment we call reading may seem real and useful only under conditions now endangered. One can hardly imagine that reading would enjoy such preeminence in the West if other developments—the printing press, for example—had never occurred. But the culture of reading requires other things as well, all of which have become rarities: relative quiet, a wealth of leisure time, a supportive circle of fellow readers. The act of reading also entails a distinctive state of mind—a state of patient, ambling curiosity—that many people today may find unfamiliar and sometimes quite difficult to achieve for long stretches of time. Reading demands something else, however, that may be its most important attribute: a willingness to tolerate deliberate alienation—a suspension of the "now" that makes reading the very opposite of mindfulness meditation. As many observers have noted, to read is to accept a special kind of loneliness, and such a loneliness may seem distasteful, even frightening, to those who lack a solid sense of the world and of one's own place within it. It was surely no accident, after all, that the fashioners of modern literacy were medieval monks, Renaissance aristocrats, and the upwardly mobile bourgeoisie, three groups unusually secure in their appointed roles.

But now, with the coming of postmodernity, the world looks less and less like a readable text. With the emergence of mass communications and the proliferation of multiple codes and signs, often incongruously juxtaposed and sometimes in fierce competition, everyone must feel a certain sense of groundlessness. And under these circumstances, many of our fellow citizens may find more or less unbearable the alienation produced by extended reading, especially when it no longer transports us to certainty, as our Enlightenment forerunners believed, but only to a seemingly endless regress of free-floating positions and perspectives. When academic interpretation has become a labor of Sisyphus, who can blame people for turning to TV and the movies, which at least promise the simulacrum of contact with the sensuous world? Yet the somatic turn has not led to the final disenchantment of reading. When Moore speaks of reading as a hermeneutics of experience, we might say that he is trying to rectify the problem by restoring a bodily dimension.[31] What he has in mind is much less like postmodern textual practices, which uncouple text and world, than their medieval counterparts—when words were like "grapes," to be "eaten and chewed."[32]

> A man with a doctrine doesn't stand a chance against a man with an experience.
>
> —Pentecostal saying

While books remain the principal medium for much of the new religious sensibility, the status of the word has changed, and with it, the character of truth. Once the ties between text and life-world are cut, as they have been in postmodernity, the insights provided by reading may lose their pertinence. The very idea of a "sign" or a "code" implies the existence of something other than a sign or code—the much maligned "signified" in the argot of French theory. But in a world of socially constructed language games, where "truth" gets defined in any way a community elects to define it, how is one to choose *which* community deserves one's assent? Is it good, for example, to think of oneself as essentially "a woman"? Clearly, the writers on gender disagree. Does it make sense to seek out one's "true self" or is the very idea of a self an illusion of bourgeois morality? Once again, the answers given by those who claim to know authoritatively fall on every side of the issue.

As the signified keeps receding from view, screened off by an endless variety of perspectives, people may feel the need to reach *beneath* the level of signs and codes, and it is this need that might explain the current flourishing of religious fundamentalisms. But the new religions make their journey to truth by a different path from the way of the fundamentalists—not through a nostalgic return to the "right reading," but through practices that range from simple prayer and visualization to yoga and possession by the Holy Spirit. The truth produced by these practices, however, has less in common with the "truth" of philosophy or theology than it does with the knowledge made by scientists, since its merit lies not primarily its propositional character—in claims reached by a purely deductive reason—but in its capacity to produce real-world results, in the self and in the self's relation to others. At least for those who follow the new religions, truth of this kind enables one to act: it frees one from ambivalence and so produces health as well as wisdom, at least ideally.

Yet the pursuit of such a truth paradoxically returns its pursuers to an older, premodern kind of knowledge. Knowledge in the modern sense separates the object and the observer from the larger world that contains them both. We say, for example, that we "know something" when it stands out vividly as a thing-in-itself, amenable to an analysis designed to expose the object's internal logic—its parts. To know a poem, for instance, is to know how it is "put together," and the same might be said of knowing a flower or a style of architecture. But the word *knowing* may also denote a kind of fusion, as in the King James Bible: a collapse of the boundary between I and thou, or thou and that. To know a poem in this sense is to see a world "through it," so that the world, far from receding, becomes intensely present as a whole, and as a part of one's own self-perception, memory, affect, and so on. This kind of truth *feels* true, and it feels true in a special way—by dissolving the knower's sense of isolation. Precisely because such a knowledge extracts the observer from the grip of discriminating judgment, it runs the risk of appearing useless and purely fanciful—just as alleged by early empiricists like Descartes and Bacon—but this older path to truth offers something that our textualist knowledge cannot reliably provide: an experiential solution to the problem of multiple paradigms, which ordinarily intensify our alienation, and it does so without resorting to the authoritarian ideal of a single truth applicable to everyone.

Such a knowledge, as I say, can never be a knowledge about specific things; rather, it restores the *awareness of context* that makes it possible to see how specific things fit together. And as people in the West have recognized intermittently at least since the time of Plotinus, "light" may be the best metaphor to describe the intimation of this unity-in-diversity, which has no qualities of its own but which makes visible the qualities of everything else. Precisely because that sense of coherence still remains so distant from our daily lives in the modern world—precisely because we

experience the absence of coherence so often and so painfully—light has resurfaced
as a "root metaphor" in the new discourse of religion, cutting right across denomina-
tional lines.[33] Among those inspired most directly by Christian tradition, however,
the experience of light also assumes the form of a direct encounter with a "personal
God."

In *Embraced by the Light,* for example, which has sold three million copies so
far, Betty Eadie describes her encounter with God after a postpartum hemorrhage
caused her heart to stop while she lay unattended in her hospital bed:

> I saw a pinpoint of light in the distance. The black mass around me began to
> take on more of the shape of a tunnel, and I felt myself traveling through it at
> an ever greater speed, rushing toward the light. . . . As I got closer the light
> became brilliant—brilliant beyond any description, far more brilliant than
> the sun.[34]

And at the center of the light, Eadie saw the figure of Christ:

> I felt his light blending into mine. It was the most unconditional love I have
> ever felt, and as I saw his arms open to receive me I went to him and received
> his complete embrace and said over and over, "I'm home. I'm home."[35]

In a sense, there is nothing new about Eadie's revelation. Thanks to extensive media
coverage, many millions of Americans are familiar with near-death experiences of
the kind that she describes. But Eadie's revelation is distinctive in a way it might be
easy to overlook, since she is no Mohammed or Joseph Smith: she has *a* message but
is not *the* messenger. Again and again in many subtle details, Eadie stresses the
ordinariness of her life, neither unusually good nor unusually bad.

Eadie's heaven seems remarkably ordinary too, and her Jesus talks to her
because, it seems, he will gladly talk to anyone. As she describes him, Jesus is not at
all the wrathful judge at the end of time, but a gentle and friendly older brother.
When her excitement prevents her from speaking, for example, he laughingly tells
her to slow down. But Eadie's vision is distinctive in yet another way. Her most
urgent questions are concerned with how to manage life from day to day rather than
with the fate of her soul after death. And this concern with the proper way to live
culminates in a question about the diversity of religious beliefs. "I wanted," she
writes, "to know why there were so many different Churches in the world":

> The answer came to me with the purest of understanding. Each of us, I was
> told, is at a different level of spiritual knowledge. All religions upon the earth
> are necessary because there are people who need what they teach. . . . Having
> received this knowledge, I knew that we have no right to criticize any church
> or religion in any way.[36]

Eadie's concern with the diversity of sacred knowledge is no accident. The
daughter of a white father and a Lakota mother, she was raised on the Rosebud

Reservation and her vision of the afterlife may owe as much to Lakota shamanism—the same tradition that produced Black Elk—as it does to Western theology. And like the intensely eclectic Black Elk, Eadie seems quite prepared to modify Christian beliefs if such revisions seem appropriate to her, as they do when she discovers that the Father and the Son are not "one being" as she had been taught in Catholic school. Yet the most striking feature of her revelations is not their particular content, but their authorization by the testimony of her own experience, possibly another inheritance from Lakota traditions.

Eadie's account may remind us of dream narratives from other times and places—if not the visions of Black Elk then perhaps those of the English mystic Julian of Norwich—but we still need to ask what it means that she should tell such a story now, speaking from the very heart of postmodernity. It seems to me that Eadie's account is not a throwback to "primitive" modes of experience, but postmodern in a more radical sense than the term ordinarily signifies—so radical, in fact, that our academic paradigms may not be up to the job. Like all people in our time, Eadie recognizes the multiplicity of perspectives or positions, but she may have found—experientially—what many postmodernists have not: a way out of the endless hall of mirrors.

We might say that in the presence of multiple perspectives, Eadie shifts her attention from an exterior to an interior "plane of visibility." And on this plane, the vertiginous multiplicity of viewers and positions, subjects and objects, resolves itself into a "primal" dyad, an "I" and "Thou" whose mutual recognition erases the boundary between them. Rather than explain this shift of planes in psychoanalytic terms as a wish-fulfilling fantasy or a regression to childhood, we might think of it instead as a cognitive shift, an *intensification of focus* on the experience of separation itself. The interior plane that Eadie explores is not apart from the exterior world, but deeply within it, though unnoticed by everyday awareness. In a state somewhere between consciousness and the unconscious—the state Moore associates with "soul"—Eadie observes the split between self and world "up close," without distractions and without wandering, as Foucault does, from one moment of alienation to the next. Although she might not explain her insight as I have explained it here, Eadie discovers a unity underlying the subject/object split, a unity that she describes as an outpouring of light and unconditional love.

The truth that Eadie discovers is a truth about relations—about how things fit together to make up the world—and it calls not only for a new kind of knowledge but also for a new ethics. If Foucault's *oeuvre* can seen as typical of poststructuralism in general, then we might agree that people working within that tradition regard all claims to unity or wholeness as repressive impositions of "sameness" on an "unruly" diversity of perspectives. But the unity that Eadie witnesses actually requires diversity. "God" has "decreed" it: as Jesus tells her, *all* the different churches teach the truth. For Eadie and those who accept her testimony, the appropriate response to difference is neither a "foundationalist" nostalgia for agreement nor a transgressive overturning of all positions, but the search for an underlying "family resemblance." While difference has become the academy's highest god, the new religions value pluralism, which Moore contrasts to the rigidity of fundamentalist thinking. "From the point of view of the soul," he writes, "the many churches and innumerable understandings of Christianity are its richness, while any attempt to make all churches one" is "a threat to the very life of religion."[37] This emphasis on the relative or proximate character of attempts to describe a reality beyond words goes hand in hand with a commitment to personal freedom in the pursuit of religious insight, and also with a utopian vision based on tolerance and mutuality. But such a community of mutual tolerance, at least as many of these writers conceive it, is fundamentally incompatible with the competitive, normalizing ethos of the marketplace. Moore, for example, celebrates the ideal of "monastic poverty," which he defines "not as a scarcity of money and property but rather as 'common owner-ship.'" In her collection of prayers, *Illuminata,* Williamson insists that on this earth "Our primary work . . . is to love and forgive. Our secondary work is worldly employment."[38] And in his book, *Hymns to an Unknown God,* Sam Keen proposes a somewhat broader program of resistance to the logic of capitalism. His program includes repudiating nationalism, shrinking the chasm between the rich and the poor through progressive taxation, reducing the number of hours worked each week to create more jobs while expanding leisure time, and developing forms of manufacturing less destructive to the environment.[39] This is clearly not the religion of T. S. Eliot, but it is not just pseudo-religion either, as detractors of the New Age faiths commonly imply.

The term New Age is, of course, a disparagement, yet as I started to suspect at the *Santuario,* we *are* entering a new age. Like me, the people under the cottonwood trees belonged to a cosmopolitan society, a multiverse of religions and realities, each persuasive and sustaining to its believers. In a world subject to a single rationality, if such a world has ever existed, the line between truth and falsity will be clear for most people most of the time. But in a world defined by multiple rationalities, no single paradigm will seem adequate to the continuous encounter with diversity. I may hear on the radio, for instance, that Jesus of Nazareth is the Christ, the son of God and redeemer of sinful humankind, but I may also learn, perhaps from Bill Moyers on TV, that the Buddha, Lord Shakyamuni, attained enlightenment five centuries before the birth of Jesus and taught that everyone could undergo the same experience. In the face of these divergent claims, which arise from two very different paradigms, I may adopt the postmodernist strategy by placing all beliefs without exception *sous rature,* crossing out the Buddha, so to speak, and crossing out the Christ. Or I can spend the freshest hours of every day "interrogating" the relations of power implied by the Gospel of St. Mark or the Lankavatara Sutra. Of course, both of these responses, if mistaken for ends instead of means, presuppose that alienation is our inescapable fate, and not only alienation but something even worse. Pressed to explain his understanding of social life, Foucault once described it as "a war of everyone against everyone else." While Foucault may be right, in a certain sense, this is not the response recommended by people like Moore and Williamson. For them, a more compassionate and useful response to contradiction is a synthetic exercise of imagination. The point is not to decide who was right, the Buddha or the Christ—surely we have seen enough intolerance—but to construct a way of seeing inclusive enough to accommodate *both* claims as truth.

This is, I believe, the cultural logic at work in bestselling books like John Butcher's *The Tao of Jesus*.[40] As its title openly acknowledges, *The Tao* attempts to demonstrate the unity beneath two ostensibly opposed religious paradigms—Christianity and the Taoist way of China—so opposed that most of us would probably say the project could hardly be less promising. The legendary founders of Taoism, Lao Tzu and Chuang Tzu, understood the noumenon as an impersonal Way rather than as a personal God. Instead of valorizing the struggle to lead an ethical life in Old Testament prophetic tradition, they repudiate thinking in terms of right and wrong as inherently destructive. And whereas Jews and Christians have traditionally viewed the natural world with distaste or, at times, even outright hatred—Jesus encounters Satan in the wilderness, don't forget—the Taoists valorize a return to "original nature," which is not just trees and birds but also the primordial state of awareness itself.

One might endlessly continue listing differences of this kind, or one might conclude, with Paul Ricoeur, that writers like the author of *The Tao of Jesus* do great violence to both Taoism and Christianity.[41] To substitute "Tao" for "God," after all, is to represent God in a radically altered way: as the formlessness behind all form, the emptiness that makes presence possible—not the primordial *I am* of Exodus but the primordial *I am not*. Yet we might say that this response is a product of the older, textualist regime, presupposing as it does that beliefs exist within isolated, incommensurable systems. For better or worse, however, ideas are endowed with this airtight self-containment only in the pages of intellectual history, from which the real complexity of motives and actions gets excluded at the outset. In reality, the meaning of the text never lies within the text itself, but emerges from the interpreter's relations to the world. This is why, of course, both slaveholders and abolitionists could cite the same Bible with perfect honesty in defense of their respective positions. And it is why, in our time, no scholarly reading can ever be definitive, regardless of how closely it attends to the nuances of words, or to the historical "conjunctures" that the text supposedly expresses.

Christianity and Buddhism, the Taoist way and Islam—these are now mixed together in a single life-world along with democracy, science, Marxist thinking, capitalism, deconstruction, and Darwin, and we can scarcely help but recognize that their values and terms have entered into universal circulation. Simply to learn the definition of "Tao" is already to be changed—is already to inhabit a world where the idea must somehow find a meaningful place. While poststructuralists have correctly understood that encounters among cultures are often "relativizing," they have generally failed to understand that the "relativity" of "incommensurable" paradigms cannot remain a permanent condition: their view, too, is an illusion of the scholar's training—the neat divisions of academic labor and the card catalog, which owe far less to the process of understanding than to the logistics of storing and retrieving information.

Syncretism—the continuous pragmatic fusion of life-worlds—violates the logic of the library, but it makes sense as an ethics of engagement with the Other when alternative forms of life have placed in doubt one's own beliefs. To praise, as Butcher does, "the Tao" that "becomes flesh and dwells among us" is not to overturn the Gospel, but to renew its *inner* dimension through the encounter with Chinese tradition. And if syncretism sanctions all beliefs as potentially true, it also makes each person responsible for creating a private truth, which is true not because it can be universalized—that's the textualist formula—but because it restores the knower's sense of connectedness to the world and to others. We might say that critical reason, carried to extremes, evacuates the subject by forcing its beliefs into a public domain where they must undergo an ordeal of interminable challenge. Under these conditions, the delicate structures of memory and feeling upon which all belief necessarily rests—even scientific belief—can be torn to pieces so thoroughly that dissociation and disenchantment may become habitual. When proponents of the new religion speak of "inner healing," they are describing a reconstruction of memory and feeling in ways that place belief beyond the reach of public assault, a strategy not at all unreasonable when one acknowledges that every belief is susceptible to deconstruction.

Groups of men who go into the woods to beat drums make an easy target for those predisposed to think ill of them, but it seems to me that academics in the humanities should try to understand the social forces that have made such conduct increasingly widespread—and, in fact, necessary. For many writers on modernity, at least since C. B. Macpherson, it has become an article of faith that no other society in history so indulges the individual, and in this same spirit, the late historian Christopher Lasch was only too ready to denigrate all efforts at a "craft of life" as symptoms of a decadent "narcissism."[42] But other observers, starting with Max Weber, may come closer to the reality when they point out that the modern world has made the self the particular focal point of social control. Surely no society has gone farther than ours in the regimentation of experience. What the first twelve years of schooling leave undone, the media bring to completion, collapsing the fragile wall that divides public image from private life and social status from self-respect.

   Within the academy we keep trying to produce a heightened social consciousness by insisting that the subject is nothing more than an "effect" of objective social forces—that the self, in other words, is nothing in itself. But many of our counterparts outside the academy believe that society's renewal will begin with the creation of selves more flexible, secure, and independent, selves more capable of *resisting* the social forces that we tend to see as fundamental and irresistible. Like us, the New Agers have come to think that domination in our time takes the form of control over images of ourselves that we unreflectingly internalize. To be real at all, in other words, I must conform to the image of "a beautiful woman," or a "manly man," a "good mother," a "success," and so on. But our counterparts also understand what we in the academy have often overlooked—that in the long run the images themselves matter less than our psychological dependency on the institutions that authorize them. While we tend to believe that the best response to an oppressive public image is an energetic critique, the practice of critique may overturn ideas while leaving unchanged more fundamental structures of identification. As we all know, even brilliant social critics can be desperate for approval, and in the theater of political action, quite committed liberators can exploit, manipulate, and even murder the very people they set out to liberate. Those of us committed to critical consciousness have too readily assumed that criticism alone can compensate for relations of power that make it impossible to think or say certain things in public forums where the wrong sorts of speech often carry enormous penalties—the high regard of one's colleagues, for example, or the possibility of publication in a prestigious journal. Or, to give a simpler example, we can critique TV from now until the end of time, but nothing much has changed unless we turn it off.

If equality is our concern, and if the minimum requirement for a relation of equality is the capacity to say no to others without fear of retaliation, then the making of a strong inner life becomes absolutely indispensable. So long as I depend for my self-worth on the powerful, the learned, the wealthy, the famous, and so on—so long as I locate outside my own control whatever I define as the highest good—words like *equality* and *freedom, liberation* and *truth* are little more than empty abstractions. And for this reason, a central tenet of the new religions is a return to the idea that "the kingdom of god is within you." The valorization of the everyday has many dimensions, but the existential and the political seem inextricably related in much of the writing. As J. K. Bailey reasons in *Already on Holy Ground:*

> For too long we've reserved the divine presence for a coterie of bishops and cardinals, *sadhus* and gurus, self-appointed preachers and brilliant philosopher-scholars—as if they were the guardians of *our* religious experience. Perhaps we believed we weren't smart, holy, or committed enough, or we presumed the core of spiritual life lay in some grand future awakening. But in waiting for the blinding light to strike us, we ignored the tiny sparkle of a star in the night sky that could bring joy to the heart and help us to remember the Divine.
>
> In experiencing this presence, no event is too minute for our attention. . . . The potential for light is as present with mechanics amid the grease and grime of the neighborhood Amoco station as it is with Zen monks at a monastery in Kyoto.[43]

To academic humanists, people who have spent whole decades in the labor of acquiring specialized knowledge, this claim is bound to sound offensive, another version of the "easy transcendence" that Mark Edmundson, an English professor and a harsh critic of the New Age, has belittled as lacking in "difficulty," which he apparently equates with genuineness.[44] Yet it seems to me that difficulty in itself may not be a virtue; instead, it may simply function as another class marker, something like saying "Harvard" without leaning hard on the *r*'s. At its best, however, "difficulty" can serve the purpose of emancipation by making possible the "exercise of the self" that Foucault commended, a practice of self-cultivation that short-circuits the psychological dynamics of dependency. But Foucault was not the first person in the West to follow this path: the Stoic tradition in antiquity rested on the same concept of discipline. To this way of thinking, only a strong self is capable of demonstrating genuine compassion and genuine respect for others, since only such a self no longer has anything to fear from others, or to gain from their manipulation.

It would be easy to point out, of course, that even the practice of self-cultivation must be socially constructed and that the self is therefore basically social. But we might just as well start with some other term: everything is basically biological or mathematical or chemical or economic. To start with the social is not to get to the real bottom of things, but only to *choose* a bottom of a certain kind. Moore's truth is no less true than Derrida's "truth," just as theory's truth is no less "true" than poetry's. Each way of engaging with the world produces a different *kind* of recognition on terms that the way itself defines, and so the question posed by the new religions in our time, with their profoundly pragmatic orientation, also has to be a pragmatic one. What advantages do people now perceive in supporting the changes I have described at length here, and what social interests can explain their defection en masse from the culture of text?

The question, as I say, is a pragmatic one, but the answer I will give is *political,* though political in the deepest sense, not as an allegiance to this program or that party, but as an expression of people's struggle to control as much of their lives as they actually can. Although literacy seems to have some links with the rise of democratic polities, the culture of the text in the modern world is a culture of hierarchy, if only because the masters of the text interpose themselves between the reader and the work. And that mediation has become the alibi for the rule of a restrictive but immensely empowered class of specialists: philosophers, historians, critics, and pedagogues. Priesthood and the culture of the text go hand in hand, and the waning of the text goes hand in hand with the desire for something better. "The history of the world," writes Marianne Williamson,

> is the history of control . . . over masses of people who finally rise up against [that] control. . . . Seizing someone's soul is the ultimate form of control, because without the soul, we are without our love. Without our love, we're without our power. In this sense, we are as controlled a society as has ever existed. . . . [But now] the slaves are beginning to agitate.[45]

The common thread running through all the discourses here is a profound suspicion about any system that divides up the labor of cultural production to preserve a hierarchy. And in this same leveling spirit, Sam Keen takes issue with "the reactionary efforts of Islamic, Jewish, or Christian nations governed by religious authorities [who] threaten the civil liberties, women's rights, and sexual freedoms we have struggled so hard to achieve. . . . I can't go back to traditional religion. Neither can I live within the smog-bound horizon of the secular-progressive faith."[46]

The communities imagined by those who "can't go back" are typically communities of practice—of ritualized communion—rather than communities of dogmatic consensus, and perhaps the most eloquent testimony to this change is the much-debated, much-maligned Million Man March. On that ambiguous occasion, so hard for us in the academy to interpret, Black Muslims and black Christians, and many men of color without any faith at all, gathered to affirm a collective identity against an indifferent and immobilized state, that consummate product of bureaucracy. What mattered most to many of those involved was not Farrakhan's bizarre theology, or even his political analysis, but the transformative drama of pilgrimage, which forges bonds of commonality through the practice of the pilgrimage itself.[47] For the textualist, the idea of religion without fixed belief seems to be a contradiction. But the power of practice, as the theologian Karen Armstrong has argued, and as most of us have only begun to learn, is precisely that it remakes the world in ways that belief can appreciate only in part and belatedly, when the *miraculum*—"the wonder"—has already passed.[48]

> I understood that life is lived most fully in the imagination. . . . We
> are sent here . . . to find joy in our creations.
> —Betty Eadie, *Embraced*

If religion as a practice may seem threatening to many academic humanists, the New Age has taken a still more alarming turn, though it may ultimately prove to be a miracle in its own way: a turn toward *arts* as practice, *toward* the making of art and *away* from its consumption, critical or otherwise. As we know from the historical record, the idea that a poem or painting exists primarily to be "analyzed" is actually quite recent. English departments, for example, were created to "teach literature" before anyone actually knew what "teaching literature" might concretely involve. Arguably, the triumph of academic criticism cannot be separated from the essentially administrative role of English studies, which arose to normalize the tastes of the nation.[49] As the sociologist Eric Livingston alleges, our critical practices serve primarily to legitimize qualitative distinctions between the "informed" readings of experts and the "misreadings" of ordinary people, who generally read for pleasure or "life lessons."[50] And as other observers have pointed out, criticism helps preserve the boundary separating laypeople from the august ranks of "real writers."

The rarification of the arts—their sequestration from everyday life and their metamorphosis into objects of abstruse expert consumption—typifies the very essence of disenchanted modernity as Weber described it, and this development corresponds quite closely to other forms of political and social disenfranchisement. But the academy's appropriation of the arts may have social consequences more important in the long run than even the plummeting rate of voter participation or the widespread dissatisfaction with, say, the public school system. Fundamentally, the lesson of all the arts is the same: ways of seeing, ways of thinking, ways of feeling can be changed, and each of us can change them. The arts, we might say, dramatize the human power of "world making," to take a phrase from Nelson Goodman, and they do so by freeing the artist from the ordinary constraints of practical feasibility, empirical proof, and ethical uprightness. Once the arts have become nothing more, however, than an object of specialist inquiry, they often cease to teach this crucial lesson and teach instead exactly the opposite: ways of seeing, thinking, and feeling might be changed, but only by exceptional people.

Like so much that comes out of the new religions, popular books such as *Writing Down the Bones* and *The Artist's Way* lend themselves to easy dismissals as naïve. Instead of talking about the conventions of discourse communities or the history of genres, the author of *Writing Down the Bones,* Natalie Goldberg, represents the composing process as an inner discipline on a par with meditation:

> In Zen meditation you sit on a cushion called a zafu with your legs crossed, back straight, hands at your knees or in front of you. . . . You face a white wall and watch your breath. No matter what you feel—great tornadoes of anger and resistance, thunderstorms of joy and grief—you continue to sit, legs crossed, back straight, facing the wall. You learn not to be tossed away no matter how great the thought or emotion. That is the discipline: to continue to sit. The same is true in writing.[51]

For some time now within the university, the inner-directed or "expressivist" perspective that Goldberg adopts has become virtually anathema. Yet the embarrassment of academic theorists, or perhaps I should say, their contempt, may obscure the repressive character of their own social situation. By methodically dismissing as irrelevant the inner experience of writing, compositionists have created a quasi-scientific knowledge—a knowledge of conventions, tropes, and so on—that strengthens their claim to legitimacy. At that same time, however, the formation of this knowledge tacitly affirms their exclusive sovereignty over a process that Goldberg still annoyingly imagines as hers.

It goes without saying that every form of artistic practice involves something like conventions, and that much of learning to be a novelist or a painter is a matter of "technique." Yet many accomplished artists think of technique as the means to a higher, experiential end. In *The Artist's Way,* for example, Julia Cameron fills the margins of her text with the words of distinguished artists and philosophers who comment on art making as an inner discipline. One of the quotes comes from Jackson Pollock who observes, "The painting has a life of its own. I try to let it come through," and another comes from Edgar Dégas, who insists that "Only when he no longer knows what he is doing does the painter do good things."[52] If we dismiss these claims as self-indulgent or narcissistic, we misrepresent the character of the experience that many artists value, an experience of self-overcoming achieved through an *intensification of subjectivity.* The way in becomes the way out. As Aaron Copland observes in another passage that Cameron cites, "Inspiration may be a form of superconsciousness, or perhaps of subconsciousness—I wouldn't know. But I am sure it is the antithesis of self-consciousness."[53] The experience that Copland identifies here transcends the perspective of isolated individuality through the activity of a synthetic imagination. And Copland is hardly alone in this belief. If the fine arts reveal any overriding tendency in the last half of the twentieth century, it is in their movement away from the valuing of art as virtuoso object and toward a celebration of art as a process, a form of involvement with the world that anyone can engage in. When composition theorists denigrate expressivism, they turn their backs on this vital tradition of expressionism. At the same time, they may ignore something even more important, which lies at the very heart of the expressionist tradition: the potential for a radical democratization of cultural life itself.

Although the New Age certainly runs the risk of co-optation by the market—as books like *Chicken Soup for the Soul* demonstrate—the same might be said of oppositional thinking in every form.[54] But precisely for this reason, the time has come, perhaps, for us to reconsider the modern and postmodern tendency to denigrate the inner life. Perhaps the cultivation of an inner life is the *most* revolutionary thing we can do. Certainly I am not alone in saying so:

> Today this private space [of inner freedom] has been invaded and whittled down by technological reality. Mass production and mass distribution claim the *entire* individual, and industrial psychology has long since ceased to be confined to the factory. The manifold process of [psychological colonization] seems [now] to be ossified into almost mechanical reactions. The result is not adjustment, but *mimesis:* an immediate identification of the individual with *his* society, and through it, with the society as a whole.[55]

Here the writer suggests that our problem is not too little awareness of the social but too much. Despite the appearance of endless freedom, consumer society is, he claims, essentially totalitarian in its expansion of the "realm of necessity" to include those regions of human experience formerly exempt from its logic. In a consumer society, even our *dreams* come to serve "productive" ends. At this point I should confess that the passage I've just quoted does not belong to a masterpiece of the New Age, but to the canon of the academic left—and indeed to the handful of works in that canon that might qualify as best-sellers: Herbert Marcuse's *One-Dimensional Man,* which has gone through twenty-five printings. True, Marcuse saw religion as an obstacle to freedom, but in this respect his thinking became ahistorical and undialectical. While at certain times and in certain places religion *has* promoted a cultural logic of self-denial, one might fairly claim that in our time the New Age thinkers have envisioned some of the least repressive forms of collective interaction. Thanks to people like Durkheim and Freud, we have come to conceive of religion as *essentially* foundational and repressive, when in fact it can play an oppositional role, even a subversive one. Any number of critics, Marx included, have dismissed religion on the grounds of its otherworldliness, but they have failed to understand the varied *uses* of otherworldliness itself—which is not necessarily an autistic response to unpleasant realities, but may also make possible a refusal to accept those representations of the real that are officially held up as incontestable truth. The power of otherworldliness is the power to refuse, not only the official reality, but even the terms upon which that reality can be called into question legitimately.

Religion is so important to the New Age, just as it was important to William James, because it confers this power by virtue of its essential liminality, its capacity to expose all truth as partial and relative (and therefore, finally, untrue) by pointing outside of the whole system—to God, heaven, the Tao, the Dharmakaya and so on.[56] Liminality makes religion *dangerous,* as the critic Marianna Torgovnick reminds us, and the danger has required, at various moments in the past, elaborate structures for its containment: enormous ecclesiastic hierarchies and armies of dogmaticians.[57] But these efforts to stabilize liminality entail an irresolvable contradiction, and so the history of religion has always been what it will always be, a history of common practice, not common belief. For similar reasons, every effort to produce a "rational" or "scientific" religion is destined to fail, since these efforts set out to eliminate the one thing that believers value most even when they might not describe it in my terms: an *unconditional* freedom, and not from the world but in it.

Once again an insight from the New Age may be more truthful than we wish to admit—the insight that the arts share common ground with the kind of experience we think of as religious. It seems to me, in other words, that unless the humanities can offer people something like an experience of unconditional freedom, they have nothing to offer at all. If a poem or painting or a philosophy is always *only* a product of social forces, an economy of signs, or some unconscious mechanism, then why not simply study sociology or economics? If all we have to show for our reading and writing lives is a chronicle of ensnarements, enslavements, and defeats, then why should anybody tramp so far afield—through, say, the six hundred pages of *Moby Dick*—when we can learn the same lessons much more easily from *People* magazine or the movies? In itself, the forms of activity we speak of as "the arts" can be put to countless uses for countless reasons, but we might do well to ask if ideology critique is the best of those uses. Does it seem credible that the millions of years of evolution that have brought forth humankind's marvelous intelligence have now come to their full flower in our disenchanted age? Was it all for *this?* Or could it be, instead, that disenchantment and the failure of humanities as sources of popular meaning and inspiration are now impelling us toward the one encounter we have tried for more than a century to avoid: James's "intellectual republic," a cultural democracy?

9

"Art Serves Love"

The Arts As a Paradigm for the Humanities

For the better part of the twentieth century, the humanities aspired to the power and prestige of the sciences. The path to equality, many humanists believed, lay in a reconstruction of their enterprise: their idea was to forge a science of culture, as in the case of English, history, and art history; or else, as in the case of philosophy, to support the culture of science by making a foundational contribution to its self-understanding. A central assumption of this book is that this gambit has failed. Most of the scientists I know remain quite content to ignore the writings of philosophers who have tried to justify scientific findings and methods, which in any case need no justification of the sort that philosophers are trained to provide. (After all, if philosophers someday reached the judgment that the claims of, say, quantum physics were illegitimate, scientists could hardly be expected to discontinue their research.) At the same time, English and its allied disciplines have never managed to produce a knowledge that meets the bare minimum of requirements for scientific validity.

First, the "knowledge" developed by Marxism, structuralism, and its poststructuralist successors cannot meet the standard of predictiveness. If culture really were a text subject to laws of transformation, as Marx, Lévi-Strauss, Foucault, Derrida, and others pretend, then our culture professionals should be able to predict what our society will look like in thirty, fifty, or another hundred years, just as physicists can predict the trajectory of a spacecraft and the half-life of plutonium. But even Marx has failed dismally by that measure, while Foucault's effort in *The Archaeology of Knowledge* seems half-hearted, if not actually parodic.[1] Derrida appears to get away unscathed because he predicts the perpetual appearance of the unpredicted, but he cannot tell us where the unpredicted will next turn up.[2] Second, the privileged knowledge of English and its allies—high theory—is immune to the sort of falsification that scientific theory must withstand. No amount of evidence will ever suffice to disprove Marx, Freud, Adorno, Derrida, Lacan, and Foucault because they each provide an all-embracing system that predetermines how the evidence will be viewed. What Sartre is supposed to have once said about Marx's followers—that they pay no attention to particular events because they already know how history will turn out—holds true for high theory in general. Third, the discoveries of our current leading humanists cannot be replicated in the objective manner of scientific research. A person unfamiliar with Derrida and assigned to read, say, Rousseau's *Confessions,* would be unlikely to draw independently the same conclusions that Derrida draws from his reading of Rousseau in *Of Grammatology.*[3] Although Derrida has countless imitators, the truth is that only Derrida can read as Derrida does because his way of reading is an art, not a science. Derrida purports to describe a textual dynamic that exists independent of human intentionality, but his work is actually an expression of his unique personality, inventiveness, learning, and rather waggish but overbearing style. Needless to say, knowledge in the sciences does not depend to the same degree on the personality of the scientist. If Einstein had never lived, someone else would have discovered the principle of general relativity. But if Derrida had never lived, deconstruction would not exist, just as *The Stranger* could not have existed without Camus.

The humanities cannot follow the lead of the sciences because they communicate something the sciences cannot communicate—the primacy of our experience and the uniqueness of that experience. Although the sciences see with human eyes and speak with human language, they describe a world that will exist, and has existed, without a human presence. Gravity operates whether we notice it or not, and it will operate long after humankind has vanished. But the proper concern of the humanities, deconstructions of subjectity notwithstanding, is the world that exists with humans in it, the world from which science draws the raw material for its highly refined investigations. But what do we mean when we speak of "the world with humans in it"? Perhaps the humanities have aspired to the status of a science not simply because the sciences now enjoy preeminence, but also because humanists have never fully grasped the implications of being human. Actually, there is no such thing as "the world with humans in it"; there is only the world with this person and that person. The world with me in it is the world seen through my eyes. And this world—uniquely particular—is remarkable in ways that our predecessors have often overlooked. Viewed long enough and closely enough, the world as seen through my eyes can assume a universal character, both for you and for me, and it can reveal this character because and not in spite of its particularity.

This lesson the arts have always taught, and I believe that the humanities must learn it as well. Every generation has to rewrite history, for example, because every generation needs a different history, and not only different generations but different people living in the same generation. The purpose of history, of philosophy, of literary scholarship is not to record a truth independent of you and me, but to offer us the truths of greatest usefulness right now. There can be no other human truth. Regrettably, this view has few defenders in the academy right now. Our conservatives continue to insist that truth must be true for all times and places. They find it unthinkable that Plato might someday go unread and they call endlessly for a return to the classics, which they contrast to the ad hoc thinking of their own day, forgetting that the classics were the ad hoc thinking of another. Although academic leftists have different sources of inspiration, they demand from learning much the same universal character. On their terms, the legacy of the past comes up short because it fails to express the outlook of the oppressed and the excluded, whom they tacitly regard as real heroes of history and the ultimate inheritors of all its cultural achievements. But history—I feel confident—will reveal no final winner and no consummating moment of universal transparency. There is only today, and today, and today, in an endless series of days lived by countless individual people. To excoriate a book or article because it fails to represent the perspective of some person somewhere, possibly even in the future, is to expect the wrong sort of thing from culture. A work of history or philosophy can be true, but only as art is true, not as science.

In this chapter I will argue that the humanities can escape from the "culture wars" between the right and the left only by reinventing themselves as arts of living, arts of self-cultivation. But I also recognize that we have so far overlooked this possibility because we have more or less ignored the character of the arts themselves as an activity. However radical our critics of culture now imagine themselves to be, they have often remained profoundly backward looking in one important respect: they still tend to believe that in every age only a few special people manage to see matters clearly, an outlook they share with their opponents on the right. Ironically, left and right are staunchly allied in their unwillingness to recognize in ordinary people the creative powers long accorded to the makers of high culture. We have yet to develop, in other words, an understanding of cultural life that supports our ideals of democracy. But the present moment offers us another opportunity, just as every present moment will until the end of time itself.

Now that high theory and the critique of culture are winding down, we have the chance to rediscover the value of the arts as a paradigm for the humanities in general. Consider the case of Frank Lentriccia, one of my personal heros when I was still much taken with theory and critique. In the photo on the back of *Criticism and Social Change,* a hot-blooded young Lentriccia stares out at the reader with an expression of cool defiance. He was, in the words of one reviewer quoted on the cover, "the Dirty Harry of . . . critical theory."[4] Even more powerfully than the book itself, which I could not set down until I'd read it to the end, Lentriccia's *stare* inspired me, all the way through my dissertation and into my years as an assistant professor. For me, he was the model of the "oppositional intellectual," the sort of critic I earnestly wanted to become: ruthlessly analytical but also a defender of the little guy, inexhaustibly learned but also down-to-earth and *engaged.* Troubled as I was by half-repressed doubts about the point of my own discipline, I was prepared to believe every word he wrote. Echoing Marx, Lentriccia had announced that the point of English "is not only to interpret texts . . . but also [to] change our society."[5]

Of course, this was fifteen years ago, and since then many things are different, not least of all Lentriccia himself. In a scandalous 1996 essay, he recanted almost every word of his career.[6] As he describes the change, the moment of crisis arrived in a graduate class when a student began by denouncing William Faulkner as a racist. In this student's response and in others he describes, Lentriccia saw his finely honed critical weapons of choice brandished like a meat ax. Surely Faulkner was more than a racist, and surely Faulkner's novels are somewhat better than case studies in social pathology. The arch provocateur suddenly found himself asking what had gotten lost on the way to the revolution.

What had gotten lost, Lentriccia argues, was "the literary," which he describes as a form of lived experience to be valued in its own right and not as an extension or expression of anything else—of politics or economics, gender relations, and so on. In his long march away from any subsequent long marches, Lentriccia discovered a fundamental incompatibility between two traditions he had always taken for one— the tradition of literature and the arts, and the tradition of criticism. Forced to choose, he finally sided with the novels he loved, turning his back forever (probably) on criticism and the education of future critics.

Needless to say, Lentriccia's essay was the occasion for ill feelings. If we're willing, after all, to accept his terms, then critics start to look rather narrow, hard, and mean, while as flesh-and-blood individuals they are sometimes quite the opposite. But Lentriccia makes a crucial point, despite his residual tendency to blow away the opposition, Dirty-Harry style. I would put it this way: the aspiration of the student in his graduate class—to hold Faulkner's work accountable for its claims— is fundamentally mistaken because a work that qualifies as literary or as art never makes a claim of any kind; instead, it dramatizes the act of claiming. Although Lentriccia seems more or less content to stop with his critique of criticism, I want to pick up where he ends by arguing that the arts are actually processes and not representations or arguments.[7] And if this is true, then the purpose of a novel, play, or poem is not to convey some determinate "meaning," but to make possible a change that goes deeper than representation could ever bring about—a change in what I call the reader's "opening" to the world.

Lentriccia himself offers some hints about the nature of this opening when he confesses, at the start of his essay, to having lived a double life, one as a critical assassin, the other as a covert lover of literary art, whose "silent encounters" with the great works were "ravishingly pleasurable." By day, so to speak, he did what many critics do:

> I would show my students that what is called "literature" is nothing but the most devious of rhetorical discourses (writhing with political designs upon us all), either in opposition to or in complicity with the power in place. In either case, novels, poems, and plays deserved to be included in the Sunday section called News of the Week in Review.[8]

But at the same time, Lentriccia continued to pursue a hidden and shameful pleasure. Despite his growing preeminence, he came to value most what his students appeared to value least—the "literary experience of liberation," which he compares to travel and to sexual excitement:

> All that you know is that you live where you live and that you are who you are. Then you submit to the text, you relinquish yourself, because you need to be transported. . . . The first time that I traveled it was 1956 and I was sixteen. I was in bed. Ever since, I like to do it in a bed, or reclining on a couch, or on the floor, with my knees drawn up—just like the first time, the book leaning against my thighs, nestled in my groin.[9]

No doubt, there are readers who don't do it in bed; who don't feel that poems and novels solicit an act of submission; who have never had the experience of losing themselves in a story. Yet it seems to me that Lentriccia describes an experience familiar, more or less, to many millions of people—the kind of people who "love books" and read them with a pleasure that borders on ecstacy—that is, *ecstasis,* a movement of consciousness from the self to a place beyond the self. These may not be the ones who now gravitate to advanced study in English, but the genealogy of ecstatic reading reaches back, as I will later argue, at least to the Middle Ages. Why, then, has it come to an end with us?

Part of the reason, or so I believe, is our debt to John Crowe Ransom's "Criticism, Inc."[10] Maintaining the place of English in a system of learned professions so thoroughly absorbs our energies that experience of the kind Lentriccia praises has become virtually an embarrassment, as it should be if we are indeed a profession on the pattern of the sciences. After all, it scarcely matters whether engineers love engineering or not—the point is to build a bridge that won't go crashing down. One might say that any knowledge premised on the model of technical expertise presupposes from the start the irrelevance, even the perniciousness, of "affective" influences. Clearly, many scientists love to do research, but their feelings are never allowed to count as evidence or knowledge. I can still remember my first college course in English—"Introduction to the British Novel"—where the instructor, echoing Ransom, cautioned us quite specifically that "appreciation" should remain a private affair and had no proper place in our class. I suspect that most of us in the humanities have received some version of this advice, and so it is small wonder we have yet to ask ourselves what appreciation might actually involve and why it might be crucial to the humanities, and to English especially, in a way that may have no parallel in the sciences. Isn't it possible that what matters about literature is not its character as an object of inquiry? Perhaps the key to understanding literature is the kind of experience it makes possible, irrespective of its form and content.[11]

That art is a mode of experience no one, to my mind, has shown with greater eloquence than Marcel Duchamps in his famous "ready-made" entitled *Fountain,* an inverted urinal signed by the fictitious artist "R. Mutt." As soon as we view the urinal as "art," it undergoes a fundamental change in its relation to the everyday world: we no longer know where to place it and we may suddenly feel more free or more awake to possibility. A structuralist or semiotician might say that we are never *really* free—that we have simply shifted the item from one category to another: from "urinal" to "art object." But if this were all that Duchamps had done, it's hard to imagine why his viewers in 1917 would have found that "object" as exciting— and disturbing—as they did.[12] Somehow Duchamps managed to transform the category of "art object" itself. The experience of art differs from the experience that the structuralists have in mind precisely because it feels open-ended, and they can't explain away this open-endness simply by pointing to the factors—psychological, political, social, linguistic, and so on—that are supposed to predetermine our perception of the world.[13] We might turn the tables on our determinist friends by saying that theirs is the perspective of people who have forgotten how to encounter the world as anything other than a drab repetition of the already known. But the problem with determinism goes even deeper, since its adherents assume that once we have identified categories of understanding or ensembles of signs, we always know how to employ them. The power of Duchamps' R. Mutt urinal is precisely the power to place us *between* categories and constellations of signs in a way that makes us aware that what we might do next is a genuine question, endlessly open-ended.

I would like to suggest that structuralism and semiotics unintentionally bring to a close the whole tradition of imagining art as a *thing*, and with it the still broader tradition that regards critical analysis as the foundation of understanding. While much has been gained from describing conscious life in terms of supposedly objective structures, we have paid far less attention to the *transformation* of structure—that is, to the various ad hoc and deliberate *processes* by which our signs, structures, tropes, and paradigms undergo change.[14] Although the French poststructuralists attempted to put change squarely at the center of their enterprise, their obsession with the primacy of "the text," their atavistic desire to identify lawlike mechanisms ("writing," *différance* and so on), and their loathing for the very notion of personal experience have steered us down a cul de sac. And as a consequence of their legacy, we in English have yet to consider the possibility that humankind, over tens of thousands of years, has devised a wide array of cognitive strategies, some of which resemble criticism as we now practice it, while others, though quite dissimilar, are no less enabling. To suppose that critical analysis represents the highest form of awareness, and that all other forms of awareness are nothing more than reification, mystification, or, as the Marxist like to say, "interpellations of ideology," is to turn our backs on many of the most important cognitive achievements of our species. As a distinct way of encountering the world, art should not be understood as thought that has failed to rise to the level of criticism, or as criticism by other means—or as incomplete unless made whole by the critic's commentary.

If we accept Lentriccia's account of literary experience as a useful place to start, then we can say, at least, what the experience of art is not:

1. It's not interpretation. People caught up in the process of, say, reading poetry or novels are not immediately concerned with making sense of the work in terms of some "larger" issue outside the world evoked by the work itself. Nor are readers especially concerned with the formal properties of the work, such as the rhyme scheme.

2. It's not criticism. Readers "in the act" are not ordinarily concerned about making qualitative distinctions among writers or works, or about deconstructing the writer's conscious or unconscious sympathies and aversions. As I shall argue later, interpretation and criticism are both activities in their own right, distinct from the experiernce of art.

3. It's not history and it's not philosophy. Aristotle was correct to distinguish between history and fiction, attributing to fiction (drama, actually) a universal character absent from historical narratives.[15] By the same token, hardly anybody can be persuaded that philosophy is the same enterprise as the writing of short stories or novels. Art, I want to argue, is its own sort of thing, a distinctive form of activity and

experience as well. At the same time, I also wish to press the case that there is art, so to speak, in the activities of historians, philosophers, and even scientists.

Art can be found in all these different activities, but we might say that art-making is more "primitive" than the others.[16] That is, history and also philosophy must first accomplish cognitively and experientially what art accomplishes, but then they must do something more, meeting tests that the arts are not expected to meet. In the broadest sense, the term "art making" identifies a family of practices that enable us, once they have done their work, to go on to ask questions about logical consistency or fidelity to historical evidence or technical skillfulness. Before we can grasp something genuinely new or unfamiliar, that something must take its proper place in a world that already exists, and our making, our synethic activity, creates this coherence, whether we choose to call it art or not. The arts in a more restricted sense, as poetry and painting and so on, have the special task of dramatizing this ground-floor activity on which all of the humanities build.[17]

To say that art making as practice and experience is more primitive does not means that it has no social history. The case can be made, for example, that Lentriccia's version of literary reading began with Augustine, the Bishop of Hippo, who synthesized late-Classical conventions of exegesis with the Jewish tradition that considered reading a religious act.[18] As Augustine's thought unfolds over the thirty years of his maturity, reading becomes a means of grace—becomes, in fact, *the* redemptive practice. But one might argue that redemptive reading reaches its apogee in twelfth century with works like Hugh of Saint Victor's *Didascalicon*. In his discussion of Hugh's world, Ivan Illich contends that Hugh would not have understood the modern idea of reading for a supposedly objective content. In Hugh's world, the purpose of reading was the reader's ascent to "wisdom," which he understood as an inner condition—a transformation of consciousness:

> For Hugh the page radiates. . . . Reading, for Hugh, is a remedy because it brings light back into a world from which sin had banned it. According to Hugh, Adam and Eve were created with eyes so luminous that they constantly contemplated what now must be painfully looked for. . . .
>
> Hugh asks the reader to expose himself to the light emanating from the page . . . so that he can recognize himself, acknowledge himself. In the light of wisdom that brings the page to glow, the self of the reader will catch fire.[19]

Some modern accounts of reading may come close to Hugh's way of thinking—reader-response theory, for example—but they lack not only the commonplace medieval belief in a "higher" reality, but also any appreciation of the sensuous dimension that readers in Hugh's time took for granted:

> The modern reader conceives of the page as a plate that inks the mind, and of the mind as a screen onto which the page is projected and from which, at a flip, it can fade. For the monastic reader, whom Hugh addresses, reading is a much less phantasmagoric and much more carnal activity: the reader under-

stands the lines by moving to their beat, remembers them by capturing their rhythm, and thinks of them in terms of putting them into his mouth and chewing.[20]

If Illich is correct in arguing that our culture of literary reading has its roots here, then Lentriccia's remarks may seem less petulant and world evading than they do when we think of critical reading as our baseline, so to speak. In fact, the ascent of criticism may have played an important part, not only in the "darkening" of the text—in the devaluation of reading as a redemptive practice—but also in its disembodiment. Whatever we may do with signs and codes, we cannot chew them "like grapes."

For medievals such as Hugh, by contrast, the act of reading was an experience of transport as well as transformation. In our secular and often cynical age, the idea that reading "transports us to another world" survives only as a pale metaphor, and this loss of depth may in part account for the decline of "the literary" in our culture generally. But I find it consoling to recognize that even in the modern world, the act has retained some portion of its former character, especially among nonprofessionals. Here, for example, is what reading meant to an American seventy-odd years ago:

> The thing that I believed was genius came to me first on one of those Christmas holidays which I spent in Baltimore, at the home of my uncle. . . . I had always enjoyed these holidays . . . but on this particular Christmas, my uncle's home meant to me a shelf of books. I read Shakespeare straight through in that holiday, and though it sounds preposterous, I read the whole of Milton in those same two weeks. This is the way I was living; literature had become a frenzy. I read while I was eating, I read lying down, sitting, standing and walking, everywhere I went. . . . My mind on fire with high poetry, I went out for a walk one night. I do not know my age at the time, but it was somewhere around eighteen or nineteen, a winter night, with hard crunching snow on the ground, and great bright lights in the sky. . . . Suddenly this thing came to me, startling and wonderful beyond any power of words to tell; the opening of gates in the soul, the pouring in of music, of light, of joy which was unlike anything else. . . . I stood riveted to one spot, and a trembling seized me, a happiness so intense that the distinction between pleasure and pain was lost.
>
> If I had been a religious person at this time, no doubt I would have had visions of saints and holy martyrs, and perhaps have developed stigmata on hands and feet. But I had no sort of superstition, so the ecstacy took a literary form.[21]

The writer of these words was Upton Sinclair, a spokesman for American socialism who nearly won a hard-fought campaign to become the governor of California. If we substitute "wisdom" or the "holy spirit" for "genius" in this passage, then we begin to see how much the writer shared with his monastic predecessors eight hundred years before. Sinclair's ecstacy was an overflowing of pleasure, but a pleasure that may become increasingly unfamiliar in our hyperinstrumentalist age. To read Shakespeare and Milton as Sinclair did in his uncle's study is not at all to encounter "texts" but instead to encounter other "fictional worlds," in the happy phrase coined by Thomas Pavel, though I would add that these are worlds that we as readers make instead of worlds we "see" because they exist already.[22] And as Sinclair's own account testifies unself-consciously, the person who stands at the threshold between worlds may experience this liminality not as a loss or a crisis, but as an intimation of some ultimate freedom—an opening of "the gates of the soul" upon the Great Mysterium itself. Even for those who choose, as Sinclair did, to talk about such moments in secular terms, the experience of reading can go hand in hand with an intensified awareness of our connectness with things, a greater opening to the actual. If Sinclair had never experienced the "pouring in" of music, light, and joy, I wonder if he would have been equal to the conflict and unhappiness that events were already preparing for him. Somehow, I'm not so sure.

We might say, of course, that Sinclair's experience confirms certain insights offered by criticism in our time. We might, for example, conclude that his reading of Shakespeare operates as a kind of deconstruction worked upon the hegemonic semiotic order of the 1920s. And we might also offer his account as a rough and ready proof for the reality of *jouissance,* the Derridean/Barthian pleasure produced by an interpretive excess that sometimes overwhelms the stability of our signifiers. But to offer experience as a proof of Derrida's or Barthes' critical programs is to accept the idea that the experience Sinclair describes precedes the theory, and that our theories are only attempts to come to terms with certain practices and experiences that occur no matter how we actually explain them. It's significant, and outright amazing to me, that the readers I've cited—Hugh of Saint Victor, Sinclair, and Lentriccia himself—describe the act of reading in remarkably similar ways. What we see is a close family resemblance among practices spanning a thousand years, practices that may even be universal, since we would not need to search for very long to find similar practices in the Asian and Islamic traditions.

We will never recognize the family resemblance, though, until we concede, perhaps with some alarm, that the experience each writer describes is not actually determined by the text, in and of itself. Hugh wasn't reading fiction, of course, but the Bible, which he held to be absolute Truth. Sinclair was reading Shakespeare (who bored another reader, Leo Tolstoy). And Lentriccia was reading a book few people even remember these days, Willard Motley's crime novel *Knock on Any Door.* What matters, in other words, is not the text itself—pulp fiction or the *Odyssey, Sense and Sensibility* or Wittgenstein's *Tractatus*—but the practice of reading and the experience it produces. Of course, a reader is always free to employ the text in ways other than the one that Lentriccia describes. A linguist might comb through the pages of Shakespeare for evidence of a deep structure unaffected by linguistic change since the late 1500s; a historian might employ key passages to parse the class relations of Elizabethan England. But to read any work as "literature" is to use it freely as a device—a technology, if you want—for undergoing a certain change in awareness, now confined largely to the literary but once held to be the reason for reading of all kinds. The technology, I should add, may fail and the change may not happen. Just as one might go to confession and still not feel forgiven, or just as one can do yoga for hours and still have jangled nerves, so the proper conjunction between the words, the world, and the reader is too complex to orchestrate effectively every time.[23]

My choice of these last examples—the sacrament of confession, and the yogic practice of meditation—is deliberate, because all three accounts of literary reading, Hugh's, Sinclair's, and Lentriccia's, suggest a close connection to ritual. Literary reading *is* a ritual, in the root sense of the word as an act that *joins* the performer with something or someone, first performatively and then (if all goes well) experientially and psychologically.[24] But joined with what? While Ivan Illich traces reading-as-ritual back to the monasteries, the ritual of literary reading as we know it today is no longer a religious discipline but one that we might speak of as artistic. We might conjecture that religious ritual transports us out of ourselves into a world "above" and "beyond"—metaphorically, the realm of heaven—or else it brings heaven down to us. One might explain any particular ritual in a variety of ways, but no religious ritual that I know of fails to promise this mobilization of the transcendent, from low to high or high to low. By contrast, artistic ritual would seem to follow a rather different trajectory, not out of the world but more intensely into it.

I scarcely need to add that a century of formalism has helped to sever the arts (and the humanities) from discussions of experience generally. And at the same time that the idea of experience has fallen into discredit among intellectuals, people in the West have come to conceive of ritual as unchanging and inflexible, the quintessential instance of routinization and the very opposite of the disruptiveness that lies at the heart of avant-gardism in the arts. This way of thinking, however, overlooks what is, perhaps, the most obvious aspect of ritual of every kind—its distinctness from everyday life. The practice of ritual symbolically creates a space freed from the parameters of mundane awareness. Ritual involves repetition, certainly, but not, strictly speaking, routinization because ritual takes place outside normal time in a "primordial world." We might say, with the anthropologist Roy Rappaport, that successful ritual arrests the passing of mundane time and returns its practitioners to an apparently eternal "now" of pure presence or pure absence, a "time out of time."[25] Of course, rituals produce this suspension of the mundane to different degrees, but often the central rituals of a society are those that bring people most directly face to face with a reality perceived as sacred because it exceeds the interpretative resources at their disposal. In the world of mundane time, the communion host is only a wafer of unleavened flour, the wine is only the fermented juice of grapes; but for devout practitioners, these can become the *same* bread and wine as those consumed at the Last Supper, which was itself a ritual. A comparable argument can also be made for our experience of a work of art. Although we "know" that the Hans Hofmann painting on the wall before us is nothing more than squares of paint on cloth, the canvas is also, experientially, the golden doorway into another world, a threshold or *limen* we are invited to cross.[26]

The "other world" of religious ritual is *fundamentally* other. While the activities of ritual with their attendant symbols—breaking bread, eating bitter herbs, constructing sand mandalas, sounding a shofar or a conch shell—may lend themselves to endless interpretation, the ritual process, as the anthropologist Victor Turner calls it, is not an *interpretive* activity; not one, in another words, that calls on participants to engage in exegesis.[27] We might even say that religious ritual does its real work when the desire for discursive explanation ceases, since "understanding" simply means that we have placed things in their familiar conceptual places. The impulse to ritual begins, by contrast, with a loss of confidence in the existing order of things, even when practitioners enact their ritual with the goal of restoring that order—during moments of personal or social crisis. In *Boiling Energy,* Richard Katz's study of Kung religious belief, he describes three stages in the healing ritual—stages that we might call (although Katz himself does not) encounter, transport/transformation, and release:

> At the start . . . the mood is casual and jovial. . . . Then, almost imperceptibly, the mood intensifies. The singing and clapping become more spirited, the dancing more focused. Most of the healers at the dance are now dancing; the adolescents have either retired to the periphery or begun dancing in a more serious manner. Joking and socializing continue. The atmosphere is earnest, but not somber.
>
> As midnight approaches, with the flickering fire illuminating the singers and dancers, a healer or two begins to stagger, then perhaps one falls. They may shudder or shake violently, their whole body convulsing in apparent pain or anguish. The experience of *kia* [the descent of *num* or divine energy] has begun. And then, either on their own or under the guidance of those who are more steady, the healers who are in *kia* go to each person at the dance and begin to heal. . . .
>
> Gradually a calm sets in as the dance moves into the early morning hours. Some dancers sleep for a brief period; the talk is quiet, the singing soft . . . Before the sun becomes too warm, the kia and healing subside, and the singing gradually softens, then ends. The dance is over.[28]

Unlike healers in other traditions—the Tungus shamans, for example—the Kung do not leave their bodies and ascend to heaven. Instead, the *num* or divine life-energy descends into their mortal bodies as the "boiling energy" of Katz's title. Infused with this energy, healers act as living circuit breakers, sending the restorative current surging through their community. That heaven comes down to the Kung tells us a great deal about the particular character of Kung society, but we might find quite similar rituals, however differently explained, in Pentecostal churches right here in the United States. In both cases, the healer first leaves day-to-day reality and then enters another, transcendent domain. In the condition that the Kung call *kia,* which closely resembles the descent of the Holy Spirit, the healer "sees clearly," as though "lighted up," and possesses the power to heal. Finally, as the ritual concludes, participants return to everyday life with a restored sense of well-being— of connectedness with the world.

At the heart of Kung ritual is an encounter with a force that healers may or may not understand theoretically but that direct experience presents to them as superior to understanding. In this regard, the Kung practice of healing with *num* energy resembles rituals in many societies. Here, for example, is an account from the filmmaker Maya Deren, in the culminating moments of her own experience at a Haitian *voudon* ritual:

> For I know now that, today, the drums, the singing, the movements—these may catch *me* also. I do not wish that . . . The drums pause; then, almost immediately, begin again, accumulating, this time, into a Mahi. This has a gay quality and is a dance step which I particularly delight in, although it rapidly tires the muscles of the calves and thighs. At first the drummer is considerate and "breaks" often enough to permit the limbs to relax and rest. But as the dance goes on, these "breaks" become more rare and the sense of fun gives way to a sense of great effort. The air seems heavy and wet and, gasping, I feel that it brings no refreshment into my pounding lungs. . . . Each cell of my body and brain anguishes upward and yet I cannot lift myself by my own motion; but, like some still unborn, unliving thing, [I] am drawn up, slowly at first by the sound's power. Slowly still . . . as one might rise up from the bottom of the sea, so I rise up, the body growing lighter with each second . . . uprising higher, mounting still higher . . . the sound grown still stronger . . . the thundering rattle, clangoring bell, unbearable, then suddenly: surface; suddenly: air; suddenly: sound is light, dazzling white.
> How clear the world looks in this first total light.[29]

In religious discourses from many cultures—late Classical, Medieval Christian, Islamic, Hindu-Buddhist, Hasidic, Native American—one might find numerous similarities; too many, in my view, for us to dismiss them as coincidence.[30] The lesson that I draw, however, from these numerous correspondences is not (necessarily) that God or the gods are real, but that there are more things between heaven and earth than are dreamt of in our current text-centered way of thinking. Obviously, a deft critic might subject the "text" of the *voudon* ritual to a range of ingenious readings, but so long as we imagine the event, experienced as continuous change, to be a static and impersonal text, we will continue to believe mistakenly that human beings always encounter the world pretty much as we do sitting at our desks.

If ritual is, as I suggest, a formalized mode of activity that serves to connect practitioners with something beyond themselves, and if the hallmark of this connection is a change in the condition of their consciousness—a change like the one Maya Deren recounts—then we might think of literary reading as another form of ritual, though not necessarily a religious one. Even if literary reading today has become a distinctly secular affair, it still bears a close family resemblance to its sacred predecessor, at least outside the academy. As accounts like Lentriccia's suggest, however, the ritual of literary reading differs in a significant way from religious ritual because it refuses the path of absolute transcendence. In literary reading, the movement is not out of the world altogether—into Daren's synesthetic white light, for example—but into another world, or if you wish, an Other world, always marked by its difference from the real. Certainly, I can take a trip down the Mississippi, but I cannot take a trip in the same way to Faulkner's Yoknapatawpha County. It has become conventional in English to argue that every reader must imagine Yoknapatawpha for himself, but the truth is somewhat more complex. Nobody really *sees* Faulkner's fictional world with his mind's eye: we simply know that it is somewhat like the place we live, and also somewhat different. Deconstruction, in its attentiveness to this always "other" quality of the literary, has gone a long way toward showing why no two readings of Faulkner can ever be the same, and why English studies has no stable literary object that we might dissect like an anatomical specimen. But because we have stopped there, with the alleged "impossibility" of reading in a normative way, we have failed to consider the likelihood that "literature" is not primarily a noun but a verb: not an object but a process.

If there were such a verb as "to literize"—though I'm infinitely thankful there's not—it would define an activity that most text-centered theories overlook. To literize, I'm arguing, is to establish a particular relation between the world presented by immediate experience and always-other world evoked by language. Here is what one writer, Eudora Welty, remembers about her earliest moments of literary experience:

> In my sensory education I include my physical awareness of the *word*. Of a certain word, that is: the connection it has with what it stands for. At around age six, perhaps, I was standing by myself in our front yard waiting for supper, just at that hour in a late summer day when the sun is already below the horizon and the risen full moon in the visible sky stops being chalky and begins to take on light. There comes the moment, and I saw it then, when the moon goes from flat to round. For the first time it met my eyes as a globe. The word "moon" came into my mouth as though fed to me out of a silver spoon. Held in my mouth the moon became a word.[31]

I suggest that we have given the name "literary" to those sorts of experience in which language heightens, in the mode of pretend or possibility, an awareness of our connectedness to things. And language does so in part, as many of our theorists have claimed, by creating a distance or a difference—a detour—from immediate sensory life. But difference is only one moment in a more extended process, a process that never simply leaves us in a condition of worldlessness. Instead, it brings us back again to the everyday, and by stages closely comparable to the stages of Kung ritual.[32] Can we not see in the process that Welty describes a triparte movement that corresponds to the inner journey of the Kung healer—from Here to There and back again? Obviously, the globe of light that Welty saw in the sky was not the same as the word *moon*. And yet the word *moon* carries Welty from "Here" to "There," from the earth to the sky and back. The word *moon* allows Welty to eat the moon, to make it part of her sensuous life, much as Christian communion takers eat the body of Christ, and much as Lentriccia felt reading to be a sensual, sexual pleasure. In each case, there is a crucial moment of "joining," just as the Latin root of "ritual" suggests. By overemphasizing dissociation—the "gap" between the word and its referent—poststructuralists have undervalued the synthetic character of language in particular and the arts in general, but they have done so for a reason that deserves a second look: the moment of synthesis, of contact, takes place not on the level of words but on the level of life as lived or as imagined, while the words themselves are always empty vehicles. The word *moon* will *never* be the same as the object in orbit above our heads, but word and moon can be fused *experientially*—in the associational fabric of our memory and feeling.

To those who still long for the certainties of science, an achievement of the kind Welty commemorates is bound to seem disappointing. If we permit ourselves to reflect, however, that the recent decline of "French theory" is only one sad moment in a century of reversals, then we might at least consider a turn to the arts instead. But this turn, as I have tried to indicate so far, may produce a sweeping transformation of the way we imagine the arts themselves. Once we can look closely at the subject without high theory obstructing our view, we are dragged back to the arts as a mode of experience—in fact, as a form of ritual. And once we begin to think along these lines, we may discover that the truths offered by the humanities differ fundamentally from the truths of science. Rembrandt's painting, after all, can scarcely be called more true than Carravaggio's; what mattered about the work of both artists in their times was not fidelity to some ultimate level of fact but the artists' ability restore and intensify, for themselves and for others, a sense of contact with the world at its most immediate. By the same token, no one can decisively say that Richard Poirier's reading of Robert Frost's poetry is incorrect; no one can say with absolute certainty that Roosevelt knew in advance about Pearl Habor or that William James influenced Ludwig Wittgenstein. The truth of the humanities does not lie primarily in what they *say* but in what they enable us to *do*.

Ritual at once demonstrates and dramatizes the existence of this other, nonscientific kind of truth—the truth of contact.[33] If we ask any form of ritual to produce an accurate representation of something, then we are bound to see the "text" of the ritual as useless, even deceptive. There is, for example, no necessary relation of fact, logic, or resemblance between a sacramental wafer and the body of Jesus: one could just as easily eat fish, since Jesus called himself a "fisher of men," or the hearts of palm, since Jesus' donkey trod upon palm fronds as he entered Jerusalem. Granted, the wafer is a kind of bread and Jesus ate bread at the Last Supper, but what makes Holy Communion tranformative is the repetition of an activity—doing what Jesus did. It is not the bread that makes communion holy, but the process that transforms the bread itself, and that transports Christ into the assembly of believers. Much the same might be said of the events in a story: what links them, finally, is the synthetic practice of storytelling. Along the way, the storyteller can throw in almost any event, no matter how incongruous or unexpected, without ceasing to "tell a story."[34]

The practices of art making recreate the world for the purposes of renewing contact with it. Even works that are self-consciously "realist" could not qualify as "art" at all unless they managed, if only implicitly, to reconfigure in some way the conventional matrix of sounds, ideas, associations, and so on. In fact, we might say that art is art only by virtue of this reconfiguring, as in the case of the R. Mutt urinal. Ordinarily, we bet our lives on the predictability of our interactions with the world. Hearing the noise of a bus approach as we cross the street, we pick up our pace to the curb. To react to the noise by assuming that absolutely anything might happen— that the bus might turn into a flock of birds or that the street itself might lift us high above danger—could prove to be a fatal mistake. But it is the function of art making to compose a new world counterfactually. Art allows us, through synthetic activity, to reconstruct our sensuous and intellectual relations without immediate regard to consequences, and the result, perhaps paradoxically, is a deepened intimation of reality. This playful reordering of our experience is a basic human need and a distinctive source of pleasure that requires no defense on "ultimate" or metaphysical grounds, any more than sexuality or eating require some philosophical justification.

From moment to moment, people ceaselessly fashion their own lived worlds, synthesizing manifold impressions into a whole that is primarily emotional and sensory. The arts, we might say, enact in a ritualized manner this most basic human labor, even when the material products of these arts ostensibly represent fragmentation, loss, confusion, and so on. Even *Guernica,* even the layered splatters of Jackson Pollock, call upon us to bring forth a meaningful world at the moment of our seeing them.[35] I say "call upon us" because no artist can deliver to us such a world fully realized, never mind that our creative activity may escape our own attention. Strictly speaking, a person does not see a painting: a person employs the painting as an opportunity to see, using it as the raw material out of which he or she can relive and renew a felt sense of connection.

Of course, the arts may be used for propaganda, for nation building, for "education" in the most reductive senses of the word. But the arts are fundamentally promiscuous, and this is why we need them at the center of the humanities. So long as academic humanists set themselves up as the cultural police, they will continue to take us farther and farther away from any deepened appreciation of our own inextinguishable freedom. If ten thousand years of art making have taught us nothing else, from the caves of Lascaux until now, they have taught us that the human being is not just the creature who knows, nor even the creature who plays, but the creature who *awakens.* Every moment of human life, when we feel truly alive, is a moment of awakening into a world somehow unlike the world we knew a moment before. It is, on the one hand, this propensity for awakening that will endlessly overturn all our utopias, leaving even our finest creations to crumble in neglect. But this native-born capacity for awakening is also, on the other hand, our saving grace, since it means that the products of our worst imaginings cannot last forever.

Of course criticism is an activity too, no less than painting or writing poetry, but criticism as a process has a different trajectory. Criticism begins with a unique stabilization of our perceptions, one that inhibits tranformation and transport. Before criticism can get underway, it needs to constitute a stable object, and it does so by "freezing" relations among words, images, objects, even sentiments. How many times have we found something unexpected in a familiar book or an often-heard piece of music, no matter how carefully we've read it or listened to it before, and no matter how often? But criticism—even in its deconstructive variant—suppresses this complexity at the outset for the purposes of passing judgment, not only the complexity within the work itself but also the complexity of our thoughts and feelings about it. In this sense, criticism is fundamentally *conservative*. As Robert Scholes has argued approvingly, criticism is always an act undertaken on behalf a group, an "us": what Scholes neglects to say is that "us" generally means our most powerful institutions.[36] Precisely because critical judgment gets undertaken in the service of an "us," a preexisting group or an institution, the categories on which it must rely are typically conventional and normative.

But if scholarship in the humanities should turn its back on the practice of criticism, what might it become instead? Luckily, there is an alternative and that is "interpretation." When we interpret—when we use a painting to see or a poem to engage in our own practice of art making—we express through this activity a faith in the possibility of elective affinities, noncoercive connections to the world and to other people, which are actually expressions of love. In the practice of interpretation, at least beyond the classroom and the barriers of the profession, we often feel ourselves to be moving toward a disclosure of some fundamental secret, and along the way we get distracted and delayed by any number of stimulating complications. Although people frequently imagine that a painting or a novel presents a finished order or an overarching philosophy, it actually makes seeing or hearing or thinking more difficult. In the activity of interpretation, we may feel that we have opened a door into some strange place, either terrible or wonderful. Perhaps paradoxically, it is this experience of ritualized estrangement that finally intensifies our sense of both connection and of freedom: the loss of a familiar world provides the stimulus for renewed synthesis on terms we ourselves must discover or define. And this is why we actually have no need for standardized critical approaches that tell us in advance the proper way to engage with a work of art—deconstruction, New Historicism, and so on. No sooner do we use a painting to see, no sooner do we use a poem to think and feel, than we are already caught up in the ritual. Every work of art by its nature is automatically estranging, enticing, and potentially renewing, and any response that makes us feel "more alive," in Frank Lentriccia's words, is always exactly the right response.[37]

Criticism aims at truth on the model of the sciences, but the most important outcome of interpretation is virtuosity, as in the case of any artistic activity. The virtuoso has the ability to act in a way that is more or less *satisfying* to himself and others, more or less enabling, enobling, or refreshing. In this spirit, we can admire, even envy, an interpretation that we ourselves would never care to embrace. No one who understands the creative aspect of interpretation will be troubled to consider that the most learned and able critics often disagree about the "meaning" of a passage in, say, Wallace Stevens. To interpret a Stevens poem is to employ it as an opportunity for the creation of exactly such disagreements, and we judge the interpreter, as we judge the artist, by the fulfillment of a goal he himself has created. But virtuosity should not be conflated with technical proficiency: it offers something much more valuable, the chance for a richer interior life, and by extension, a richer communal life as well. Why is it that one interpretation will seem somehow satisfying to me when any number of alternative readings might be equally warranted by the text? Why is it that when I read a poem or story, I reach *this* particular conclusion, rather than some other? Surely the answer has to do with all the things that make one human life among six billion lives into *my* life uniquely. Reading may be a "social act," but it is also an act that produces a progressively greater self-awareness—as Hugh of Saint Victor understood—at the same time that it produces a deepened and broadened awareness of the world beyond the self. Interpretation achieves this end by moving us back and forth between domains, between the self and the world, so that our presence to ourselves is never given matter-of-factly, but must always be achieved in the encounter with potentially endless multiplicity. If criticism reinforces the "us," interpretation presupposes an "I" and a "thou": the world with this person, and that person, in it *together.* In the process of interpretation, we are always "alone with others," to take a phrase from the philosopher Stephen Batchelor, always set free to create the conditions of our sociability.[38]

Instead of imagining our mission as the search for a sciencelike certainty—perhaps in the service of political change, perhaps just to prop up our profession—we in the humanities should understand that knowledge, in the strictest sense, is not our primary concern. Rather, our concern is a particular *use* of knowledge, a use that loosens the hold of society over us, and we should not condemn this loosening as inherently antisocial, since the process of art making releases all of us from the rigidity of culture itself. If this true—if the humanities serve their proper end when they refuse to subordinate human beings to the artifacts of human activity—then the academy might play a political role less like the one it has played for some time now, and more like one from another time, in another place. I have in mind the Athens of Sophocles, author of the Oedipus plays.[39]

When I was an undergraduate, I learned to read *Oedipus the King* as a cautionary tale about the dangers of *hybris,* the arrogance of the play's protagonist. As everyone knew after "World Drama Survey," the gods visit on the dynamnic young king a terrible and unforeseen lesson: that his autonomy and resourcefulness were only an illusion. If we accept this conventional reading of the play, then we might conclude that a humbled Oedipus discovers by the end that the gods *will* be obeyed—that they have been his masters all along, and that because of his overweening pride, undeserved disasters have fallen on the city he ruled. But this reading now strikes me as insensitive to the complexities of Sophocles' actual story. Oedipus may have been guilty of arrogance, and he gives way at times to a truly murderous temper, yet many scholars have pointed out that the Greeks would have seen him as morally blameless for the parricide and incest he *unknowingly* commits.[40]

But if Oedipus is morally blameless for the murder of his father and the marriage to his mother, how should we understand the play? I suspect that few of the Athenians who first witnessed its performance at the festival of Dionysus would

have failed to appreciate a key detail: the savior of Thebes from the ravages of the
Sphinx is Oedipus instead of a more conventional choice, the shaman/seer Tiresias,
whose stock-in-trade was tranformation and transport through ritual. While the
blind Tiresias waits in vain for Apollo's guidance, Oedipus acts on the counsels of
reason. Though I am not the first to make this argument, I now believe that
Sophocles' protagonist represents the spirit of critical rationality in the Periclean
age.[41] As we learn from the series of revelations that destroy Oedipus inexorably,
reason could not protect him when he needed it most.

The story, of course, does not end there, with reason's failure. In the second of
the two Sophocles plays, Oedipus gets taken up to Olympus by the gods. But what
does this change in his status imply? I would say that to become a god as Oedipus
does is to see like a god: to see the terrible together with the beautiful, the rational
together with irrational, the knowable together with the unknowable. Oedipus
begins as a critic, so to speak, but in the course of events he discovers another way of
being, a discovery that costs him so terribly because he was so thoroughly convinced
that the limits of the world are the limits of discriminating intellect. As he eventually
learns in the most painful way, critical reason operates only in the realm of the
familiar and cannot achieve what Oedipus lacks as his life falls apart: a way of
making sense—of making whole—events that seem impossible at first to assess. For
the rationalist, it's reason or nothing, system or nothing, but Oedipus discovers that
reason is only the right hand of understanding, so to speak. In the person of
Oedipus, Sophocles argues for what we might call the *hodos,* the way, of the arts: if
reason is the right hand of our understanding, art making is the left.

When Oedipus has learned that reason rests on a life-world broader and
deeper than reason, an imperterbable calm descends on him, a sense of connection
no misfortune can destroy, and not calm alone but also joy.[42] According to Socrates
in the *Phaedrus,* reason works by transcending every particular until the sensible
world itself evaporates, leaving only pure, disembodied forms, but the *hodos* of
Oedipus moves "out" instead of "up," bringing more and more of the actual world
into the theater of his awareness—and his affections:[43]

> This day, my daughters,
> you shall have no father left to you.
> For all my life is done. . . .
> It was not easy, children, *that* I know,
> and yet one little word can change all pain:
> that word is LOVE; and love you've had from me
> more than any man can ever give.[44]

The freedom that Oedipus at last achieves is not a freedom from this world of
insecurity and pain, as in Platonic philosophy, but a release from the illusion of his
own separateness—which is the sickness of too much reason, the sickness of critique. And *this* is Sophocles' answer to the philosophers, his warning to the citizens
of Athens. To them he sends a message to this effect: "The triumph of critical reason
can bring nothing short of ruin to the polis. Our polis, our democracy, will survive

only if we understand that all of us are blind, that no can see the entire truth. This blindness is our common ground, and the birthplace of our equality." Oedipus, we might say, learns how not to know, how to live in a condition of modest and creative uncertainty that is more inclusive than reason. What he resists, good rationalist that he is, and what he must be made to learn by the fate that the gods have apportioned to him, is learning itself. To live in a condition of "not knowing" is to cultivate a greater receptivity to things and a more flexible understanding, a refusal to insist that the present must always exactly repeat the past.

In effect, Sophocles tells his fellow citizens, "Our thinkers see parts but they cannot see wholes. Wholeness, the known *and* the unknown, will reveal itself only to the poet's sightless eye." Democracy needs the poet's blindness—democracy needs the arts—because equality is possible only in a climate of pervasive uncertainty: since no one can ever know for sure, anyone might offer a crucial piece of the puzzle. And since *anyone* might know something worthwhile, *everyone* should be heard. But unknowing has another and perhaps more important dimension: in a democracy, what matters most is not any particular answer but the inclusiveness of participation in our questioning. When we dispense with the dumb show of "representative government" and aim instead at government by the governed, democracy is the form of politics that comes closest to an art, since participation ceases to be a means to an end becomes instead an end in itself. Precisely because the arts are ritual enactments of our freedom to *make* our lives, they teach the openness of the human condition even when they seem to argue for the very opposite, and even when they get taken up as instruments of cultural normalization.

Every teacher in the humanities already knows this, on some level. The problem for most teachers in introductory classes is not that the novel or painting or historical event seems meaningless to students but the very opposite: the problem is how to *constrain* interpretation within "acceptable" or "responsible" limits. But what are those limits? Even the most accomplished readers disagree, often with great vehemence. The problem for the teacher, in other words, is to ensure that the student's practice of interpretation does not undermine the authority of Criticism, Inc. But precisely because the experts themselves must each say something new, they inevitably destabilize their own claim to a definitive understanding of the subject at hand. Like it or not, the subject at hand always compels us to speak as nothing less and nothing more than our fallible individual selves.

Oedipus is the first interpreter in the Western imagination, and also the first true individual, the first person in legend or literature to have an inner life. Although traditional Greek society understood identity as a public affair—the public performance of a normative role—Oedipus becomes the complete outsider, unwelcome in any city on the whole of the Peloponnesus. Yet the great lesson of the Oedipus plays is the ennobling and liberating character of his separateness, which finally leads him to the realm of the gods, a lesson utterly lost on those who associate all forms of self-awareness with "possessive individualism." As Sophocles understood, and the point would get taken up again by Tocqueville two thousand years later, the principal danger of democracy is not that people will give themselves over to sheer anarchy, but that the power of popular opinion will become a tyranny worse than any dictatorship.[45] We should not forget that antiquity's greatest critics of democracy, Plato and Aristotle, understood Socrates' execution to be the decisive failure of the whole democratic experiment. The two philosophers renewed a search for unchanging foundations precisely because they believed that if truth were nothing more than a matter of consensus, as many of our postmodernists hold, then the strongest voice would always carry the day. And in this fear they were right: the desire to achieve consensus all too easily becomes coercive. When no one dares to challenge the wisdom of the collectivity—or rather, the wisdom of its charismatic leaders—an entire society can go astray. It's worth remembering that Hitler was *elected.*

For Plato—and indeed for the modern West—the alternative was the administered state. In place of popular sovereignty, Plato's Republic embodies the principle of rule by the best and the brightest. And as everyone knows, Plato banishes the poets from his Republic precisely because they are willing to think counterfactually—to think, that is, in ways that the elite have banished from their own lives as well as from the lives of those they rule. Plato's real quarrel, however, is not with the poets but with politics itself, and with the tendency in a democracy for politics to become increasingly expansive and intrusive. Politics, in the sense that Aristotle means when he defines it as the art of the possible, becomes impossible in Plato's Republic, where reason's unrepealable laws reign supreme.[46] By contrast, in the real Athens of Plato's time, everything had become political, so that any belief that challenged the *sensus communis* might be regarded as virtual treason. This was political correctness with a vengeance, and we have seen it more than once in the twentieth century, from the left and from the right. The best corrective seems to be administration from on high: when democracy means Jim Crow, after all, who wouldn't want an intrusive bureaucracy? And yet, as we have learned, or should have learned from our own nation's recent history, the best and the brightest can also make egregious mistakes. For this reason, rule by the best and brightest should politely give way to rule by the ruled themselves. As John Dewey argued, the solution to democracy's failures is more democracy, not its abandonment.[47] But even Dewey never fully understood that democracy requires a freedom *from* democracy.

We should not forget that Oedipus is a person for whom the private becomes entirely, and uncontrollably, political, so that the whole city of Thebes must pay for transgressions he alone commits while the most intimate details of his private life fall under the scrutiny of every citizen. Surely now, after the bedroom scandals of Clinton years, we can read the Oedipus plays as warning the Athenians to place limits on the reach of the political into personal life. As social beings, we are knowable to others only insofar as our behavior conforms to some category or other; but our lives are meaningful to us personally only to the degree that they exceed all such categories. We are the creatures who awake, and who never cease to awake, only because we never cease to be a question, a mystery, to ourselves.

And this question, we might say, was the one posed by the Sphinx to Oedipus: What walks on four legs in the morning, two legs at noon, and three legs as the sun begins to set? The truth, a truth we have yet to learn, is that no political system—not democracy and certainly not the Marxist fantasy of total collectivity—can solve the riddle of the Sphinx. If there is any difference, however, between democracy and its authoritarian rivals, that difference lies primarily in *their* readiness to furnish us with answers all quite neatly worked out and revisable only on pain of banishment, the gulag, or death. We should understand, however, that Oedipus *also* fails to answer the Sphinx properly. In keeping with his character as a rationalist and bureaucrat, he replies with the smart but empty abstraction, "Man." If only he could have openly declared, "*I myself* am that mysterious creature," how different his life might have been. By admitting to his own unknowability, Oedipus would have freed himself from the ruinous belief in his natural superiority.

"I myself"—this is the first and last lesson taught by the arts, and the one most crucial for our political future. Anyone who bothers to review the centuries of literature, music, the visual arts, historical writing, and philosophy is bound to be struck not so much by the continuity as by the overwhelming *diversity*. But this diversity is not simply remarkable, a lucky accident: it is also inescapable because each of us has to answer the Sphinx's question for ourselves in fashioning the lives we actually lead. While it may be true that unconscious forces goad us inescapably, and while unexpected consequences are bound to overtake us, just as they overtake Oedipus, it is profoundly false to view the self in the structuralist fashion as nothing more than the focal point of various determinants, or else, as the poststructuralists think, of various accidents. The self, we might say, persists only through its own creative activity: we choose it and then we lose it in the welter of unforeseen events, but then we create it again, and again and again. For as long as we live, we continue this synthesis, until the self we have fashioned assumes the character of our *fate,* as Emerson understood.[48] This is the self that Oedipus gradually discovers in his homeless wandering. And the continuous deepening of this self, its continuous destruction and re-creation, takes him closer and closer to the gods, for whom choice and fate have become the same. The Greeks understood this experience as *apotheosis,* becoming godlike, but we in our time might understand it as a return to nature. In its best moments, the created life, as opposed to the life that we are compelled to live, assumes the character of a "natural process" that unfolds like the unfolding of leaves from a bud, or of grass from a seed. It is surely no accident that any number of artists have recognized this same fateful process in the slow maturing of their work. After blindly groping, sometimes for years, they suddenly see in everything that came before a hidden *telos,* an unfolding that appears in retrospect to have been inevitable all the time. In reality, the recognition of this "inevitability" is itself a creative act.

Yet in a certain sense, the self is not our own creation. While the sciences have shown us for two centuries our connection to a universe enormous and strange beyond our powers of description, the arts have shown us much the same thing from a different direction—starting from *inside.* The great secret of the arts is the great secret of culture in general: at the heart of our humanity we find something beyond humanity. This too is a lesson first learned by Oedipus. The deeper we move within ourselves when we follow the *hodos,* the way, of not knowing and of making, the closer we come to an intimation of a world within which the self is only one small but integral part. It is a legacy of the critical tradition to see the world as though from a distance, but human beings are always *in* the world. And because we are always in it, we might say that our own creativity does indeed allow us, as I claimed in chapter 7, to participate in the creativity of the universe itself—that is, if we choose to do so.

If we choose. The age of Oedipus the expert has come to an end only in the annals of Attic tragedy: today's Americans seem no more troubled by their political passivity than they did in the Eisenhower years, and the Populist struggle of the nineteenth century has ceased to live on in our nation's daily life even as a memory. But those of us who still believe in government *by* the governed, not simply by consent of sandbagged "voters" but by action on the part of able citizens—we might begin to transform our passive politics by first changing the character of private life. And here the arts may have a crucial role to play, if we can somehow extricate them from the velvet of pretentious erudition in which they now lie smothered. A nation of internet novelists and camcorder movie-makers, Sunday-afternoon painters and bankers who spend downtime at poetry slams might not become a second Athens, but it could all the same produce Americans slightly less in awe of their leadership and slightly more assured of their capacity for freedom. How those of us who are not artists, even of the Sunday-afternoon kind, but who teach and write inside the university, might help to bring about such a development is the question I will turn to next.

10

Travels to the Heart of the Forest

Dilettantes and Professionals in the Twentieth Century

So completely have professionals remade knowledge in their own image that most of us might find it hard, and possibly absurd, to seek knowledge from anyone else. After all, the university and its disciplines exist only for the sake of knowledge. And the disciplines have brought us, some might say, the most complex, transformative achievements of all time—so complex and transformative that we can scarcely name the least of them without falling back on clichés: the discovery of DNA and black holes, the invention of the microchip and the polio vaccine. Who, after reading Max Weber's *The Protestant Ethic and the Spirit of Capitalism,* or Ian Watt's *The Rise of the Novel,* or J. L. Austin's *How to Do Things with Words,* would want to challenge the fundamental wisdom behind the modern system of academic professions? As it turns out, however, growing numbers of people inside the system itself have begun to voice their deep misgivings about professionalism and its human consequences.

The philosopher Hilary Putnam has, for one, dismissed several decade's worth of analytic philosophy on the grounds that it is "fundamentally frivolous"— fundamentally unrelated to anything except "the 'intuitions' of a handful of philosophers." For all its brilliance and sophistication, Putnam frankly concedes, the discipline of academic philosophy no longer carries any "weight" in the lives of most Americans.[1] At the same time, another respected malcontent, the economist Richard Parker, has written on the implications of a full-page ad, placed some years ago in *The American Economic Review,* calling for a conceptual revolution in *that* field. Among the co-signers decrying "the monopoly of method" and the obsession with elegant, otherworldly formulas were a number of Nobel winners, including Paul Samuelson, Herbert Simon, and Jan Tinbergen.[2] "Much of what economists [used to] do," Parker concedes, "is being done more effectively outside economics departments," while the Ph.D. in economics has become "a stepping-stone" into a "hermetically circular world."[3] But the humanities are hardly exempt from such a charge. From within the discipline of history, Alan Megill and Donald McCloskey note with alarm "a growing split" between professional historians, who have largely abandoned the narrative form, and a wider public that has abandoned these historians in turn. A century ago, by contrast, historians like Gibbon in Great Britain and Prescott in the United States. still rivaled major novelists as widely read public figures. For whom, Megill and McCloskey ask, are current academic histories intended, and why has a once enormous audience disappeared almost overnight?[4] Something has gone wrong across the disciplines. A philosopher, an economist, and a pair of historians—what these doubters all share is not just a profound dissatisfaction with academic knowledge, which keeps saying more and more about less and less, but also an aversion to the way of life that the making of this knowledge appears to demand: the *culture* of specialization.

As the last hundred years have shown all too graphically, entire countries can collapse in a year, in a week, but a world without the current division of knowledge appears to many humanists far less possible than the world without its now-familiar national borders. Yet the modern system of academic professions is only slightly older than the automobile. Weber and Durkheim both belonged to an emergent profession, sociology; Marx, notably, did not. That Darwin began his intellectual journey as a free-lance "naturalist," and that *The Origin of Species* precedes the full professionalization of biology—these details we often forget, and our forgetfulness has prevented us from asking a crucial question: Does the system of professions actually *ensure* that everyone, experts as well as amateurs, will feel powerless in the long run?

The principal subjects of this chapter are two very different men representing two very different futures for the humanities, and not only for the humanities but also for knowledge in general. The first of these two futures has also been our recent past: the humanities as professions on the model of a science. And the man behind the model, in this chapter at least, is the anthropologist Claude Lévi-Strauss, the scientist who has held the greatest sway over humanities for the last forty years. The other man, by contrast, is far less widely known: in fact, I have never encountered anyone else who has even heard his name. Yet this man, Earl Parker Hanson, may have shown us the way out of our current impasse, if we are prepared to follow him.

Sometimes Hanson's writing reads like anthropology, and his great travelogue *Journey to Manaos* might be mistaken at certain moments in the narrative for a classic of social science like *The Sexual Life of Savages* or *Coming of Age in Samoa*. In much the same way, the casual observer might have mistaken Hanson himself for an associate of seasoned anthropologists like Bronislaw Malinowski or Margaret Mead. In the early 1930s, Hanson left the United States to live among the "natives" of northwestern Brazil, where he observed, recorded faithfully, and struggled to explain strange events and even stranger customs. But Hanson was not an anthropologist, and his *Journey to Manaos* actually belongs to the genre anthropologists contemplate with a pronounced uneasiness: the amateur genre of travel writing, which resembles anthropology closely enough to raise doubts about the differences between serious research and the dilettante's passing impressions.[5] The doubts raised by books like the one that Hanson wrote go a long way toward explaining why Lévi-Strauss should start his own, far more famous travelogue *Tristes Tropiques—Sad Tropics*—by announcing right up front, "I hate traveling and explorers." "Adventure," Lévi-Strauss continues, has no proper role to play "in the anthropologist's profession."[6] Yet his distaste for adventure and adventurers has sources deeper than simple snobbery—sources that will be my subject here. To someone who embraces his profession as the last, best hope for order in a profoundly misguided world, nothing could seem less welcome than the spectacle of dilettantes crashing noisily around.

Those of us now entering the new century have a special need to look closely at books like the one that Hanson wrote. Precisely because travel narratives come from outside the self-enchanting circle of specialization, they give us a chance to think more honestly about the motives that have made academic knowledge so thoroughly . . . academic—motives openly professed, as I hope to indicate, by leading figures in many fields during their formative years. Heinrich Wölfflin in art history and Northrop Frye in English are two of the great system builders whose writings I will place beside Lévi-Strauss's work as symptomatic of the "system" I would like to see replaced. But the view from outside the circle may help us, as well, to account for the persistent discontents that have blurred the boundaries of the disciplines until none of us can say with much assurance what it means to "interpret" a poem or "study" a painting, to write history or elucidate the central values of a civilization. The humanities have lost much of their credibility, even within their own ranks. And they will not get that credibility back by continuing to search for universal principles or quasi-scientific laws of the kind that Taine and others first set out to find. The humanities, instead, have to offer people freedom, and beyond that, to express real solidarity with the inner life of ordinary citizens. After examining the forms of credibility developed by patriarchs like Wölfflin and Frye, I will look at several prominent defectors from the culture of specialization. And then, when I will turn at last to Hanson himself, an amateur who wrote the great bulk of his prose more than fifty years ago, I want to argue that the current crack-up of the disciplines was bound to happen sooner or later. What Hanson discovers instead of hidden laws at the heart of the Amazon forest is a primal scene, a basic human reality, that anthropologists have not been alone in repressing: the endless breakdown of culture—the endless breakdown of our codes, conventions, systems, and stories— and the resourcefulness of the ordinary person, who is obliged to make do prag- matically with the materials at hand. As belated witnesses to this primal scene, humanists may no longer feel themselves compelled to mimic Lévi-Strauss's famous contempt for the struggles and hopes of average people. Instead, we might accept it as our task to assist in the emergence of another, less oppressive kind of knowledge, the kind that dilettantes like Hanson have been crafting all along, somewhere out there in the bush.

Despite appeals to method and disinterested scholarship, the turf grabbing and empire building of the disciplines is basically a *moral* problem, a problem of unequal social relations and the obstacles to thinking that these produce. And it is just these relations and obstacles that give shape to the myths and metaphors used to justify specialized inquiry. For example, when Lévi-Strauss proposes in *Tristes Tropiques* to tell the story of his travels in the days before he got his advanced degrees, he feels compelled to add that a sense of "shame" about that time kept him silent for the next two decades.[7] Following his youthful indiscretions, of course, he went on to become the creator of cutting-edge cultural theory, and he proceeds through the next four hundred pages of his book to elevate his profession far above its amateurish rival. From his remarks, the casual reader might very well conclude that his profession is both the subject and the hero of *Tristes Tropiques*—and Lévi-Strauss's self-awareness as a specialist makes the book unique in the history of the disciplines. But if *Tristes Tropiques* stands apart from other classic texts of anthropology in its confessional character, it is also broadly typical of work in that field, since it claims for its research a special mission, and at a time of crisis overtaking all the world:

> Now that the Polynesian islands have been smothered in concrete and turned into aircraft carriers solidly anchored in the southern seas, when the whole of Asia is beginning to look like a dingy suburb, when shantytowns are spreading across Africa . . . what else can the so-called escapism of traveling do than confront us with the more unfortunate aspects of our history? Our great Western civilization, which has created the marvels we now enjoy, has only succeeded in producing them at the cost of corresponding ills. . . . The first thing we see as we travel round the world is our own filth, thrown into the face of mankind.[8]

As Lévi-Strauss would have it, the story of the West's global triumph has turned out to be a tale of abject failure—our failure to perceive things as they *really* are, which he also sees as the failing of the dilettante traveler. In fact, with his usual hyperbole, Lévi-Strauss makes travel writing the symbol of *everything* bad about the modern world. The "adventure" that began with the Enlightenment, the rights of man, and liberal democracy now culminates, he tells us with a Gallic sweep, in the nightmare of the modern world, where reason has become organized insanity, freedom terminates in rampant lawlessness, and representative government degenerates into mass seduction and deceit. By now, he scolds, with the self-created ruins all around us, we should have learned a few fundamental truths: first, we've never really known where the human race was headed; second, human beings have never been the masters of their own lives; and finally, the freedom sought through traveling is nothing more than a comforting mirage. But sadly, these are lessons we have never learned, or so Lévi-Strauss believes. Even now, adventurers keep setting off in search of new beginnings, only to learn at the end of their latest trip that prior travelers have already transformed once-exotic and pristine islands into the tropical versions of industrial slums.

Of course, *Tristes Tropiques* is itself a brilliant example of travel writing, but an example turned against the reader's wish still to believe what every dilettante wants to believe: in the possibility that you or I, without any special training and only average intelligence, might enjoy a few moments of true contact with the world in some new and faraway place. But as Lévi-Strauss himself assures us, this aspiration is bound to end in bitter disappointment, as he knows so well from his own experience because he too was once an amateur—on his first voyage out from France to South America, when anthropology was still unfamiliar to him. "I wonder," he asks rhetorically, if "after all these years, I could ever again achieve such a state of grace. Would I [ever] be able to relive those feverish moments when, notebook in hand, I jotted down second by second the words which would . . . fix" the fleeting "forms" made by such things as clouds in the evening sky.⁹ But the question *is* rhetorical. Nothing could be more seductive than the dilettante's search for an obvious meaning in the onrush of events, and nothing could be less appropriate to the anthropologist's special mission. If the Western faith in the ordinary person's intelligence has culminated in a world of filth, then anthropologists alone can put a stop to it all. Beneath the shifting, varied surface of appearances, endlessly enticing to the untrained eye, some very brilliant, very learned professional must uncover the impersonal mechanisms that govern the very act of seeing, in the minds of South Pacific fishermen no less than Oxford dons. And with the unveiling these elusive mechanisms, the Western passion for adventure—for freedom and immediate contact with the world—will die its inescapable death.

As we learn from the pages of *Tristes Tropiques,* Lévi-Strauss himself is the one who pulled it off—the one who found the hidden mechanisms. His pilgrimage through the jungle of Brazil turns out to be a journey backward into prehistory—or, as he call it, the "savage mind"—and it continues until he discovers what he terms "mythemes," the fragments of myths that he takes to be the fundamental building blocks of all human thought. And along with the mythemes he discovers as well the laws of "structural transformation" that supposedly control the mutation of these mythemes over time and across space. Triumphantly quoting his idol, the philosopher Jean-Jacques Rousseau, Lévi-Strauss declares that "The Golden Age, which blind superstition had placed behind us . . . is *inside us"*—by which he means that the elusive order sought in every generation has been at work within the human mind all along.¹⁰ And because this undetected ideal order is always present there, Lévi-Strauss finds it expressed in everything that humans make and do—as tattoos on the faces of Brazil's native Caduveo women, as whorls on Shang Dynasty incense burners, as animals engraved and painted on Kwakiutl storage boxes. The basic building blocks of thought! In his earlier days as a dilettante, he had perhaps felt some inkling of this discovery as each strange, exciting moment hinted at some concealed significance, always just about to reveal itself. But the revelation never happened, and it never could, so long as he remained just an amateur. Instead, the great discovery would have to wait until the years of rigorous training had instructed him in the virtues of detachment, not only a detachment from his own feelings, motives, and memories, but also a deliberate indifference to everything told to him by the subjects of his research, the South American Indians whose thoughts and emotions he took care to reject as no less irrelevant than his own. *Behind* the thought, *behind* the feeling, lay a deeper structure, always unthought, unfelt, and unnoticed, visible only to the most expert eye. Carved wooden boxes from the Puget Sound or jade figurines from China, mythological tales or modern detective fiction—everything had to be wrenched out of its context of meaning and shown to exhibit a significance undetected by the "natives." What the jade carver never sees, although Lévi-Strauss does—in flattened images of dogs joined at the mouth or in spirals bound together at their starting points—are the telltale signs of conflicts, rivalries, and tribal taboos. What the spirals reveal, in other words, are the tensions that the people conceal from themselves, and Lévi-Strauss's work assures us, if it assures us of nothing else, that we are all unknowingly forced to express these hidden tensions in an unconscious but universal language.

Tristes Tropiques represents this all-embracing system as the glory of professional anthropology. And only seven years later, in the closing paragraphs of another book, The Savage Mind, Lévi-Strauss would grandly proclaim the end of history as well as the end of the West. All humans can really do is move the mythemes around into patterns already "hard-wired" in our brains. With the emergence of structuralism—his new branch of anthropology—the "entire process of human knowledge thus assumes," he wrote, "the character of a closed system" not in any sense different from the world of the "savages," whose "spirit" the science of anthropology has reestablished at the very heart of the modern world.[11] But if savagery and civilization are reconciled by the discovery of his universal laws, Lévi-Strauss achieves another, far more intimate reunion at the close of his book: a reunion of his private life with his professional knowledge, now that he has killed the little dilettante inside. In these closing moments, he reflects on the basic nature of knowledge, which can never be fashioned directly from the stuff of experience. Only by regarding the object again and again in an impersonal and systematic light can the observer at last draw closer to a world that otherwise remains too immediate and self-evident to reveal its secret order. For this reason—because the attainment of understanding first requires a corresponding loss of immediacy—travel writers in the depths of the jungle are destined to remain unenlightened, while anthropologists at their desks with pens in hand can achieve the wisdom of the Buddha, whose priests, Lévi-Strauss implies in passing, are anthropologists of a certain kind as well.[12]

Buddhist sages, culture heroes, and courageous emancipators—anthropologists in the pages of Tristes Tropiques take their place beside this august company. As for the book's unprofessional readers, they are left to conclude that travel should be left to the very few who know how to do it best. But Lévi-Strauss was not the first to pass on this particular lesson, which all the modern humanities have been eager to learn—and to teach. A generation earlier, for instance, the art historian Heinrich Wölfflin had paused at the start of his pathbreaking Principles of Art History to argue with the baldest disingenuousness, "It is hardly necessary here to take up the cudgels for the art historian and defend his work before a dubious public."[13] Yet Wölfflin meant his Principles to do exactly that. While his "dubious public" still regarded the arts (correctly) as a more or less accidental matter of individual expression using the available materials, he wanted to demonstrate that the evolution of styles stood in desperate need of professional study. "It is," Wölfflin underscores, "a dilettantist notion that an artist could ever take up his stand before nature without any preconceived ideas."[14] Rejecting such a notion, he insists that the systematic study of art must ascertain precisely what the painting or the sculpture, considered in isolation, cannot disclose: the socially constructed, historically evolving "forms of beholding" that predetermine the work of any artist at any particular moment.[15] Although "men have," Wölfflin holds, "at all times seen what they wanted to see, [this fact] does not exclude the possibility that a law remains operative throughout all change. To determine this law would be a central problem, the central problem of a history of art."[16] Offering his own Principles as a test case for his

new discipline's claim to disclose this invisible law underlying visible forms, Wölfflin announces his complete success, just as Lévi-Strauss would announce his own
triumph later, at the close of a radiant final chapter. One system governs everything,
and he has found that system. "In spite of all deviations and individual movements,"
he writes, "the development of style in later [European] art was homogeneous, just
as European culture as a whole can be taken as homogeneous."[17] Beneath the
surface of apparently endless change, Wölfflin claims to trace out the evolution of a
single great Western Spirit to which every work, no matter how "original" or
"eccentric," has made its unintended contribution.

Wölfflin's search for the invisible sources of the visual arts and Lévi-Strauss's
anthropological journey into the reaches of savage mind—both of these we today
might recognize as variations on a single theme encompassing other nonscience
disciplines as well. If the struggle for professional dominion over the arts began two
decades before Lévi-Strauss set off for Brazil's interior, the struggle of English
departments to appropriate all matters literary culminated in the decade after his
return to France. It was then that Northrop Frye called for the refashioning of *his*
discipline by insisting that literature, no less than physics or chemistry, must be
made "the subject of a systematic study." And the name Frye gives to this program
of study is not just "criticism" but actually "science." "Certainly," he reasons, "criticism as we find it in learned journals and scholarly monographs has every characteristic of a science. Evidence is examined scientifically; previous authorities are used
scientifically; fields are investigated scientifically."[18] Like Wölfflin before him, Frye
wants to show that his subject must be rescued—and rescued by specialists—from
the everyday person's way of thinking; and for this purpose he needs to demonstrate
that there is "an order of words corresponding to the order of nature in the natural
sciences."[19] While Frye begins his program by conceding that the study of "art," in
contrast to the study of "nature," can never achieve the precision of a "'pure' or
'exact' science," he still pushes the analogy as far as it will take him—so far, perhaps,
that his invocation of science may tell us less about his actual beliefs than about the
sweep of his ambitions and the depth of his anxieties as a humanist in an increasingly technologized university.[20]

More than Wölfflin and certainly no less than Lévi-Strauss, Frye links the
future of his discipline to a messianic repudiation of the laity and its entire manner
of living. All around him he beholds the evidence of an "an irrational world," a
society, as he put it, "of perverted imagination." "Advertising, propaganda, the
speeches of politicians, popular books and magazines"—these he represents as
symptoms of a culture subject to unprecedented spiritual danger.[21] If Lévi-Strauss
recoils with horror at the filth we have thrown in the faces of other peoples, Frye is
revolted by the filth that he believes we have heaped upon ourselves. And like his
French counterpart, he turns finally to myth (rather than mythemes) for salvation,
although for him myth is the royal road, not to universal laws of the mind but to the
symbol systems that lie at the core of each society's culture.[22] According to Frye, the
mythology of every healthy culture is always necessarily a "total structure, defining
as it does a society's religious beliefs, historical traditions, cosmological speculations—in short, the whole range of its verbal expressiveness"—and to this great

"matrix" of structural patterns and archetypal images every writer must return, knowingly or otherwise.[23] Those who return to the matrix in ways that renew and extend its coherence, as James Joyce does when he invokes Homeric legend while describing a day in the life of a Dublin public relations man, help to create what Frye calls a "real society."[24] But those who draw upon the archetypes in ways that foster greater incoherence—the writers of advertising and pulp fiction, for instance— pervert the imagination and bring their society one step closer to a final dissolution. Yet precisely because the writing that sustains "real" society is so hard to tell apart from the writing that perverts it, only someone with the training of a literary critic has the skill needed to adjudicate. And this task of adjudication demands an elaborate institutional network bringing together the rhetorician and philologist, the literary psychologist, the literary social historian, the historian of ideas, and finally, the literary anthropologist, who takes the archetypes as his principal concern.[25] While Frye concedes that other fields, especially anthropology and Jungian psycho- analysis, have explored the archetypes more thoroughly than most literary scholars, and while these literary scholars "are bound to appear for some time" little better than "dilettantes," he still seizes for his fellow critics the whole terrain of mythology, since the order of the myths is first of all an order of words, and English words belong, he reasons, to English departments.[26]

   With Lévi-Strauss's ascent to the status of seer and Frye's division of inter- pretive labor a decade after that, we witness the full flowering of a phenomenon Burton Bledstein has termed the "culture of professionalism." According to Bleds- tein, the university in the first half of this century not only "segregated ideas from the public" but promoted a rigorous segregation of ideas within the university itself. "A department emphasized the unique identity of its subject, its special qualities and language, its special distinction as an activity of research and investigation. Any outsider who attempted to pass judgment . . . was acting presumptuously."[27] Yet this segregation did more than organize knowledge in a certain manner, as Bleds- tein observes; it produced a different *kind* of knowledge, constructed for the pur- poses of mastery rather than cooperation—a knowledge made to reflect the image of a world in which human beings mattered only as herdlike masses or as abstract types susceptible to manipulation. The new power of the specialist was—as it still is, even in the poststructuralist academy—the capacity to tell "ordinary" people who they "really" are and what their actions "really" mean, independent of their own conscious doing and thinking. And precisely because the central paradigms of the humanities are almost always configured for this end, we will never again find a place for the ordinary person—as an intelligent social actor rather than a cultural dope—until we are willing to reconceive the nature and the uses of knowledge.

   The American anthropologist Clifford Geertz was among the first to try his hand at this job when he maintained more than twenty years ago that the French structuralists had managed to build "an infernal culture machine [which] . . . annuls history, reduces sentiment to a shadow of the intellect, and replaces the particular minds of particular savages in particular jungles with the Savage Mind immanent in us all."[28] But Geertz seems never to have noticed the hackneyed character of Lévi- Strauss's whole enterprise, since the story that the structuralists liked to tell about themselves was the same one that every nonscience discipline had been telling for half a century and continues to tell today. What distinguishes *Tristes Tropiques* from other apologies for academic professionalism is simply the candor and the eloquence—and, *bien sûr*, the poetic virtuosity—of its attack on the idea that ordinary people can make sense of the world they inhabit. It was Lévi-Strauss, after all, rather than the notorious poststructuralist Michel Foucault, who first argued that "the ultimate goal of the human sciences is not to constitute man but to dissolve him."[29] And while poststructuralists like Derrida, Lacan, and Foucault have abandoned their predecessor's search for scientific certainties, they have continued to repeat a lesson first learned at the feet of Lévi-Strauss himself: that culture acts when people *think* they have acted, that language speaks when they *think* they have spoken. To explain why it is that humans do what they do, any systematic inquiry must begin by discounting their stated reasons and explicit motives.

Critics of professionalism like Bledstein have commonly taken on the system rather than the kind of knowledge it perpetuates. Some observers have noticed, however, that the problem goes beyond institutions to the mental habits they inculcate. Once a passionate systematizer in his own right, Ludwig Wittgenstein became profoundly disenchanted with the efforts of specialists who were, as he put it, "occupied with building an ever more complicated structure." Even their "clarity," he decided, "is sought only as a means to this end, not as an end in itself."[30] If Wittgenstein in the 1930s renounced the search for hidden foundations, turning his attention instead to the pragmatic forms of everyday life, a similar sense of dissatisfaction overtook the anthropologist and linguist Edward Sapir. Although Sapir never ceased to believe that people depend on the linguistic resources at their disposal, he experienced an acute crisis of confidence in his discipline's suppression of the individual's capacity for intelligent thought and action. According to his biographer Richard Handler, "Sapir came to insist that cultural wholes are analytic constructions having no reality, as wholes, as entities, in human behavior. When anthropologists speak of 'a culture' they refer to a pattern or system that they themselves have constructed in the analysis of their data."[31] Though such constructs had legitimate uses, Sapir warned against the "fatal fallacy" implicit in presupposing that cultures (or languages or systems of knowledge) have a power of their own and can predetermine in a lawlike way the behavior of individuals. Against those who had declared well before Lévi-Strauss the disappearance of "man" as a knowing, self-conscious actor, Sapir concluded that "the true locus of culture is in the interactions of specific individuals and, on the subjective side, in the world of meanings which each one of these individuals may . . . abstract for himself from his participation in these interactions."[32] Where his opponents saw "superorganic" structures, Sapir saw meanings and choices; where they saw the persistence of impersonal "forces," he saw a ceaseless process of conscious innovation and exchange.[33]

Sapir wrote his defense of "specific individuals" in 1932, but it failed to bring about the revolution of sensibility he intended. For *that* change to begin, we have had to wait another seventy years, when the rewards of professionalism are proving less and less satisfying for the growing numbers of academic intellectuals, who have discovered that the cost of their authority is a subtle but severe narrowing of their power to think, and to speak, on their own.[34] Carried to its logical conclusion, the systematization of inquiry has made inquiry far more difficult—if we mean the asking of questions where they most urgently need to be asked and not where the practice of questioning has grown ritualized and perfunctory. Haunted by a suspicion that the academic humanities no longer meet anyone's real-world needs, the first wave of self-conscious "theorists" writing in the late 1960s—not only in English but in other fields as well—followed Lévi-Strauss's lead by trying to define "deep" structures or principles determining the production and reception of knowledge. Their great differences aside, Thomas Kuhn ("paradigms"), Stanley Fish ("communities"), Jonathan Culler ("codes and conventions") and Hayden White ("master tropes") were all characteristic of their generation in responding to the crisis with a return to this founding gesture of professional authority.

But the gesture, so convincing when the disciplines were still young, had become by the end of the 1970s so manifestly unpersuasive that even the journal *Daedalus,* arguably *the* voice of academic professionalism, dedicated a double issue to the unstable state of knowledge. And there, one of the contributors—the historian M. I. Finley—would identify the search for hidden laws as the problem rather than the solution. Modestly entitled "'Progress' in Historiography," Finley's essay might been more aptly named, "The Emperors' New Quasi-scientific Clothes." Surveying the terrain of research in his field, he is moved to declare that there are *no* determining foundations of any kind, "no Kuhnian paradigms, no established doctrines . . . even about the . . . historian's subject matter."[35] Taking issue with colleagues who perceive in the burgeoning of historical knowledge a self-correcting, self-enlarging gestalt, he maintains that the "study and writing of history" are always "a form of ideology" in the ordinary sense of the word: an expression, that is, of the specific social interests of the people involved.[36] The practice of history "cannot be codified" or regulated, Finley contends, because of its irrepressibly pragmatic nature, and he goes on to insist that even professionalism, "the cult of Research" for "its own sake," must be recognized as an "ideological stance," one arising from an attempt to shield the discipline from social problems outside the campus.[37] Behind the facade of professional consensus and the illusion of incremental progress, there remain, Finley charges, disagreements arising from differences in the everyday lived world, and it is to this world in its complexity that historians should turn their attention.

But history was not the only field whose professional uniformity concealed a more fundamental dissonance. In the same issue of *Daedalus,* Svetlana Alpers described a comparably scandalous scene among her colleagues in art history, whose discourse she represents less as an orderly and dispassionate "conversation" than a series of arguments, beginning with founders like Wölfflin and extending through Panofsky and Gombrich to Baxandall onward. While Alpers sets out to expose the rifts behind the fiction of unbroken continuity, she also raises a larger question about professionalism by asking why these rifts went unnoticed for so long. And the answer she gives has to do with the institutional suppression of self-doubt for the sake of getting on with the "real business," namely scholarship. In a passage fit for Finley's naked emperors, Alpers notes that "art historians [characteristically] see themselves as being in pursuit of knowledge without recognizing how they . . . are the makers of that knowledge."[38] No less than Finley, she rejects the assumption that something called "the discipline" operates like a hidden hand to predetermine the actions taken by practitioners; rather, the practice of art history is a perpetual questioning of what both "art" and "history" mean. Instead of answering the question raised by her title—"Is Art History?"—she wants her readers to admit, at least among themselves, that there can be no decisive answer.

Alpers's point is not simply that her colleagues should conduct their business in plain view, openly displaying the private commitments that scholars have been trained to conceal quite carefully, but also that they should acknowledge the force of these same commitments in the works they study. The miracle of a painting like the one that art historian T. J. Clark made the subject of a now-famous monograph— Courbet's *Burial at Ornans,* which outraged nineteenth-century middle-class viewers with its depiction of a crude provincial funeral—lies in the artist's deliberate violation of the established rules of painting.[39] If scholarship reshapes knowledge through its partisan innovation, then artists like Courbet do the same, and by acknowledging their capacity to change culture, Alpers breaks decisively, I would say, with Lévi-Strauss's "scientific" fatalism, which he defends in *Structural Anthropology* by misquoting Marx to this effect: "Men make their own history, but they do not know that they are making it."[40] What Marx actually wrote, however, is that "Men make their own history, but they do not make it just as they please."[41] The *consciousness* of making history, and with it the consciousness of being debarred from certain kinds of choice and action—these Alpers hopes to place squarely at the core of her discipline, not because they have been missing but because they were there, unnoticed and unvalued, all along. For Alpers and Finley, the heart of the forest lies wherever we are, and they warn that to search for an order beyond or beneath our own self-understanding is to become like enchanters who have finally enchanted themselves. Why *did* Courbet paint his awkward, enigmatic villagers rather than happy peasants or a graceful urban elite? T. J. Clark gives one kind of answer, his fellow art historian Michael Fried gives another, but the question can never be decided permanently since every new observer, professional or not, will bring to the painting something else, something more.

It is just this "something more," this power to go beyond the limits of the "known," that each of us possesses irrespective of schooling or station. And it is just this same power that professionalism in the humanities has diligently suppressed. Far from creating a knowledge that is truly universal—that represents everyone in general because it represents no one in particular—academic humanists have persistently remade accounts of the social world in their own parochial image, and here once again Lévi-Strauss qualifies as the great exemplar. When *Tristes Tropiques* at last takes us to the Amazon, the Indians become, not progressively stranger and harder to interpret, as they might have seemed to a dilettante tourist, but more and more exactly like their ethnographer. Lévi-Strauss remarks, for example, on the exceptional "refinement" of the Bororo, especially in matters "sociological," and he describes the Nambikwara as so hypercivilized that their "pronunciation is marked by an affectation and preciosity of which they are perfectly aware."[42] Even their sexual lives are distinguished by the greatest tact, so that despite "the amorous fondling in which [Nambikwara] couples indulge so freely and so publicly, and which is often quite uninhibited," Lévi-Strauss testifies that he "never once noticed even an incipient erection"—surely the sign of an almost Parisian refinement.[43] The Bororo and Caduveo belong, he claims hyperbolically, to genuinely "learned societies"; they have professions, vocations, and hierarchies of expertise just like modern Europeans.[44] Best of all, they have something closely approximating Lévi-Strauss's version of social science:

> Bororo society offers a lesson to the student of human nature [for] . . . their wise men have worked out an impressive cosmology and embodied it in the plan of the villages and the layout of the dwellings. They arranged and rearranged the contradictions they encountered, never accepting any opposition without repudiating it in favor of another, cutting up and dividing the groups, joining them and setting them one against the other, and turning their whole social and spiritual life into a coat of arms in which symmetry and asymmetry are equally balanced.[45]

In the method of Bororo "wise men," whose logic so remarkably resembles structuralism, Lévi-Strauss finds a daily confirmation of his method, as he does once again among the Caduveo, who suggest to him, in the perfect symmetry of their relations, the playing cards from *Alice in Wonderland*. "These Indians," he writes, "had [their] kings and queens, and like Alice's queen, the latter liked nothing better than to play with the severed heads brought back by their warriors."[46] Although he wants to tell his Eurocentric readers, as he certainly should, that the "savages" were never really savage at all, a basic and perhaps more important truth still gets lost, a truth about his own motives. What he discovers at the heart of the Amazon is nothing more and nothing less than what he wanted to discover, while the actual men and women he encounters there, who never cease to talk among themselves in the course of their daily affairs, are silenced and made to disappear. And so, at the same time, are we all.

Among the many thousands of words that fill the pages of *Tristes Tropiques,* not more than twenty sentences transcribe things said by the "natives," but when people like the Caduveo have an occasion to speak in their own voices—when they speak and are listened to—they say something quite unlike what Lévi-Strauss seems to have heard. They reflect eloquently, for example, on the problems of their lives, as they did in this creation myth told to a very different researcher more than eighty years ago:

> Onoenrgodi [the Creator] divided up the earth among all [the] people. To the Paraguayans and the Portuguese he gave houses, cattle, and arms. The Tereno got maize, manioc, and the like. . . . Then the caracara bird came and said: "Master, you haven't thought of the Caduveo at all." Onoenrgodi replied: "That's true; I didn't think of 'my people.' . . ." [Then] Onoenrgodi went to Caracara and said: "There are only four Caduveo and there's no land left for them, but when they die I'll revive them again." Caracara answered: "No,

why should they revive? Let them fight with other Indians instead and steal their land, women, and children." . . . But the Caduveo were hungry, and they cried. Onoenrgodi said to Caracara: "I'll prepare some food for them." Caracara replied: "Why? They should hunt and gather honey." . . .

[Then the] god said: "When they have no more clothes left I'll make them new ones." But Caracara said again: "No, don't. They have cotton and can spin and weave."[47]

Far from existing outside of time and apart from conscious experience, myths like this one constituted a special form of oral history that helped the Caduveo address the urgencies of their lives at a moment when the future had become almost unthinkably dark. Perceiving their condition through the lens of such myths, they could see themselves as undiscouraged, even indestructible. Through the stories of daring tricksters, suave seducers, and cunning thieves, they turned their stigma as pariahs into a badge of the highest distinction; and in this response they could not bear less resemblance to the doomed and decadent "playing cards" of Lévi-Strauss's description, passive victims of our Western filth. While "the white man" makes a brief appearance in a number of surviving Caduveo myths, these myths never grant *him* the capacity to have caused the tribe's misfortunes—only a god like Onoenrgodi could have given them their fate. And in the face of divine disfavor, the Caduveo were determined to thrive. Through their myths, in other words, this insignificant tribal people, probably never more than several hundred strong, once managed to succeed where our academic humanities have often failed, by creating a sense of themselves as intelligent and capable. And if these myths have anything to say to us now, it is that we, no less than the Caduveo, can tell such stories and exert such a power.

Finley and Alpers both speak from within an institution—the university—that has progressively become a prison-house for those who once imagined it as a privileged, open space. While neither writer takes the time to explain with much precision how this imprisonment has come about, the jail in which they find themselves is the same one in which their predecessors contrived to lock up everybody else. The two scholars, in my view, do not go nearly far enough by insisting that historians should have the right to redefine "history," or that artists and the scholars who study their work can transform the rules for exploring representation. Neither Finley nor Alpers seems to recognize that such a change, if it is to occur at all, obliges academic intellectuals to give up their long-accustomed and largely self-appointed role as the arbiters of culture, truth, and taste. Either everyone makes knowledge or else no one really can, not even specialists. Far from looking to the disciplines as the place where knowledge properly gets made, we might see them instead as social locations where this making has become especially constricted.

If knowledge is "produced," as we academics like to think, and if it therefore lends itself to production by different people for different ends, then we might ask why the university has failed to produce forms of knowledge affirming the non-specialists' capacity to act. No matter what the fashion of the day may be—structuralism or semiotics, deconstruction, psychoanalysis, Marxism, or New Historicism—we have held back the last word for ourselves, whether the text under scrutiny is *Pride and Prejudice* or *Ferris Bueller's Day Off.* Gerald Graff's widely quoted slogan "Teach the conflicts" still enjoins a teaching of the conflicts we alone have provoked. And even the tradition of reader-response criticism—which claims to defend the rights of readers to develop their own responses to the text—has been more concerned with defining an idealized and abstract "act of reading" rather than with taking the trouble to ascertain how and why actual readers make the meanings they actually make.[48] But perhaps the time has come to think differently—to concede that the search for hidden structures or lawlike rules, on the level of the sentence or the level of the state, is always, as John Dewey argued more than once, an act of domination by other, covert means.[49]

> A class of experts is inevitably so removed from common interests as to become a class with private interests and private knowledge, which in social matters is not knowledge at all.
> —John Dewey, *The Public and Its Problems*

Lévi-Strauss may have told us *his* story about knowledge, but another one might be told, a story that reminds us that knowledge is less fixed and more accessible than the system of learned professions has led ordinary people to believe. Four years before Lévi-Strauss first landed in Sao Paulo to begin his research on the Amazon basin tribes, Earl Parker Hanson, a self-proclaimed "career" adventurer with a background in engineering, made his way down the Orinoco River from the highlands of Venezuela to the city of Manaos in northwestern Brazil, recruited by the Carnegie Institution to take readings of the earth's magnetic fields. Like an explorer in the travel books, Hanson hired porters; he got lost in terrain still blank on his maps from the American Geographical Society; he shivered with tropical fevers; he ran out of supplies. En route something happened, and kept happening, to Hanson, the kind of thing that Lévi-Strauss never mentions. "Little by little," he confesses unprofessionally, "I began to feel my preconceived, stereotyped notions about the tropics breaking down."[50] Having left the United States during the worst years of the Great Depression, he finds the collapse reaching deeply even there. At Maracaibo, he sees that the oil fields are "dead," the unemployed "swarming like ants," and in San Fernando de Apure, a white backer of the dictatorship, an *andino,* complains, "We . . . have given our territory of Amazonas back to the Indians."[51] Kept up all night by burrowing parasites called *chivacoas,* Hanson rises to hear on his radio that Japan has invaded China, and months later, in Manaos itself, he learns that the Lindbergh baby has been kidnapped. "Like millions of people at exactly that same time," he writes, "I felt trapped. . . . What were we coming to? What was the way out?"[52]

Instead of leaving the disorder of modernity behind as Lévi-Strauss blames travelers for trying to do, Hanson sees that our modernity is now everywhere—or rather, he falls prey to a growing suspicion that modernity has never really existed at all. As he travels from one river landing to the next, he notices the precision of the

Indians, who build better houses than their white and *mestizo* counterparts, and whose villages often look more prosperous and orderly:

> I had always "known" that the Indians of the forested lowlands were a shiftless, lazy lot. I had not realized that this impression was one which had been handed on partly by the white men who had uprooted them, taken their lands and destroyed their social structures, and who have undoubtedly always found them poor workers in a white society in which race prejudice would always keep them from amounting to anything no matter how hard they worked.[53]

And if the Indians were not savages, they were not noble savages either, corrupted by the coming of white colonists, Western culture, and a money economy. Behind the anthropological fiction of a people with a "fallen" and degraded version of a culture formerly pure, he discovers elaborate Indian networks of production and trade—local, ad hoc, and decentralized—and one day at the house of a tribesman "dressed in immaculately clean clothes made from old flour sacks," he sees muzzle loaders side by side with blowguns. "The sight surprised me," he writes. "I had been looking for *wild* Indians for weeks and . . . not finding any. Suddenly I realized that I had been among Indians all the time who still used the blowgun and the poisoned dart."[54] If Lévi-Strauss bears witness to disaster, the erosion of old norms, and the spread of a dismal mediocrity, Hanson sees something else: the perpetual making and unmaking of culture, language, and day-to-day social arrangements, by people—active, thoughtful like the Indians—who are well aware of their dilemmas; more aware, in some respects, than Hanson was of his own.

Further on in his travels Hanson learns about the manufacture of curare for the coating on poison darts, and he is told about a shaman who enters trances and converses with tribes far away.[55] He passes dilapidated rubber boom towns, built laboriously in the European style, but sleeps among the Indians in their houses.[56] He quarrels with Catholic missionaries of the Salesian order over efforts to convert the locals; he searches for the famed hallucinogen *yagé*.[57] While none of these events make sense all at once, Hanson does exactly what the "natives" need to do every moment of their lives, trying out new ways of interacting with the world when the old ones no longer seem to work. And by doing so Hanson demonstrates that the event that Lévi-Strauss most fears, the breakdown of cultural order, takes place ceaselessly in matters as unexceptional as casting off from a dock or dealing with an injury. To the degree every human act demands an effort of thought, every act is nothing less than a remaking of culture itself, as Hanson himself discovers unforgettably when he injures his foot on the path to his hammock.

"At midnight," he remembers, "the pain in my foot woke me up. I couldn't sleep with that torture going on, and I lay awake a long time, conjuring up the worst that might have happened to me"—"the end of my expedition."[58] Although Hanson is convinced that breakage of some kind has occurred, his Venezuelan *patron* strongly disagrees. "Let me see your foot!" Ezekiel commands. "Broken? It

isn't broken. *Es farciado.*" In debating the relative merits of the two interpretations—"broken" or *"farciado"*—the travelers soon reach the limits of Lévi-Strauss's
method, since the issue will never be resolved by resort to deep structures of
language or the mind. And even if such structures really existed, they would be of no
pragmatic use in such a case, any more than we can use the rules of grammar to
decide if the earth is flat or round. But there is still another problem with the search
for deep structures: there are no structures for applying or transforming the structures themselves when the unexpected happens. In short, Hanson and Ezekiel have
to take a chance. If the foot is actually broken, then they should ferry Hanson over to
the clinic, but if it happens to be *farciado* (a word whose formal definition Hanson
never actually learns), they should subject it to Ezekiel's "murderous" therapy. They
take a chance: "Ezekiel pulled, and pushed, and twisted. He massaged and
slapped. . . .and sent sharp pangs of pain into my head."⁵⁹ Overnight the foot
improves and *farciado* enters Hanson's growing lexicon—not because it has a place
in any preexisting order but because the word enabled him to act in the world.

To imagine that knowledge can ever be more systematic or less accidental
than this is to overlook the fact that people have a need for knowledge only after
things have stopped making sense. While the literary critic Stanley Fish is certainly
right to point out that no one gets out of bed in the morning and reinvents civilization, the creation of new knowledge begins when the "wrong" questions start to
intrude: difficult, unforeseen questions that can never be answered with certainty.
And through the act of addressing questions of this kind, people find themselves
caught up, willingly or otherwise, in a predicament—a state of uncertainty—that
most professionals will go to any length to keep concealed from their clients. But
uncertainties alone make needed changes in culture possible. Here, for example, is
what Hanson writes about his porter Laureano during the first weeks they spent
together:

> I abhor sentimentality over Indians, Negroes, and other abused and misun-
> derstood races, even more than I do the usual, and often necessary, determina-
> tion to "keep them in their places." But in Laureano I realized I had some-
> thing special—a man who was intuitive enough to recognize all the facets of
> [each] position I allowed him to take in my relations with him, and who never
> once "took advantage."⁶⁰

Everything encourages Hanson to see Laureano as someone unambiguously
"placed"—as a mere "savage," an *indio*—not only the many lessons that Hanson
had learned growing up in the United States but also what he hears from bitter
andinos, murderous generals, parasitical merchants, and the standard conniving
bureaucrats. Yet one afternoon in the river village of Maroa, Hanson's way of seeing
undergoes a dramatic transformation. After crossing the plaza and entering a
church, he notices gravestones set in the floor, most of them bearing the last name of
"Bueno"—Laureano's family name—which Hanson had forgotten. So long perceived as a familiar "type" within the constellation of Brazilian types, Laureano at
last identifies himself to Hanson as the son of a local Indian leader, a *jefe* who was

forced to flee his native town following an unsuccessful struggle against the central government.[61] Laureano, it turns out, has grown up on the run, the first member of his family for many generations to be landless and illiterate. But in spite of his relative powerlessness, he displays through the act of telling his story on his own terms a power reserved by Lévi-Strauss solely for anthropologists and other intellectuals: the power that people always have to understand both themselves and the world they share with others.

Though Lévi-Strauss intended *Tristes Tropiques* as the last great critique of all pretensions to this power, Hanson ends his amateur's narrative by believing in nothing else. And when he reaches the Indian town of Maroa he finds his own version of Lévi-Strauss's lost Amazonian paradise. But instead of disclosing a primordial law that must be obeyed, consciously or otherwise, Maroa suggests the possibilities of a world in which the past no longer exerts the force of an irresistible destiny. To Hanson, the people of Maroa looked somehow "rooted, thoroughly at home." "It was," Hanson remembers, "a place in which time did not matter. The past was dead and the future inscrutable; only the moment counted, today and this year's crops, this year's hunting and fishing."[62] Maroa comes to signify for Hanson not simply another, better way to live, but another, better way of understanding social life—as both "rooted" *and* open to transformation.

Could we live in Maroa? *Why not* try to think beyond the disciplines? And *why not* give up the assurances that deterministic thinking provides—if only because a future that repeats the past will surely be darker and harder to bear than most determinists are ready to suppose. As Maroa recedes from view and Hanson's boat drifts down the river that defines Brazil's northwestern border, he encounters Indians living under conditions very different from the happy ones he had just witnessed. While Hanson speculates at certain hopeful moments that these Indians might break free from the past just as their counterparts in Maroa have, he sadly registers the forces arrayed against them—and their misery reminds him of grim Depression conditions back in the United States. Different as the two societies appear, both are oppressed, he concludes, not primarily by force, though force never ceases to matter, but by their obedience to what he calls the "old social dogmas" that "no longer fit the facts of our changing" circumstances.[63] If force makes new arrangements unlikely for the Indians along the river, Hanson still believes that his fellow Americans up north have the capacity to "resort to revolution"; and revolution—the "effort of a people to exercise control over the social changes affecting them"—he comes to see as anything but exceptional. "In fact," he writes, "we do resort to it almost continually. Revolution, which shows itself in violence only in extreme cases, is *normal* . . . in a dynamic world, just as tyranny, which is oppressive only in extreme cases, is normal to the striving for stability, be it found in Europe, Venezuela, or Alabama."[64] And by proposing this account of perpetual change in the search for a livable permanence, Hanson manages to anticipate insights subsequently "discovered" by academic social theorists like Victor Turner, Pierre Bourdieu, Anthony Giddens, and Sherry Ortner. The important point for us now is not simply that a dilettante got there first, although I think this small fact matters enormously, but that we ourselves, professionals, are headed in the same direction.

What Hanson understood, and what Lévi-Strauss would not concede, is that even our conceptions of order and permanence keep changing unpredictably. And while Hanson's precocious recognition of this truth is remarkable in itself, far more remarkable is the discontent that has enlivened the work of a small number of academic humanists: Henry Louis Gates and Richard Rorty, Patricia Nelson Limerick and Harvey Cox, Robert Thurman and Stephen Ambrose.[65] Works such as Gates's *Colored People* and Ambrose's *Citizen Soldiers*—and even more, the television projects these two men have launched—testify to a profound dissatisfaction with learned disciplines that maintain their authority by concealing the contingency of knowledge, its character as a response to each person's situation here and now. Writing with grace and depth about matters the academy has reduced to purely linguistic "signifiers"—identity, adversity, adventure, friendship, courage, family— they occupy a place beyond the existing disciplines, and from this place they demonstrate that the order of academic inquiry is as susceptible to change as everything else.

In this way they resemble another Frenchman, not Lévi-Strauss but a compatriot who went "native." "Wherever one goes on those rivers," Hanson recalls, "one hears about a French scientist who had made marvelous discoveries among the Indians. . . . He was probably mythical. But when I heard about him I was told that two 'rescue-expeditions' had reached him, had tried to bring him out, and had met with . . . obstinate refusal."[66] Like the legendary Frenchman of the Amazon, the one who stayed on to live among his ethnographic subjects, these latter-day descendants of Wittgenstein and Sapir share a desire to open knowledge up to life as lived, and to our dangers, fears, and needs. But the price these humanists pay for this desire is the recognition of a perpetual—and amateurish—uncertainty that places all authority in question. And under these conditions they are obliged to become what Lévi-Strauss most fears and reviles: adventurers in the root sense of term; people who are willing to take the risk of an *adventura,* an "event," a process of "arrival" whose outcome no one can foresee.

Whether this return of the human to the humanities can withstand the attacks already launched against it may depend on the capacity of its defenders to name— and to celebrate—the value of uncertainty, as I have tried to do here. For certain professionals, the ones for whom profession has become a cult, any talk of this kind is bound to sound like a decline, a fatal lowering of standards. But of course, humans don't exist for the sake of knowledge; knowledge exists to sustain and enrich our lives. And human life is an adventure, inescapably. Lévi-Strauss, you might recall, undergoes an *adventura* only once in *Tristes Tropiques,* when he encounters the edenic Nambikwara. But from the moment that he remembers their "simplicity" and his unexpected feeling of kinship with them, his text becomes exactly what he has disparaged all along—travel writing. As he walks through a crowd of Nambikwara who lie sleeping beside fading campfires, he reflects on their frailty in a world of infinite dangers, more even than they can dream of. Then, abruptly, when their amorous laughter interrupts his solemn meditations, he finds himself overwhelmed by the spectacle of an "immense kindness, a profoundly care-free attitude and . . .

something which might be called the most truthful and moving expression of human love."[67] Such a freedom and such a love, which elude expression on the terms allowed by structuralism, Lévi-Strauss must attempt to describe in the groping fashion of one who does not quite know what to say. Any dilettante could do as well.

Yet by avoiding, with this one exception, the dilettante's unmethodical struggle to learn from his particular encounters with the actual people, Lévi-Strauss himself perpetuates the characteristically modern form of violence that has reduced the Nambikwara to a tattered remnant at the end of the world: the violence of a social order that withholds from the vast majority of people control over their everyday lives, and that justifies this separation by constructing knowledge as intrinsically removed from their own experience. Knowledge has replaced the sword, in other words, as the principal instrument of social control. In turning from the chaos of human interactions to an unchangeable order of ideas, Lévi-Strauss remains indebted to a legacy that the sociologist Alvin Gouldner has called a heritage of "defeat," of "man's failure to possess the social world he [has] created." Instead of trying to bring forth a better world by the process of trial and error, social scientists and other cognoscenti devote themselves to brilliant explanations of why the system cannot be changed. The "objectivity" of men like Lévi-Strauss—and Gouldner might as well be speaking here about the humanists Wölfflin and Frye as well—is "not the expression of a dispassionate and detached view of the social world; it is, rather, an ambivalent effort to accommodate to alienation *and* to express a muted resentment of it."[68] That Lévi-Strauss's successors in so many disciplines, and even many of his critics, should follow his dehumanizing lead only shows how completely we continue to idealize knowledge, and how deeply we fear the possibility of a world made in real collaboration with the people we academics would prefer to dismiss as the unwitting pawns of culture: our neighbors, our students, the people who paint our houses and fix our cars.

Lévi-Strauss may decry the absolutism of the West—its suppression of alternatives— but the option offered by the structuralists and their successors is less an escape from that absolutism than an urging to accept it as inescapable. When these academics formulate their theories, they think less of people like the gentle Nambikwara and more of people like the violent Caduveo. And at least as Lévi-Strauss has rendered them, the Caduveo subject both their rivals and themselves to imperatives quite unlike the Nambikwara's "kindness" and "love." As he wrote eleven years before *Tristes Tropiques,* the hidden laws of consciousness leave their visible marks on the Caduveo in the form of facial tattoos, and he implies that every social order is compelled to inflict such a "defacement" on its members. He assumes, in other words, that unless our culture scars us with enduring wounds, human beings can have no "real" faces at all.[69] But against this sadistic image of a scarified human face, which signifies the triumph of culture over the helpless bearers of culture, we might juxtapose another: the image of Maroa, Hanson's free city on the river, where people come and go, unmarked and unmolested.[70] At a time when knowledge has never seemed more breathtakingly complex or more crushingly abstract, we need to put it in its proper place: we need to cultivate a more creative attitude—one part disbelief and one part curiosity—toward all theories and systems, terminologies and rules. What the dilettante Hanson offers us is not the emblem of a face scarred by a Law always hidden from its own victims, but the ideal of a world whose gentle features, human features, still remain to be imagined. Why don't we begin?

Postscript

Could Teaching, of All Things, Prove to Be Our Salvation?

Just before noon on September 11, 2001, while I was working at home on revisions to this book, my wife Barbara phoned to tell me that New York City was under siege. Of course I thought she was joking. Like millions of Americans that morning, I sat speechless as the World Trade Towers burned and fell, again and again in endless televised replays.

In the immediate aftermath, it become commonplace to say that nothing would ever be the same, and in a certain sense this was true. Candidate Bush had eschewed "nation building," but President Bush found himself preoccupied with the forging of multicontinental coalitions while sending many thousands of troops overseas—the exact figure still remains under wraps—to a semiarid plateau more than seven thousand miles away from his "ranch" in Crawford, Texas. But this was not the only change. Long regarded with suspicion by most Americans west of the Hudson, New Yorkers were suddenly transformed into global ambassadors of a nation that had shown it could "pull together in crisis," its police and fire squads hailed as heros, its abrasive and scandal-tainted mayor elevated to *Time*'s "Person of the Year," in the company of Gandhi and Winston Churchill. And if the memory of massacres at My Lai and Kent State had soured aging boomers on the use of armed forces, the popular press compared troops landing in Kabul to the liberating armies of D-Day. At this moment, no one can even begin to foresee the ramifications of such developments.

Yet at the same time, nothing has changed in at least one important sense. The education most Americans now receive is essentially the same as a century ago, in form if not in content. Yes, more Americans finish high school, more get to college and take degrees, but the organization of basic knowledge, the stock-in-trade of the humanities, assumed its current appearance well before the invention of airplanes and cars, before the two World Wars, before people understood the structure of the atom, before the United Nations, before the discovery of penicillin, and before the mapping of space beyond our solar system. For many people working in the humanities, however, the failure to address such developments is not a failure at all: as they see it, their purpose is to keep the past alive for its own sake and not because it might happen to have some utility now. They might agree that people need to know a bit about world politics, contemporary geography, advances in science, and so on, but they might say that all of this is evanescent and superficial. Anyone can keep tack of current events simply by reading the papers, but the knowledge that really matters stays the same no matter what the future brings. We humanists value foundations, traditions, and canons, whether we wish to preserve them in amber or subversively explode them. This is why eleventh graders in the state where I live—who may someday bear arms in Africa or Indonesia—still read Hawthorne's "Young Goodman Brown" and memorize events from U.S. history that get forgotten the day after the exam. My guess is that the current innovation of national standardized testing will only make matters worse: students will get better at standardized tests, but nothing will have altered the enormous disparity between the world that young Americans actually inhabit and the image of the world preserved and purveyed by the knowledge apparatus.

After 9/11 at my university there were teach-ins and a special lecture series, but no one in the flurry of information seemed to recall a debate that flamed up and then died out less than a decade earlier, a debate that had consumed the time and energy of key faculty for several years on end. It had begun in response to the "Qualls Report," a document that called for fundamental change in undergraduate education here at Rutgers. Under the direction of Barry Qualls, chair of the English Department and later Dean of the Humanities, a committee had acknowledged openly what everyone knew but seldom vocalized: that college students across the United States graduate without an adequate understanding of their society, their world, and their times. But agreement about the problem did not produce agreement about potential remedies. If the committee had begun its discussions by attempting to define a core curriculum, it soon ran up against an immovable wall: no one could concur about whose knowledge counted as "essential." Very quickly every discipline and subdiscipline made the claim that its particular specialization could not be cut from the list. Students needed to know about Reconstruction, the nature-versus-nurture debate, Quattrocento painting, Aristotle on politics, Wordsworth and Keats, as well as recent achievements in psychology, philosophy, and the sciences. Not only did the members of the committee disagree about what constituted "cultural literacy," but they could not even reach consensus on the definition of culture itself, in spite of their evident respect for one another and the good intentions they all shared.

After many fruitless hours stuck at this impasse, the committee took a radically different tack: instead of beginning with the effort to define the kinds of knowledge educated people ought to have, it tried to identify the problems that college graduates might be expected to face in the next twenty years or so, not as doctors or lawyers or Indian chiefs, but as ordinary citizens. And here, it turned out, agreement came more readily. Of course, a list of this sort would look different now. No committee member ten years ago could have foreseen how quickly human cloning might become a reality, just as no one could have anticipated the machinations of al-Qaeda. The committee overlooked other matters as well. Since 1990, the ruination of the world's environment has continued to accelerate, and the growing convergence of opinion on global warming has failed to produce any meaningful response. In 1990, the Kyoto Agreement lay seven years ahead. Today, it has apparently died and gone to the heaven reserved for noble but stillborn ideas. Who would have guessed ten years ago that the next world war might begin, not in the Middle East as so many have suspected, but on the border between India and Pakistan? And who then could have predicted bioterrorism? The list drawn up by the Qualls committee might look distinctly dated now. Yet to point out that the present moment's urgencies will become tomorrow's old news is not to deny the importance of events as they unfold in the here and now. I would say the committee had exactly the right idea.

What Qualls and his associates concretely proposed instead of a core curriculum were courses designed around "dialogues" on the issues of consequence to society as a whole. The idea was to give students the intellectual tools—the information and the interpretive paradigms—to explore both the problems of the coming century and their possible solutions. As originally imagined, the "dialogues courses" were supposed to instigate a rich cross mixing of the disciplines, as enticing to the faculty as they would be to students. According to the final plan, the Dean's office would release a list of dialogues courses for each coming year, and on the way to graduation all our students were supposed to complete several of these special courses. While the conventional divisions of knowledge would remain in place, supported by the iron scaffolding of departments and disciplines, the dialogues courses would eventually become the centerpiece of undergraduate intellectual life.

What actually happened? Initially, very little. As the report circulated downward from the deaconal level to individual faculty, they quickly grasped that nothing in the university's structure of promotion and reward would compensate them for the special efforts they would have to make if they got involved. They felt uncomfortable, as well, teaching out of their field: historians knew little about ecology, English professors might explore "economies of signs" but in fact they knew next to nothing about economies of dollars. To make matter worse, the teaching done in the dialogues courses would seldom translate easily into publication, and the willingness of some faculty to participate might keep them locked below decks with the undergraduates instead of mounting freely to the vistas of graduate study. Besides, they would have to work with strangers from other departments who might look at them askance, or at whom they might look in much the same manner. The faculty responded, in other words, with all the reservations inculcated by their long and arduous training, and by the culture of the University itself, which would, indeed, punish them through benign neglect when raises were handed out. No one at our Research 1 institution gets a raise for better teaching. Ultimately, the administration, which had called for the report and convened the committee, distanced itself from the whole debate, preferring not to squander its political capital on a contest so clearly destined to end with the innovators' defeat.

More was at stake, however, than the dreams of a few idealists and the intransigence of the professoriate. Consider 9/11. Consider, too, that right now, by most estimates, species are disappearing at a rate without precedent since mammals first appeared on earth. Should global warming becoming a reality, we are not likely to enjoy a future of springlike weather at Christmas. Years of record drought in

Afghanistan, record cold in Mongolia, record floods in Bangladesh—these may offer us a foretaste of things to come, not outright cataclysm but a slow, steady, and irreparable deterioration of the natural order. On its own, this deterioration might pose mortal challenges to many societies around the globe, but it is just now intersecting with an orgy of first-world-style consumption and first-world-style pollution to match, combined with a projected fivefold increase in the world population since 1900. While the triumph of Western democracy, such as it is, may seem virtually assured, environmental degradation could easily undermine not only economic progress but political stability as well. If people are willing to fight wars over oil, they will surely spill blood over water when that resource becomes desperately scarce, as many observers now predict. We may assume that the extensiveness and redundancy of our social systems will safeguard us against disaster, but the world's economy in 1929 collapsed within a few weeks, while the Soviet Union fell apart just as fast and just as unexpectedly.

What have we done to prepare the next generation for these problems and possibilities? At my institution six or seven years ago, the great majority of the faculty apparently resolved that we couldn't do much, and probably shouldn't. For the soundest of institutional and historical reasons, we were quite willing to perpetuate an arrangement guaranteeing that *none* of the coming century's major problems will be studied formally at the university: for the most part, whatever students happened to learn about these matters they will have to learn on their own. As for their professors, we continue to believe—or at least to claim—that a knowledge of Plato, a reading of Shakespeare, a brush with current historiography, an immersion in possible worlds theory, or an acquaintance with the New York Fluxus artists circa 1960, will somehow enable young Americans to make better decisions than if they actually had more pertinent information at their ready command. As far as I'm concerned, this is the sheerest superstition.

But the story does not end with the shelving of the Qualls report. The one place at our university where the proposal could be instituted was our writing program. That it happened there, and only there, was no accident. Although housed in an English department, the program had a long record of interdisciplinary instruction. In fact, it drew its teachers, for the most part TAs or adjunct instructors, from across the spectrum of the humanities and social sciences. Its marginal status, without so much as a budget line of its own, and its position at the bottom of the ladder of prestige, made it an ideal place for innovation. With so few tenured faculty employed in the teaching of writing, and with such poor compensation for those engaged with that work, the stakes were too low to spark much of a fight. One day, with few dust-ups to speak of, English 101 became the foundation course for a program of interdisciplinary study that reached about eleven thousand undergraduates every year.

Most students in college composition classes nationwide do exactly what they did in high school, writing about short stories, novels, poetry, and plays—literary pseudo-scholarship masquerading as something else. Or the students read "short essays" that might have appeared originally as opinion pieces in the major daily papers, something by Shelby Steele on affirmative action, for instance, or by Katie

Roiphe on the perfidy of various feminists, or a classic from the archives like E. B. White's "Once More to the Lake" or Nora Ephron's infamous "Breasts." Alternately, students learn to practice cultural critique, unmasking class anxieties in *ER* or celebrating gansta rap as counterhegemonic. The thinking behind such absurdities, which only the force of long tradition can obscure, is that English 101 should somehow bridge the gap between the home world of the students themselves and the specialized concerns of the university. But what an image of that "home world" most courses conjure up! Can the students or their instructors really bring themselves to believe in it?

The teaching of E. B. White in 2002 is the product of an all-too-familiar compromise in English 101: the students pretend to learn, and will do so in good humor so long as little effort is required from them, while the faculty, often indifferent and underpaid, pretend to teach. The same might be said, however, of lower-level courses across the curriculum. Complaints about this predicament have become a permanent fixture of university life, much like statues of forgotten Confederate generals in empty, sun-baked Southern parks. But the champions of teaching have misunderstood why it might have value for us once again: not because teaching possesses some intrinsic merit, like hard manual labor or cold morning baths. Teaching has lost its value precisely because the humanities no longer see their fate as linked to the future lives of ordinary citizens. Instead of asking how we might enable those citizens to act in the world that is likely to emerge ten or fifteen years from now, we have imagined ourselves as our society's principle actors, while those citizens, our students, have become superfluous in our eyes. But what should really matter, and what might really save us, is our attention to the problems they will have to address, and the skills they will need in order to improve on our common life. Our job is not to lead, but to prepare and support.

After several years of trial and error, it became possible for beginning students at my institution to read Benjamin Barber on civil society, Martha Nussbaum on women and human rights, Malcolm Gladwell on the dynamics of change in commercial culture, and Michael Pollan on Monsanto's genetic engineering. Students had the opportunity to write papers on health care in the Third World, global trade and environmental decline, the Internet and rates of voter turnout, artificial intelligence and religious tradition. Certainly, the writing classes taught students how to write; but more important, these classes taught them how to use academic knowledge, fixed and formalized as it probably has to be, in order to make sense of a perpetually shifting real-world terrain. As texts for reading and writing, Benjamin Barber or Karen Armstrong demand a great deal more than a four-page theme on teenagers and abortion, and not simply because the prose is conceptually difficult and presupposes a wide range of background knowledge. Instead of urging students to take sides on an issue whose contours are already familiar and well-defined, thinkers like Barber and Armstrong expect those who engage with their ideas to move beyond the accustomed contours. Barber and Armstrong enact synthetic thinking, and they require it as well.

These demands we acknowledged openly in the preface to the reader we assembled for the writing program's flagship course, which still carries the antiquated title of "Expository Writing." Here's one part of what we told the students themselves:

> Although the articles and essays in this book deal with subjects as diverse as the anthropology of art and the ethics of science, the book is not really "about" art or science or any of the other subjects explored by the readings. Instead, this book is about the need for new ways of thinking, and it does not pretend that those ways of thinking already exist. Never before have people faced uncertainty in so many different areas. How, for instance, will the information technologies affect our personal lives? As corporations spread across the continents, will our identity as Americans continue to be important, or will we need to see ourselves in other ways? Will genetic technology lead to a Brave New World of "designer babies" and made-to-order soldier-clones or will its breakthroughs revolutionize food production and eliminate genetic disease?
>
> Unlike most questions posed by textbooks, the right answers to these questions aren't waiting for us in the teacher's edition. Not even the best educated and the most experienced can foresee with certainty how the life of our times will turn out. Our problems today are not only much more sweeping than humankind has encountered before, they are also more complex. Globalization is not just an issue for economists, or political scientists, or historians, or anthropologists; it is an issue for all of them together. The degradation of the biosphere is not just an ecological matter, but a political, social, and cultural matter as well. The uniqueness of our time requires us to devise new understandings of ourselves and the world. One purpose of this course is to provide a place for these understandings to emerge.
>
> It may seem strange, perhaps, that we would have such lofty goals in a course for undergraduates. Surely the experts are better equipped than college students to respond to the issues our world now confronts. But this assumption may be unjustified. In a certain sense, the current generation of students needs to reinvent the university itself, not by replacing one department or methodology with another, but by building broad connections across areas of knowledge that still remain in relative isolation.

Clearly, this is a manifesto and not the innocuous course description it pretends to be. It tells students that the university's knowledge has reached its historical and institutional limits, and that their role as social actors after graduation will require them to think and act in ways beyond the imaginings of most of their professors.

Earlier, I claimed that English 101 had become "the foundation course for a program of interdisciplinary study that reached about eleven thousand undergraduates every year." While that figure is entirely accurate, and even a bit conservative, the foundation stands alone as of this writing, uncrowned by the soaring architecture of any new curriculum. Perhaps this is how change always has to come. In a certain sense, after all, the situation of the academic humanities is nothing short of hopeless: few of those ensconced within the institution's cocoon have any pressing reason to pursue systemic change. For this very reason, however, any future life the humanities might enjoy will depend on our students—those raw, unlettered citizen-dilettantes—and on our efforts to prepare them for their world, not ours, should we make such effort at all. And this too we said, more or less, in the preface to our book:

> The humanities will have succeeded in their work only when students take the knowledge of the university beyond the university itself. In a certain sense, this means that students have to become their own best teachers: they need to find in their own lives—their own goals, values, and commitments—an organizing principle for a learning experience which is bound to seem disorganized. The great, unspoken secret of the university now is that the curriculum has no center: specialization makes sure of that. Historians write primarily for historians; literary critics for other literary critics. As students shuttle back and forth between these specialized domains, the only coherence they can take away from their education is a coherence they have made for themselves.

Ironically the humanities may find themselves better off if they abandon all hope of recovering a centrality they have never really had, not in Plato's time nor Shakespeare's nor Lionel Trilling's. The very effort to protect something called "the past" from something called "the present," already testifies to the limitations of our temporal perspective. When we gaze a thousand years into the past, or a thousand years into the future, the worlds we envision there are only reflections of our world right now, and it is to this fragile, fearful world that we must turn with all our energy, intelligence, and care.

NOTES

Chapter 1   Taking the Humanities Out of the Box

1. The historian Burton J. Bledstein has traced the emergence of a distinctive "culture of professionalism" in the United States after the Civil War. The American Medical Association led the way with its founding in 1847. Among many other organizations, the American Chemical Association followed in 1876, the American Society of Naturalists in 1883, the American Institute of Electrical Engineers in 1885, the American Mathematical Society in 1888 and the American Physical Society in 1889. The humanities pursued the same course with the founding of the Modern Language Association in 1883, the American Historical Association in 1884, the American Philosophical Association in 1900, and the College Art Association in 1911. See *The Culture of Professionalism: The Middle Class and the Development of Higher Education in America* (New York: W.W. Norton, 1976), esp. 80–128. As his title suggests, Bledstein links the emergence of professionalism in the nineteenth century with the quest for membership in the middle class. Professionalism was the means of dignifying certain forms of work and ability, while educational attainment served to justify a new and "fairer" form of hierarchy. For a more recent treatment of professionalism, one quite different in its emphasis, see Andrew Abbott, *The System of Professions: An Essay on the Division of Expert Labor* (Chicago: University of Chicago Press, 1988). In contrast to Bledstein, Abbott sees the professions as constituting a system in its own right, not simply as an extension of middle class hegemony. Both accounts, in my view, capture aspects of professionalism important to the argument I develop here. Professions *do* convey social advantage within a class society; they *also* have their own intrinsic dynamics, about which I am less sanguine than Abbott appears to be. He sees the professions as providing "continuously independent life chances" for individual academics in a highly competitive arena. I see that arena as less open than he does for individual academics, and more isolating for the academy as a whole.

For a history of English studies, see Gerald Graff, *Professing Literature: An Institutional History* (Chicago: University of Chicago Press, 1987). For the field of history, which broke off from the American Social Science Association, see Thomas L. Haskell, *The Emergence of Professional Social Science: The American Social Science Association and the Nineteenth-Century Crisis of Authority* (Urbana: University of Illinois Press, 1977); John Higham, *History: Professional Scholarship in America* (Baltimore: Johns Hopkins University Press, 1965), and Peter Novick, *That Noble Dream: The "Objectivity Question" and the Historical Profession* (New York: Cambridge University Press, 1988). For philosophy, see Bruce Kuklick, *The Rise of American Philosophy, Cambridge, Massachusetts, 1860–1930* (New Haven: Yale University Press, 1977). For art history, see Craig Hugh Smyth and Peter M. Lukehart, eds., *The Early Years of Art History in the United States: Notes and Essays on Departments, Teaching, and Scholars* (Princeton: Dept. of Art and Archaeology, Princeton University, 1993).

2. The classics and rhetoric withered away within a generation, from the 1880s to about 1900. See Frederick Rudolph, *Curriculum: A History of the American Undergraduate Course of Study Since 1636* (San Francisco: Jossey-Bass, 1977), 180–88. For the history of rhetoric and its displacement by composition see Albert T. Kitzhaber, *Rhetoric in American Colleges, 1850–1900* (Dallas: Southern Methodist University Press, 1990); Gregory Clark and S. Michael Halloran, eds., *Oratorical Culture in Nineteenth-Century America: Transformations in the Theory and Practice of Rhetoric* (Carbondale: Southern Illinois University Press, 1993); John C. Brereton, ed., *The Origins of Composition Studies in the American College, 1875–1925: A Documentary History* (Pittsburgh: University of Pittsburgh Press, 1995). Although composition courses replaced the teaching of rhetoric in twentieth-century American universities, the field of rhetoric has virtually risen from the grave by attaching itself in recent years to the teaching of writing.

Two articulate and thoughtful attempts to inspire a revival of the classics are Victor Davis Hanson and John Heath, *Who Killed Homer: The Demise of Classical Education and the Recovery of Greek Wisdom* (New York: Free Press, 1998) and Page duBois, *Trojan Horses: Saving Classics from the Conservatives* (New York: New York University Press, 2001). Hanson and Heath admit, however, that a revival will not be easy. As they note, in the period from 1965 to 1974, the number of students taking courses in college Latin dropped from 40,000 to 25,000, where it has since remained, more or less. Between 1971 and 1991, the number of classics majors dropped by 30 percent (3).

3. The *Digest of Educational Statistics, 2000* offers some surprising insights. Since 1960, the number of bachelor's degrees has tripled nationally, increasing from about 400,000 to about 1.2 million. Since 1970, the number of B.A.s majoring in English has dropped from 64,342 (seven percent of all B.A.s) to 49,708 (four percent). History and the social sciences, listed together in the *Digest,* have dropped by more than 20,000, from eighteen percent to ten percent of the total. Philosophy and religion, also aggregated, have never managed to rise to a single percent, but their fraction has been halved since the 1970s.

Within the humanities, the conventional wisdom is that the culture of commerce has stolen the students away, but the reality is far more complex. True, enrollments in business courses have risen by 100,000 more than thirty years ago, but that amounts to a jump from thirteen percent to only nineteen percent. Other gainers include the health professions, up from three percent to seven percent; psychology, from four percent to six percent, and communications, from one percent to four percent. None of these are fields that necessarily promote greed or vulgarity. Computer science, imagined by some humanists to be a juggernaut, now claims only two percent of total B.A.s. It is significant as well that the number of graduates majoring in the performing arts has increased by 20,000 (from three percent to four percent). General liberal arts study has also registered a modest gain, from less than one percent to two percent, and the same holds true for multidisciplinary and interdisciplinary studies, again rising from nearly zero to two percent. From these statistics I would infer that the problem is not with business, but with the humanities themselves. See National Center for Educational Statistics, "Postsecondary Education," *Digest of Educational Statistics, 2000, http://nces.ed.gov/pubs2001/digest/ch3.htm*

4. In constant 1999–2000 dollars, total expenditures for public education have risen from less than $20 billion in 1960 to more than $160 billion in 2000. Expenditures for private colleges have risen from about $5 billion to nearly $80 billion (*Digest of Educational Statistics, 2000*). A glance at any campus today will make it clear how much of that money has gone into science and technology. According to the National Science Foundation's *Survey of Research and Development Expenditures at Universities and Colleges* (1998), R&D expenditures at U.S. colleges and universities have increased by twenty-nine percent in the period between 1993 and 1998, with a six percent jump in 1997–1998 alone. "Academic R&D Spending Continues Steady Growth in FY 1998," *Data Brief,* Division of Science Resource Studies, National Science Foundation, 14 August 2000: 1. As the *Digest* shows, however, the numbers of science majors have not generally increased; in some fields, they have actually declined. These enrollment figures suggest that much of the $26 billion total for 1998 went into pure research and the graduate training that supports it.

The Bureau of Labor Statistics reports that about thirty-three percent of all university faculty worked part time. *Occupational Outlook Handbook 2000–01,* 29 December 2000, *http://www.bls.gov/oco/ocos066.htm* But according to the American Association of University Professors, part-time faculty are concentrated primarily in humanities disciplines, especially English, history, composition programs, mathematics and the modern languages. "Background Facts: Part-Time Faculty," *http://www.aaup.org/Ptfacts.htm*

A typically careful survey conducted by the American Historical Association indicates that in the period from 1979 to 1999, the number of part-time faculty in that field increased from 6.3 percent to twenty-four percent. The author of a report on the survey, the historian Robert B. Townsend, indicates that the 1999 figure would be even higher if the study had factored in graduate students. According to the survey, the number of full-time faculty in history has dropped from ninety-four percent to sixty-seven percent in the space of twenty years. Much the same story could be told about English. "Part-Time Faculty Surveys Highlight Disturbing Trends," October 2000, *http://theaha.org.ptcom/pt_survey.htm*

5. The watershed event in the so-called "culture wars" was the publication of Allan Bloom's culturally conservative polemic *The Closing of the American Mind* (New York: Simon and Schuster, 1987). Other landmarks in the conservative canon are Harold Bloom's *The Western Canon: the Books and School of the Ages* (New York: Harcourt Brace, 1994), and Jacques Barzun's *The Culture We Deserve* (Middletown, Conn.: Wesleyan University Press, 1989) as well as his more recent *From Dawn to Decadence: 500 Years of Western Cultural Life: 1500 to the Present* (New York: Harper-Collins, 2000). The Blooms are both, to my mind, quite brilliant but also fundamentally misguided in their willingness to embrace Western high culture so uncritically. Barzun has a more complex understanding of the past but he still denigrates as

"decadent" much of great value in the last hundred years or so. By contrast to the work of these writers, Roger Kimball's *Tenured Radicals: How Politics has Corrupted Higher Education* (New York: HarperCollins, 1990) is often crude and intemperate. While the right has dominated mass-market publishing, a few articulate left-progressive thinkers have attempted to answer them. These thinkers include Gerald Graff, author of *Beyond the Culture Wars: How Teaching the Conflicts Can Revitalize American Education* (New York: W.W. Norton, 1992) and Lawrence W. Levine, in *The Opening of the American Mind: Canons, Culture, and History* (Boston: Beacon Press, 1996). Graff and Levine have pursued the course that I prefer, turning their backs on the extreme elements within the academic left while refusing to cede the field to the conservatives.

6. Robert N. Bellah, "The True Scholar," *Academe: Bulletin of the American Association of University Professors* (January–February 2000): 18–23. In his article, Bellah relies on statistics published in *Harvard Magazine* during 1998, but these do not exactly coincide with the statistics I have collected covering a somewhat longer period. The authors of the article he cites make misleading claims as well. They note ominously, for example, that the number of majors in computer and information science doubled between 1970 and 1994. While the claim is true, strictly speaking, the two areas together still constitute less than five percent of all B.A.s granted. Bellah himself ignores or downplays some of the evidence his source provides. According to the *Harvard* authors, two of the fastest growing areas were the health professions and public administration—a shift that might indicate a growing spirit of humanitarian concern and civic activism, not the triumph of gross cupidity.

7. Garrett Hardin quotes Carl Linneas on a Swedish famine in 1769, during the lifetime of Dr. Johnson. *Living Within Limits: Ecology, Economics, and Population Taboos* (New York: Oxford University Press, 1993), 220. Friends of Finnish ancestry have told me about the Years of Horror, 1866–1868, when crop failures drove many Finns to immigrate to the United States.

8. See, for example, Humphrey Taylor, "The Mood of American Workers," Harris Poll #4, Wednesday, 19 January 2000, *http://www.harrisinteractive.com/harris _poll/index.asp?PID=5* Also see Lydia Saad, "American Workers Generally Satisfied, but Indicate Their Jobs Leave Much to be Desired," The Gallup Organization, 3 September 1999, *http://www.gallup.com/poll/releases/pr990903.asp* Although workers polled by the Gallup Organization expressed a lower level of job satisfaction than workers polled by Harris, only fourteen percent described themselves as "dissatisfied." The Harris Poll noted especially high rates of job satisfaction among workers over fifty.

A report by the AARP's Public Policy Institute notes that in 1979, half of preretirees indicated that they would like to work after retirement, preferably part time or in less demanding jobs. By the late 1990s, that figure had risen to seventy percent for all workers and eighty percent for baby boomers. See Sara E. Rix, Economics Team, "Social Security Reform: Rethinking Retirement-Age Policy—A Look at Raising Social Security's Retirement Age" (Washington, D.C.: AARP Public Policy Institute, November 1999).

9. Department of Defense statistics show the following percentages for mi-

norities in uniform: Army 40.8 percent; Navy 35.4 percent; Marine Corps 32.4 percent; Air Force 25.4 percent; Department of Defense 34.4 percent. The percentages of officers are as follows: Army 20.6 percent; Navy 16.9 percent; Marine Corps 32.4 percent; Air Force 25.4 percent; DOD 16.9 percent "Minorities in Uniform," 5 September 2000, *http://www.defenselink.mil/pubs/almanac/almanac/people/minorities.html*

The *Chronicle of Higher Education*'s *2000–2001 Almanac* paints a very different picture. The Almanac does not calculate percentages, but its figures indicate that minority faculty at all levels (including "lecturer" and "other") amount to only thirteen percent of the total. Among full professors, nonwhites amount to only ten percent. "Number of Full-Time Faculty Members by Sex, Rank, and Racial and Ethnic Group, Fall 1997," *http://chronicle.com/ weekly/almanac/2000/facts/3803folks.htm* But many of these minority faculty are actually in the sciences. According to statistics provided by the National Academy Press, in 1995 only two percent of humanities Ph.D.s were black, two percent Asian, and three percent Hispanic. In other words, ninety-three percent of humanities Ph.D.s were white. "Humanities Doctorates in the United States: 1995 Profile," 1997, *http://books.nap.edu/books/0309058449/html/5.html*

10. In his biography of Faulkner, Joseph Blotner notes that Faulkner made the truly grand sum of $19,374.99 in 1936. Blotner's account seems to indicate that this was four or five times Faulkner's annual wage in the preceding years. See Joseph Blotner, *Faulkner: A Biography,* vol. 2, (New York: Random House, 1947), 950–56.

11. Throughout the United States and Canada, classical stations are closing down in response to a dwindling audience while many symphonies operate in the red. For an account of the experiment with jazz and world music, see "Classical Music: An Endangered Art?" Minnesota Public Radio transcript, *http:/news.mpr.org/features/199706 . . . risib-_classical/docs/lebrecht. shtml* In order to increase the faltering audience of KUSC in Los Angeles, program director Wally Smith took his station in this controversial new direction in 1995. Two years later, he was forced to resign. It appears that Smith was unable to generate a large enough number of new listeners to offset the dissatisfaction of the station's more traditional audience, who eventually managed to scare off the University's licensee. Nevertheless, in a retrospective assessment, *Los Angeles Times* critic Mark Swed applauded the effort. KUSC, he argued, may have gone "too far, too fast," but it was headed in the right direction.

The four-part Minnesota Public Radio series on classical music also includes an interview with Bobby McFerrin, who in 1991 became the Artistic Director of the Saint Paul Chamber Orchestra. Like Smith, he encountered determined resistance from musical conservatives, despite the crucial need to expand the support base. Unlike Smith, however, McFerrin still holds his job as I complete this chapter.

Two years after Smith's dismissal, however, the University of Southern California received a $25 million donation to endow what is now the Thornton School of Music, a tacit endorsement of its music school's innovative curriculum. According to Paul Boylan, dean of music at the University of Michigan, the Thornton School combines the very highest level of traditional training in music with new programs responsive to the best of music in popular culture." Diane Krieger, "Reaching for a High Note," *USC Trojan Magazine* (Winter1999), *http://www.usc. edu/dept/pubre/troj . . . winter99/Thornton/Thornton_pg1.html*

12. Mozart spent most of his life as an independent performer-composer who lived off the incomes generated by his various activities: teaching, composing, performing at subscription concerts, and of course, drawing large crowds, on occasion, to his operas. See John Roselli, *The Life of Mozart* (Cambridge: Cambridge University Press, 1998), esp. 71–72. And as Maynard Solomon details, Mozart was quite eager for applause, popularity, and good receipts; see *Mozart: A Life* (New York: HarperCollins, 1995), 285–305. Solomon also observes that Mozart "carefully analyzed the economics of the music world; in particular, he realized that Vienna did not constitute a monolithic audience but contained a multiplicity of audiences with appetites for various kinds of music" (286).

Beethoven, as David Wyn Jones observes, "craved recognition, and, more basically, as he repeatedly wrote to friends and potential publishers [of his music], he needed to compose in order to live"—in order, that is, to maintain his livelihood. *The Life of Beethoven* (Cambridge, Eng.: Cambridge University Press, 1998), 172. For a discussion of the marketing of Beethoven as a brooding recluse, see also Tia DeNora, *Beethoven and the Construction of Genius: Musical Politics in Vienna, 1792–1803* (Berkeley: University of California Press, 1995).

"The box office," Verdi declared, "is the proper thermometer of success," quoted in John Rosselli, *The Life of Verdi* (Cambridge, Eng.: Cambridge University Press, 2000), 2.

13. Bruce Weber, "A Boston Museum Director Is Criticized for Doing What He Was Hired to Do," *The New York Times,* 23 December 1999. Rogers's subordinates were particularly incensed at his habit of displaying art without consulting them. One curator was quoted as deploring the "way the paintings are exhibited . . . All the important jewels of the collection have been massed together in the tapestry gallery, so that these important things that are the center of the collection become a corridor. You can't possibly concentrate on them when you get them massed in close quarters, and it teaches the public a disrespect for art." Another cause for offense was Rogers's decision to cancel the museum's expensive scholarly journal, *http:/ www.nytimes.com/yr/mo/day/news/arts/boston-museum.html*

14. See Svetlana Alpers, *Rembrandt's Enterprise: The Studio and the Market* (Chicago: University of Chicago Press, 1988). For a discussion of the commercial interests of the Impressionists and their successors Matisse and Picasso, see Michael C. Fitzgerald, *Making Modernism: Picasso and the Creation of the Market for Twentieth-Century Art* (New York: Farrar, Strauss and Giroux, 1995). The Impressionists wanted wide acclaim, and they ended their careers as the beneficiaries of "an international network of collectors and critics" (7). Picasso was famous for declaring, "Le marchand—violà l'ennemi." Yet he was a very astute entrepreneur who lived, as Cecil Beaton recalled, in "the manner of a Grand Seigneur" (3–4). Matisse too was known in Paris art-dealer circles as "a very hard bargainer" (10).

15. See Gary Witherspoon, *Language and Art in the Navajo Universe* (Ann Arbor: University of Michigan Press, 1977); Urs Ramseyer, *The Art and Culture of*

Bali (New York: Oxford University Press, 1977); and Soetsu Yanagi et al., *The Unknown Craftsman: A Japanese Insight into Beauty,* rev. ed. (New York: Kodansha International, 1990).

16. My primary source here is Michael Schudson, "Beyond the Informed Citizen," *http://prairie.org/detours/ResPublica/features/Feature4.html* See also Schudson's *The Good Citizen: A History of American Civic Life* (New York: Free Press, 1998). Schudson's argument—that the Progressives actually set out to *limit* democratic participation in the political process—is quite consistent with mine in Part I of this book. For a discussion of the growth of voter participation after the Civil War, see Glenn C. Altschuler and Stuart M. Blumin, *Rude Republic: Americans and Their Politics in the Nineteenth Century* (Princeton: Princeton University Press, 2000). For an analysis of the current situation, see Frances Fox Piven and Richard A. Cloward, *Why Americans Still Don't Vote: and Why Politicians Want It That Way* rev. and updated ed. (Boston: Beacon Press, 2000).

17. The author of these words was the fifteenth-century philosopher Nicholas of Cusa. See Alexander Koyré, *From the Closed World to the Infinite Universe* (New York: Harper Torchbooks, 1958).

18. See *Untimely Meditations,* trans. R. J. Hollingdale (New York: Cambridge University Press, 1983), esp. 62, 77–95. As Nietzsche insists in his essay, "On the Uses and Disadvantages of History for Life" (1874), "Forgetting is essential to action of any kind, just as not only light but darkness too is essential for the life of everything organic" (62). For Nietzsche, historical consciousness can be crippling, and the critical revision of history—in the manner of deconstruction—he viewed as a symptom of fear. The best response was creative, not revisionary—the response of the "uncultured" Greeks. Of course, Nietzsche was not a democrat—in that regard his epigones have gotten him right.

19. Rorty has made this argument most forcefully in *Achieving Our Country: Leftist Thought in Twentieth-Century America* (Cambridge, Mass.: Harvard University Press, 1998). There, and in subsequent writings and interviews, he rejects much of postmodernist cultural politics as a nostalgia for "philosophy," for the attempt to ground worldly actions on some quasi-transcendental foundation. For an even more candid and succinct presentation of these views, see also Joshua Knobe, "A Talent for Bricolage: An Interview with Richard Rorty" *The Dualist* 2 (1995): 56–71.

Fish writes so copiously—and so repetitively—so that one could pick up almost any book at random, but two most important recent ones are *There's No Such Thing as Free Speech and It's a Good Thing, Too* (New York: Oxford University Press, 1994) and *Professional Correctness: Literary Studies and Political Change* (Oxford: Clarendon Press, 1995).

The differences between Fish and Rorty should not be overlooked, however. Long ago, Rorty gave up on philosophy as a profession with a subject matter of its own, as the interview with Knobe makes clear. What Rorty seems to want is a public philosophy in the Deweyan mode concerned with social problems and possible solutions. By contrast Fish's pragmatism leads to a reaffirming of professionalism and a defense of its insulation from "political" concerns.

One of the most revealing documents in this regard is "Stanley Fish Replies to

Richard John Neuhaus," *First Things* 60 (February 1996): 35–40. There Fish makes
the case that for the professional literary critic, the study of Milton has nothing to do
with a possible change in the critic's own inner life. The point of literary criticism
instead is to make a change in the way the community of critics views their own
understanding of Milton. On the face of it, this would seem to suggest that criticism
is an utterly pointless undertaking, if we presume that the literature should somehow matter to us in a personal way, which is how most people view the issue, not
least of all writers themselves. Given that the whole culture of the arts in the West
has long presupposed a connection between art and life, Fish's argument is bound to
seem ingenious but unsatisfying. The same holds true for Rorty's defense of a
politics that remains agnostic about ultimate concerns. We can't really pursue the
good life in this particular way or that one unless we believe in the idea of "the good
life." It's clear that Rorty wants a better world, at least; it's not so clear that Fish does,
unless "better" means securing for his discipline—and by extension, for himself—a
greater degree of prestige and respect.

20. *The Collected Works of Ralph Waldo Emerson,* ed. Alfred R. Ferguson, vol.
1, *Nature, Addresses, and Lectures* (Cambridge, Mass.: Belknap Press, 1971), 57.

21. Consider Emerson's argument in "The Over-Soul": "Ineffable is the
union of man and God in every act of the soul. The simplest person, who in his
integrity worships God, becomes God, yet forever and ever the influx of this better
and universal self is new and unsearchable." Ibid., ed. Alfred R. Ferguson and Jean
Ferguson Carr, vol. 2, *Essays: First Series* (Cambridge, Mass.: Belknap Press, 1979),
172–73.

22. In one variant of this iconographic tradition, told to me by art historian
Glenn T. Webb, the three sages are shown laughing because all three have just been
startled by the roar of a nearby lion—the sound, in other words, of their own
mortality.

23. Whitman's attitude toward Emerson was ambivalent. In the essay "Emerson's Books (The Shadows of Them)" Whitman recalls the time in his youth when
he had "Emerson-on the-brain," but much of the essay faults the "Master" for his
failure to achieve a truly organic and democratic vision, beyond the structures of the
day. Though "the author has much to say of freedom and wildness and simplicity
and spontaneity, no performance was ever more based on artificial scholarships
and decorums (he calls it culture). . . . It is always a *make*, never an unconscious
growth." *The Works of Walt Whitman, The Collected Prose,* vol. 2 (New York: Funk
and Wagnalls, 1968), 329. James also criticizes Emerson for his abstractness, as in
The Varieties of Religious Experience, but Emerson remained an important and
acknowledged inspiration throughout his career. See *The Varieties of Religious Experience* (New York: Modern Library, 1999), 37–40.

24. As Whitman argues in *Democratic Vistas,* "Something a man is (last
precious consolation of the drudging poor), standing apart from all else, divine in his
own right, and a woman in hers, sole and untouchable by any canons of authority"
(*The Works of Walt Whitman,* vol. 2, 217). The radical equality that James argues for
has a rather different and less Emersonian basis: "neither the whole of truth, nor the
whole of good, is revealed to any single observer, although each observer gains a

partial superiority of insight from the peculiar position in which he stands" *The Works of William James, Talks to Teachers on Psychology* (Cambridge, Mass.: Harvard University Press, 1983), 149.

25. Ferguson, *The Collected Works,* vol. 2, 159.

26. William James, *The Works of William James, A Pluralistic Universe* (Cambridge, Mass.: Harvard University Press, 1977), 130. Emerson makes a rather similar observation in "The American Scholar" when he observes, "The world,—this shadow of the soul, or *other me,*—lies wide around. Its attractions are the keys which unlock my thoughts and make me acquainted with myself. I run eagerly into this resounding tumult" (Ferguson 59).

27. Ibid., 131.

28. See Allan Megill and Donald N. McCloskey, "The Rhetoric of History," in *The Rhetoric of the Human Sciences: Language and Argument in Scholarship and Public Affairs,* ed. John S. Nelson et al. (Madison: University of Wisconsin Press, 1987), 221–38.

29. The article, by physicist Alan Sokal, was "Transgressing the Boundaries: Toward a Transformative Hermeneutics of Quantum Gravity," *Social Text* 46/47 (Spring/Summer 1996): 217–52. Sokal announced the hoax in "A Physicist Experiments with Cultural Studies," *Lingua Franca* (May/June 1996): 62–64.

30. Anthony Giddens, *Modernity and Self-Identity: Self and Society in the Late Modern Age* (Stanford: Stanford University Press, 1991), 84.

31. As Arnold argues in his essay "The Function of Criticism at the Present Time," "There is the world of ideas and there is the world of practice." Although he makes this distinction in a passage contrasting English society to the French, he goes on to argue for a corresponding division of cultural labor. "It is," he writes, "because criticism . . . has so little detached itself from practice . . . that it has so ill accomplished . . . its best spiritual work" *The Portable Matthew Arnold* (New York: Viking, 1969), 243, 250.

32. William James, *Some Problems of Philosophy: A Beginning of an Introduction to Philosophy* (New York: Longmans, Green, and Co, 1911), 7.

33. For an extremely coherent, accurate, and (for me) persuasive discussion of this issue, see Paul R. Gross and Norman Levitt, *Higher Superstition: The Academic Left and Its Quarrels with Science* (Baltimore: Johns Hopkins University Press, 1994).

34. Clement Greenberg was the exemplary modernist critic in the sense that he succeeded in controlling not only the reception of art by patrons and the public but even the standards informing artistic production for almost twenty years. Few other figures in this century have exerted so far reaching an influence, though many have tried. He was, we might say, the exception that created the rule. See Florence Rubenfeld's controversial *Clement Greenberg: A Life* (New York: Scribner's, 1998). For a discussion of his influence on Jackson Pollock and others, see Claude Cernuschi, *Jackson Pollock: Meaning and Significance* (New York: Icon/HarperCollins, 1992), 263–310.

35. See Max Weber, *Economy and Society: An Outline of Interpretive Sociology,* vol. 1, trans. Guenther Roth and Claus Wittich (Berkeley: University of California Press, 1978), 266–71.

Chapter 2   Democracy Sets in the West: From Able Citizens to Ignorant Masses

1. M. I. Finley, *Democracy Ancient and Modern,* rev. ed. (New Brunswick, N.J.: Rutgers University Press, 1988).
2. Ibid., 20.
3. Ibid., 18–19.
4. Ibid., 24–25.
5. Ibid., *Economy and Society in Ancient Greece* (London: Chatto and Windus, 1981), 64.
6. Elias Bickerman, "The Hellenistic World," in John A. Garraty and Peter Gay, *The Columbia History of the World* (New York: Harper & Row, 1972), 181–89. See also Simon Price, "The History of the Hellenistic Period," 315–37, and Jonathan Barnes, "Hellenistic Philosophy and Science," 365–85, in *The Oxford History of the Classical World,* ed. John Boardman et al. (New York: Oxford University Press, 1986). Price tends to whitewash the whole period, describing the murderous and monomaniacal Alexander as "one of the archetypally romantic figures" (315); nevertheless, the facts of political and social life speak powerfully for themselves. See also Naphtali Lewis, *Greeks in Ptolemaic Egypt: Case Studies in the Social History of the Hellenistic World* (Oxford: Clarendon Press, 1986).

For a discussion of the linkages between Alexander's empire and the deteriorating condition of the Greek homeland, especially economic decline, see Margaret O. Wason, *Class Struggles in Ancient Greece* (New York: Howard Fertig, 1973), 164–214.

7. Bickerman, 187.
8. Finley, *Democracy Ancient and Modern,* 20–21.
9. Ibid., 105.
10. Eduardo Galeano, *Memory of Fire: 1, Genesis,* trans. Cedric Belfrage (New York: Pantheon, 1985), xv.
11. For the Greeks, what we now call the "humanities" were inescapably political, history perhaps most of all. See Cynthia Farrar, "Ancient Greek Political Theory as a Response to Democracy," in *Democracy: The Unfinished Journey, 508 B.C. to A.D. 1993,* ed. John Dunn (New York: Oxford University Press, 1992): 17–39.
12. Jean-Pierre Vernant, *Myth and Society in Ancient Greece,* trans. Janet Lloyd (New York: Zone Books, 1990), 92.
13. Ibid., 89.
14. Finley, *Democracy Ancient and Modern,* 170.
15. Robert H. Wiebe, *The Search for Order 1877–1920* (New York: Hill and Wang, 1967), 2. For the further development of Wiebe's thinking, see also his brilliant *Self-Rule: A Cultural History of American Democracy* (Chicago: University of Chicago Press, 1995). As he observes there, democracy's decline cannot responsibly be blamed on "an individualism that has always been intrinsic to" American culture, or on political polarization, which is merely a symptom of the disease. Rather, the cause is "the centralized, hierarchical structure of relations that first took shape between the 1890s and the 1920s" (266).

16. John Dewey, *The Public and Its Problems* (Denver: Alan Swallow, 1954), 111.

17. The term "island community" is Wiebe's. See "Crisis in the Communities" in *The Search for Order,* 44–75.

18. Ibid., xiii.

19. See Robert N. Bellah et al., *Habits of the Heart: Individualism and Commitment in American Life* (Berkeley: University of California Press, 1985), as well as *The Good Society* (New York: Vintage, 1992); and Amitai Etzioni, *The Spirit of Community: Rights, Responsibilities, and the Communitarian Agenda* (New York: Crown, 1993) and *The New Golden Rule: Community and Morality in a Democratic Society* (New York: Basic Books, 1996).

20. Wiebe, *The Search,* 44. However, this process of local disempowerment had begun even earlier than Wiebe suggests, the "first wave" washing over the continent during the Jackson era. See Charles Sellers, *The Market Revolution: Jacksonian America, 1815–1846* (New York: Oxford University Press, 1991). Wiebe seems to me correct nevertheless in identifying centralization and institutionalized hierarchy as a new and distinctly modern stage in the process.

21. The term "cultural populist" is my own coinage. Among many academics on the left today, the word *populist* has become a term of derision, roughly equivalent to "white supremacist" or "Christian fundamentalist"—a false assumption but one, alas, altogether consistent with the truncated vision and elitist sensibilities handed down to us from the 1960s. The Populist movement during the period that I deal with here, however, championed grassroots democracy against the economic and political forces that had undermined it. There is now an enormous body of scholarship on what the historian Lawrence Goodwyn has described as "the largest democratic mass movement in American history," and several decades of scholarship following his book have only deepened the understanding that he provides. See Goodwyn's *The Populist Moment: A Short History of the Agrarian Revolt in America* (New York: Oxford University Press, 1978); Robert W. Larson, *Populism in the Mountain West* (Albuquerque: University of New Mexico Press, 1986); Worth Robert Miller, *Oklahoma Populism: A History of the People's Party in the Oklahoma Territory* (Norman: University of Oklahoma Press, 1987); Theodore R. Mitchell, *Political Education in the Southern Farmers' Alliance, 1887–1900* (Madison: University of Wisconsin Press, 1987); Robert C. McMath Jr., *American Populism: A Social History, 1877–1898* (New York: Hill and Wang, 1993); Jeffrey Ostler, *Prairie Populism: The Fate of Agrarian Radicalism in Kansas, Nebraska, and Iowa 1880–1892* (Lawrence: University Press of Kansas, 1993); Gene Clanton, *Congressional Populism and the Crisis of the 1890s* (Lawrence: University Press of Kansas, 1998); Elizabeth Sanders, *Roots of Reform: Farmers, Workers, and the American State, 1877–1917* (Chicago: University of Chicago Press, 1999). One important theoretical source for me has been Norman Pollack, *The Humane Economy: Populism, Capitalism, and Democracy* (New Brunswick, N.J.: Rutgers University Press, 1990). As Pollack points out, Populism was not liberalism: "Liberalism strengthened monopolistic enterprise by synchronizing it with government; and Populists regarded this process as the antithesis of democratic modernization" (168). Also important is Michael

Kazin's *The Populist Persuasion: An American History* rev. ed. (Ithaca, N.Y.: Cornell University Press, 1998), which explores American populist sentiments before and after the Populist movement. Kazin is particularly concerned with the conservative appropriation of populist language since the 1980s. For a recent restatement of the pre-Reagan-era populist tradition, see Jeff Gates, *Democracy at Risk: Rescuing Main Street from Wall Street: A Populist Vision for the Twenty-First Century* (Cambridge, Mass.: Perseus, 2000). See also the many books of Hazel Henderson.

22. For a theoretical discussion of the administered society as a new and distinctive form of social life, see Willard F. Enteman, *Managerialism: The Emergence of a New Ideology* (Wisconsin: University of Wisconsin Press, 1993).

23. If academic leftists hold "Populism" in contempt, they tend to use the term "Progressive" as a synonym for "democratic" and "right thinking." But here again, the history is more complex. In fact, the Progressives were sometimes openly undemocratic and inegalitarian, a complex legacy that our latter-day Progressives either do not understand or deliberately overlook. For discussions of the relation between Populism and the Progressive movement that displaced it, see Wiebe, *The Search,* 164–95 and Sanders, 387–408. As in the case of Populism, recent scholarship has largely confirmed and greatly extended the account developed by Wiebe. See for instance, John Stafford Lugton, *Pragmatism and the Progressive Movement in the United States: The Origin of the New Social Sciences* (Lanham, Md.: University Press of America, 1987); Andrew Feffer, *The Chicago Pragmatists and American Progressivism* (Ithaca: Cornell University Press, 1993); Kenneth Finegold, *Experts and Politicians: Reform Challenges to Machine Politics in New York, Cleveland and Chicago* (Princeton: Princeton University Press, 1995); Leon Fink, *Progressive Intellectuals and the Dilemmas of Democratic Commitment* (Cambridge, Mass.: Harvard University Press, 1997); and Michael Schudson, *The Good Citizen: A History of American Civic Life* (New York: Free Press, 1998). One work of particular importance for my understanding of the shift from Populism to the Progressives was Oscar and Lilian Handlin, *Liberty in Peril, 1850–1920; Liberty in America, 1600 to the Present* vol. 3 (New York: HarperCollins, 1992), esp. 253–98. Another important source is Arthur Lipow, *Authoritarian Socialism in America: Edward Bellamy and the Nationalist Movement* (Berkeley: University of California Press, 1982), esp. 136–59. Lipow makes a distinction, however, that I do not make, between the Progressives and the Nationalists, although he acknowledges much overlap. For me, the important point is that Populism was comparatively localist and egalitarian in spirit, whereas Progressives thought in terms of an administered national state.

24. Charles Eastman, *From the Deep Woods to Civilization: Chapters in the Autobiography of an Indian* (Boston: Little, Brown, 1916), 3.

25. Ibid., 74.

26. Ibid., 112–13.

27. Ibid., 17.

28. Ibid., 29.

29. Ibid., 195, my emphasis.

30. Dewey, *The Public and its Problems,* 98.

31. Eastman, *Deep Woods,* 127.

32. Ibid., 132–33.

33. Hamlin Garland, *A Son of the Middle Border* (New York: Grosset and Dunlap, 1923), 35.

34. The phrase "local knowledge" is from Clifford Geertz, *Local Knowledge: Further Essays in Interpretive Anthropology* (New York: Basic Books, 1983).

35. Garland, *Son*, 68.

36. Ibid., 89.

37. Ibid., 112–13.

38. Ibid., 154–55.

39. Mary Austin, *Earth Horizon* (Boston: Houghton Mifflin, 1932), 100.

40. Ibid., 127–28.

41. The transformation that Austin and Garland describe would become in the century that followed a worldwide phenomenon. See Mark Hobart, "Introduction: The Growth of Ignorance?" in *An Anthropological Critique of Development: the Growth of Ignorance* (New York: Routledge, 1993), 1–30.

42. Austin, *Earth*, 100.

43. Ibid, 101–02.

44. I have borrowed the terms "core" and "periphery" from Immanuel Wallerstein's work on the dynamics of regional economies. My concern here is with the connections between cultural systems and economic ones. See *The Modern World System* (New York: Academic Press, 1974).

45. Austin, *Earth*, 102–04.

46. Ibid., 119.

47. Ibid., 121.

48. Ibid., 151–52.

49. Garland, *Son*, 258.

50. Ibid., 351–52.

51. Ibid., 306–07.

52. Ibid., 323.

53. See Hippolyte A. Taine, *History of English Literature*, vol 1, trans. H. Van Laun (1883; New York: Frederick Ungar, 1965). A detailed discussion of Taine's impact on English studies follows in Chapter 4.

54. Garland, 460.

55. Ibid., 440.

56. See in this regard John Whiteclay Chambers II, *The Tyranny of Change: America in the Progressive Era, 1890–1920,* 2nd ed. (New York: St. Martin's Press, 1992), esp. 132–71.

57. Robert Ezra Park, *Human Communities: The City and Human Ecology* (New York: Free Press, 1952), 31. For some indication of Park's enormous influence not only on urban sociology but on urban planning, see John D. Fairfield, *The Mysteries of the Great City: The Politics of Urban Design, 1877–1937* (Columbus: Ohio State University Press, 1993).

58. Park, *Human Communities*, 33–34.

59. Ibid., 90.

60. Ibid., 37.

61. Robert E. Park, "The Urban Community as a Spatial Pattern and a Moral Order," in *On Social Control and Collective Behavior: Selected Papers,* ed. Ralph H. Turner (Chicago: University of Chicago Press, 1967), 55–84. Park originally presented "The Urban Community" as his Presidential Address at the 1925 meeting of the American Sociological Association. The quotation comes from page 59; see also 81.

62. Park, *On Social Control,* 223.

63. Nels Anderson and Eduard C. Lindeman, *Urban Sociology: An Introduction to the Study of Urban Communities* (New York: Knopf, 1928), 271.

64. Austin, *Earth,* 140–41.

65. Ibid., 142.

66. Ibid., 185.

67. Ibid., 274.

68. Ibid., 283. This remark appears in the context of an account of Austin's meeting with William James, whom she regarded as a kindred spirit.

69. T. S. Eliot, *Selected Prose of T. S. Eliot,* ed. Frank Kermode (New York: Harcourt Brace Jovanovich, 1975), 273.

70. Austin, *Earth,* 266.

71. Ibid., 274.

72. Ibid., 361.

73. Ibid., 368.

Chapter 3   The Greate Divide: The Professions Against Civil Society

1. Samuel Haber, *The Quest for Authority and Honor in the American Professions, 1750–1900* (Chicago: University of Chicago Press, 1991), x–xiv. Haber argues that the modern idea of the professions as "impartial arbiters" of the common good has roots in the colonial period. As he adds, "That outcome, however, was not apparent until well into the nineteenth century" (8–9).

2. Ibid., 360–61.

3. For recent work on the rise of medicine, see Lester S. King, M.D., *Transformations in American Medicine: From Benjamin Rush to William Osler* (Baltimore: Johns Hopkins University Press, 1991); John Harley Warner, *Against the Spirit of System: the French Impulse in Nineteenth-Century American Medicine* (Princeton: Princeton University Press, 1998); Rosemary Stevens, *American Medicine and the Public Interest,* updated ed. (Berkeley: University of California Press, 1998); and Kenneth M. Ludmerer, *Time to Heal: American Medical Education from the Turn of the Century to the Era of Managed Care* (New York: Oxford University Press, 1999). For the history of law, see Wayne K. Hobson, *The American Legal Profession and the Organizational Society, 1890–1930* (Ph.D. diss., Stanford University, 1977); Gerard W. Gawalt, ed., *The New High Priests: Lawyers in Post–Civil War America* (Westport, Conn.: Greenwood Press, 1984); James C. Foster, *The Ideology of Apolitical Politics: Elite Lawyers' Response to the Legitimation Crisis in American Capitalism, 1870–1920* (New York: Garland, 1990).

4. Haber, *Quest,* 58.

5. Ibid., 350.

6. Ibid., 142–43, 327.

7. Ibid., 327.

8. Ibid., 323.

9. Sir James Paget, "The Cultivation of Medical Science," *Popular Science Monthly* 19 (1881): 774–784. The passage comes from 774. I am indebted to Haber for a reference to this source. See Haber, 457, n. 71.

10. Ibid., 776–77.

11. Ibid., 783–84.

12. C. C. Langdell, "Teaching Law as a Science," *American Law Review* 21 (1887): 123. See also Haber, *Quest,* 217–18, 426, n.10.

13. Ibid., 124, my emphasis.

14. Alexander Bain, "The University Ideal," *Popular Science Monthly* 22 (February 1883): 459. Compare Bain's claims about specialization in Greece to the observations of Pierre Vernant, "Social History and the Evolution of Ideas in China and Greece from the Sixth to the Second Centuries B.C.," *Myth and Society in Ancient Greece* (New York: Zone Books, 1990), 79–100.

15. Ibid., 469.

16. Nicholas Murray Butler, *The Meaning of Education: Contributions to a Philosophy of Education,* rev. ed. (New York: Scribner's, 1915), 264.

17. Ibid., 265.

18. Ibid., 101.

19. Ibid., 108–09.

20. Herbert Spencer, "Social Forces in American Life," *Popular Science Monthly* 22 (February 1883): 492.

21. Ibid., 493.

22. Edward Alsworth Ross, *Social Control and the Foundations of Sociology,* ed. Edgar F. Borgatta and Henry J. Meyer (Boston: Beacon Press, 1959), 5.

23. Howard Zinn, *A People's History of the United States* (New York: Harper-Perennial, 1990), 248.

24. Elizabeth Gurley Flynn, *The Rebel Girl: An Autobiography of My First Life (1906–1926)* (New York: International, 1973), 36.

25. Zinn, *People's History,* 263–64.

26. Ross, *Social Control,* 22.

27. Ibid., 4, 66.

28. Ibid., 8.

29. Ibid., 114.

30. Eugene Wera, *Human Engineering: A Study of the Management of Human Forces in Industry* (New York: D. Appleton and Company, 1921), vii.

31. Ibid., viii.

32. Ibid., 117.

33. Ibid., 349.

34. Ibid., 361.

35. Ross, *Social Control,* 62.

36. Wera, *Human Engineering,* 308.

37. Butler, *Meaning,* 6.

38. Walter Robinson Smith, *Principles of Educational Sociology* (Boston: Houghton Mifflin, 1928). For echoes of Ross, see the discussion of "social control as an educational objective," 32–39. Two works by Ross get listed following this discussion under the heading "Selected Readings" (40). Ross appears at the end of other chapters under "Readings."

39. Ibid., 132.

40. Ibid., 88.

41. Ibid., 25.

42. Ibid., 20.

43. Ibid., 21.

44. Ibid., 351, 363–65, 368–69.

45. See *Biennial Survey of Education, 1930–32* (Washington: Government Printing Office, 1935), esp. 6–7, and *Biennial Survey of Education in the United States, 1944–46* (Washington: Government Printing Office, 1950), esp. 14. See also Gerald W. Bracey, "What Happened to America's Public Schools," *American Heritage* 48, no. 7 (November 1997): 38–52.

46. See for example the sections "Child Labor Legislation" and "Hour Laws for Men," in John R. Commons et al., *History of Labor in the United States, 1896–1932,* vol. 3 (New York: Augustus M. Kelley, 1935, 1966). See also Richard Schneirov, *Labor and Urban Politics: Class Conflict and the Origins of Modern Liberalism in Chicago, 1864–97* (Urbana: University of Illinois Press, 1998).

47. Donald K. Pickens, *Eugenics and the Progressives* (Nashville: Vanderbilt University Press, 1968), 46. For a broader overview of the left's involvement in eugenics, see Matt Ridley, *Genome: The Autobiography of a Species in 23 Chapters* (New York: Perennial, 2000), 286–300.

48. Pickens, *Eugenics,* 53.

49. Smith, *Principles,* 325.

50. Nicole Hahn Rafter, ed., *White Trash: The Eugenic Family Studies, 1877–1919* (Boston: Northeastern University Press, 1988), 1–30.

51. Ralph Chaplin, *Wobbly: The Rough-and-Tumble Story of an American Radical* (Chicago: University of Chicago Press, 1948), 41.

52. Flynn, *Rebel Girl,* 36–37.

53. Ibid., 38.

54. Philip S. Foner and Sally M. Miller, *Kate Richards O'Hare: Selected Writings and Speeches* (Baton Rouge: Louisiana State University Press, 1982), 35–36.

55. Flynn, *Rebel Girl,* 41.

56. Jean Y. Tussey, ed., *Eugene V. Debs Speaks* (New York: Pathfinder Press, 1970), 258.

57. See for instance Marx's *Critique of the Gotha Program,* where he tends to dismiss as halfway measures certain democratic legislative reforms of the day.

58. As Debs wrote in 1916, "The mission of the Socialist Party is to destroy industrial despotism and establish industrial democracy; to abolish class rule and

inaugurate true freedom and self-government" (Tussey, *Debs Speaks,* 236). During his trial for a violation of the Espionage Act, Debs explicitly invoked Washington, Jefferson, Franklin, and Paine, "the rebels of their day," as well as the abolitionists William Lloyd Garrison and Wendell Phillips, and the feminists Elizabeth Cady Stanton and Susan B. Anthony (283–84). See also Nick Salvatore, *Eugene V. Debs: Citizen and Socialist* (Urbana: University of Illinois Press, 1984), 270–72, 308–45.

59. Chaplin, *Wobbly,* 344. Chaplin himself retreated from radicalism on the Russian model, as did O'Hare, Flynn, Goldman and many other leaders of the left. See "Introduction," in Foner and Miller, *Kate Richards O'Hare,* 1–31.

60. Alix Kates Shulman, ed. *Red Emma Speaks: An Emma Goldman Reader,* 3rd ed. (Amherst, N.Y.: Humanity Books, 1998), 111. The dating of the essay from which this passages comes, "The Individual, Society and the State," is uncertain, but it seems similar to others published prior to 1910.

61. Ibid., 73; Emma Goldman, *Anarchism and Other Essays* (New York: Dover, 1969), 36.

62. Goldman, *Anarchism,* 35.

63. Ibid., 37.

64. Tussey, *Debs Speaks,* 196.

65. See Goldman's "Afterword to My Disillusionment in Russia," in Shulman, *Red Emma,* 383–420.

66. For a discussion of some of the parallels between Western and Russian modernism, see Susan Buck-Morss, "The City as Dreamworld and Catastrophe," *October* 73 (Summer 1995): 3–26.

67. John Dewey, *The Middle Works, 1899–1924,* vol. 11, *1918–1919,* ed. Jo Ann Boydston (Carbondale: Southern Illinois University Press), 52.

68. Ibid., 51–52.

69. Ibid., 44–45.

70. Ibid., 43.

71. Ibid., 52.

72. Ibid., 56.

73. Ibid., 56–57.

74. Goldman, *Anarchism,* 213–14.

75. Edward Alsworth Ross, *Seventy Years of It: An Autobiography* (New York: D. Appleton-Century Company, 1936), 26.

76. Ibid., 2.

77. Ibid., 7.

78. Ibid., 13.

79. Ibid., 21.

80. Ibid., 31.

81. Ibid., 32–34.

82. Ibid., 44.

83. Ibid., 69.

84. Ibid., 70.

85. Ibid., *Social Control,* 46.

86. Ibid., *Seventy Years of It*, 95.
87. Quoted in C. Wright Mills, *The Sociological Imagination* (New York: Oxford University Press, 1959), 27–28.
88. Ibid., 34.
89. Ibid., 105–06.
90. Ibid., 106.

Chapter 4   The Trouble with English: The Rise of the Professional Humanities and Their Abandonment of Civil Society

1. Edward Alsworth Ross, *Seventy Years of It* (New York: D. Appleton-Century, 1936), 27–28.
2. M. D. Learned, "The President's Address," *Publications of the Modern Language Association of America* (Baltimore: PMLA, 1910), xlvi–xlvii.
3. Ibid., xlviii.
4. Henry Seidel Canby, *College Sons and College Fathers* (New York: Harper and Brothers, 1915), 175. Of course, as one of the founders of the Book-of-the-Month Club, Canby is often reviled by academic literary critics. Nevertheless, his judgment seems to be confirmed by the explosion of mass market publishing in the twentieth century.
5. Ibid., 175–76.
6. Ibid., 159–161.
7. Ibid., 210.
8. Charles Hall Grandgent, "The President's Address," *Publications of the Modern Language Association of America* (Baltimore: PMLA, 1913), xlv.
9. See, for example, Pierre Riché, *Daily Life in the World of Charlemagne,* trans. Jo Ann McNamera (Philadelphia: University of Pennsylvania Press, 1978), especially Chapter 10, "The Lay Aristocracy: A Life of Sport and War," 74–83. While Riché certainly acknowledges the existence of a "Carolingian Renaissance," he also understands that the Franks were fundamentally a "warrior culture."
10. Grandgent, "President's Address," xlviii–xlix.
11. Ibid., li.
12. Ibid., lii.
13. Ibid., lviii.
14. Ibid., lix.
15. For an account of the literary societies, see Frederick Rudolph, *The American College and University: A History* (Athens: University of Georgia Press, 1990), 136–55. See also Roger L. Geiger and Julie Ann Bubolz, "College as It Was in the Mid-Nineteenth Century," in *The American College in the Nineteenth Century* ed. Roger L. Geiger (Nashville, Tenn.: Vanderbilt University Press, 2000): 80–90. For a discussion of the women's reading clubs and their displacement by largely male academic professionals, see Ann Gere, *Intimate Practices: Literacy and Cultural Work in U.S. Women's Clubs, 1880–1920* (Urbana: University of Illinois Press, 1997).

16. See, for instance, Algernon Tassin, *The Oral Study of Literature,* 5th ed. (New York: F. S. Crofts, 1939).

In *College Sons and College Fathers* Canby tries to explain the enterprise of English to a hypothetical public audience in this way: "I should probably begin by asserting that the purpose of teaching English is to give light for the mind and solace for the heart" (213). But how to do it? In a more pedestrian spirit, he divides his colleagues into two camps, the "inspirationists," who aim to "make them think," and the German-inspired quasi-scientists (226–27). Canby refers to an institution known as "recitation rooms" and then opines, "it is depressing to sit in a recitation-room, estimating, while one [student] recites and your voice is resting, the volume and the flow of the streams of literary instruction washing over the undergraduates" (221). Depressing indeed!

Bliss Perry was the first Professor of English, as opposed to a Professor of Belles Lettres, appointed at Harvard. In his memoir, he describes the nearly complete incoherence of the department in 1907. "Here," he wrote of his colleagues, was a "brilliant array of primadonnas. . . . But it was difficult for a stranger to discover any common denominator of their activities." See *And Gladly Teach: Reminiscences* (Boston: Houghton Mifflin, 1935), 243.

17. Berenson was, famously, the great embodiment of nineteenth century connoisseurship—and the enemy of modernism. He represents one tendency of art history as a discipline. Another tendency is represented by the great theorizers like Heinrich Wölfflin. The later Berenson, however, could sound very much like a high modernist—very much, in fact, like T. S. Eliot. In *Seeing and Knowing,* for example, Berenson writes, "A tradition, a convention, needs constant manipulation to vivify it, to enlarge it, to keep it fresh and supple, and capable of generating problems and producing their solutions. To keep a convention alive and growing fruitfully requires a creative genius." *Seeing and Knowing* (Greenwich, Conn.: New York Graphic Society, 1953), 35. For a study of Berenson that does justice to his real complexity, see Mary Ann Calo, *Bernard Berenson and the Twentieth Century* (Philadelphia: Temple University Press, 1994).

18. Thorstein Veblen, *The Theory of the Leisure Class: An Economic Study of Institutions* (New York: Huebsch, 1918), especially "The Higher Learning as an Expression of the Pecuniary Culture," 363–400. While Veblen recognizes the impact of the new mass culture on academic institutions, he does not regard the older humanities as a critical counterweight. Rather, he sees them as emblematic of the uselessness and archaism that are the hallmark of leisure-class culture. The point of the humanities is to provide each student with the knowledge that will mark him as a "true-bred gentleman of leisure" (385).

19. Grandgent, "President's Address," lxiii.

20. Hippolyte Taine, *History of English Literature,* vol 1, trans. H. Van Laun (New York: Frederick Ungar Publishing Company, 1965), 12,17.

21. Ibid., 17–18.

22. Of course, Turner was not what we would now call a multiculturalist. See John Mack Faragher's balanced and sensitive overview of Turner's work in *Rereading Frederick Jackson Turner: "The Significance of the Frontier in American History"*

and other Essays (New York: Henry Holt, 1994). As Faragher notes, Turner believed the frontier had made democracy possible by expanding to an unprecedented degree life opportunities for ordinary people. With the closing of the frontier, Turner believed that new forms of opportunity were required—especially through access to higher education—if American democracy were to survive (8–9).

23. Taine, *History,* 17.

24. Nevertheless, Taine saw literature as providing a unique entree into "the psychology of a people." For him, literature was more revealing than "constitutions, religions" or "a heap of historians with their histories" (34–35).

25. Irving Babbitt, *Literature and the American College: Essays in Defense of the Humanities* (Boston: Houghton, Mifflin, 1908), 108. Babbitt makes explicit reference to English departments in one essay, "The Doctor's Degree," a critique of over-specialization. "At one extreme of the average English department," he writes, "is the philological mediaevalist, who is grounded in Gothic and Old Norse and Anglo-Saxon; at the other extreme is the dilettante [the writing teacher] who gives courses in 'daily themes' and, like the sophists of old, instructs ingenuous youth in the art of expressing itself before it has anything to express" (130).

26. Ibid., 162–63.

27. See ibid., 152–158.

28. Ibid., 23.

29. Ibid., 244.

30. Ibid., 97.

31. Ibid., 8.

32. Ibid., 9–10.

33. Ibid., 10.

34. See Peter Brown, *The Body and Society: Men, Women and Sexual Renunciation in Early Christianity* (New York: Columbia University Press, 1988), 5–32.

35. Babbitt, 80.

36. For many conservatives, Dewey has become a straw man. See Allan Bloom, *The Closing of the American Mind* (New York: Simon and Schuster, 1987). Bloom describes Dewey, along with John Stewart Mill, as exemplars of "liberalism without natural rights": "No attention had to be paid," in their schema, "to the fundamental principles or the moral virtues that inclined men to live according to" those principles (29). Like Babbitt, Bloom was an admirer of the Greek and Roman classics, and while many classicists—probably most—would repudiate Bloom's position, Babbitt might have written exactly these same words.

37. J. E. Spingarn, "The New Criticism," *Criticism in America: Its Function and Status* (New York: Harcourt, Brace, 1924), 13.

38. Ibid., 25.

39. Ibid., 27–29.

40. Ibid., 31–32.

41. Ibid., 38–41.

42. Spingarn borrowed the term from Goethe, as he acknowledged (23).

43. Ibid.,128.

44. Ibid., *Creative Criticism and Other Essays* (Westport, Conn.: Hyperion Press, 1979), 128, 145–46. These opinions were evidently quite resonant with some readers. They loom large in the Introduction to William A. Drake's *American Criticism, 1926* (New York: Harcourt, Brace, 1926), x–xiv.

45. Irving Babbitt, "Genius and Taste," in *Criticism in America*, 156.

46. Ibid., 164–65. Babbitt gets particularly exercised by Spingarn's "facile assurance, so agreeable to democratic ears, that 'we are all geniuses'" (170).

47. Babbitt seems to have disliked Wilde, as his remarks in "Genius and Taste" make clear. He alleges that Wilde and Spingarn are allied in celebrating "the emancipation of the imagination from any allegiance to standards, from any central control" (158–59).

48. Spingarn went on to become a founder of Harcourt, Brace and Company. A prominent figure within the NAACP, he established in 1913 the annually awarded Spingarn Medal, for outstanding achievement by an African American.

49. In the late twenties, the left-leaning cultural historian Vernon Louis Parrington wrote approvingly of Brooks as one of a group of "young critics of established ways," and especially of middle-class morality and the nascent consumer culture. *The Beginnings of Critical Realism in America, 1860–1920* (New York: Harcourt, Brace, 1930), 376. Only three years later, the Marxist critic Granville Hicks had already grown disenchanted with Brooks's failure to formulate "some sort of social program, on the theory that a new social order would bring into existence a new set of values." *The Great Tradition: An Interpretation of American Literature Since the Civil War* (New York: Macmillan, 1933), 252. By the spring of 1945, writing in *The Virginia Quarterly Review*, the conservative critic Allen Tate dismissed Brooks as a "literary nationalist" whose "influence is no longer very much felt by anybody who seriously writes." *Essays of Four Decades* (Chicago: The Swallow Press, 1968), 535–36. Of course, for Tate, as for Hicks, the real problem lay in Brooks's approving attitude toward popular culture, or rather, toward cultural democracy. Here, as in so many other places, left and right converge.

Perhaps the most balanced and thoughtful treatments of Brooks's life and work are James Hoopes' *Van Wyck Brooks: In Search of American Culture* (Amherst: University of Massachusetts Press, 1977), and Raymond Nelson's *Van Wyck Brooks, A Writer's Life* (New York: E. P. Dutton, 1981).

50. In an influential essay originally published in 1915 in *The Forum*, Brooks described that the tension fundamental to American culture, and he traces it back to the dichotomy between Jonathan Edwards and Benjamin Franklin, whom he represents as what we now call, after Weber, "ideal types." See "Highbrow and Lowbrow," in *Contemporary American Criticism*, ed. James Cloyd Bowman (New York: Henry Holt, 1926): 161–74. See also Lawrence W. Levine, *Highbrow/Lowbrow: The Emergence of Cultural Hierarchy in America* (Cambridge, Mass.: Harvard University Press, 1988). Levine does not mention Brooks, but he quotes from Brooks's close friend, ally, and fellow New Jerseyan, Randolph Bourne (145).

51. Van Wyck Brooks, "The Critics and Young America," in *Criticism in America: Its Function and Status* (New York: Harcourt, Brace, and Co., 1924): 116–

51. As Brooks argues there, "Puritanism was a complete philosophy for the pioneer and by making human nature contemptible and putting to shame the charms of life it unleashed the acquisitive instincts of men" (121).

52. This was, of course, Weber's insight in *The Protestant Ethic and the Spirit of Capitalism,* especially the final chapter , "Asceticism and the Spirit of Capitalism." Although Brooks does not cite Weber in "The Critics," his language follows Weber's very closely at times.

53. See John Demos, *A Little Commonwealth: Family Life in Plymouth Colony,* 2nd. ed. (New York: Oxford University Press, 2000).

54. Brooks, "The Critic," 119.

55. Ibid., 146.

56. Ibid., 144.

57. Ibid., 135.

58. Ibid., 128.

59. Ibid., 148–49.

60. See for instance Van Wyck Brooks, *An Autobiography* (New York: E. P. Dutton, 1965), 479–80, 484–85. On the other hand, in *The Writer in America* (New York: Avon Books, 1964), Brooks had some rather harsh things to say about many prominent literary figures such as Scott Fitzgerald and William Faulkner. Throughout that book Brooks took exception to the pessimism and hopelessness of much modernist fiction, and he issued a call to "rehumanize literature." The first step toward this end, he wrote, "is to think better of man" (178).

61. René Wellek notes that Brooks's five-volume history of American literature, *Makers and Finders,* won a Pulitzer and nearly achieved best-seller status, and he reminds his readers also that Carl Van Doren called that work "not only the best history of American literature, but . . . one of he best literary histories in any language." Nevertheless, Wellek judges Brooks's achievement "a dismal failure." There is, he writes, "scarcely any analysis of actual books, nothing about a continuity of literary themes or forms." *A History of Modern Criticism: 1750–1950,* vol. 6, *American Criticism, 1900–1950* (New Haven, Conn.: Yale University Press, 1986), 14.

62. See José Ortega y Gasset, *The Revolt of the Masses,* trans. Anthony Kerrigan (Notre Dame, Ind.: University of Notre Dame Press, 1985). Saul Bellow, who wrote the foreword for this edition, performed the same service for Allan Bloom in *The Closing of the American Mind.*

63. T. S. Eliot, *Selected Prose of T. S. Eliot,* ed. Frank Kermode (New York: Harcourt Brace Jovanovich, 1975), 39.

64. Ibid., 40.

65. Ibid., 38.

66. Ibid., 38.

67. Ibid., 38.

68. Ibid., 40.

69. Ibid., 41–42.

70. Ibid., 37.

71. See the selections from "The Idea of a Christian Society" in ibid., 285–91.

72. See Adrienne M. Golub, "Towards a Newer Critique: The Missing Link: The Influence of T. S. Eliot's Ultra-Conservative Criticism on Clement Greenberg's Early Rhetoric and Themes," *Art Criticism* 12:1 (1997): 5–37.

73. Quoted approvingly in G. J. Warnock, *J. L. Austin* (London: Routledge, 1989), 5. I suggest that Austin's work might profitably be viewed as one important part of the same modernist regime to which Eliot also contributed. In Austin's thinking, "ordinary language" plays much the same role as "tradition" in Eliot's, and the philosopher plays much the same role as the critic. This is why, I suspect, that Austin has enjoyed such an enduring reputation in departments of English, much more enduring, probably, than in philosophy departments. Austin's is a fundamentally conservative theory of language, even if it privileges the "ordinary" over the literary, a move that Eliot would never countenance. It says, first, that we need to respect longstanding conventions because they are longstanding. Second, it holds out to the philosopher a unique role as the arbiter of language. The philosopher is the one who has the last word, so to speak, about how to do things with words.

Chapter 5　The Poverty of Progress: James Agee, Lionel Trilling, and the Alienation of Knowledge

1. Laurence Bergreen, *James Agee: A Life* (New York: E. P. Dutton, 1984), 158–82.

2. Ibid., 240–41.

3. James Agee, *Let Us Now Praise Famous Men* (Boston: Houghton Mifflin, 1941, 1986), 322–33.

4. Ultimately, they would be liberated, not by political revolution or social change, but by technological innovations that made the hand-picking of cotton unprofitable. For a discussion of this transformation and its effect on the families that Agee described, see Dale Maharidge and Michael Williamson, *And Their Children Came After Them: The Legacy of Let Us Now Praise Famous Men* (New York: Pantheon, 1989), xvi–xvii, 3–32.

5. Agee, *Let Us Now*, 324.

6. Sigmund Freud, *An Outline of Psycho-Analysis*, trans. James Strachey (New York: W.W. Norton, 1989), 83.

7. Agee, *Let Us Now*, 14.

8. Ibid., 425.

9. Ibid., 426.

10. Ibid., 427–28.

11. Ibid., 183.

12. Ibid., xxxiii.

13. Lionel Trilling, "Greatness with One Fault in It," *Kenyon Review* 4 (Winter 1942): 102.

14. Although a close second to Trilling's review would have to be Paul Ashdown's amazingly unperceptive "Introduction" to *James Agee: Selected Journal-*

ism (Knoxville: University of Tennessee Press, 1985) where he writes, "Like George Orwell," Agee "tried to make himself over as a proletarian. But this was also a form of intrusive deception" (xxx). Once Agee "got the tenant farmers out of his system, his writing became more controlled and more forceful" (xxxv).

15. Agee, *Let Us Now,* 42.

16. Ibid., 15.

17. In an review of Vittorio de Sica's film *Shoeshine,* Agee deplores the disappearance among intellectuals of what he calls the "humanistic attitude." "Even among those who preserve a living devotion to it, moreover, few seem to have come by it naturally, as a physical and sensuous fact, as well as a philosophical one; many fewer give any evidence of applying it with any of the enormous primordial energy which, one would suppose, the living fact would inevitably liberate in a living being." *Agee on Film,* vol. 1 (New York: Perigree Press, 1983), 278.

18. Although Trilling began his career writing for the *Menorah Journal,* he wanted, in the words of Mark Krupnick, to be both a Jew and "an English-style gentleman." *Lionel Trilling and the Fate of Cultural Criticism* (Evanston: Northwestern University Press, 1986), 28. A few years later, Trilling became even more decisively committed to "a cosmopolitan ideal of culture." As Krupnick observes, any willingness to be "provincial and parochial" seemed "to Trilling in the [1940s] nothing less than a sin against the self" (32).

19. Lionel Trilling, *The Liberal Imagination: Essays on Literature and Society* (New York: Viking Press, 1950), ix.

20. Ibid., xv.

21. Ibid., 212.

22. Ibid., 181, 255.

23. Agee, *Let Us Now,* 80–81.

24. Ibid., 88.

25. See Maharidge and Williamson, *And Their Children Came,* 30.

26. Agee, *Let Us Now,* 301. As things turned out, Maggie Louise was not to realize her dream. See Maharidge and Williamson, 78–86. As they note, "Maggie Louise . . . became a failure, at least according to the expectations Agee's work created for her. . . . But if Agee had returned to Alabama in 1946, or later, he might have envied her. She was in a love-filled marriage, raising her children and, unlike Agee, doing right by them" (86).

27. Ibid., 303.

28. Ibid., 298.

29. Ibid., lii.

30. Ibid., 311.

31. Ibid., 227, my emphasis.

32. Ibid., 11.

33. For a recent analysis that confirms much of Agee's understanding of modernity and consumerism, see Juliet B. Schor, *The Overworked American: The Unexpected Decline of Leisure* (New York: Basic Books, 1991), esp. "The Insidious Cycle of Work-and-Spend," 107–138.

34. Agee, *Let Us Now,* 11.

35. Ludwig Wittgenstein, *Culture and Value,* ed. G. H. Von Wright and Heikki Nyman, trans. Peter Winch (Chicago: University of Chicago Press, Eng.: 1980), 4e.

36. Ibid., 7e.

37. Agee, *Let Us Now,* 12.

38. Ibid., 16.

39. Ibid., 155.

40. Trilling, *Liberal Imagination,* 131–32.

41. Ibid., 144.

42. Ibid., 148.

43. Ibid., 149.

44. As Wittgenstein wrote in 1930, "What Renan calls 'the bon sens précoce' of the semitic races . . . is their *unpoetic* mentality, which heads straight for what is concrete. This is characteristic of my philosophy, "Things are placed right in front of our eyes, not covered by any veil.—This is where religion and art part company" (Wittgenstein 6e).

45. Robert Penn Warren, *Democracy and Poetry: The 1974 Jefferson Lecture in the Humanities* (Cambridge Harvard University Press, 1975), 72–73.

46. Ibid., 76; but see Agee, *Let Us Now,* 237–39.

47. Warren, *Democracy,* 73.

48. Ibid., 74.

49. Jonathan Culler, *The Pursuit of Signs: Semiotics, Literature, Deconstruction* (Ithaca: Cornell University Press, 1983), 5.

50. Ibid., 11–12.

51. Bergreen, *James Agee,* 367–74.

52. See John Evangelist Walsh, *The Shadows Rise: Abraham Lincoln and the Ann Rutledge Legend* (Urbana: University of Illinois Press, 1993).

53. Joseph Wood Krutch, *Experience and Art: Some Aspects of the Esthetics of Literature* (New York: Harrison Smith and Robert Haas, 1932), 50.

Chapter 6   The Wages of Theory: Isolation and Knowledge in the Humanities

1. See Allan Bloom, *The Closing of the American Mind* (New York: Simon and Schuster, 1987), and Roger Kimball, *The Long March: How the Cultural Revolution in the 1960s Changed America* (San Francisco: Encounter Books, 2000).

2. William H. Whyte, *The Organization Man* (New York: Simon and Schuster, 1956); William Sloan, *The Man in the Gray Flannel Suit* (New York: Simon and Schuster, 1955).

3. See "Dual America," in Manuel Castells, *End of Millennium,* rev. ed., vol. 3 of *The Information Age: Economy, Society, and Culture* (Oxford, Eng.: Blackwell, 1999), esp. 130–37.

4. Herbert Marcuse, *Eros and Civilization: A Philosophical Inquiry into Freud* (Boston: Beacon Press, 1955, 1966). As Marcuse explained his project in the Preface to the 1966 edition, " 'Polymorphous sexuality' was the term which I used to indicate

that the new direction of progress would depend completely on the opportunity to activate repressed or arrested organic, biological needs: to make the human body an instrument of pleasure rather than [of] labor" (xv). Marcuse believed that the promise of polymorphous sexuality would be strong enough to overthrow the power of "dead affluence," the tyranny of "clean clothes" and "gadgets" (xxi). What are the chances?

5. Richard Reeves, *President Kennedy: Profile of Power* (New York: Touchstone, 1993), 35–36, 350.

6. Ibid., 476.

7. See Robert Penn Warren, *Who Speaks for the Negro?* (New York: Random House, 1965). Needless to say, much of the book is ripe for deconstruction today, but it represents, all the same, a determined effort to come to terms with social change, an effort I applaud whatever its limitations.

8. Reeves, *President Knowledge*, 497, 479, 474.

9. Marvin E. Gittleman et al., *Vietnam and America: A Documented History*, rev. ed. (New York: Grove Press, 1995), 348.

10. Arthur Marwick, *The Sixties: Cultural Revolution in Britain, France, Italy, and the United States, c.1958–c.1974* (Oxford, Eng.: Oxford University Press, 1999), 544.

11. Les Editions de Minuit released *De la grammatologie* in 1967. Johns Hopkins University Press followed in 1974 with the famous English translation by Gayatri Spivak.

12. Gilles Deleuze and Félix Guattari, *A Thousand Plateaus: Capitalism and Schizophrenia*, trans. Brian Massumi (Minneapolis: University of Minnesota Press, 1987); Jürgen Habermas, *The Theory of Communicative Action, vol. 1, Reason and the Rationalization of Society* trans. Thomas McCarthy (Boston: Beacon Press, 1984).

13. See Homi K. Bhabha, "Postcolonial Criticism," in *Redrawing the Boundaries: The Transformation of English and American Literary Studies,* ed. Stephen Greenblatt and Giles Gunn (New York: MLA, 1992): 437–65; also, Judith Butler, *Gender Trouble: Feminism and the Subversion of Identity* (New York: Routledge, 1990).

14. Carl Bereiter et al., "An Academically Oriented Pre-school for Culturally Deprived Children," in *Pre-School Education Today,* ed. Fred. M. Hechinger (Garden City, N.Y.: Doubleday, 1966): 107.

15. Ibid., 105, 113.

16. Ibid., 113.

17. Hans-Georg Gadamer, *Truth and Method,* 2nd ed., trans. Joel Weinsheimer and Donald G. Marshall (New York: Crossroad, 1990), 378, 549.

18. Ibid., 306–07.

19. Ibid., 448.

20. Max Horkheimer, "Tradition and Critical Theory," in *Critical Theory: Selected Essays,* trans. Matthew J. O'Connell et al. (New York: Continuum, 1982), 188–243.

21. Robert Scholes, *Textual Power: Literary Theory and the Teaching of English* (New Haven: Yale University Press), 19.

22. Gayatri Chakravorty Spivak, "A Literary Representation of the Subaltern: A Woman's Text from the Third World," in *In Other Worlds: Essays in Cultural Politics* (New York: Routledge, 1988), 244.

23. Ibid., 259.

24. For a discussion of the social isolation of academic intellectuals, see Charles Derber et al., *Power in the Highest Degree: Professionals and the Rise of a New Mandarin Order* (New York: Oxford University Press, 1990), esp. 79–108.

25. Gary T. Marx, "Reflections on Academic Success and Failure: Making It, Forsaking it, Reshaping It," in *Authors of their Own Lives: Intellectual Autobiographies by Twenty American Sociologists,* ed. Bennett M. Berger (Berkeley: University of California Press, 1990), 261.

26. Pierre Bourdieu, *Distinction: A Social Critique of the Judgement of Taste,* trans. Richard Nice (Cambridge, Mass.: Harvard University Press, 1984), 22–28.

27. Samuel Haber, *The Quest for Authority and Honor in the American Professions, 1750–1900* (Chicago: University of Chicago Press, 1991), xi–xiii.

28. Bernice Martin, "Symbolic Knowledge and Market Forces at the Frontiers of Postmodernism: Qualitative Market Researchers," in *Hidden Technocrats: The New Class and the New Capitalism,* ed. Hansfried Kellner and Frank W. Heuberger (New Brunswick, N.J.: Transaction, 1992), 126.

29. Sykes, Charles J., *Profscam: Professors and the Demise of Higher Education* (New York: St. Martin's, 1988), 37. I am certain that the problems he describes have gotten worse since then. In my own department, fully a quarter of tenured faculty are released from their teaching duties every term, sometimes to compensate for administration and sometimes to assist in research.

30. Jonathan Culler, "Criticism and Institutions: the American University," in *Poststructuralism and the Question of History,* ed. Derek Attridge et al. (Cambridge, Eng.: Cambridge University Press, 1989), 94.

31. Marshall Gregory, "From Ph.D. Program to B.A. College; or, The Sometimes Hard Journey from Life in the Carrel to Life in the World," *ADE Bulletin* 107 (Spring 1994): 20.

32. Edward W. Said, *Culture and Imperialism* (New York: Vintage, 1994), 319–21, 333–36.

33. John Dewey, "Political Science as a Recluse," *The Middle Works, 1899–1924,* vol. 11:1918–1919, ed. Jo Ann Boydston. (Carbondale: Southern Illinois University Press, 1982), 93–97.

34. As Anthony Giddens observes in *The Transformation of Intimacy: Sexuality, Love and Eroticism in Modern Societies* (Stanford: Stanford University Press, 1992), 184–204.

35. See Bernie S. Siegel, M.D., *Love, Medicine, and Miracles: Lessons Learned about Self-healing from a Surgeon's Experience with Exceptional Patients* (New York: Harper & Row, 1990).

36. T. S. Eliot "Burnt Norton," *Four Quartets,* in *The Complete Poems and Plays, 1909–1950* (San Diego: Harcourt, Brace, Jovanovich, 1980), 119.

37. See Bernard Campbell, "Ecological Factors and Social Organization in Human Evolution," in *Primate Ecology and Human Origins: Ecological Influences on*

Social Organization, ed. Irwin S. Bernstein and Euclid O. Smith (New York: Garland STPM, 1979): 291–312; Maxine Sheets-Johnstone, "On the Origin of Language," *The Roots of Thinking* (Philadelphia: Temple University Press, 1990), 134–66; and Rick Potts, *Humanity's Descent: The Consequences of Ecological Instability* (New York: Avon Books, 1996).

38. For my understanding of attunement I am indebted to Shigenori Nagatomo, *Attunement Through the Body* (Albany: State University of New York Press, 1992). Although Nagatomo is concerned largely with the experience of attunement in Soto Zen meditation practice, I believe that his insight can be applied to other, more mundane experience as well.

39. Primo Levi, "Beyond Judgment," *New York Review of Books* 17 (December 1987): 10, 12–14.

40. D. W. Winnecott, *The Child, the Family, and the Outside World* (Reading, Mass.: Addison-Wesley, 1987), 167–72.

41. The term "life-world" derives from Edmund Husserl. See *The Crisis of European Sciences and Transcendental Phenomenology: An Introduction to Phenomenological Philosophy,* trans. David Carr (Evanston: Northwestern University Press, 1970), esp. 103–35. There Husserl notes that the life-world "functions as [the] subsoil" of our conscious, purposive awareness (124). "The life-world is the realm of original self-evidences" (127). To put it simply, the process of thinking about the world or acting on the world already presupposes the existence of a coherent "world."

I am also indebted to Jürgen Habermas, in spite of my reservations about the usefulness of his sweeping insights for an understanding of democratic political processes or of democratic culture in general. Nevertheless, his subtle discussion of life-world colonization by bureaucratic structures has been invaluable. See *The Theory of Communicative Action,* vol 2, *Lifeworld and System: A Critique of Functionalist Reason,* trans. Thomas McCarthy (Boston: Beacon Press, 1987), esp. 303–31.

42. Robert F. Murphy, *The Body Silent* (New York: W.W. Norton, 1990), 193–94.

43. For a general overview of human cognitive development that challenges the primacy of language, see Paul Bloom, *How Children Learn the Meanings of Words* (Cambridge, Mass.: MIT Press, 2000), esp. 55–87. For a discussion of music and the brain see Mark Jude Tramo, "Music of the Hemispheres," *Science* 291 (January 5, 2001): 54–56; William J. Crombie, "Music on the Brain: Researchers Explore the Biology of Music," *Harvard University Gazette* March 22, 2001 *http://www.news. harvard.edu/gazette/2001/03.22/04-music.html;* and Kristin Leutwyler, "Exploring the Musical Brain," *Scientific American: Explore!* January 22, 2001 *http://www.sciam.com/ explorations/2001/012201music/* For a related analysis of visual experience, see Donald D. Hoffman, *Visual Intelligence: How We Create What We See* (New York: Norton, 1998).

44. Robert Goldwater and Marco Treves, eds., *Artists on Art: from the XIV to the XX Century* (New York: Pantheon, 1945), 421.

45. Susan Bordo, *Unbearable Weight: Feminism, Western Culture, and the Body* (Berkeley: University of California Press, 1993), 45–69.

46. Keith H. Basso, "'Stalking with Stories': Names, Places, and Moral Narratives among the Western Apache," in *On Nature, Landscape, and Natural History,* ed. Daniel Halpern (San Francisco: North Point, 1986), 102.

47. Murphy, *Body,* 106.

48. See for example Peter F. Drucker, "The Age of Social Transformation," in *Atlantic Monthly,* November 1994, 93–97; and Etienne Balibar, "Politics and Truth: The Vacillation of Ideology, II," *Masses, Classes, Ideas: Studies on Politics and Philosophy Before and After Marx,* trans. James Swenson (New York: Routledge, 1994), 151–74.

49. See James C. Scott, *Weapons of the Weak: Everyday Forms of Peasant Resistance* (New Haven, Conn.: Yale University Press, 1985). Of course we aren't peasants, but we still often find ourselves in positions of stark disadvantage.

50. Quoted in Ernst Fischer, *The Necessity of Art: A Marxist Approach,* trans. Anna Bostock (London: Penguin, 1978), 74. Picasso says much the same thing: "Mathematics, trigonometry, chemistry, psychoanalysis, music, and what not have all been related to cubism to give it an easier interpretation. All this has been pure literature, not to say nonsense, which brought bad results, blinding people with theories. Cubism has kept itself within the limits and limitations of painting, never pretending to go beyond it." Goldwater and Treves, *Artists on Art,* 418–19.

Chapter 7   World without End: Criticism or Creation in the Humanities?

1. See Emily Martin, "The Egg and the Sperm: How Science Has Constructed a Romance Based on Stereotypical Male-Female Roles," *Signs: Journal of Women in Society and Culture* 16 (1991): 485–501.

2. The privileging of contemplation over action goes back to classical Greece. In the *Metaphysics,* for example, Aristotle writes, "the man of experience is thought to be wiser than the possessors of any sense-perception whatever, the artist wiser than the men of experience, the master-worker [wiser] than the mechanic, and the theoretical kinds of knowledge to be more of the nature of Wisdom than the productive." *Metaphysics,* trans. W. D. Ross, *The Basic Works of Aristotle,* Book 1, ed. Richard McKeon (New York: Random House, 1941), 691. See also *Nicomachean Ethics,* 1104.

3. Jacques Derrida, *Of Grammatology,* trans. Gayatri Chakravorty Spivak (Baltimore: Johns Hopkins University Press, 1976). See especially "The End of the Book and the Beginning of Writing," 6–26, in many ways the founding statement—yes, founding—of Derrida's entire project. As he writes there, "The movements of deconstruction do not destroy structures from the outside. They are not possible and effective, nor can they take accurate aim, except by inhabiting those structures. Inhabiting them *in a certain way,* because one always inhabits, and all the more when one does not suspect it. Operating necessarily from the inside, borrowing all the strategic and economic resources of subversion from the old structure . . . the enterprise of deconstruction always in a certain way falls prey to its own work" (24).

4. Andrew Hacker, *Two Nations: Black and White, Separate, Hostile, Unequal,* expanded and updated ed. (New York: Ballantine Books, 1995).

5. As Adorno writes, in language no less powerful and no less opaque than Derrida's, negative dialectics is "the self-consciousness of the objective context of [socially produced] delusion; it does not mean to have escaped from that context. Its objective goal is to break out of that context from within." *Negative Dialectics,* trans. E. B. Ashton (New York: Continuum, 1987), 406. Notice how closely Derrida's notion of subversive thinking from inside resembles Adorno's in this passage.

6. For much of Foucault's career, "transgression" was the paramount value. See, for instance, *Language, Counter-Memory, Practice: Selected Essays and Interviews,* ed. Donald F. Bouchard, trans. Donald F. Bouchard and Sherry Simon (Ithaca, N.Y.: Cornell University Press, 1977), esp. 29–52. However, perhaps the paradigmatic Foucault is the taunting persona he adopts in *The Archaeology of Knowledge,* trans. A. M. Sheridan Smith (New York: Pantheon, 1982), "What, do you imagine that I would take so much trouble and so much pleasure in writing . . . if I were not preparing . . . a labyrinth into which . . . I can lose myself. . . . I am no doubt not the only one who writes in order to have no face. Do not ask who I am and do not ask me to remain the same; leave it to our bureaucrats and our police to see that our papers are in order. At least spare us their morality when we write'" (17). Later in his career, Foucault attempted to move beyond transgression toward an ethics without moral absolutes, inspired by classical Greek notions regarding self-mastery. See *The Use of Pleasure,* Vol. 2, of *The History of Sexuality,* trans. Robert Hurley (New York: Vintage, 1986), esp. 249–54.

7. In a series of books written over the last decade, Derrida has attempted to develop an ethics of self-sacrifice consistent with a recognition of the uniqueness of individual identity and the impossibility of a reward for the act of giving. I find it difficult to imagine, however, that these works can have any significant impact on the life of our times. How, for example, might Derrida's ethics help us to navigate the complexities of the Palestinian question in Israel, or the complexities of genetic technology? When Derrida weighs in on real-world ethical problems, he tends to choose the easy ones, as he did in denouncing the evils of apartheid in South Africa. See *Given Time: I, Counterfeit Money* (Chicago: University of Chicago Press, 1992), *On the Name* (Stanford, Calif.: Stanford University Press, 1995), and *The Gift of Death* (Chicago: University of Chicago Press, 1995).

8. Walter Kaufmann, ed., *The Portable Nietzsche* (New York: Penguin, 1976), 54–55. As Nietzsche argues, the danger faced by "communities founded on homogeneous individuals who have character is growing stupidity. " It "is the individuals who have fewer ties and are much more uncertain and morally weaker upon whom spiritual progress depends. . . . Precisely in this wounded and weakened spot the whole structure is inoculated."

9. Ernest Hemingway, "A Clean, Well-Lighted Place," *The Snows of Kilimanjaro and Other Stories* (New York: Charles Scribner's Sons, 1927), 32.

10. James Joyce, *A Portrait of the Artist as a Young Man: Text, Criticism, and Notes,* ed. Chester C. Anderson (New York: Penguin Books, 1977), 253.

11. Irving Howe, *Decline of the New* (New York: Harcourt, Brace, and World, 1970), 3–4.

12. Paulo Freire, *Pedagogy of the Oppressed*, trans. Myra Bergman Ramos (New York: Continuum, 189), 72.

13. Ibid., 73.

14. When Freire argues, in the first sentence of chapter 1, that "the problem of humanization has always . . . been man's central problem," he is not only wildly ahistorical, but also profoundly Eurocentric.

15. Frank Lentriccia, *Criticism and Social Change* (Chicago: University of Chicago Press, 1983), 11.

16. Gayatri Chakravorty Spivak, "Translator's Preface," *Of Grammatology,* lxxv.

17. Paul de Man, *Blindness and Insight: Essays in the Rhetoric of Contemporary Criticism,* 2nd., rev. ed,. (Minneapolis: University of Minnesota Press, 1983), "reproduces," 76–77; "nothingness," 18.

18. See Fredric Jameson, *The Political Unconscious: Narrative as a Socially Symbolic Act* (Ithaca, N.Y.: Cornell University Press, 1982). There Jameson argues that "our aim, as literary analysts, is . . . to demonstrate the ways in which modernism—far from being a mere reflection of the reification of late nineteenth-century social life—is also a revolt against that reification and a symbolic act which involves a whole Utopian compensation for increasing dehumanization on the level of daily life" (42). For Jameson, the unveiling of this "revolt" is a matter of "historicizing"; a matter, that is, of reconciling the text with the terms of the Marxist historical master narrative. Of course, this reconciliation may not be possible by remaining on "the surface of the text" (48); rather, the historicizing "analyst" must look for it in the *"impensé* or *nondit,"* the unconsidered or unstated—in other words, in the "political unconscious" (49). It is important to recognize, however, that Jameson describes this activity as "interpretation" rather than "criticism," a term he seems to avoid quite deliberately in *The Political Unconscious* when he describes his own program. Because Jameson claims to be embracing all positions within a larger historical totality, he would not describe the method of *The Political Unconscious* as "criticism" in a polemical sense, or so I would think. See also "Criticism in History," in *The Ideologies of Theory: Essays 1971–1986,* vol 1, *Situations of Theory* (Minneapolis: University of Minnesota Press, 1988): 119–36.

19. Michel Foucault, *The Order of Things: An Archaeology of the Human Sciences* (New York: Vintage Books/Random House, 1973), xi. As Foucault maintains in the "Preface to the English Edition," "this unconscious is always the negative side of [any] science," and therefore his "archaeology" is intended to expose "a level that eludes the consciousness of the [practitioner] and yet is part of [his or her] discourse." Fundamentally, Foucault's program is to expose the "will to power" behind the formation of ostensibly neutral and objective knowledge. He is concerned as well with institutions that purport to serve the general interest but which in fact arrogate to themselves unwarranted and tyrannical authority. But here again, as in Jameson's work, how do we know that the connections Foucault claims to tease

out are anything more than the products of a brilliant but obsessive and paranoid imagination? When Foucault posits structural homologies linking leprosariums to lunatic asylums, and then to schools, prisons, and workhouses, doesn't he already presuppose the connections he sets out to demonstrate? The truth is that anything can be linked to anything: the disappearance of typewriters might credibly be linked to the rising of corporate capitalism, to the growing incidence of divorce in America, or to the rise of global terrorism: that no one has noticed such connection wouldn't trouble Foucault; in fact, he would find them more compelling—and more revealing—for that very reason.

20. Matthew Arnold, *Culture and Anarchy and Other Writings,* ed. Stefan Collini (Cambridge, Eng.: Cambridge University Press, 1993), 38.

21. Ibid., 42.

22. See, for instance, 78: "Culture looks beyond machinery, culture hates hatred; culture has one great passion, the passion for sweetness and light."

23. See Thomas Henry Huxley, "Science and Culture," *The Major Prose of Thomas Henry Huxley* (Athens: University of Georgia Press, 1997): 224–38; and Laurence W. Mazzeno, *Matthew Arnold: The Critical Legacy* (Rochester, N.Y.: Camden House, 1999), 1–20.

24. See Lionel Trilling, *The Liberal Imagination: Essays on Literature and Society* (New York: Viking Press, 1950), 181–97. "The world," he wrote, "seems to become less and less responsive to literature; we can even observe that literature is becoming something like an object of suspicion" (181). Still later in the same collections, he asks "whether or not the novel is still a living form" (255) and he laments "the general deterioration of our intellectual life" (265).

25. John Crowe Ransom, "Criticism, Inc.," *The World's Body* (New York: Charles Scribner's Sons, 1938): 327–50.

26. Ibid., 329.

27. See "The Archetypes of Literature," originally published in the *Kenyon Review* prior to the appearance of *The Anatomy of Criticism* and described by Frye as a summation of much that gets argued in the larger work. *Fables of Identity: Studies in Poetic Mythology* (San Diego: Harcourt Brace Jovanovich, 1956, 1984), 7–20. In "The Archetypes," as in *The Anatomy,* Frye presupposes an evolutionary schema comparable to biological evolution, observing, for example, that in ritual "we may find the origin of [all] narrative" (15). He conceives of literary evolution in terms of "archetypes" that begin as myths linked to ritual and then evolve over time. Literature, he says, "develops from the primitive to the self-conscious." The problem with "popular literature"—for Frye—lies in its atavistic, quasi-primitive character. Its "appeal[s] to the inertia of the untrained mind puts a heavy emphasis on [the] narrative values" that Frye associates with primitive myths (17).

28. As Frye writes in *The Stubborn Structure: Essays on Criticism and Society* (Ithaca: Cornell University Press, 1970), "I recently saw a documentary movie of the rock-and-roll singer Paul Anka. The reporter pried one of the squealing little sexballs out of the audience and asked her what she found so ecstatic about listening to Anka. She said, still in a daze, 'He's so *sincere.*' The will to unite rhetorical and direct address is very clear here" (88). To call someone a "screaming sexball"—and

to believe it—is to offer yet another example of the failure of literary study to promote the understanding, wisdom, and compassion it often claims to promote. But the will to unite "rhetorical and direct address" is just as strong in Frye as it is the this young woman: What makes him think, after all, that Blake is any more or any less sincere than Paul Anka?

At any rate, popular culture poses a serious theoretical obstacle to Frye's project. Ultimately, he concedes that "Advertising, propaganda, the speeches of politicians, popular books and magazines . . . all have their own kind of pastoral myths, quest myths, hero myths" and so on. But these he describes as the products of a "perverted imagination" that must be combated, through the offices of academic criticism, for the sake of "real society" (105).

29. Robert D. Kaplan, *The Ends of the Earth: From Togo to Turkmenistan, from Iran to Cambodia: A Journey to the Frontiers of Anarchy* (New York: Vintage Books/ Random House, 1997), esp. 328–32. Academics tend to dislike Kaplan because he offers an unflattering image of "subaltern" countries and because he refuses to represent them simply as passive victims of Western domination. He has also made waves by arguing that formal democracy can be destabilizing in the absence of a strong middle class.

30. See Jean François Lyotard, *The Postmodern Condition: A Report on Knowledge* (Minneapolis: University of Minnesota Press, 1984).

31. See Outreach Communications, "Why HIPC Still Fails to Deliver to LDCs," (12/5/01), *http://home.no.net/outreach/19may3.htm* According to this press release issued by Outreach Online, the total debt stock of the world's 48 LDCs (Least Developed Countries) reached $154 billion in 1998, almost four times the 1980 level. More than half of the LDCs have experienced economic stagnation or contraction during the 1990s. For this reason, many NGOs remain skeptical about the Heavily Indebted Poor Countries (HIPC) Initiative. See also Manuel Castells, "Rise of the Fourth World: Informational Capitalism, Poverty, and Exclusion" *End of Millennium*, rev. ed., Vol. 3 of *The Information Age: Economy, Society and Culture* (Oxford: Blackwell Publishers Inc., 1999), 70–165.

32. In the year 1900, the world's population was about 1.5 billion. But today, according to World Bank figures, twenty-three percent of the world's 6 billion people live off of less than $1 a day. See "Income Poverty: The Latest Global Numbers," (7/10/01), *http://www.worldbank.org/poverty/data/trends/income.htm*

33. Serge Latouche, *The Westernization of the World: the Significance, Scope, and Limits of the Drive Towards Global Uniformity,* trans. Rosemary Morris (Cambridge: Polity Press, 1996), 61.

34. Vandana Shiva, *Monocultures of the Mind: Perspectives on Biodiversity and Biotechnology* (Atlantic Highlands, N.J.: Zed Books, 1993), 12.

35. Alain Touraine, "The Idea of Revolution," in *Global Culture: Nationalism, Globalization, and Modernity,* ed. Mike Featherstone (London: Sage Publications, 1990), 122.

It's interesting to note that M. I. Finley also a singles out Schumpeter for special criticism. An Austrian-American economist and a socialist, Schumpeter had a wide-ranging influence as an apologist for the administered society. Not only did he argue that most people want to be freed from politics in order to devote them-selves to getting and spending, but he also celebrated capitalism, as Marx had, for its creative destructiveness. See *Capitalism, Socialism, and Democracy* (New York: Harper & Row, 1950). For "creative destruction," see 81–86; for his repudiation of democracy, see 269–83. As he argues there, "the electoral mass is incapable of action other than a stampede" (283).

36. Ibid., 135.

37. John Tomlinson, *Cultural Imperialism: A Critical Introduction* (Baltimore: Johns Hopkins University Press, 1991). As Tomlinson observes, the global cultural tourist may decry homogenization, but "The Kazakhstani tribesman who has no knowledge of (and perhaps no interest in) America or Europe is unlikely to see his cassette player as emblematic of creeping capitalist domination" (109); see also 90–94, 140–69.

38. See Consumer Federation of America, "Credit Card Debts Escalate in 1997, Burdening Many Xmas Shoppers" (Washington, D.C.: Consumer Federation of America, 1997). According to this report by the nonprofit CFA, between 1990 and 1996 the nation's aggregate credit card debt more than doubled. Between December 1996 and October 1997, the total increased by another 6.4 percent to $455 billion. The estimated 55–60 million households with revolving credit card accounts carry on average $7,000 of credit card debt, and they make more than $1,000 in interest pay-ments annually. Lower-income families suffer from debt ratios far higher than those carried by their wealthier counterparts. In 1996, the average annual after-tax income for Chapter 7 bankruptcy was $19,000; the average credit card debt was $17,544.

39. I have borrowed the concept of "disembedding" from Anthony Giddens, *The Consequences of Modernity* (Stanford, Calif.: Stanford University Press, 1990), 21–29.

40. Here I should acknowledge my debt to Michael Herzfeld, *The Social Production of Indifference: Exploring the Symbolic Roots of Western Bureaucracy* (New York: Berg, 1992).

41. See Robert H. Frank and Philip J. Cook, *The Winner-Take-All Society: Why the Few at the Top Get So Much More than the Rest of Us* (New York: Penguin Books, 1996), esp.153–56.

42. Gramsci is famous among leftists for his slogan, "All men are intellec-tuals," but in fact he posits relations between intellectuals and "the masses" that are distinctly hierarchical. See esp. "The Study of Philosophy," *Selections from the Prison Notebooks*, trans. Quinton Hoare and Geoffrey Nowell Smith (New York: Interna-tional Publishers, 1987): 323–77. There he argues that the "active man-in-the-mass has a practical activity, but has no clear theoretical consciousness of his practical activity" (333). According to Gramsci, "Critical self-consciousness means, histor-ically and politically, the creation of an *elite* of intellectuals" (334). Innovation "cannot come from the mass, at least at the beginning, except through the mediation of an *elite*" (335). See also an earlier essay in the collection, "The Intellectuals," esp. 14–15 on peasants.

43. In some ways, Adorno's negative dialectic is analogous to Gramsci's no-tion of a "war of position" waged against hegemony. See Gramsci, "State and Civil

Society," in *Prison Notebooks:* 206–26. For Benjamin's Angel of History, see *Illuminations,* trans. Harry Zohn (New York: Schocken Books, 1969), 257–58.

44. See Peter Bürger, *Theory of the Avant-Garde,* trans. Michael Shaw (Minneapolis: University of Minnesota Press, 1984). There Bürger makes the essential point that the avant-garde never actually managed to free itself from "art as an institution," by which he means, among other things, the arts as professions that turn out commodifiable objects for the "art market." As he charges, the institution of art "prevents the contents of works that press for radical change in a society . . . from having any practical effect" (95). Of course, the same point could be made about theory: see Paul Mann, *The Theory-Death of the Avant-Garde* (Bloomington: Indiana University Press, 1991).

45. See Cross-National Collaborative Group, "The Changing Rate of Major Depression: Cross-National Comparisons," *JAMA, The Journal of the American Medical Association* 268.21 (2 December 1992): 3098–106.

46. Arthur Kleinman and Alex Cohen, "Psychiatry's Global Challenge," *Scientific American* (March 1997): 86–89. See also Arline Kaplan, "China's Suicide Patterns Challenge Depression Theory," *Psychiatric Times* 16.1 (January 1999) *http://mhsource.com/pt/p990101b.html*

47. Ibid., 86. China has seen an explosion of neurotic "identity" disorders as well, especially bulimia. See "China's Chic Waistline: Convex to Concave," *New York Times* 9 December 1999. *http://www.nytimes.com/library/world/asia/120999china-weightloss.html*

48. Elizabeth Wurtzel, *Prozac Nation: Young and Depressed in America* (New York: Riverhead Books, 1995).

49. See Gerald Graff, *Beyond the Culture Wars: How Teaching the Conflicts Can Revitalize American Education* (New York: W.W. Norton, 1992).

50. Nelson Goodman, *Ways of Worldmaking* (Indianapolis: Hackett Publishing Co., 1978), 57–70.

51. See Dai Qing, ed., *The River Dragon Has Come! The Three Gorges Dam and the Fate of China's Yangtze River and Its People* (Armonk, N.Y.: M. E. Sharpe, 1998). With the exception of *The New York Times,* which has regularly covered the controversy surrounding the construction of the world's largest dam, only the environmentalist press has paid careful attention. Dai Qing's book also appeared without much fanfare.

52. This term is a coinage of Jane Bennett in *Unthinking Faith and Enlightenment: Nature and the State in a Post-Hegelian Era* (New York: New York University Press, 1987), 149–50, 158–61.

53. For a devastating—and often hilarious—exposé of the poststructuralists' misappropriation of science, see Paul R. Gross and Norman Levitt, *Higher Superstition: The Academic Left and Its Quarrels with Science* (Baltimore: Johns Hopkins University Press, 1994).

54. Karl Marx and Friedrich Engels, *The Communist Manifesto,* trans. Paul M. Sweezy (New York: Monthly Review Press, 1964), 7.

55. Ellen Dissanayake, *What Is Art For?* (Seattle: University of Washington Press, 1988), 135.

56. Lin Yutang, *The Chinese Theory of Art: Translations from the Masters of Chinese Art* (New York: G. P. Putnam, 1967), 154. Translation altered.

Chapter 8   Specialists with *Spirit: The Humanities—Outside the University*

1. Matthew Arnold, *Culture and Anarchy and Other Writings,* ed. Stefan Collini (Cambridge, Eng.: Cambridge University Press, 1993).

2. See Weber's famous observation in *Economy and Society: An Outline of Interpretive Sociology,* ed. Guenther Roth and Claus Wittich, trans. Ephraim Fischoff et al. (Berkeley: University of California Press, 1978, 630: "Only Protestantism completely eliminated magic and the supernatural quest for salvation. . . . For the various popular religions of Asia, in contrast to ascetic Protestantism, the world remained an enchanted garden. . . . No path led the magical religiosity of . . . Asia to a rational, methodical control of life." See also Weber's comparison of charismatic authority versus "rational, primarily bureaucratic, authority" (241–45).

3. Arnold, *Culture,* 126–37.

4. Max Weber, *The Sociology of Religion,* trans. Ephraim Fischoff (Boston: Beacon Press, 1991), 236. In these passages Weber describes some of the pathologies of a bureaucratic society in which coercion has itself become rationalized. At times, even Weber seems to have been overwhelmed by a powerful nostalgia for a prerational order based on charismatic leadership.

5. In *The Sociology of Religion,* Weber has this to say about the religious interests of the intellectuals of his day, and his remarks apply to much more than religion: Despite "the need of literary, academic, or café-society intellectuals to include religious feelings in the inventory of their sources of impressions and sensations, and among their topics for discussion . . . no new religion has ever resulted from . . . their chatter. The whirligig of fashion will presently remove this subject of conversation and journalism, which fashion has made popular" (137). Of course, Weber was himself an intellectual, as he well recognized with his usual ambivalence.

6. William James, *The Will to Believe and Other Essays in Popular Philosophy* (New York: Longmans, Green, 1937), 12.

7. Ibid., 30.

8. Ibid., 63–110.

9. Ibid., 65.

10. Ibid., 64.

11. William James, *The Varieties of Religious Experience: A Study in Human Nature* (New York: Modern Library, 1999), 552.

12. Qtd. in Michael Kazin, "The Politics of Devotion," *The Nation,* 6 April 1998: 16.

13. See for example Mark Edmundson, *Nightmare on Main Street: Angels, Sadomasochism, and the Culture of the Gothic* (Cambridge, Mass.: Harvard University Press, 1997).

14. See Andrew Ross, "New Age Technoculture," in Lawrence Grossberg, et al., *Cultural Studies* (New York: Routledge, 1992): 531–48; also Marianna Torgovnick, *Primitive Passions: Men, Women, and the Quest for Ecstacy* (New York: Knopf, 1997), 172–88. I should add that Ross seems curious rather than interested; Torgovnick curious, skeptical, and massively condescending. The more things change, the more they stay the same.

15. Marianne Williamson, *Illuminata: A Return to Prayer* (New York: Riverhead Books, 1994), xvi.

16. Ibid., 3–5.

17. Thomas Moore, *Care of the Soul: A Guide for Cultivating Depth and Sacredness in Everyday Life* ((New York: HarperPerennial, 1994), 47; Michel Foucault, *The Care of the Self*, vol. 3 of *The History of Sexuality*, trans. Robert Hurley (New York: Vintage, 1988), 43–45.

18. See Hubert L. Dreyfus and Paul Rabinow, *Michel Foucault: Beyond Structuralism and Hermeneutics*, 2nd ed. (Chicago: University of Chicago Press, 1983), 245.

19. Moore, *Care of the Soul*, 296.

20. Ibid., xviii.

21. Ibid., xvii.

22. Ibid., 220.

23. Ibid., 175, 309.

24. Ibid., 213. See also Sam Keen, *Hymns to an Unknown God: Awakening the Spirit in Everyday Life* (New York: Bantam, 1994), 1–2, 98–90.

25. Keen, *Hymns*, 141. See also André Droogers, "The Normalization of Religious Experience: Healing, Prophecy, Dreams, and Visions," in *Charismatic Christianity as a Global Culture*, ed. Karla Poewe (Columbia: University of South Carolina Press, 1994), 33.

26. Douglas Robinson, *The Translator's Turn* (Baltimore: Johns Hopkins University Press, 1991), 3–15; see also Keen, *Hymns*, 76.

27. See Deepak Chopra, *Creating Health: How to Wake Up the Body's Intelligence*, rev. ed. (Boston: Houghton Mifflin, 1991), 167–205; and *Return of the Rishi: A Doctor's Story of Spiritual Transformation and Ayurvedic Healing* (Boston: Houghton Mifflin, 1991), 86–102.

28. See Brian Stock, *Augustine the Reader: Meditation, Self-Knowledge, and the Ethics of Interpretation* (Cambridge, Mass.: Belknap Press of Harvard University Press, 1996), 248–78.

29. Jon Kabat-Zinn, *Wherever You Go, There You Are* (New York: Hyperion, 1994), 103–26; see also Chopra, *Creating Health*, 181–84.

30. Kabat-Zinn, *Wherever*, 18–21.

31. See Thomas Moore, *The Reenchantment of Everyday Life* (HarperPerennial, 1996), 248–57.

32. For a discussion of medieval attitudes toward reading, see Ivan Illich, *In the Vineyard of the Text: A Commentary to Hugh's Didascalicon* (Chicago: University of Chicago Press, 1993), esp. 50, 58.

33. For a discussion of "root metaphors," see Victor Turner, *Dramas, Fields,*

and Metaphors: Symbolic Action in Human Society (Ithaca, N.Y.: Cornell University Press, 1974), 166–230.

34. Betty J. Eadie, with Curtis Taylor, *Embraced by the Light* (New York: Bantam, 1994), 40.

35. Ibid., 41.

36. Ibid., 45–46.

37. Moore, *Care of the Soul,* 235–36.

38. Williamson, *Illuminata,* 187.

39. Keen, *Hymns,* 239–42.

40. John Beverley Butcher, *The Tao of Jesus: A Book of Days for the Natural Year* (San Francisco: Harper, 1994).

41. See Paul Ricoeur, "Universal Civilization and National Cultures," *History and Truth,* trans. Charles A. Kelbley (Evanston: Northwestern University Press, 1965), esp. 274–78.

42. See Christopher Lasch, *The Culture of Narcissism: American Life in an Age of Diminishing Expectations* (New York: Warner Books, 1979), and Crawford Brough Macpherson, *The Theory of Possessive Individualism: Hobbes to Locke* (Oxford, Eng.: Clarendon Press, 1969).

43. J. K. Bailey, *Already on Holy Ground: Experiencing the Presence in Ordinary Life* (Center City, Minn.: Hazelden, 1996), 168–69.

44. Edmundson, *Nightmare,* 77–78.

45. Williamson, *Illuminata,* 12.

46. Keen, *Hymns,* 5.

47. For an analysis of pilgrimage as psychological process, see Turner, *Dramas,* 123–64.

48. Karen Armstrong, *A History of God: The 4000–Year Quest of Judaism, Christianity, and Islam* (New York: Knopf, 1993), 195–96, 377–99.

49. See Bill Readings, *The University in Ruins* (Cambridge: Harvard University Press, 1996), 89–118; and Anne Ruggles Gere, *Intimate Practices: Literacy and Cultural Work in U.S. Women's Clubs, 1880–1920* (Urbana: University of Illinois Press, 1997), 208–47.

50. Eric Livingston, *An Anthropology of Reading* (Bloomington: University of Indiana Press, 1995), 135–46.

51. Natalie Goldberg, *Writing Down the Bones: Freeing the Writer Within* (Boston: Shambhala, 1986), 9.

52. Julia Cameron, *The Artist's Way: A Spiritual Path to Higher Creativity* (New York: Putnam, 1992), 155.

53. Ibid., 14.

54. See Jack Canfield and Mark Victor Hanson, *Chicken Soup for the Soul: 101 Stories to Open the Heart and Rekindle the Spirit* (Deerfield Beach, Fla.: Heath Communications, 1993).

55. Herbert Marcuse, *One-Dimensional Man: Studies in the Ideology of Advanced Industrial Society* (Boston: Beacon Press, 1964), 10.

56. See Turner, *Dramas,* 231–71.

57. See Torgovnick, *Primitive Passions,* 209–19.

Chapter 9 *"Art Serves Love": The Arts As a Paradigm for the Humanities*

1. In fact, some readers have concluded that Foucault intended *The Archaeology* as a parody. See Allan Megill, *Prophets of Extremity: Nietzsche, Heidegger, Foucault, Derrida* (Berkeley: University of California Press, 1985), 227–32.

2. Derrida has, as always, brilliantly managed to cover himself on this score, all the while claiming that his method is characterized by the utmost "rigor." "It is not enough," he writes, "to install plurivocity within thematics in order to recover the interminable motion of writing. Writing does not simply weave several threads into a single term in such a way that one might end up unraveling all the 'contents' just by pulling a few strings. . . . The difference between discursive polysemy [which Derrida sees as naïve] and textual dissemination [which Derrida celebrates] is precisely *difference* itself, 'an implacable difference.'" *Dissemination*, trans. Barbara Johnson (Chicago: University of Chicago Press, 1981), 350–51. Behind this entire argument is an attempt to elude any scientific or positivistic understanding of language by claiming that the very study of language already introduces *différance*. No sooner do we try to fix language or discourse as the object of our study than it wriggles out of our grasp again in the form of "writing." The only thing that can be predicted is unpredictability. How convenient.

3. As he does in ". . . That Dangerous Supplement . . ." *Of Grammaology*, trans. Gayatri Chakravorty Spivak (Baltimore: Johns Hopkins University Press: 141–64.

4. Frank Lentriccia, *Criticism and Social Change* (Chicago: University of Chicago Press, 1985).

5. Ibid., 10–11.

6. Ibid., "Last Will and Testament of an Ex-Literary Critic: 'Dirty Harry' Comes Clean," *Lingua Franca: The Review of Academic Life* 6.6 (September/October 1996): 59–67.

7. Art may use representation or argument, but this is not what art is. There are, after all, many kinds of representations and arguments that do not qualify as art. I contend that we need to see art as a distinctive behavior or human activity in its own right. For an extended defense of this position, see Ellen Dissanayake, *What Is Art For?* (Seattle: University of Washington Press, 1988), and *Homo Aestheticus: Where Art Comes from and Why* (New York: Free Press, 1992).

8. Lentriccia, "Last Will and Testament," 60.

9. Ibid., 63.

10. In his essay, "Criticism, Inc.," Ransom specifically "prescribes" from the proper domain of criticism all "'personal registrations,' which are declarations of the effect of the art-work upon the critic as reader." See *The World's Body* (New York: Charles Scribner's Sons, 1938), 342.

11. Certainly such an approach has had at least some advocates in the last half century. One important forerunner is Louise M. Rosenblatt, *Literature as Exploration* (New York: D. Appleton-Century, 1938), as well as her later book *The Reader, the Text, the Poem: The Transactional Theory of the Literary Work* (Carbondale, Ill.: Southern Illinois University Press, 1978). See also Norman Holland, *5 Readers*

Reading (New Haven, Conn.: Yale University Press, 1975); David Bleich, *Subjective Criticism* (Baltimore: Johns Hopkins University Press, 1978). The successor to "subjective criticism" was the reader-response school, one important early advocate of which was Stanley Fish, especially in *Surprised by Sin: The Reader in Paradise Lost.* (Berkeley: University of California Press, 1991). Fish seems, however, to have grown increasingly uncomfortable with the reader-centered tradition. Much of his subsequent work can be understood as an attempt to discredit the literary experience of nonprofessionals. See for example *Is There a Text in this Class? The Authority of Interpretive Communities* (Cambridge, Mass.: Harvard University Press, 1980). By "interpretive communities" Fish really means "academic disciplines."

12. Duchamps submitted "Fountain" for inclusion the first Exhibition of Independent Painters in New York City. Actually, the piece was rejected and returned to him several hours after the start of the show.

13. The insistence upon the inescapability of certain preconscious determinants is precisely what poststructuralists share with structuralists. In "The Violence of the Letter: From Lévi-Strauss to Rousseau," Derrida adopts a position he holds to be "strictly in accord with one of Lévi-Strauss's intentions": "If writing is no longer understood in the narrow sense of linear and phonetic notation, it should be possible to say that all societies capable of producing, that is to say of obliterating, their proper names, and of bringing classificatory difference into play, practice writing in general." *Of Grammatology,* trans. Gayatri Chakravorty Spivak (Baltimore: Johns Hopkins University Press, 1976) 109. In other words, "writing in general" is a preconscious constraint to which we are subject all the time, whether we choose to be or not.

14. I am indebted here to Marshall Sahlins, *Islands of History* (Chicago: University of Chicago Press, 1985), esp. vii–xvii and 136–56.

15. As he argues in chapter 9 of *Poetics,* "the poet's function is to describe, not the thing that has happened, but a kind of thing that might happen, i.e., what is possible as being probable or necessary." *De Poetica,* trans. Ingram Bywater, *The Basic Works of Aristotle,* ed. Richard McKeon (New York: Random House, 1941), 1463.

16. The association of the arts with "the primitive," both socially and psychologically, has a long history, one reaching back at least to the Romantics. In essays like "Creative Writing and Daydreaming" and "The Moses of Michelangelo," Freud might be said to renew the Romantic view of art in the first decades of the twentieth century. Freud's is not, however, the argument I am making here. The arts are not, in my view, developmentally or socially more primitive than other modes of activity, nor do they involve regression to childhood mental states or precultural modes of perception, whatever those might be. But I am suggesting that the arts *dramatize,* often in ways that are highly sophisticated, a phenomenological process that all forms of understanding share.

My argument presupposes that art making takes place within historically contingent traditions; at the same time, I believe that there are some transcultural universals rooted in our biological heritage as a species. See for example John Willats, *Art and Representation: New Principles in the Analysis of Pictures* (Princeton:

Princeton University Press, 1997). Willets argues that all of the world's artistic traditions can be shown to employ three different "drawing systems," that is, projection systems for representing relations between objects. Clearly, cultural differences matter; clearly, too, we are the products of a common evolutionary process.

Perhaps the most controversial aspect of my argument is the claim that the arts dramatize conceptual work that must get done before the sciences can accomplish their more specialized tasks. Obviously this claim remains highly speculative. Nevertheless, see Sidney J. Blatt, "Concurrent Conceptual Revolutions in Art and Science," in *Development and the Arts: Critical Perspectives,* ed. Margery B. Franklin and Bernard Kaplan (Hillsdale, N.J.: Lawrence Erlbaum Associates, 1994), 195–226.

17. For an extremely lucid discussion—by a distinguished artist—of art as "making," see Robert Morris, "Some Notes on the Phenomenology of Making: the Search for the Motivated," *Continuous Project Altered Daily: the Writings of Robert Morris* (Cambridge, Mass.: The MIT Press; New York: Solomon R. Guggenheim Museum, 1993), 71–91.

18. See Brian Stock, *Augustine the Reader: Meditation, Self-knowledge, and the Ethics of Interpretation* (Cambridge, Mass.: Belknap Press of Harvard University Press, 1996).

19. Ivan Illich, *In the Vineyard of the Text: A Commentary to Hugh's Didascalicon* (Chicago: University of Chicago Press, 1993), 20–21.

20. Ibid., 54.

21. Upton Sinclair, *American Outpost: A Book of Reminiscences* (Pasadena: Published by the Author, 1932), 74–76. Interestingly, this experience happened outside the context of formal education. Like many people of his generation, Sinclair had found college disappointing. "It had," he wrote, "become an agony for me to sit and listen to the slow recitation of matter which I either knew already, or did not care to know" (67). While at Columbia he used Grandgent's Italian grammar handbook (87), and he took a course on Kant with Nicholas Murray Butler, who possessed, Sinclair thought, "an aggressive and capable mind, with a cold and self-centered heart" (84).

22. See Thomas Pavel, *Fictional Worlds* (Cambridge, Mass.: Harvard University Press, 1986).

23. Ronald L. Grimes makes a useful distinction in this regard: "Ritual practices such as daily meditation and weekly worship are responses to recurring needs. These rites move but do not transform. By contrast, when effective rites of passage are enacted, they carry us from here to there in such a way that we are unable to return to square one. To enact any kind of rite is to *per*form, but to enact a rite of passage is also to *trans*form." *Deeply into the Bone: Re-inventing Rites of Passage* (Berkeley: University of California Press, 2000), 7. I have not adopted Grimes's distinction between kinds of rites, and I regard all rituals as rites of passage; nevertheless, I believe that Grimes points to a crucial distinction between performance and transformation: they are not necessarily opposed, but neither are they always one and the same.

24. For my remarks on the performative character of ritual I am much indebted to Richard K. Payne, "Realizing Inherent Enlightenment: Ritual and Self-Transformation in Shingon Buddhism," in *Religious and Social Ritual: Interdisciplinary Explorations,* ed. Michael B. Aune and Valerie DeMarinis (Albany: State University of New York Press, 1996): 71–104. Following Stanley Tambiah and Frits Staal, Payne argues that we have overestimated the symbolic or textual character of ritual while scanting its fundamentally performative character. At the same time, he wants to distinguish Tambiah's *performative* understanding of ritual from the *performance*-centered approach championed by Richard Schechner. By comparing ritual to dramatic performance, Schechner tends to overemphasize the "scripted" or deterministic aspects while marginizing ritual's genuine open-endedess as experienced. See also Stanley J. Tambiah, *Culture, Thought and Social Action: An Anthropological Perspective* (Cambridge, Mass.: Harvard University Press, 1985); Frits Staal, *Rules Without Meaning: Ritual, Mantras and the Human Sciences,* Toronto Studies in Religion, vol. 4 (New York: Peter Lang Publishing, 1989); and Richard Schechner and Willa Appel, eds., *By Means of Performance: Intercultural Studies of Theatre and Ritual* (Cambridge, Eng.: Cambridge University Press, 1990).

25. Roy A. Rappaport, *Ritual and Religion in the Making of Humanity* (Cambridge, Eng.: Cambridge University Press, 1999). See especially the chapter "Intervals, Eternity, and Communitas," 216–35. There Rapport speculates, under the influence of d'Aquili and Laughlin, that the experience of the "apparently immutable" follows from a change in relations between the brain's hemispheres. In the first stage of ritual the "nondominant" hemisphere (right in most people) is stimulated while the dominant hemisphere enters a condition of diminished activity. In the second stage, the arousal of the nondominant hemisphere continues while the activity of the other is almost completely suppressed. In the final stage, the traditional division of labor between the two hemispheres is overridden and both "discharge [electrically] at once" (229). These three stages may correspond to the three stages that I identify in my discussion of Kung and Haitian rituals. They may not correspond exactly to the cerebral activity of readers of poems or viewers of paintings at a gallery, but I suspect that the experience of art involves a comparable shift from discursive intellection to more affectively enriched modes of perception and action, culminating in a fusion of the discursive and the intellective. This may be why we find some responses to a work of art more satisfying than others.

26. I am drawing here on Arnold Van Gennep's pioneering work, *The Rites of Passage,* trans. Monika B. Vizedom and Gabrielle L . Caffee (Chicago: University of Chicago Press, 1960). Implicit in my argument is the speculation that both the *num* ritual among the Kung and the Western experience of the arts can fruitfully be understood as *rites de passage*. Especially pertinent is Van Gennep's discussion of threshold experiences. Also helpful is his tripartite division of complex rituals into preliminal rites, liminal or threshold rites, and postliminal rites (21). I conjecture that preliminal, liminal, and postliminal *moments* actually occur in all rituals.

27. See Victor Turner, *The Ritual Process: Structure and Anti-structure* (Chicago: Aldine, 1969), also *Dramas, Fields, and Metaphors: Symbolic Action in Human Society* (Ithaca, N.Y.: Cornell University Press,1974), 23–59. While I have found

Turner's discussion of the ritual process profoundly enlightening, he still tends to overvalue the conceptual aspects of ritual at the expense of its psychological and somatic aspects.

28. Richard Katz, *Boiling Energy: Community Healing among the Kalahari Kung* (Cambridge, Mass.: Harvard University Press, 1982),40–41.

29. Maya Deren, *Divine Horsemen: The Living Gods of Haiti* (New Paltz: McPherson and Co., 1970), 256–61.

30. The experience of the transcendent as a "light," for example, reached through a liminal state of darkness can be found in the historical record of Christian figures like John of the Cross, in the teaching of Sufi masters, and in the various Hindu-Buddhist traditions. For a discussion that has helped to shape my thinking here, see John Hick, *An Interpretation of Religion: Human Responses to the Transcendent* (New Haven: Yale University Press, 1989), esp. 1–17, in particular 3–5, "Religion as a family-resemblance concept," and 278–296. Basically, Hick argues for the existence of a "universal structure of human consciousness," while allowing that individual cultures motivate, constrain, and inflect consciousness in a variety of ways that cannot simply be conflated into one system. Even closer to my argument in its assumptions is Andrew Newberg, M.D., et al., *Why God Won't Go Away: Brain Science and the Biology of Belief* (New York: Ballantine Books, 2001). Hick is still a theologian; Newberg et al. are scientists: as a pragmatist, I come closer in sensibility to the scientists.

31. Eudora Welty, *One Writer's Beginnings: The William E. Massey Sr. Lectures in the History of American Civilization, 1983* (New York: Warner Books, 1985), 11.

32. In the West, the first and archetypal artist was Orpheus. The anthropologist Piers Vitebski points out that "ancient Greek culture contain[ed] striking shamanistic elements" memorialized in the Orpheus myth. In his brief discussion Vitebski identifies "typical shamanic themes," but he leaves unexplored the connections between shamanism and the arts. See Piers Vitebsky, *The Shaman* (Boston: Little, Brown, 1995), 51.

33. The anthropologist Renato Rosaldo helps to clarify the links between ritual and affective experience in *Culture and Truth: The Remaking of Social Analysis* (Boston: Beacon Press, 1989). There he contrasts the traditional textualist understanding of ritual, such as Clifford Geertz's practice of "thick description," with an approach that privileges emotional "force" over exegetical "depth" and interpretive complexity (1–20). For discussions of art as contact, see Hans-Georg Gadamer, *The Relevance of the Beautiful and Other Essays,* ed. Robert Bernasconi, trans. Nicholas Walker (New York: Cambridge University Press, 1986). See also Gemma Corradi Fiumara, *The Metaphoric Process: Connections Between Language and Life* (London: Routledge, 1995); John Stewart, *Language as Articulate Contact: Toward a Post-Semiotic Philosophy of Communication* (Albany: State University of New York Press, 1995).

34. I am indebted here to Crispin Sartwell, *The Art of Living: Aesthetics of the Ordinary in World Spiritual Traditions* (Albany: State University of New York Press, 1995), esp. 3–29.

35. *Meaningful* may not be the best word, however. A satisfying relation to the

world or to others requires consonance on many levels, not simply on the level of discursive understanding. A meaningful friendship, for example, might not be readily explainable: in this case, the term "meaningful" serves only to indicate the quality and character of the contact sustained by the friends themselves. A more accurate term would be "contactful," or maybe "full-filling."

36. Robert Scholes, *Textual Power: Literary Theory and the Teaching of English* (New Haven, Conn.: Yale University Press, 1985), 22–23.

37. For a comparable perspective on interpretation from the world of the visual arts, see Jed Perl, *Eyewitness: Reports from an Art World in Crisis* (New York: Basic Books, 2000), especially "The Art of Seeing," (309–30). I find myself strongly in agreement with Perl, art critic for the *New Republic*, when he takes issue with the notion that an intelligent response to art requires (1) the application of a theoretical paradigm and (2) that such a response requires us to treat the work as though it had a single, unifying "message." "If there is so much to be said for particularity and paradox," Perl asks, "why has the unity idea triumphed so totally?" (313). For the development of a similar if somewhat more nuanced position from within the academy, see Thomas Crow, *The Intelligence of Art* (Chapel Hill: University of North Carolina Press, 1999).

38. See Stephen Batchelor, *Alone with Others: An Existential Approach to Buddhism* (New York: Grove Press, 1983).

39. All references are to *The Oedipus Plays of Sophocles*, trans. Paul Roche (New York: Mentor Books), 1958.

40. In *Oedipus at Colonus* Oedipus himself points this out as early as the first episode:

> how was I the sinner?
> I provoked to self defense in such a way
>   that even had I acted with full knowledge,
>   even then, it never could be called a sin.
> As I was, where I went I went
>   all ignorant toward a doom too known
> To those who planned it. (Roche, 97)

41. See Christopher Rocco, *Tragedy and Enlightenment: Athenian Political Thought and the Dilemmas of Modernity* (Berkeley: University of California Press, 1997), esp. 2–67; also Joel D. Schwartz, "Human Action and Political Action in *Oedipus Tyrannos*," in *Greek Tragedy and Political Theory*, ed. J. Peter Euben (Berkeley: University of California Press, 1986): 183–209.

42. In the fifth episode of *Oedipus at Colonus*, where the chorus relates the events just before his ascent to the gods, Oedipus is described as walking "unled" to a sacred spot, a "yawning orifice":

> Then sitting down undid his squalid dress,
>   and calling for his daughters bade them fetch

water to wash with from a spring
and some to pour in ritual for the dead.

It seems likely that an Athenian audience would not have failed to notice how much Oedipus has come to resemble Tiresius.

43. See *The Collected Dialogues of Plato*, ed. Edith Hamilton and Huntington Cairns (Princeton, N.J.: Princeton University Press, 1961). Socrates argues that in order to perceive the "pure forms," we must pass "from a plurality of perceptions to a unity gathered together by reasoning" (496; 249b–c). Also pertinent is the discussion of the scale of perfection in *Symposium*, whereby one progresses from love for "one individual body" to an intellectual vision of "pure oneness." "Nor will [this] vision of the beautiful take the form of a face, or of hands, or of anything that is of the flesh" (562; 211a–b).

44. Roche, *Oedipus Plays*, 153–54.

45. Alexis de Tocqueville, *Democracy in America* vol. 1, (New York: Alfred A. Knopf, 1941), 254–70.

46. I am referring to the famous first chapter of Book 4 of *Politics*. "We should consider, not only what form of government is best, but also what is possible and easily attainable by all." Aristotle, *Politics*, trans. Benjamin Jowett, in *The Basic Works of Aristotle*, ed. Richard McKeon (New York: Random House, 1941), 1205–06. Elsewhere Aristotle refers disparagingly to Plato's *Republic* and his *Laws* because the political systems they propose are impractical.

47. See, for example, *Freedom and Culture* (New York: G. P. Putnam, 1939). There Dewey wrote that the conflict faced by Americans in an industrial society is a conflict "*within* our own institutions and attitudes. It can be won only by extending the application of democratic methods . . . [to] the task of making our own politics, industry, education, our culture generally, a servant and an evolving manifestation of democratic ideals" (175). Like many social critics now, Dewey saw the dissolution of historical communities as the major threat to democratic values, but he failed to recognize that the process of democratizing social institutions and "culture generally" could become oppressive in its own way.

48. Ralph Waldo Emerson, "Fate," *Ralph Waldo Emerson: Representative Selections*, ed. Frederic I. Carpenter (New York: American Book Company, 1934), 316–42. Viewed from too constraining a perspective, fate and freedom seem to be in mortal opposition. But when surveyed from a more encompassing vista, "fate slides into freedom and freedom into fate." Let us, Emerson wrote, "build altars to the Beautiful Necessity" (342).

Chapter 10   Travels to the Heart of the Forest: Dilettantes and Professionals in the Twentieth Century

1. Hilary Putnam, *Renewing Philosophy* (New York: Cambridge University Press, 1992), 141, 197.

2. Richard Parker, "Can Economists Save Economics?" *The American Prospect* (Spring 1993), 159.

3. Ibid., 160.

4. Alan Megill and Donald N. McCloskey, "The Rhetoric of History," in *The Rhetoric of the Human Sciences,* ed. John S. Nelson, et al. (Madison: University of Wisconsin Press, 1987): 221–38.

5. Earl Parker Hanson, *Journey to Manaos* (New York: Reynal and Hitchcock, 1938).

6. Claude Lévi-Strauss, *Tristes Tropiques,* trans. John and Doreen Weightman (New York: Atheneum, 1974), 17.

7. Ibid., 17.

8. Ibid., 38.

9. Ibid., 62.

10. Ibid., 393.

11. Ibid., *The Savage Mind* (Chicago: University of Chicago Press, 1966), 269.

12. Ibid., *Tristes Tropiques,* 410–412.

13. Heinrich Wölfflin, *Principles of Art History: The Problem of the Development of Style in Later Art,* trans. M. D. Hottinger (New York: Dover, 1932), 11.

14. Ibid., 230.

15. Ibid., 226.

16. Ibid., 17.

17. Ibid., 235.

18. Northrop Frye, *Fables of Identity: Studies in Poetic Mythology* (San Diego: Harcourt Brace, 1984), 7.

19. Ibid., 12.

20. Ibid., 7.

21. Northrop Frye, *The Stubborn Structure: Essays on Criticism and Society* (Ithaca: Cornell University Press, 1970), 105.

22. Ibid., *Fables of Identity,* 21–38.

23. Ibid., 33.

24. Ibid., *The Stubborn Structure,* 105.

25. Ibid., *Fables of Identity,* 13.

26. Ibid., 17, 38.

27. Burton J. Bledstein, *The Culture of Professionalism: The Middle Class and the Development of Higher Education in America* (New York: W.W. Norton, 1976), 327–28.

28. Clifford Geertz, "The Cerebral Savage: On the Work of Claude Lévi-Strauss," *The Interpretation of Cultures* (New York: Basic Books, 1973), 355.

29. Qtd. in Geertz, 346.

30. Ludwig Wittgenstein, *Culture and Value,* ed. G. H. Von Wright, trans. Peter Winch (Chicago: University of Chicago Press, 1980), 7e.

31. Richard Handler, "The Dainty Man and the Hungry Man: Literature and Anthropology in the Work of Edward Sapir," in *Observers Observed: Essays on Ethnographic Fieldwork,* ed. George Stocking Jr. (Madison: University of Wisconsin Press, 1983), 226.

32. Ibid., 227.

33. Ibid., 210.

34. For a frank recognition of this predicament, see Thomas Bender, *Intellect and Public Life: Essays on the Social History of Academic Intellectuals in the United States* (Baltimore: Johns Hopkins, 1993), esp. 127–45.

35. M. I. Finley, "'Progress' in Historiography," *Daedalus* 106 (Summer 1977): 127.

36. Ibid., 132.

37. Ibid., 127, 137.

38. Svetlana Alpers, "Is Art History?" *Daedalus* 106 (Summer 1977): 6.

39. See Timothy J. Clark, *Image of the People: Gustav Courbet and the 1848 Revolution*, 2nd ed. (Princeton: Princeton University Press, 1982).

40. Lévi-Strauss, *Structural Anthropology*, 23.

41. Karl Marx, *The Eighteenth Brumaire of Louis Bonaparte*, ed. C. P. Dutt (New York: International Publishers, nd), 13. Anyone who bothers to consult the original German, as well, will see that Lévi-Strauss's translation is not defensible.

42. Lévi-Strauss, *Tristes Tropiques*, "sociological," 251; "pronunciation," 279.

43. Ibid., 286.

44. Ibid., "learned societies," 274; professions, 225; vocations, 236.

45. Ibid., 245.

46. Ibid., 178.

47. Johannes Wilbert and Karin Simoneau, eds, *Folk Literature of the Caduveo Indians* (Los Angeles: UCLA Latin American Center Publications, 1989), 23–24.

48. For trenchant discussions of the limitations of reader-response theory, see Mary Louie Pratt, "Interpretive Strategies/Strategic Interpretations: On Anglo-American Reader-Response Criticism," *Boundary 2* 11 (Fall/Winter 1982–1983): 201–31; and Patrocinio P. Schweickart, "Reading Ourselves: Toward a Feminist Theory of Reading," in *Gender and Reading*, ed. Elizabeth A. Flynn and Patrocinio P. Schweickart (Baltimore: Johns Hopkins University Press, 1986): 31–62.

49. John Dewey, "Philosophy and Democracy," *The Middle Works, 1899–1924*, Vol. 11: 1918–1919, ed. Jo Ann Boydston (Carbondale: Southern Illinois University Press, 1982), 50–51.

50. Hanson, *Journey*, 90.

51. Ibid., "swarming," 24; "back to the Indians," 12.

52. Ibid., 146, 201.

53. Ibid., 90.

54. Ibid., 160.

55. Ibid., 93, 174.

56. Ibid., 259.

57. Ibid., "convert the locals," 255; "yagé," 222.

58. Ibid., 97.

59. Ibid., 99.

60. Ibid., 62.

61. Ibid., 187–88.

62. Ibid., 186.

63. Ibid., 211.

64. Ibid., 212.

65. See for instance Stephen E. Ambrose, *Citizen Soldiers: the U.S. Army from the Normandy Beaches to the Bulge to the Surrender of Germany, June 7, 1944–May 7, 1945* (New York: Touchstone Books/Simon and Schuster, 1998); Harvey Cox, *Fire from Heaven: the Rise of Pentecostal Spirituality and the Reshaping of Religion in the Twenty-first Century* (Reading, Mass.: Addison-Wesley Publishers, 1995); Doris Kearns Goodwin, *No Ordinary Time: Franklin and Eleanor Roosevelt: the Home Front in World War II* (New York: Simon and Schuster, 1994); Henry Louis Gates, *Colored People: A Memoir* (New York: Knopf, 1994); Richard Rorty, *Philosophy and Social Hope* (New York: Penguin, 2000).

66. Hanson, *Journey,* 224–25.

67. Lévi-Strauss, *Tristes Tropiques,* 293.

68. Alvin W. Gouldner, *The Coming Crisis of Western Sociology* (New York: Basic Books, 1970), 53.

69. Lévi-Strauss, *Structural Anthropology,* 245–69.

70. Hanson, *Journey,* 255.

INDEX

A

Abbott, Andrew, 249*n1*
Adams, Hazard, 154
Adams, Henry, 36, 73
Adams, Samuel, 62
Adorno, Theodor, 147, 152, 153, 154, 163, 199, 278*n5*, 282*n43*
Advertising, 132; creation of crisis of meaning by, 162; as deconstruction, 161, 162; incoherence and, 228; myths of, 280*n28;* perverted imagination and, 228; social production of emptiness and, 163; stimulation of demand and, 161
Aesthetics, 17
African Americans, 35; omission from American culture, 122; writers, 34
Agee, James, 271*n14,* 272*n17,* 272*n26;* on "actual" world, 103–104; on coherence, 113; criticism of administered society by, 99; desire for basic dignity for all, 101; on education, 107, 116; failure of knowledge and, 104; on formalism, 111; modernism and, 99; pessism of, 106; praise for space, 111; on solving life problems, 110; Trilling on, 104, 105; views on American life, 100–112
Alcibiades, 29
Alcott, Louisa May, 34
Alexander the Great, 29, 31, 258*n6*
Alienation: as inescapable fate, 190; intensification of, 187; in market economy, 165; reading and, 186; transformation of, 116
Alpers, Svetlana, 230, 231, 232, 254*n14*
Ambrose, Stephen, 238
America: African-American authors, 34; agrarian order in, 32, 33; collective nature of, 47; cultural life in, 76; cultural populism in, 34; culture of the arts in, 84; depressions in, 33; education in, 241; enslavement to competition in, 54; ethnic authors, 34; excessive specialization in, 74; forms of association in, 32; groundlessness in, 45, 46; hierarchies in, 32; ideas in, 91; indifference to European literature in, 74; individualism in, 33; individual relationships of power in, 47; liberalism in, 106; literacy rate in, 74–75; local autonomy in, 33; modernity and, 54; radical writers, 34; reading in, 74, 75; regionalist authors, 34; re-

ligion in, 184; shared story of, 79; small town life in, 32, 33–37; social criticism in, 33; success of democracy in small centers of, 32, 33; transformation of life in, 32–47; urbanism in, 43, 44, 45; women writers, 34
American Bar Association, 51
American Federation of Labor, 55
Anarchy, 97, 217
Anderson, Nels, 44
Anomie, 45; pervasiveness of, 165; radical, 165
Archaeology of Knowledge, The (Foucault), 199
Aristotle, 82, 132, 204, 218, 277*n2*
Armstrong, Karen, 195, 245
Arnold, Matthew, 53, 106, 149, 155, 157, 257*n31;* credibility gap of, 155; on criticism, 152, 153, 154; as defender of tradition, 176; defense of human values by, 175; defining intellectualism, 20; disinterestedness and, 152, 153, 154; establishment of division of labor by, 20; sweetness and light of, 155, 176
Art(s): appropriation for administrative ends, 84; association with "primitive," 288*n16;* connectedness and, 172; consumer culture and, 7; as criticism, 204; Cubism, 76, 277*n50;* culture and, 22–23; culture of, 5; defining, 142; democracy and, 7; development of style in, 227; as distinctive behavior, 287*n7;* for "education," 213; erudition needed for, 6; evolution in, 86; experience of, 85, 204; expression of, 24, 88; finding, 205; forms of beholding in, 226; Futurism, 76; high, 81; history, 226; imagining, 204; Impressionism, 76, 254*n14;* invisible sources of, 227; judgment of, 86; liberal, 250*n3;* of living, 148, 201; making, 205, 212, 214, 215; as means to ends, 85; as mode of experience, 203; openness of, 168; as paradigm for humanities, 199–220; patronage and, 24; performing, 250*n3;* personal experience in, 85; of the poem, 85; Post-Impressionism, 76; as practice, 195; as process, 202; promiscuity of, 88, 213; as propaganda, 212; rarification of, 195; reception by patrons and public, 257*n34;* remoteness of, 6; representational, 24; as ritual enactments of freedom to make one's life, 217; of self-cultivation, 201; study vs. making, 23, 24, 212; truth of, 201; as way of knowing, 85; as